Praise for
The Liber Christo Method

"This field guide is just that, a manual to be carried and used to fight an ancient enemy with the ancient weapons of the Church. Dr. Dan Schneider writes with a military mindset drawing on his experience as an Army helicopter pilot and officer in Desert Storm. It is fitting that an Army soldier, now Catholic theologian, has teamed up with Fr. Chad Ripperger to provide an authentically Catholic program of liberation for the common man. They have given us a MOAB, Mother of All Books. This manual is a weapon of mass instruction, and it will truly equip the laity to go on the offensive as the Church Militant."

—Jesse Romero,
Author of *The Devil in the City of the Angels*

"Dr. Dan Schneider is one of my favorite guests on U.S. Grace Force. He is a sought-after speaker and author. He combines the richness of Catholic tradition on spiritual warfare with practical examples based on real field experience. In a time when diabolical activity is on the rise, *The Liber Christo Method* is a sure guide to liberation and a must read for today's Catholics who are serious about their Faith."

—Fr. Richard Heilman,
Founder of U.S. Grace Force

"As a member of Father Chad Ripperger's team and as a professor of theology, Dr. Dan Schneider provides practical analysis and proven tactics to help you win the war against the world, the flesh, and the devil. This manual will help you grow in holiness and get you battle ready!"

—Doug Barry,
EWTN Host of Battle Ready

THE
LIBER CHRISTO
METHOD

THE
LIBER CHRISTO
METHOD
A FIELD MANUAL FOR
SPIRITUAL COMBAT

DAN SCHNEIDER, PHD
FOREWORD BY
FR. CHAD RIPPERGER, PHD

TAN Books
Gastonia, North Carolina

Nihil Obstat: Rev. Marcelo Javier Navarro Muñoz, PhD
 Censor Librorum

Imprimatur: +Most Reverend Peter Baldacchino
 Bishop of Las Cruces
 Las Cruces, New Mexico, USA
 July 21, 2022

The *Nihil Obstat* and *Imprimatur* are official declarations that a book or a pamphlet is free from doctrinal or moral error. No implication is contained therein that those who have granted *Nihil Obstat* and *Imprimatur* agree with the contents, opinions, or statements expressed.

Cover Design by www.davidferrisdesign.com

Library of Congress Control Number: 2022951451

ISBN: 978-1-5051-2905-2
Kindle ISBN: 978-1-5051-3056-0
ePUB ISBN: 978-1-5051-3057-7

Published in the United States by
TAN Books
PO Box 269
Gastonia, NC 28053
www.TANBooks.com

Printed in India

Contents

Foreword

The last year that the Doloran priests personally kept statistics (now they are kept by our case manager) on the number of people that they were meeting was in 2015. That year, we had 2,000 contacts, we discussed the cases of 600 people over the phone, we saw 150 people, and of those 150 people, only 3 were possessed. About one-third of the people that we saw did have legitimate diabolic obsession and oppression issues. However, those can normally be taken care of by their pastor, and many people can actually self-liberate, if they do the right things.

The amount of time that is spent by the exorcist vetting the various cases to find the ones that actually need his help can become prohibitive. Furthermore, around the same time, there was a great deal of discussion by exorcists about what to do with what they called "aftercare." This is essentially what happens with people after they have been liberated from possession. Many of these people are in a situation where they lack catechetical instruction—their only contact with a priest is the exorcist—and so they have no contact with the local parish or church. They often need psychological help or counseling as well, and during the liberation process itself, it becomes clear that they are at times in irregular marriages, have not received all of the sacraments, or have been struggling with some form of habitual mortal sin. The former issues become a problem because the priest, once the person has been liberated, must move on to the next case and so he cannot spend time with the person who was liberated. This is why there was such a protracted discussion about aftercare. As to the latter issues, often a person's liberation was dragging out unduly because of sacramental issues or attachment to mortal sin. Again, this resulted in the exorcist having to spend extra time that could normally be used to focus on the possessed rather than on cleaning up ancillary issues.

Another issue that exorcists would regularly come across is that, of the people that were possessed, only about one-third would actually go the distance and become liberated. About a third would be informed of everything that he or she would have to do in order to become liberated and, in the end, decide not to begin the exorcisms because he or she simply just did not want to do and suffer what was required. Another third would start the process of going through the exorcisms, but once it became difficult, they would stop coming to the sessions because they simply did not have the sufficient virtue to go the distance.

It is for all of the above reasons that the Doloran Fathers worked with Mr. Clement in order to develop a protocol that would address these particular issues. To begin, the exorcist is analogous to a brain surgeon, and when one thinks he might have some type of cerebral issue, one does not go immediately to a brain surgeon, asking him to diagnose him or actually do a specific kind of brain surgery. Rather, one starts with his general practitioner, and he begins the process of vetting the problem so that the brain surgeon can focus on brain surgery. This medical model was adopted by Liber Christo to ensure that the various issues that did not require exorcism would still be adequately addressed and that people would be directed to where they can find help. At the same time, it would maximize the number of people that needed help actually receiving help.

Moreover, many people were able to self-liberate from lower-level forms of diabolic obsession and oppression simply by following the protocol, especially the prayer prescription. What became very clear over the time in which this protocol has been used is that most people who suffer from diabolic issues are spiritually undisciplined. The protocol is designed to develop the proper discipline and virtues in the individual so that many of the diabolic issues, which do not require an exorcist or even a priest to pray over them, can simply be cleared up by the afflicted himself. The second phase of the protocol also started addressing issues such as lack of catechetical instruction and also the need for psychological help or counseling before they saw the exorcist, which also often clear up the specific problem that the person is suffering. Since a priest is required to accompany the individual through the various stages of the protocol, this solved the problem of people not having a connection to the local parish or other priests. Moreover, the priest would then also be able to help the person straighten out sacramental issues, which again often cause an amelioration of the diabolic afflictions.

One other issue that required a great deal of time on the side of the exorcist was interviewing the people and doing prayers with them for a while to determine what the actual status of the case was; that is, he had to do a sufficient diagnostic. Again, this required a certain amount of time so that he was not able to spend it actually helping people but rather diagnosing cases. The Liber Christo protocol was designed to provide an initial diagnostic so that by the time it became clear that person actually needed to see the exorcist, much of the knowledge that is necessary in order to solve the case was already known.

It is the hope of the Doloran Fathers and the members of Liber Christo that this book will provide a basic outline for those who are going through the protocol as well as for priests to be able to guide people through the protocol.

It is also our hope that even those who do not go formally through the protocol will be able to make use of this book so that in following the prayer prescription and having a knowledge about how to become disciplined in the spiritual life so as to engage spiritual warfare, they will be able to avoid spiritual problems in the future but also work out the problems that they may have already. May God bless those who read this book, implement its counsels, and to follow the protocol.

Fr. Chad Ripperger, PhD

Preface

Thil manual is part of a three-book series on the strategy and tactics of spiritual warfare. By definition, a manual is a handbook or an instruction book to guide its reader to mastery of a particular subject. Accordingly, this book is intended as a tactical field manual, or a *how-to* book, for those in close engagement with the enemy. For those unfamiliar with military terminology, "tactics" include "the art and science of employing all available means to win battles and engagements."[1] Accordingly, this book is intended to teach the reader how to engage, and win, the spiritual battles of this present day.

Successful tactics on the battlefield do not need to be complicated. To this day, the US Army Rangers still deploy the tactics of Robert Rogers's *28 Rules of Ranging*, a manual on guerrilla warfare written in 1757. In Rogers's rules, you read such things as "all Rangers must be ready on any emergency to march at a minute's warning" and "when pushed upon by the enemy, reserve your fire till they approach very near, which will then put them into the greatest surprise and consternation, and give you an opportunity of rushing upon them with your hatchets and cutlasses to the better advantage."[2] His first standing order, however, shows the need for simplicity, preparedness, and attention to detail in combat. It reads simply, "Don't forget nothin'." Although warfare has changed considerably since Rogers wrote these rules, the basic principles are the same. All soldiers, for example, have a pre-combat checklist of the things needed to conduct combat operations. That list includes not only a clean

---

[1] Department of the Army, *Army Tactics*, ix.
[2] Dunnigan, *Perfect Soldier*, 40.

weapon and ammunition but also water and even extra socks (wet feet get infected and infected feet cannot march). This manual is intended to teach you the basics of spiritual warfare.

Although it may not appear so to the observer, all warfare is conducted by rules of engagement. Thus, Rogers begins his instruction with, "All Rangers are to be subject to the rules and articles of war." Bear in mind three essential factors of effective tactical engagement vis-à-vis the demon; that is, the demon is a strictly ordered, spiritual being who follows the rules of engagement as established by God through natural law and divine positive law. This means that he will either yield or not yield according to the answer to three questions:

1. Does this person have requisite authority?
2. What is the state of merit of the petitioner, and is he or she in a state of grace?
3. What specifically is the petitioner asking?

The reader should notice these three principles referred to throughout this book.

As Rogers's rules show, the battle is won by paying attention to detail, strictly adhering to standard operating procedures, which allow for safe and effective fighting, and knowing the rules of engagement. This manual is part of the Liber Christo method, which is a four-phase diocesan protocol for handling cases of diabolic affliction as developed by Fr. Chad Ripperger and the Society of Our Most Sorrowful Mother (SMD). As such, it is the fruit of the field experience of Father Ripperger and that of his long-time assistant, Kyle Clement.[3]

While the SMD teams use this manual in their apostolate, it can also be used by Catholics seeking to "clean up" any lingering effects of spiritual affliction. The reader who employs these prayers and tactics should do so upon consultation with his local pastor or spiritual director. Apart from the old

---

[3] I will sometimes write in the first-person plural, such as *we* and *our*, which refers to our collective thoughts and experience.

television show, there is no such thing as a lone ranger. A soldier works within a hierarchy of command and control, and for most Catholics, this begins with our parish priest. A wife should also speak with her husband about these prayers and let him be the "team leader" on this spiritual campaign.

A Catholic approach to liberation always involves the sacraments. Our approach is based upon this reality, while also including many prudential elements as a result of years of experience which, in our judgment, maximizes the effectiveness of the protocol. The reader should also note that this manual represents the second phase of the four phases in which we help to identify and remove obstacles to grace. Equally important is this first phase, whereby the household follows a strict prayer discipline for thirty consecutive days before picking up this book. This first phase prayer regimen is listed briefly in appendix A. Our experience is that the demon responds as much to the imposition of order as he does to the prayers themselves. That first phase is, by analogy, a pre-combat checklist which ensures one's readiness to sustain the duress and demands of battle. Thus, a life ordered to prayer presupposes the ability to effectively engage the enemy. Accordingly, one should not see this manual as a "quick fix" which contains special prayers previously unknown to Catholics. Rather, this is a plan for sustained tactical operations.

The goal of our program is not the cessation of pain but reconciliation with God the Father. By *reconciliation*, moreover, we mean two interwoven concepts. Properly speaking, reconciliation is the process by which divine friendship is restored after having been lost due to grievous sin. Thus, referring to the sacrament of Penance, the Council of Trent refers to "the *reconciling of the faithful* who have fallen after Baptism."[4] Reconciliation, then, is defined as the conference of grace which produces the salutary effect of "deliverance from the guilt of sin and, in the case of mortal sin, from its eternal punishment; hence also *reconciliation* with God, justification."[5] First and

---

4 Council of Trent, Sess. XIV, c. I.
5 Hanna, *Catholic Encyclopedia*, 623.

foremost, then, this program leads you to the most important form of deliverance—that is, from the guilt and eternal punishment due to mortal sin.

The former chief exorcist of the diocese of Rome, Fr. Gabriel Amorth, affirmed the power of the sacraments when he asserted emphatically that "confession is stronger than exorcism!"[6] According to the late exorcist, "Satan is more enraged when we take souls away from him through confession than when we take away bodies through exorcism."[7] He asserts that sacramental Penance is "the most direct means to fight Satan." This sacrament, he says, "tears souls from the demon's grasp, strengthens against sin, unites us more closely to God, and helps to conform our souls increasingly to the divine will." He counsels all Catholics—especially those afflicted by evil spirits—to make frequent, even weekly, confessions.[8]

Many seeking deliverance, therefore, first need to return to the state of grace through a good confession. By *state of grace* is meant the restoration of divine friendship and, thus, the condition of a soul as pleasing to God because it is free from mortal sin. To be clear, mortal sin leaves the soul completely unprotected from the wiles of the devil. What about those individuals, however, who are in a state of grace and still find themselves spiritually afflicted due to curses, abuse, previous occult activity, or living in infested homes? This person still requires reconciliation, but in a nuanced sense. By way of analogy, consider the canonical process that must take place when a church building is violated. By definition, a church which has been desecrated in some manner (a fact which is more commonplace among today's anarchic, anti-Catholic movements) must formally be *reconciled*. In canonical parlance, this type of reconciliation means "the act of reblessing or reinstating." By definition, "it must be reconciled by the bishop before it can be used for sacred services."[9]

---

6   Amorth, *An Exorcist Tells His Story*, 86.
7   Amorth, 67.
8   Amorth, *An Exorcist: More Stories*, 195.
9   Nevins, *Maryknoll Catholic Dictionary*, 481.

Those in a state a grace who still suffer diabolic affliction as the result of being "violated" by other people through curses, abuse, et cetera may also need reconciliation. As in a desecrated church, where the demon is invited into a sacred place through an evil act, the demon's presence to such a person is ultimately offensive to God, even though He permits it at times. Thus, by *reconciliation*, we refer not only to the restoration of divine friendship to those who had lost it due to mortal sin but also to the process of removing the demons from the person's body, exterior goods, et cetera. This person also needs reconciliation as the presence of the demon (analogously) is a violation of a sacred space (a soul possessing sanctifying grace), just like the violation of a consecrated church building. Due to the institutional nature of the diabolic presence, both instances are offensive to God, and both require an *institutional and ecclesial response*. Our four-phase protocol is part of that formal response by the local church.[10]

As for the individual in need of reconciliation of either (or both) types, sometimes God asks him to suffer, for in that suffering he taps into the redemptive power of Calvary. As suggested by Father Amorth above, penance (both sacramental and the sacrificial, interior disposition and practices which atone for sins) helps in spiritual combat by assisting us *to conform our souls increasingly to the divine will.* The process of reconciliation, moreover, means bringing oneself and one's spiritual faculties into conformity with the will of God. Although the presence of diabolic affliction may have prompted you to seek help, liberation in the Catholic sense means reconciliation at the level of the soul (the removal of the obstacles to grace) and the spiritual faculties (conformity of intellect and will). Bear in mind this nuanced definition of *reconciliation* as you read this manual.

Just as Rogers's rules presupposes that the ranger is physically and mentally fit, having completed both basic training and specialty training in guerrilla warfare, so too does this

---

[10] A summary of our medical model and four-phase protocol is found in appendix A.

book presuppose a baseline of psychological, emotional, and spiritual fitness. Those with a history of mental health issues should consult with their mental health professional in addition to their parish priest. For more, see your parish priest or visit https://www.liberchristo.org/.

Unless otherwise specified, the suggested prayers are either public domain or come from Father Ripperger's book *Deliverance Prayers for Use by the Laity*. Each lesson includes some basic prayers with additional ones located in the appendix which is tied to each chapter.

"The Spirit of the Lord is upon me. Wherefore he hath anointed me to preach the gospel to the poor, he hath sent me to heal the contrite of heart, to preach deliverance to the captives, and sight to the blind, to set at liberty them that are bruised, to preach the acceptable year of the Lord, and the day of reward."

—Luke 4:18–19, DV

Overview

Slaying Your Giants

"The Philistine then moved to meet David at close quarters, while David ran quickly toward the battle line to meet the Philistine."

—1 SAMUEL 17:48

A prime example of guerrilla warfare from the Old Testament is the popular story of David and Goliath (see 1 Sm 17), where a young shepherd boy uses unconventional methods to defeat a seasoned Philistine warrior. While the weapons used by soldiers in warfare have advanced over the ages, soldiering itself is rather timeless. David's choice of weapon was primitive but effective—the common shepherd's sling and stones smoothed by the running waters of a wadi. Ancient armies also utilized slingers. Archeologists have discovered primitive slingstones engraved not only with military unit insignia but also messages such as "take that!" or "ouch!" or "for Pompey's backside." Modern soldiers also inscribe their rockets and missiles with flags, unit markings, and similar messages. Before etching the cross of Christ onto your stones, however, let us first show you how to wield the sling safely and accurately.

Christians have long seen David's defeat of Goliath as a symbolic prefiguring of Jesus Christ's defeat of the devil on the cross.[11] In the second century, for example,

---

[11] The early Christian exegetical tradition of re-reading the battle between

Saint Hippolytus of Rome wrote that just as David dispatched the giant by cutting off his head, Jesus "crushed the head" of the devil (an allusion to Gn. 3:15) whom Hippolytus referred to as "the demon Goliath."[12] For Hippolytus, the five stones of David were symbolic of the five wounds of Christ. The staff prefigured the authority of "the King and High Priest, Christ" and the sling which launches the stone is the new Law (the old Law was contained in five books of Moses) and, therefore, "the laws of the Church." These, as I wrote elsewhere, are the armaments of victory—the cross of Jesus Christ, priestly authority, and the teachings of the Church. Goliath's defeat prefigured Christ's victory over the devil, sin, and death.[13] Thus, the cross of Jesus, where He received His five wounds, is not a sign of defeat but rather of ultimate victory. In a similar way, Saint Augustine specifically linked the sword of David to the cross, noting that "having smitten and overthrown" the Goliath with the sling, David "took the enemy's sword, and with it cut off his head. This our David also did, He [Jesus] overthrew the devil with his own weapons." We do the same, Augustine wrote, when we reject the devil's lies and profess the ancient Christian faith.[14] These are your weapons—stones, slings, staff, and sword.

David and Goliath for a Christian performance dates to the second century AD. Specifically, several early Fathers of the Church (some cited here) used a typological interpretation of the Bible story as symbolically pointing to Christ's defeat of the devil on the cross. I presented an analysis of this at the 2022 Midwest Region of the Society of Biblical Literature conference, "Warfare in the Biblical World," in a paper entitled "Weaponry in Biblical Warfare: David's Defeat of Goliath as Prefiguring the Cross in Augustine of Hippo." I am also grateful to Kyle Clement who presented a modern application of the spiritual battle in light of David and Goliath, which built upon the patristic and rabbinic traditions in a presentation in Omaha, Nebraska in 2018. This present book fleshes out into further lessons the patristic use of David's stones as metaphor for confronting evil, systematizing the praxis and prudential experience of Father Ripperger and Clement, as well as my own.

[12] Hippolytus of Rome, *On David and Goliath*, 34. Schneider, "Weaponry in Biblical Warfare," 3.
[13] Schneider, "Weaponry in Biblical Warfare," 4.
[14] Saint Augustine of Hippo, *Exposition on Psalm 144*, 1.

"When the Israelites saw [Goliath]," however, "they all retreated before him, terrified" (1 Sm 17:24). The demon's first weapon is fear. David, however, sized up his opponent, calculated the risks, and acted in faith. You must do the same. First, however, you must know your enemy, his origins, and his weapons and tactics. A *demon* is a malevolent, non-bodily, invisible creature of whom Saint Peter says prowls around "like a roaring lion looking for [someone] to devour" (1 Pt 5:8). The Fourth Lateran Council (AD 1215) affirms that "the devil and other demons have indeed been created by God as good by nature . . . [but] they, of themselves, became evil." Thus, a demon is a fallen angel who was created good by God but fell from heaven due to pride and disobedience.

The same council also said that "man . . . sinned at the suggestion of the devil." Accordingly, one of the names that Bible uses for the devil is "the tempter" (see Mt 4:3) who entices us to sin. According to Saint James, "Blessed is the man who perseveres in temptation, for when he has been proved he will receive the crown of life that he promised to those who love him" (Jas 1:12). The devil continues to tempt, however, by luring and enticing a person with "his own desire. Then the desire conceives and brings forth sin, and when sin reaches maturity it gives birth to death" (Jas 1:14–15). Thus, before "devouring" a spiritually dead soul, he first lures and entices it into sin.

He then moves from tempter to accuser. A working definition of a demon is a "lawyer from hell." That is, a legalistic and opportunistic prosecutor, he scours the horizon for any violations, waiting for the opportunity to pounce and levy an accusation. One biblical title for the devil is "the accuser," as seen in Revelation where Saint John recounts that "the accuser of our brothers is cast out, who accuses them before God day and night" (Rv 12:10). What does he accuse? Especially grave sins such as sexual deviancy, abortion, abuse and incest, and participating in occult activity all open doors to diabolic accusation and allow the demon's subsequent involvement in a person's life. When you commit a grave sin, you grant a privilege to the demon who, in turn, now accuses *you* "before God day and night." That is, due to some sinful behavior of yours, he lays claim to you—"Look, God, he gave me *permission* to be here!" Accordingly, this program will teach you how to remove any so-called legal claims of the enemy by opening the lines of grace to your soul (which belongs by right to God the Father due to the baptismal seal).

This "legal battle" is fought in a most peculiar way. The demon responds to the imposition of order as much as to deliverance prayers themselves. As I stated elsewhere, those who seek lasting liberation must acquire "a continual and habitual practice of the Catholic faith built on a monastic foundation of prayer and discipline."[15] David did not pick up the sling for the first time when confronted by Goliath. Day after day, alone among the sheep, he practiced and perfected the skill. Following his example, the *Liber Christo* model accompanies you to the gunnery range, so to speak, to teach you how to fight your daily spiritual battles. A key to accuracy with your sling is the spiritual discipline of *ascesis*—that is, self-discipline and mortification. This includes a theology of suffering and the centrality of sacramental confession as two formidable weapons.

Accordingly, a sustained and lasting liberation must be preceded by a sacrificial and Eucharistic theology which imbues all aspects of your life (spiritual, sacramental, familial, etc.). This process will include saving not just you but your whole family. For that to happen, God may require that you learn to offer your suffering for them. Remember,

---

[15] Liber Christo, "Companion Guide," 6. The "Freedom Through Christ Companion Guide" is a 2019 self-published work by Liber Christo based on conferences and teachings of Father Ripperger and Kyle Clement. The "Companion Guide" was compiled for use by lay associates working on exorcist teams implementing the Liber Christo Four-Phase Protocol both for the Society of the Most Sorrowful Mother and local diocesan exorcists across the country. After its initial draft, I edited and re-wrote the manual several times to get it into its final form for the summer 2019 Liber Christo annual conference and its present use. For purposes here, I will cite the "Companion Guide" and denote for the reader the source of the material contained therein. When applicable, I also cite the development of a concept or its praxis in the exorcist community in recent years.

David's battle was single combat, which was a one-on-one fight to the death between two warriors who represented the best from each opposing side. The two men fought center stage, in the no-man's land between the two armies, while the other warriors looked on but did not engage. David was fighting not just for his own survival but for that of the entire house of Israel.

Similarly, you may be fighting for much more than yourself. Saint Faustina Kowalska stated, "If the angels were capable of envy, they would envy us for two things: one is the receiving of Holy Communion, and the other is suffering."[16] If angels have a holy envy of our ability to unite our bodily suffering with that of Jesus Christ (or what many grandmothers simply called the "offering up" of life's difficulties) there must be something powerful to it. Thus, this program includes the neglected aspects of a penitential posture requisite for liberation. That is, while we will teach you set prayers that assist in liberation, there is no "magic bullet" or quick fix. As Father Amorth writes, "There is always a strong temptation for charismatics, sensitives and exorcists . . . of finding the quickest way to heal, by going outside the common sacred means to obtain grace." Those who seek quick solutions outside of the ordinary channels of obtaining grace, he says, "unwittingly fall into the trap of magic."[17]

Liberation is not static, nor is it merely the cessation of pain and suffering. On the contrary, as I wrote, "freedom *from* diabolic affliction and its effects . . . also means freedom *for* new life in Christ. The ultimate goal . . . is the salvation of souls—which is 'the supreme law in the Church.'"[18] You will only slay your giants—the infernal and ancient enemy—with the Church's ancient weapons in hand. These ancient weapons include the sacraments and embracing suffering in reparation for one's sins and the sins of others, which we will flesh out in more detail.

---

16 Kowalska, *Diary of Saint Maria Faustina Kowalska*, no. 1804.
17 Amorth, *An Exorcist Tells His Story*, 162.
18 Liber Christo, "Companion Guide," 6. *Code of Canon Law*, no. 1752.

From Shepherd to Warrior

David was a shepherd boy whose father had sent to the battlefield to bring food to his brothers. The two armies faced each other, and David arrived just in time to see a Philistine warrior named Goliath mock and challenge the Israelite army. Standing nearly ten feet tall by some accounts, Goliath was a formidable opponent. The Philistine champion was not only a towering figure but also seasoned, "a warrior since his youth" (1 Sm 17:4, 33). He challenged the men of Israel with a showdown seen only in Homeric epics. The stakes were high: "He stood and shouted to the ranks of Israel: 'Why come out in battle formation? I am a Philistine, and you are Saul's servants. Choose one of your men and have him come down to me. If he beats me in combat and kills me, we will be your vassals; but if I beat him and kill him, you shall be our vassals and serve us'" (1 Sm 17:8–9).

Vassals is a polite gloss for "slave." The Greek word used is, in fact, the lowest form of menial slave, or *doulos*. Many demons have attested to, under command by an exorcist in solemn session, a very sobering reality to the victor of this spiritual battle. To wit, if a person dies in a state of mortal sin, that person will be the slave, for eternity, of the demon who enticed him to mortal sin. The torment of enslavement, both experienced now and for eternity, is the goal of the demon.

What keeps most people enslaved is fear. Because of fear, the story continues, not a single soldier from the Israelite army accepted the Philistine's challenge. Even King Saul, who himself "stood head and shoulders above the people" (1 Sm 9:2), was afraid to meet Goliath in battle. In fact, Scripture tells us that King Saul himself "was tormented by an evil spirit" due to his own disobedience to God's commands and pride (cf. 1 Sm 13:13–14; 15:12; Dt 17:20). An astute reader may note how the sacred author describes the inner disposition of Saul that was not only the source of his fear but also that which attracts the demon. The king was not only disobedient (see 1 Sm 15:19) and proud (erecting a trophy in his own honor, see 1 Sm 15:12), he was vain (fearing man rather than fearing God, see 1 Sm 15:24), angry and resentful (see 1 Sm 18:8) to the point of rage (see 1 Sm 18:10), murderous (see 1 Sm 19:1), melancholic (see 1 Sm 16:14) to the point of despair (see 1 Sm 28:5), performed liturgical rituals that only a priest should do (a usurpation of authority in 1 Sm 13:8–9), and finally abandoned God and consulted a witch (see 1 Sm 28:8–11) in direct violation of God's command against conjurers, fortune tellers, and the like (see Dt 18:10–14). He exhibits what we term as "psychological compatibility with the demon," and these things must be eradicated from a soul as prerequisite for liberation. Simply stated, if you want to attract the demon to you, and quickly, do the things that Saul did.

David, conversely, was "a man after God's own heart" (1 Sm 13:14) who replaced Saul as king. His fearlessness flowed from his deep faith in God. Only David, a shepherd boy who had become the king's armor bearer, accepted Goliath's challenge. Do not be surprised, however, if you find little encouragement in your desire to find liberation. The demon will do everything in his power to keep you in fear and under his control. No one thought that David could defeat the Philistine giant, not even his own brother, who ridiculed him just as he was walking out to face Goliath. Listen to this voice and you may hear echoes of the tempter who tries to keep you from seeking liberation: "When Eliab, his oldest brother, heard him speaking with the men, he grew angry with David and said, 'Why did you come down? With whom have you left those sheep in the wilderness? I know your arrogance and your dishonest heart. You came down to enjoy the battle!" (1 Sm 17:28).

Even King Saul reminded David that he is a mere youth while Goliath "has been a warrior from his youth" (1 Sm 17:33). Thus, it is often those closest to us who seek to prevent us from seeking liberation.

On the plains of Bethlehem where David tended sheep, however, he himself learned how to fight off apex predators like bears and lions—not with swords and spears, but with something both advanced and primitive: a slingshot. Casting off Saul's armor, David applied guerrilla warfare tactics similar to Rogers's rangers. He went to a river and picked out "five smooth stones" and put them into his ammo pouch (1 Sm 17:40). This does not imply that David lacked faith but rather showed his preparedness for any contingency in battle (not unlike like Rogers's rules which said that each ranger must have "sixty rounds powder and ball and be ready to march at a minute's warning"). Although not mentioned in the narrative account of the battle, some speculate that David may have known that Goliath had four brothers (or sons), also giants, according to later accounts of the Philistine Wars. According to the Old Testament, there were four other Philistine giants in Gath who "were born as descendants of the giants in Geth, to Rapha, as a household, and they fell by the hand of David and by the hand of his slaves" (2 Sm 21:22 LXX).

More than likely, however, the sacred author's mention of *five* is a symbolic reference to the Torah (the Law of God) which is found in the first five books of the Old Testament (or Pentateuch, in Greek). In addition, *stone* was considered the most lasting writing material in antiquity, and thus, the Ten Commandments were written on stone tablets (see Ex 24:13). Because the contents of stone vessels were not subject to impurity as were earthen vessels, stone jars were used for ritual purification (cf. Jn 2:6).

The flowing water of a wadi would have produced the smoothest stones, which increases the accuracy of the projectile. This is a key principle to liberation. The "smooth stones" that are imbued with the power of God are to be found in adherence to the Law of God. The waters which produce the stones point to the waters of Baptism, and the *five* points to the five wounds of Christ (as the early Church Fathers noted). Baptismal dignity, fidelity, and adherence to the doctrinal and moral teachings of the Catholic Church are essential elements of liberation. To the extent that one strays from these, he presents vulnerabilities for the demon to exploit. While we have had many cases where liberation consisted in saying a specific prayer, albeit not known which one until much later in the process, there is no quick path to liberation. Victory lies in right belief (orthodoxy) and right practice (orthopraxy).

Armed, then, with the Law and in the name of God the Father Almighty, David came confidently against Goliath. He had recounted to King Saul the reason for his confidence. As a shepherd tending sheep, "whenever a lion or bear came to carry off a sheep from the flock, I would go after it and attack it and rescue the prey from its mouth. If it attacked me, I would seize it by the jaw, strike it, and kill it" (1 Sm 17:34–35).

Having killed both a lion and a bear, he knows how to kill this giant—with faith in the living God and human effort, cunning, and skill. With his trust totally in God, David *raced toward* Goliath and cried out: "You come against me with sword and spear and scimitar, but I come against you in the name of the LORD of hosts, the God of the armies of Israel that you have insulted" (1 Sm 17:45). Moving in at close quarters, waiting for the precise moment, he used unconventional tactics that would make Robert Rogers proud: "David put his hand into the bag and took out a stone, hurled it with the sling, and struck the Philistine on the forehead. The stone embedded itself in his brow, and he fell on his face to the ground. Thus David triumphed over the Philistine with sling and stone; he struck the Philistine dead, and did it without a sword in his hand. Then David ran and stood over him; with the Philistine's own sword which he drew from its sheath he killed him, and cut off his head" (1 Sm 1:49–51). Seeing their hero killed, the Philistine army turned in flight and were cut down by the Israelite soldiers (see 1 Sm 17:52–54).

Do you believe that you have the skills to defeat your enemy, however huge he may seem, and that God will guide your stone? We will show you tactics that are as the slingshot was to David, both primitive and advanced at the same time. You, however, must have the faith and courage to "put your hand into the bag" and reach for the stone. You must also *race toward* Goliath with the ancient weapons of the Catholic Church in hand. The stakes are high: slavery to the loser but peace and the reward of eternal life with God in heaven to the victor.

Many early Christians saw this epic fight between David and the Philistine as symbolic of the victory of Jesus Christ on the cross and also each Christian's battle against evil spirits. As David proclaimed to Goliath, "All this multitude, too, shall learn that it is not by sword or spear that the Lord saves. For the battle is the Lord's, and he shall deliver you into our hands" (1 Sm 17:47). Accordingly, this manual will walk you through twelve lessons designed to take you, like David, from shepherd to warrior. Think of this manual likewise as placing "five smooth stones" into your ammo pouch: (1) Renouncing of Evil Influences; (2) Repentance, Metanoia, and Forgiveness; (3) Examination of Conscience and Confession; (4) Learning Power and Authority; and (5) Prayer, Weapons, and Tactics. David took five steps in preparing to meet his opponent—he chose a stone, placed it into the sling, armed with a spinning force, aimed, and finally released the projectile. The chapters of this book will follow a similar five-fold inner logic.

Learning the Rules of Engagement

"All Rangers are to be subject to the rules and articles of war." Part of the enemy's strategy is to keep us from knowing the rules of engagement. Recall how Saul tried to give his armor to David, but the heavy conventional armaments were too cumbersome for the young shepherd, so David "stripped them off" (1 Sm 17:39). So, too, this battle you are about to engage in requires a "stripping off" of much of what you thought that spiritual warfare entails. For this reason, we have also included individual lessons within the five stones, which build one upon the other. We have deliberately chosen twelve lessons because the biblical number twelve represents the power and authority of God. Specifically, it symbolizes God's power and authority as seen in ecclesial governance. Just as "five" symbolized the Law, so "twelve" represents the appointive and jurisdictional authority of God on earth as seen, for example, in the twelve tribes of Israel (see Gn 49:8) and the twelve apostles chosen by Jesus to guide the Church (see Mt 10:1), who gave us twelve articles of faith in the Apostles' Creed. Thus, as you pick up each of the five "stones," you will receive instruction on how to wield them safely and effectively within the authority and creedal belief of the Church.

As Father Ripperger noted in his foreword, most people who struggle with spiritual affliction do not need an exorcist and can self-deliver through a return to the practice of the Faith. By *self-deliverance*, we mean the liberation from diabolic influences by tapping into the stream of grace afforded to Catholics. A simple definition of *grace* is *divine life*—the life of God—at work in the life of a Christian. The Greek word for grace is *charis*, a word that means "grace, favor, delight." Implied in the word also is a "vitality"—the very life and power of God vivifying and purifying everything it touches. In the divine economy, grace flows through the seven sacraments of the Catholic Church. You can receive more or less of this divine vitality, however, depending on the disposition of your soul and the impediments present there. This disposition means a dispossession from the things of the world so that you can better identify and remove any impediments.

To that end, you must identify the accuser and how he entered your life whether by sin, trauma, curses, or the occult. In addition, your participation in the sacraments restores and strengthens divine friendship and the flow of God's vitality. It is possible for a person to be liberated and not sanctified and to be reconciled and not sanctified. However, even as reconciliation (in the sense of the church analogy above) may come and go, a key feature of liberation is that it flows from sanctity of soul. The primary goal is reconciliation with God the Father, but this fits within the ultimate goal of the Christian life as sanctification, or the pursuit of holiness.

The demon, meanwhile, will obfuscate. To prevent that flow of grace, he employs various tactics: hiding, trying to convince you to stop praying, tempting you to return to past sins and destructive behavior, et cetera. Demons particularly hide, according to Father Ripperger, "in areas of weakness," all the while "probing and testing the limits to see what they can get away with."[19] Thus, you can unmask the demon by a thorough Penance, the development of virtue, good mental hygiene, and learning how to *reject, renounce,* and *rebuke* the vices and spirits which afflict your soul.

Note the inner logic of this formula as it increases in severity according to the intentionality of the penitent.[20] In dealing with any vice or spirit:

1.   Separate yourself from it with an act of the will.
2.   Cut yourself free of any entanglements due to your participation with it.
3.   Address it directly (and cast it away) in the name of Jesus Christ and from the authority given by God the Father over your own body and soul.
4.   Once a demon and concomitant vice/spiritual defect is uncovered, you now reject, renounce, and finally rebuke it to allow grace to then do its work.

As Saint Paul wrote, "For freedom Christ set us free; so, stand firm and do not submit again to the yoke of slavery" (Gal 5:1). Your time of enslavement ends when you decide to do whatever it takes to get free. At no time, however, are you a passive recipient; you must remain vigilant and active in your own liberation. To paraphrase the words of Saint Augustine, "God who created you without you, will not save you without you."

---

[19] Ripperger, *Dominion,* 108.
[20] This formula is the fruit of the field experience of Kyle Clement, who authored this prayer in 2004 at the request of exorcist Fr. James Erving, OMI. The inner logic of the *ad hoc* rejection statement comes largely in response to the exorcist team working occult and *brujaria* cases in south Texas at that time. The formula was then shared at early conferences (2005) at Mundelein and the broader exorcist community.

"Have Your Musket Clean as a Whistle, Hatchet Scoured"

Before a soldier learns "guerrilla tactics," he must first master the basics of soldiering. Lest we get ahead of ourselves, let the reader be reminded that conversion is the first movement of a person seeking healing and liberation. As Father Amorth affirms about the importance of conversion, "the efficacy of the exorcism is more directly related to the willingness to convert . . . than to the exorcism itself."[21] That is, repentance and metanoia precede liberation. We learn this from the words and deeds of Jesus. An astute reader of the Bible notes the significance of the first words and the first actions of Jesus. His first words to begin His public ministry should give us pause: "This is the time of fulfillment. The kingdom of God is at hand. Repent, and believe in the gospel" (Mk 1:15). That the "kingdom of God" is the Church is shown in Jesus's first deeds where He calls the first disciples Peter and his brother Andrew ("Come after me and I will make you fishers of men," Mk 1:17). Then, as if He is showing those disciples (and us) what the bringing about of the kingdom of God will look like, He immediately teaches, notably with such "authority" that it not only creates "astonishment" in his listeners but also evokes a manifestation by a possessed person. Jesus then immediately performs an exorcism (see Mk 1:21–28). In fact, His first day of public ministry was comprised of with preaching (v. 21) which led to an exorcism (vv. 23–27) and healing (vv. 29–31)—and more driving out of demons (vv. 32–34). Thus, we can suggest a pattern of the appropriation of the Gospel message as in the Church's missionary activity: repentance and belief, the Petrine ministry, teaching, and deliverance from evil spirits.

Christ uniquely equipped "the Twelve" (that is, the apostles) to continue these three duties of teaching, exorcising, and healing, in what eventually became known as the threefold *munera* proper to the ordained priesthood. A *munus* is a duty,

---

[21] Amorth, *An Exorcist Tells His Story*, 108.

office, or obligation, and Christ imposed this threefold duty upon the hierarchy of the Church—bishops and priests—to bring about the Kingdom of God, often amidst diabolic resistance. The demon recognizes this whether we do or not. We have encountered many priests, however, who are reluctant to engage in "deliverance ministry" for fear of retaliation. Quite simply, if a priest hears confessions, baptizes, and preaches, he is already in "the deliverance ministry" because the power and authority of the "Kingdom of God" continues through the agency of the Church. By performing the ordinary duties of his priestly ministry, therefore, the Catholic priest leads many souls to self-deliverance. Thus, we will often counsel you to "see your parish priest" because the pastoral and sacramental care of the local parish is where the graces of healing and self-liberation are dispensed.

The goal of this program, then, is to immerse you in the threefold missionary activity of the Church where grace is dispensed. As Catholics, our participation in the life of God has a bodily—sacramental and liturgical—aspect to it. Why? Man is a body-soul composite. That is, the human soul is united to the human body, and man acquires knowledge of sensible things through the bodily senses. This body-soul nature of man is that which renders us capable of union with God, who took on human flesh.

Thus, Rogers says that a ranger must "have your musket clean as a whistle, hatchet scoured" so that he is ready to engage the enemy at a moment's notice. A dirty musket is not accurate, and an unsharpened hatchet will not cut. Our infernal enemy—who is a pure, preternatural spirit with far superior intellect and cunning—knows whether our spiritual "muskets" are "clean as a whistle." He can sense the dullness of a dirty hatchet, so to speak. In the next section, we will discuss how to clean your musket and put an edge back on your hatchet.

Chapter One

Renunciation of Evil Influences

*"[David] played with lions as though they were young goats,
and with bears, like lambs of the flock."*

—SIRACH 47:3

I n this section, we discuss the occult and other areas where the "demon Goliath" operates. As Catholics, we believe that each person will get his body back in a glorified form in heaven, while the damned also suffer *bodily* torment in hell. Thus, the nature of curses—whether freemasonic or other forms of witchcraft—always involves bodily rituals. For this reason, we will explain in some detail how curses work, what makes a person vulnerable to them, and how to get out from beneath their effects. To be clear, our base armor which protects us against curses and other wiles of the devil are the sacraments. The demon attacks the sacramental construct, and we will explain how the sacraments work for our protection against evil.

A soldier must conform his body, his will, and his intellect to the task of soldiering. The tasks of a spiritual soldier are no different. Many who are afflicted by evil spirits think they need the "right" prayer or the most "anointed" exorcist to drive out the demon so that they can experience normalcy again. That is, they seek a quick fix that focuses on the cessation of pain and a return of a better quality of life rather than holiness and union with God. Not only is this mindset unrealistic, but also it often prolongs affliction to the extent that true metanoia is delayed. In fact, most who seek help from spiritual affliction have never learned to pray or have never applied any spiritual rigor on themselves because of the short-term pain it causes.

For this reason, we propose a "medical model" which is designed to address the spiritual and psychological wounds that linger from your past so as to begin the healing process (see appendix A for an overview). Anyone who has undergone physical therapy knows that a muscle must be loaded and given resistance, sometimes even pushed to its limit, so as to gain the strength needed to heal itself. While leaving a wounded muscle alone may avoid temporary pain, it will eventually atrophy and require more and more pain management. The right use of therapy, although painful at first, will eventually remove pain and restore mobility. In many cases, a disciplined regimen of physical therapy will eliminate the need for pain medicine or even surgery. Most people further the problem by living in a perpetual state of "spiritual pain management" through the self-medication of drugs and alcohol, worldly distractions, illicit sex, and other such things. Quite frankly, you may be that person who is guarding and self-medicating a deep wound in such a way—and the demon who is feeding off it is quite content. In military parlance, you are the "walking wounded," but it is time to get back in the fight.

Inside the Wire: Ordinary and Extraordinary Diabolic Activity

Knowing your enemy is part of soldiering. Rogers would routinely send out patrols with the purpose of scouting "their enemies' forts or frontiers for discoveries" to learn their size, movements, habits, and activities. To prevent the enemy from doing the same, Rogers told his men, "When you camp, half the party stays awake while the other half sleeps." Modern rangers add to that by setting up a defensive perimeter of claymore mines strung together by interconnecting detonating wires. They call this perimeter "the wire," and the mine itself is stamped with the reminder: *Front Towards Enemy.* If an enemy breaches the defense, he is "inside the wire."

Traditionally, diabolic activity is distinguished between *ordinary* and *extraordinary.*[22] Temptation—physical or psychological—is part of the ordinary (common to all) way the devil operates.[23] According to Father Amorth, "The devil's mission in the world is to seduce souls, to lead each man and woman on the wayward paths of sin; and the principal path of this tragic mission is the path of temptation."[24] Fr. Francesco Bamonte, president of the International Association of Exorcists, describes temptation as when "the enemy attempts to seduce us with sense realities, acting on our senses (sight, touch, hearing, smell, and taste)." This seduction, he says, also includes our memory, imagination, and intellect.[25] That is, the demon traffics in the senses and seeks to manipulate how we appropriate the external world into our higher, internal faculties. His goal, according to Father Bamonte, is "to arouse the consent of our free will to do evil in hopes of stimulating and further reinforce our dependence upon him."[26] That is, the ordinary activity of the evil one is to use the sensory data presented to us to habituate us in sinfulness in thought, word, and deed.

God will never allow you to be tempted beyond what you can endure, however, and when you conquer various temptations, you grow in virtue, self-mastery, and mastery over the enemy. Temptation is, as Father Ripperger writes, "a school of humility" because it reveals the deficiencies in our formation and causes us to "distrust ourselves because of our

---

[22] Ripperger, *Dominion*, 219. Aumann, *Spiritual Theology*, 404. Amorth, *An Exorcist Tells His Story*, 32. Bamonte, *Diabolical Possession*, 55.

[23] For an in-depth explanation of temptation, see Ripperger, *Dominion*, 220–40.

[24] Amorth, *An Exorcist Explains the Demonic*, 63.

[25] Bamonte, *Diabolical Possession*, 40.

[26] Bamonte, 40.

weaknesses."[27] He notes also that by "fighting demons and vanquishing them, the demons become weaker, not only in the lives of the individual who fights them but in the lives of others as well." Thus, he states, "people have to understand that it is not unfair for God to allow this because He is actually giving them something greater."[28] The demon becomes an instrument of both our sanctification and education. Saint Bonaventure gives four reasons why God allows demons to influence a person: to reveal God's glory, to punish sin, to rebuke a sinner, or to educate a person.[29] That is, God allows all demonic activity (whether ordinary or extraordinary) for a greater good.

Although the demon may probe your perimeter through various temptations, therefore, when you resist temptation, you keep the enemy "outside the wire." When given the opportunity, however, the demon will slip past the claymore mines, get "inside the wire," and exert himself beyond ordinary temptation. Extraordinary diabolic activity, according to Father Ripperger, "is that which goes above and beyond what is normal or the ordinary diabolic influence, which all men must endure."[30] Father Bamonte describes it as "the devil's intervention on matter."[31] Father Amorth lists six ways of extraordinary diabolic activity: physical pain, demonic possession, diabolical oppression, diabolic obsession, diabolic infestation, and diabolic subjugation.[32] Notably, Father Bamonte emphasizes that extraordinary diabolic activity is the result of original sin and can often be due to "one's own culpability" to include sins of:

- superstition and occult practices, such as participation in (or even being present at) sessions with psychics or fortune tellers;

---

[27] Ripperger, *Dominion*, 239.
[28] Ripperger, 241.
[29] Cited in Smit, *De Demoniacis*, 79.
[30] Ripperger, *Dominion*, 241.
[31] Bamonte, *Diabolical Possession*, 54.
[32] Amorth, *An Exorcist Explains the Demonic*, 35–37.

- use of amulets and talisman; recourse to mediums, sorcerers, witches, tarot card readers, or having attempted any of these on your own;
- the practice of certain meditation techniques like transcendental meditation, Reiki, opening oneself to "chakras" or other New Age practices;
- submitting oneself to "spiritual cleansing," being present at voodoo, Macumba or other rituals; and
- membership in secret societies or satanic groups.[33]

He explains further that one can be vulnerable to demonic influence particularly when combined with "alienating vices" such as "alcohol abuse, drugs, sexual perversion, and blasphemy." Such activities, he says, "weaken the individual and open him up to the devil's extraordinary activity."[34] The motives for participation in witchcraft, says Father Amorth, are "wealth, power, vice, and more."[35]

While the enemy probes your "wire" through temptations, he can use other tactics, such as curses, to gain quicker access. As Father Bamonte notes, the demon can exploit such vulnerabilities ("alienating vices") through the actions of someone else who has performed occult rites and curses against him. That is, certain behaviors alienate you from God's friendship and protection, which can make you vulnerable to curses and the effects of the occult activity of others.

Here we present the devil's extraordinary and intensifying activity "inside the wire" of a person's interiority along a threefold scale of oppression-obsession-possession. These are defined as:[36]

Oppression—a form of extraordinary diabolic influence in which a demon attacks one's externals; first stage in the

---

[33] Bamonte, *Diabolical Possession*, 56–57.
[34] Bamonte, 57. Father Bamonte also notes "the rare vocation of victim soul."
[35] Amorth, *An Exorcist Explains the Demonic*, 151.
[36] This lexicon is adapted from Liber Christo, "2019 Conference Manual," 22–24 and Ripperger, *Dominion*, 538–57.

progression toward classic possession and often experienced as a heaviness, malaise, melancholy, or depression. As the influence of the diabolical increases during this phase, the individual begins to lose focus, especially on vocational obligations.

Obsession—*Spiritual* obsession can be seen in marked neurotic and abnormal mental symptoms due to the persevering efforts of an evil spirit to gain mastery over him; the second stage in the progression toward classic possession where one is besieged psychologically—that is, intellectually and emotionally—by demons. There will be psychological as well as physical indicators of the diabolical presence. It is during this phase that the demon begins to "move in" (increased and persistent activity in the interiority of a person). A *psychological* obsession is recurrent and persistent thoughts, urges, or images that are experienced as intrusive and unwanted.

Possession—the phenomenon in which the devil invades the body of a living person and moves the faculties and organs as if he were manipulating a body of his own. Three types of possession are as follows:

Classic: usually a gradual progression through the stages of oppression and obsession.

Partial: usually through a pact made in exchange for a favor with a demon such that the demon is present to that activity and when the person seeks God, demonic affliction arises; sometimes can be ethnic/cultural related.

Transient: where rights are given by someone else, usually familial such as in Freemasonry or other witchcraft, and the demon becomes present when the rights are challenged; akin to "peanut allergy" such that the effects arise situationally. The demonic claim will (as a rule) spike when the activity associated with the possession/curse is performed.

The **Praenotanda** of the Solemn Rite lists three primary signs indicative of possession: speaking/understanding languages unknown to the person, or other occult knowledge (making known distant or hidden events, knowledge of things beyond one's state in life); and display of power, superhuman strength (or strength beyond one's age or condition, to include shape-shifting); other indications include aversions to the sacred (i.e., a vehement aversion to God, the Holy Name of Jesus, the Blessed Virgin Mary or the saints, blessed objects, sacred ritual, sacred images, etc.).[37]

A **manifestation** is when a demon shows himself, normally in some physical manner. Spiritual attacks can also cause interior afflictions, such as darkness, despair, and sorrow.[38] Father Bamonte cites Fr. Antonio Royo Marín in describing the experience of affliction as "profound and unsurmountable repugnance for his duty or an intense desire to do what is prohibited, proposing to the mind all sorts of illicit and indecent fantasies which continue regardless of one's efforts to reject . . . a sense of anger, doubt, anguish, desperation, rebellion and antipathy . . . disproportionate affective impulses which do not correspond to one's personality."[39]

The following activities create a breach in your perimeter, thus opening the way for demonic affliction. In addition, many of these mock the sacraments or the various sacramentals that seek to bring grace to the soul:

Affliction—physical and/or mental distress experienced by a human; may have differing and multiple causes ranging from purely psychological to purely spiritual; generally, there is a combination of causation and augmentation where the demon fills the void.

Astrology—a pseudo-science which professes to judge the alleged occult influence of the stars upon human affairs.

---

[37] Weller, *Roman Ritual*, vol. II, 169. See also Bamonte, *Diabolical Possession*, 76.

[38] Bamonte, *Diabolical Possession*, 67. These can also find their origin in psychological causes, which our protocol is designed to discern.

[39] Bamonte, 67.

Clinging Spirit—an evil spirit that has become attached to an individual, normally sticking to him from the outside without actual possessing or obsessing the individual.

Curse—also called a hex; the intention of harming another through diabolic intervention; using black magic to bring misfortune or even death to the victim; a malediction or spell usually spoken, a counterfeit or inverse of a blessing which is made present or causes affliction to the extent one's relationship with God is impaired, e.g., the individual must have a spiritual vulnerability to suffer the effects of a curse. Unforgiveness is the greatest vulnerability to curses.

Divination—the act of foretelling the future or discovering the unknown through the aid of evil spirits. This is a species of superstition and always a grave sin against the virtue of religion.

Dolor—a form of extraordinary diabolic influence which consists of demons acting physically on the flesh of the person in such a way as to cause pain and even, at times, bruising and lacerations.

Incantation—the use of ceremony and formula of words spoken or chanted to produce a magical effect; this is often done in witchcraft to conscript a demon.

Incubus/Succubus—demons who have sex with women and men.

Infestation—extraordinary diabolical activity on a location, which may be as various as a house, pet, vehicle, object of art, etc.; usually indicative of a malefice or curse.

Malefice—the use of magical arts upon persons or objects with the intention of causing harm (sometimes even to do some good, although by evil means) to another or to his temporal goods by the intervention of a demon.

Necromancy—a form of spiritualism which attempts to get into communication with the spirits of the dead by invocation.

Pact—a signed document promising one's soul to the devil; a pseudo-contract made with the devil or demon.

Portal—inversion of the Catholic Church in which rituals are done in order to open up a channel or avenue by which demons can affect the surrounding areas. The demon who is placed to ensure the security of a portal is called a *portron*.

Snare—diabolical activity by which external circumstances or individuals are used to entrap a person spiritually or in the order of nature.

Vex/Vexation—a ritual curse or spell done to cause harm to another person; to trouble, afflict, harass, or distress physically or psychologically.

Witchcraft—a form of black magic practiced seeking the help of the devil and evil spirits; includes casting spells, sorcery, enchantment, etc.

These and other such activities create an **Open Door**, which is something that disposes an individual to a particular diabolic influence, caused either by oneself, another, or the pure permissible will of God. Other definitions relevant to the discussion, which help secure our spiritual perimeter, include the following:

Blessing—statement and/or action invoking divine favor upon a person, place or object; flows from one's relationship with God; it can be priestly, spousal, and lay.

"Chapter 3"—slang reference to Title 12, Chapter 3 *Rituale Romanum*, also known as the Leonine "Prayer against Satan and his fallen angels." Pope Leo XIII incorporated this prayer into the solemn rite of exorcism, which had previously contained Chapter 1 (*Praenotanda*), Chapter 2

(Solemn Exorcism), and now by inclusion, Chapter 3, the above-mentioned prayer. By recent proclamation from the Congregation for the Divine Faith, this prayer is now regulated and only available to priests for public use with episcopal permission.

Deliverance—the liberation of a person from diabolic influence and affliction; a form of minor exorcism which is counter distinguished from liberation, which is often associated with the person no longer being under diabolic possession.

Deprecatory Form—a petitioning of the Lord for a desired effect. In the deprecatory form, one asks the Lord, Our Lady, the angels, or a saint to be the agent of God's truth in an ultimately open way to the need for God's justice or the need for reconciliation.

Exorcism—the expelling of demons and freeing a demoniac from the influence of demons through the spiritual authority which Jesus entrusted to the Church; the expelling of evil spirits in cases of possession and obsession according to the right prescribed in the Roman ritual, and presently performed by a priest with the permission of his bishop; classified as major (with use of the solemn rights of the Church) or minor (deliverance prayers, prayer of minor exorcism using various rites and not requiring permission of the local Ordinary).[40]

Healing—the reordering of the faculties that have been damaged by sin; reconciliation with God the Father through the sacraments.

Imprecatory Form—the direct commanding of the demon of an incorporeal being, a fallen angelic presence. It is the commanding of that creature by another creature, but it must follow the natural law. Use of the

---

[40] "Exorcism is directed at the expulsion of demons or to the liberation from demonic possession through the spiritual authority which Jesus entrusted to his Church." *CCC* 1673.

imprecatory form is relegated to one who has not only the power but the authority to command it, such as the husband/father over his wife and children.

Liberation—the removal of the impediments to reconciliation with God the Father through the sacraments. Liberation comes about through: (1) the strengthening of the free will in a person, (2) an increased sanctification in a soul, and (3) re-ordering of life.

Obex—from the Latin meaning "barrier or wall," a hindrance, impediment, or obstacle which blocks the flow of grace to the soul; can be spiritual, moral, or psychological.

LESSON ONE: IDENTIFYING EVIL INFLUENCES

The inner logic of a thirty-day prayer prescription is based on our experience that "the demon responds to the imposition of order as much as to the prayer itself."[41] As a result, the thirty-day prescription may cause memories of past injuries to the surface, causing some acute, but telling, pain. Later, we will discuss how the demon has access to (and can even block) the memory, but for now, we will focus on how the demon enters through sin and lingers in the spiritual wounds of the mind and soul.

According to Saint John Henry Newman, "To live is to change, and to change often is to become more perfect." Suffering is also part of living and often marks points of change, for better or for worse, in a person's life. Many people have suffered interior trauma which, when negatively interiorized, can prevent positive change and growth toward spiritual perfection. At one level, *trauma* is a deeply subjective and volitional response to evil (whether physical, psychological, or spiritual). When a person lacks sufficient virtue to process the event in a healthy way, negative patterns of thought and behavior can

---

[41] Liber Christo, "Companion Guide," 51.

be formed (which can present a vulnerability for a demon to exploit). At other times, someone can suffer trauma, or the effects of trauma, without any volitional involvement. Children, for example, do not have full use of reason (or even have no use of reason in some cases) and can still experience the effects of trauma. The question for them is not *that* they suffered trauma when young but *how they will process it* once they have the use of reason. If either of these describe you, a good mental health professional can help you along this path.

For purposes here, the use of reason determines whether you allow a traumatic event in your life to draw you closer to God or cause you further alienation from Him. The modern definition of trauma tends, moreover, to be any experience of an abnormal (broadly defined) or deeply negative nature, which results in a wide appropriation of a variety of traumatic stressors. Such a broadly subjective definition of trauma can mean any experience that one finds as unbearable or insurmountable. Harvard professor and trauma expert Richard J. McNally recently noted, "In recent years, we have witnessed a conceptual bracket creep in the definition of trauma whereby ordinary stressors are now deemed capable of producing PTSD. The disorder is now being diagnosed among people whose stressful events range from exposure to crude jokes in the workplace to giving birth to a healthy baby—and much else in-between. Indeed, one study showed that nearly 90% of Americans qualify as trauma survivors—as trauma is currently defined."[42]

Because of the highly subjective nature of interior responses to life's events, some trauma can even be self-induced. A perceived rejection by one's parents, for example, can become a subjective reality in one's mind. Left unchecked, this, in turn, can expose a person to a spirit of rejection and an orphan spirit.

A popular theme in some healing ministries today is what is called *repressed memory recovery*. According to this theory, a memory can be so traumatic that it gets repressed entirely and no longer available to the person's consciousness. If the

---

[42] McNally, "Post-Traumatic Stress Disorder," 9.

memory is present, they claim that it has no cohesive narrative to the person. Only by "recalling" previous repressed memory through various techniques (often such as yoga and Eastern prayer forms) can one discover the hidden trauma which now oppresses him. Thus, there is a subjective disconnect and lack of narrative memory in one's life.

This practice is very dangerous, to the point where a statement signed by more than sixty-five prominent scientists and experts in the field of psychology denounced it before the Massachusetts Supreme Court, calling it "arguably the worst catastrophe to befall the mental health field since the lobotomy era."[43] This is germane to our discussion in that it shows the dangers of the subjectification of trauma. It also reveals how the psychological compatibility of the fallen human with a perceived trauma can attract the demon. The reader should bear this in mind when we later provide instructions in the next section to "resist telling the story" and be very suspicious of mystical phenomena.

Accordingly, any injury we suffer—or even perceive to have suffered—can lead to a host of emotions, such as unforgiveness, regret, remorse, sadness, et cetera. The phrase *perception is reality* can be applied here in the sense that the subjective appropriation of events can override the objectivity of the same events and become a *de facto* reality to the person. If we do not respond properly to the event, moreover, a high emotionality associated with the event can create a spiritual vulnerability to the demon—particularly the more we dwell on them interiorly and continue to "tell the story" to anyone and everyone.

What does that spiritual vulnerability look like? Simply stated, a psychological obsession can open the soul to a spiritual oppression or obsession. For this reason, we prefer a narrower definition of trauma. In recognizing the subjective response to the negative (and sometimes even terrible) events

---

[43] Brief for the False Memory Syndrome Foundation as Amicus Curiae, *Commonwealth v. Paul R. Shanley*, SJC-10382, http://www.fmsfonline.org/links/fmsfamicusshanley.html#note74.

in someone's life, McNally notes the existence of "preexisting personal vulnerabilities factors" as well. With regard to the diabolic, these personal vulnerabilities can mean an overemphasis of the emotional response, which may lead to a symbiotic attraction with the demon. That is, human anger attracts a demon of anger, human lust a demon of lust, human rebellion a demon of rebellion, et cetera. Thus, our past experiences can present vulnerabilities to evil influences.

Redemptive Suffering: The Envy of Angels

Trauma, then, must be bought into the objective through the use of reason and volition. Only in the Christian economy— the incarnation, suffering, death, and resurrection of God— does suffering have redemptive value. Many traumas remain only subjectively appropriated and never integrated into the objective reality of the cross, meaning that one's subjective response must be affixed to that object reality. Thus, we distinguish between trauma and violence because many wounds are the result of self-induced trauma (as McNally notes above). This is to say, violence is objective, and trauma is subjective, having to do with the way one reacts to, or what one perceives as, an offense. Trauma is the psychological response to an event that may or may not have been violent.

This means that one can have either a holy or an unholy response to traumatic events. As Kyle Clement notes:

> An example of the holy response that rejects the "victim" mentality is St. Maria Goretti, who was murdered during an attempted rape. During the attack she defended her purity and prayed for her attacker (Alessandro) that he would not commit this mortal sin and grave offense to God. After years in prison, Alessandro finally converted through her intercession (by his own words). Upon eventual release from prison, he entered a Capuchin monastery to live a life of penance and even stood with her family during her canonization ceremony

in Rome. This . . . provides the key for us to unlocking true freedom.[44]

This story from the life of a modern saint highlights the importance of the subjective response along the trauma-violence continuum. An experienced exorcist will tell you that Saint Maria Goretti is a powerful intercessor, perhaps because many cases today involve sexual trauma and disorder. Her charism is not simply sexual purity, however, but also emblematic of a perfected response along the violence-trauma continuum. She did not have a traumatic response to the bodily violence she suffered, but rather *she chose to become another Christ.* Like Christ, she suffered physical violence, but her objective offering for the soul of her attacker trumped her subjective response to the event. In the process, many graces were poured out.

Saint Maria Goretti's life, therefore, reveals great value that suffering holds in the economy of salvation. She exemplifies the sanctified response to traumatic events and is a powerful intercessor for those who have suffered sexual trauma or abuse. As I wrote, "Most Catholics are familiar with the phrase 'offer it up' in response to some minor inconvenience. There is much wisdom and spiritual fruit, however, in this simple truism. To be able to see the events of our lives in the light of their salvific potential is truly liberating."[45] Resentment over past hurts will both blind you to the opportunity for reparation and, as a result, block the flow of grace and healing. Conversely, if you have suffered trauma in your life, God has not only allowed it to happen but also handed you a powerful spiritual weapon. As Saint Paul writes, "where sin increased, grace overflowed all the more" (Rom 5:20). To the extent of the depth of the wound, there is a corresponding potential for more grace.

While vicarious suffering perfectly lines out with reality and revelation, demons reject it in their wills. The mantra of modern Satanism, for example, is "do what thou wilt," which

---

[44] Adapted from Liber Christo, "Companion Guide," 38.
[45] Adapted from Liber Christo, "Companion Guide," 38.

is a direct inversion of the surrender of Jesus, who prayed, "not my will but yours be done" (Lk 22:42). Saint Paul further proclaims, "The message of the cross is foolishness to those who are perishing, but to us who are being saved it is the power of God. . . . For the foolishness of God is wiser than human wisdom, and the weakness of God is stronger than human strength" (1 Cor 1:18, 25). The word for "message" is *logos*, which means "logic, reasoning, statement, expression of inward thought." Thus, Saint Paul even states, "I rejoice in my sufferings for your sake, and in my flesh, I am filling up what is lacking in the afflictions of Christ on behalf of his body, which is the church" (Col 1:24). To the Romans, he says, "I urge you therefore, brothers, by the mercies of God, to offer your bodies as a living sacrifice, holy and pleasing to God, your spiritual worship" (Rom 12:1).

Another saint who understood the value of suffering (and the logic of the cross) was Saint Teresa Benedicta of the Cross (Edith Stein). A Jewish convert and scholar who became a Carmelite nun, she was killed by the Nazis in the Auschwitz concentration camp. As she was being led away with her sister, she offered herself as an oblation for the Jewish people, saying, "Come, Rosa, we are going for our people." She fulfilled what she had written about at Carmel. "When someone desires to suffer," she wrote, "it is not merely a pious reminder of the suffering of the Lord. Voluntary expiatory suffering is what truly and really unites one to the Lord intimately." This is because, she said, "Christ the head effects expiation in these members of His Mystical Body who put themselves, body and soul, at His disposal for carrying out His work of salvation."[46] Whether the offering be great or small, you become intimately united to Christ and continue His salvific work.

By redemptive suffering, then, we mean the vicarious offering up of one's hardships (interior or exterior) so as to make satisfaction for sins. This means either the voluntary offering of one's suffering in reparation for one's own sins or for the sins of

---

[46] Saint Teresa Benedicta of the Cross, *The Hidden Life*, 92.

others. All sin offends God, and our voluntary suffering makes satisfaction for the temporal punishment due to sin, helping to restore union with God.[47] This means adapting a penitential posture towards the Lord and recognizing that sins of thought, word, and deed offend God. This includes prayers of reparation for the offenses against the Sacred Heart, sacrileges and blasphemies committed against the Holy Eucharist, and the indifference of souls towards the merciful hearts of Jesus and Mary.

Offering your suffering for your past helps unfetter the demon's chains and causes you to become more like Christ. This is the first stone to reach for when confronting Goliath. Recall from the discussion above how the early Christian writers saw the cross as the sword which slayed "the demon Goliath." In our experience, souls progress towards liberation to the extent of their ability to offer their sufferings "to fill up what is lacking" in Christ's suffering by becoming "a living sacrifice" through prayer and reparation. Redemptive suffering helps move the trauma from the subjective to the objective reality of Christ's cross and its merits.

Rogers also taught this to his rangers: "Don't use your musket if you can kill 'em with your hatchet." In other words, do it quietly and conserve your ammo. Redemptive suffering is a quiet, but effective, way to engage an enemy who has gotten inside your perimeter. Simply stated, the demon has access to the faculty of the memory, and the more one ruminates on a memory apart from Christ, the more the demon can begin to affect the memory. Conversely, when you offer your suffering in reparation for the sins of a relative whose soul is the most in danger, or for the person who has abused you or hurt you deeply (or for the purification of the Church, for your parish priest and local bishop, etc.) the diabolic grasp begins to loosen. The demon cannot stand beneath the weight of a soul united to Christ in such a manner. When he sees that hatchet, he quickly retreats.

---

[47] See *CCC* 1472–73.

A Psychological Compatibility

To be clear, the distinction needs to be made between those who open the door to extraordinary diabolic influence because of that compatibility (a demon of lust being attracted to a lustful person, rebellion attracted to the rebellious, etc.) and a person who becomes diabolically influenced while leading a holy life. The latter are those who may have been cursed or others who, by the pure will of God, the demon is allowed to influence (e.g., events in the later stages of purification in the life Saint Teresa of Avila, or Analiese Michele in the second possession, or some who are allowed to be influenced as victim souls). For example, in the case of a curse (if left unchecked), the demon can set about building that psychological compatibility which can occur later in the affliction. When we speak of *psychological compatibility* or a *symbiotic attraction* between the person and the demon, however, we imply those who open the door to the diabolic and not the rare cases of victim souls or stories from the lives of the saints. The reader should focus on the former, as very, very few fall into the category of the latter.

That being said, the demon will seek to perfect his control, often through what Father Ripperger calls "intertwining of the demon's empowerment and his own psychology with the psychology of the individual."[48] He takes advantage of psychological woundedness, as defined above, and uses a tactic of enmeshment to entangle the interiority of the afflicted person. As Father Ripperger notes, although at the beginning the "intertwining of the psychology of the demon and the person is not very strong," the more one "gives consent to the demon driving the obsession or thought patterns, over the course of time the demon becomes so powerful in the relationship to the human being's psychology that a codependence, at least in the order of thought and emotion, arises."[49] An essential part of liberation, therefore, is the

---

[48] Ripperger, *Dominion*, 294.
[49] Ripperger, 294.

unravelling of any compatibility which gives access to the demon to manipulate intellection and volition through the imagination. Thus, the definition of healing as reconciliation with God the Father means the presence of sanctifying grace in the soul through Penance *and also* the conformity of wills. Part of the process of the reconciliation of a desecrated church, for example, means destroying anything used or left there for evil purposes. By analogy, interior attachments which are intertwined with evil must also be destroyed.

Metanoia precedes manifestation in the sense that the demon will obfuscate until forced out. While the conventions of warfare in the days of Rogers meant brightly colored uniforms and linear battle arrangements, Rogers's rangers used camouflage to conceal their movement. The breaking of the enmeshment with the demon through the discipline of the protocol, we have found, causes a pattern break. It allows you to see the demon where he previously was able to hide. Your conversion causes him to react. In some cases, he may react by projecting visions, locutions (interior voices), and the like. Part of the pathway to custody of the interiority is the rejection of such mystical phenomena, as they are easily mimicked by the demon and, therefore, difficult to discern. This is not to say that spiritual gifts or charismata do not exist, but rather we recognize how subtle the demon is in manipulating our emotions by faking spiritual consolations.

Resist Telling the Story

Another of Rogers's rules can be applied here. "Don't sit down to eat," he cautioned, "without posting sentries." This means that a ranger knows that his enemy will attack him when his guard is down, not when he is ready for battle. Keep your spiritual guard up. Post sentries around your interior and keep your emotions in check. Admittedly, feelings of sadness, hurt, shame, or anger can arise when one suffers trauma of various kinds. However, if those emotions are not united with the suffering of Christ but rather given full voice, the negative reaction in the memory makes the person vulnerable to diabolic affliction. In addition, when someone persists in appropriating negative feelings and emotions, he often develops a victim mentality which also prolongs healing. To be clear, a person can be a victim in the sense of suffering some violence of which he was undeserving in relation to the person committing the violence. However, to give full expression to the hurt is to sit down to eat without posting a sentry.

Father Ripperger defines custody of the mind as "the virtue by which one does not let into the imagination anything sinful."[50] As part of custody of the mind, we discourage you from "telling your story" in describing your feelings vis-à-vis the event. To be clear, there are times in which someone must work through the events of their lives, particularly in a professional setting. Here, however, "telling the story" means unnecessarily rehashing the events of the past. Since the demon has access to our memories and can manipulate them to stir up emotions, repeatedly telling your story can empower the demon by giving him continued interior access. The real issue is that people often talk about the event unnecessarily when most of the time it does not need to be talked about. In the repeated retelling of the event, emotion often becomes intertwined with the event itself, making it very difficult to maintain objectivity.

For this reason, *Liber Christo* encourages you to *disappropriate* (that is, separate and isolate) your emotions from the event by linking them to Christ. This serves not to suppress your feelings but to place them in right order through an act of the will where they are subject to the intellect. An effective tactic is to place the traumatic memory somewhere along the continuum of the Paschal Triduum (the three days of Holy Thursday, Good Friday, and Holy Saturday). Are you feeling alone and abandoned? Join Jesus in the garden when the disciples abandoned Him. Is your suffering too hard to bear? Unite yourself to Mary

---

[50] Ripperger, 541.

at the foot of the cross. Do you feel rejected and ridiculed? Link those emotions to Jesus who was ridiculed by the religious leaders as He hung on the cross. By this simple technique, you begin to form the habit of separating the emotion from the memory. This not only removes the enemy's weapon against you but also teaches you the value of mental prayer in gaining custody of your thoughts—an essential element of spiritual warfare.

Nonetheless, our suffering takes on meaning when united to Christ. As Isaiah prophesied, "By his wounds we were healed" (Is 53:5). Accordingly, apart from a professional therapeutic or spiritual/pastoral setting, strive to tell your story only to Jesus Christ or Our Lady in prayer and focus rather on *your response* to the event. While emotions of distrust, depression, anger, unforgiveness, and others may linger, the question remains: What will you do with these emotions? Because disordered emotions attract the demon, they present a vulnerability and should be integrated into the objective reality of the Passion of Jesus Christ. In fact, if left unchecked, a psychological obsession over a past trauma—such as a divorce, a child who has left the Faith, financial hardship, the loss of a loved one, et cetera—can expose the soul to a spiritual oppression or (even) obsession.

As I wrote, "Our response to the wounding by others is critical to how quickly we may experience true healing and freedom from its effects." Thus:

> A wound occurs as a result of our feelings of offense at the actions of another. Our response to the wounding by others is critical to how quickly we may experience true healing and freedom from its effects. We can react to these injuries, attacks or insults in either a negative way or positive way. Admittedly, it is natural to feel emotions of anger, hurt or sadness at the initial time of an injury. When we continue to harbor negative feelings and act accordingly, however, we may gradually develop a "victim" mentality. Once we allow

this emotion to influence our thoughts, the demon quickly moves in.[51]

In the medical world, one speaks of response or reaction. If a doctor prescribes medicine and things improve, he will state that the body is *responding* to the medication. If, however, things do not go well, he will state that there is a *reaction* to the medicine, and it must be changed. When someone experiences trauma, he can either respond in a positive way or react in a negative way.

In the physical realm, *healing* also requires an active, ongoing engagement for a sustained healthy lifestyle. With spiritual healing, you must also take an active role, to include forming the habits which help you to achieve stability of mind and body. Spiritual healing is not based on your feelings (subjective) but rather on the state of your soul as reconciled with God the Father (objective). The former is subjective (and easily mimicked by the demon) and the latter is objective (and grounded in the sacraments and a state of grace, which helps us to resist the demon). Emotions, moreover, can be moved by the demons and, therefore, should not be the principle of judgment of a person's state of soul. You may experience an emotional release when you "get it off your chest," but when expressed outside of a professional (medical or spiritual) setting, emotions may return you to a place of unforgiveness, a lack of charity, and even despair.

A Ranger Buddy at Your Six

Every ranger has a "ranger buddy" on the team to help him through the rigorous training. This fellow ranger helps carry your load when you are down, looks out for you, and is there when things get hardest and darkest. In military language, he has your "six" (the *six* refers to the six o'clock position on the dial, meaning your back, or what is behind you that you

---

[51] Liber Christo, "Companion Guide," 37.

cannot see). God has given to you a guardian angel as your ranger buddy. As Jesus said, "For I say to you that their angels in heaven always look upon the face of my heavenly Father" (Mt 18:10). The *Catechism* states, "From its beginning until death, human life is surrounded by their watchful care and intercession. Beside each believer stands an angel as protector and shepherd leading him to life. Already here on earth the Christian life shares by faith in the blessed company of angels and men united in God."[52]

Part of an angel's mission is to fight off demons, whom Saint Peter refers to as a "roaring lion" (1 Pt 5:8). Listen to the words of the psalmist: "For he commands his angels with regard to you, / to guard you wherever you go. / With their hands they shall support you, / lest you strike your foot against a stone. / You can tread upon the asp and the viper, / trample the lion and the dragon" (Ps 91:11–13).

The Greek word *angelos* means "messenger," and, far superior to us, they serve as messengers of God to communicate His plan of salvation and will for us.[53] Thus, "as purely spiritual creatures, angels have intelligence and will: they are personal and immortal creatures, surpassing in perfection all visible creatures, as the splendor of their glory bears witness."[54]

As Father Ripperger notes, angels "help man in attaining heaven" both in directing man's actions to the good and also to "free man from the that which impedes" him from heaven. They are called "guardian" angels because "the ultimate effect of [their] custody is [man's] salvation."[55] In his assignment to

---

[52] *CCC* 336.

[53] See *CCC* 238–336. The *Catechism* quotes Saint Augustine who says: "'Angel' is the name of their office, not of their nature. If you seek the name of their nature, it is 'spirit'; if you seek the name of their office, it is 'angel': from what they are, 'spirit,' from what they do, 'angel.'" Thus, "With their whole beings the angels are servants and messengers of God. Because they 'always behold the face of my Father who is in heaven' they are the 'mighty ones who do his word, hearkening to the voice of his word.'" *CCC* 329.

[54] *CCC* 330.

[55] Ripperger, *Dominion*, 51–52. For an in-depth discussion on guardian angels, see Ripperger, *Dominion*, 51–70.

watch your *six*, your guardian angel has several principal tasks
that include:

1.   Ward off danger of body and soul
2.   Strengthen you in times of temptations
3.   Illumine holy thoughts and desires
4.   Offer prayers to God
5.   Correct you after sin
6.   Help at hour of death
7.   Conduct soul to heaven/purgatory (consoles there)

Your angel does not see things or communicate in the same
way as you do. According to the Thomistic understanding of
the human person, the human intellect understands concepts
through abstraction by means of images (or "phantasms") in
the imagination which can then assist the person to gain a
more perfect insight into a particular thing.[56] This is different
than how the angels know and communicate, which is by direct
illumination or projection. They prompt us with "good temptations" by placing images and concepts in the imagination. They
cannot read our minds or know the future, nor can they infuse
things directly into the higher intellect. They, nonetheless,
help our intellection by prompting us via phantasm so that we
engage with the natural light of reason. Thus, they influence
our thoughts indirectly so as to prompt us to assent to the
truths of the Catholic faith and also to choose to do good.[57]

The fallen angels, or demons, also retain their angelic nature
and likewise can project a phantasm, or an image in the imagination, so as to manipulate against the good and the holy.
While the demon cannot act directly upon the human intellect or will, he does have access to the body and, consequently,
the imagination, memory, and emotions.[58] Father Ripperger
(following Saint Thomas Aquinas) shows how "they can only

---

[56] See Saint Thomas Aquinas, *Summa Theologica* I q. 111, art. 1; De Ver.,
q. 11, art. 3.
[57] See Saint Thomas Aquinas, *Sentences*, II D. 8, q. 5; cf. *Summa Theologica* I,
q. 111, art. 2; q. 106, art. 2.
[58] See Tanqueray, *The Spiritual Life*, no. 221.

cause a phantasm which has something prior in the memory, i.e., they must use prior sense data." This is significant in that the demons can only use as the source of temptation the "data stored in the memory."[59] By merging, distorting, and manipulating a person's memory, however, they can project various images into the imagination so as to distort the reality of past events, other people, objects, et cetera.

One area of access to the imagination is the "data storage" of the memory and its concomitant emotions. For this reason, part of the logic of the thirty-day withdrawal into the desert is to deprive the demon of sensory images to use against you. This, in turn, has two principal benefits: it helps to purify the memory and calm the emotions.

Emotions are subject to the senses, and the body cannot be trusted as an objective indicator of our relationship with God. That is to say, emotional satisfaction is not a reliable indicator of spiritual progress. Thus, we also encourage you to ignore all mystical phenomena because these can be easily mimicked by the demon, especially where there are deep emotional wounds in a soul. As an exercise to explain how this concept works as it applies to liberation, stop for a moment and bring to your memory a very painful experience from your past. This may be the death of a loved one, abandonment, divorce, sexual abuse, et cetera. As that memory becomes more vivid and detailed, notice the emotions that also arise. You may notice flushes of anger, shame, fear, resentment, lust, or guilt. Once the memory and the emotions are co-present in your mind, try to separate (or disappropriate) the emotion from the memory. This is not an easy task because the memory is imbued with the emotion related to the perception of the event. The recalling of a memory, therefore, also brings the emotions previously associated with it. Even positive emotions like nostalgia or delight accompany good memories. When painful memories are not fully integrated by a willful act of linking with the suffering of Christ, however, they present an acute spiritual vulnerability.

---

[59] Ripperger, *Introduction to the Science of Mental Health*, 533.

Since demons have access to our memory through the images present there, they can manipulate our emotions by "triggering" a memory and distorting those images. With the emotion present in the imagination, they can then project phantasms (images)—even false perceptions of an event itself—into the imagination. Once you appropriate that emotion, the demon can begin to manipulate your thoughts via the imagination. A demon may even project thoughts seemingly voiced with your own interior speech. This means that you could have difficulty discerning your own self-talk, prayer, and the discernment of the will of God from diabolic locutions. This is why the custody of the mind that is gained through the re-ordering of the life to prayer in this protocol is so essential to liberation.

While demons may know your past, they do not know your future. They do, however, "attempt to stir up the memory to illicit an emotional response" from you. Thus, "when emotions are high and we are interiorly unstable/unrested, they then project a new version of the memory into the imagination. The more a person dwells on the past, the more demons come in to work in distorting the memory. One of the first emotions which the demon projects is *shame*, with the rest of the cluster close behind: *embarrassment*, *self-accusation*, *worthlessness*, *self-condemnation*, and *humiliation* [which] directly militate against our core identity as beloved children of God."[60]

Accordingly, we affirm that "emotions are part of being human and valid human experiences . . . [and] not every emotion is diabolically influenced." Nonetheless, "a high emotionality can present a vulnerability to the soul. This is to say, the demon is attracted to emotionally charged situations and events."[61] For this reason, self-mastery over the emotions by custody of the mind is essential to interior freedom. The adversary circles around emotionally charged events.

---

[60] Liber Christo, "Companion Guide," 54.
[61] Liber Christo, "Companion Guide," 53.

Angels, Emotions, and
Clusters of Evil Spirits[62]

Your ranger buddy, your guardian angel, is only one type of angel; there are myriads of types of angels with various missions working within their specific order and choir.[63] Exorcists and theologians have long wrestled with how to categorize angels and demons. According to Saint Thomas, each angel (glorified or fallen) is unique—that is, each is his own species—which makes categorizing demons a nearly impossible task.[64] They do, however, "tend to work in clusters that hover around human emotions, particularly where vice is present."[65] For purposes here, note how a principal defect brings with it other concomitant vices and spirits. These, in turn, create vulnerabilities which attract certain demons.

In this section, we begin with the principle that *angels go where they are asked, and demons go where they are not resisted.* Thus, the demons work in clusters which build upon human weaknesses, especially where no resistance is given. Note how the defects in human formation attract evil spirits working within these groupings, as if like unto like. Herein lies what is referred to as a *symbiotic attraction* between the wounded human and fallen angel, and therefore, the need to identify areas of psychological compatibility is key to liberation. Thus, the more you repair the defect in formation, the more you

---

[62] The vices and spirits listed here are from Ripperger, *Minor Exorcisms*, 419–28. Used with permission.

[63] The nature and mission of the angels is beyond the scope here. The Fathers of the Church, tracing back to Pope Saint Gregory the Great, generally hold that there are nine orders of angels grouped into three choirs. Cf. Ripperger, *Dominion*, 37.

[64] In recent years, the concept of clusters of spirits comes from several annual conferences on Healing in the Roman Catholic Tradition held from 2005 to 2012 at the University of St. Mary of the Lake in Mundelein, Illinois. Kyle Clement contributed to those workshops and presented on this topic at the WSFI Spiritual Warfare Conference at Mundelein in 2015. "Clusters" is a means of classifying demons as they relate to spiritual defects so as to begin the process of gaining interior separation from them.

[65] Liber Christo, "Companion Guide," 53–54.

grow in holiness—and the less the demon can influence you. Rather than an overly rigid schema of classification of angels and demons, I suggested elsewhere that it is better to see these clusters of spirits as in a "paint wheel" which organizes paint colors within "similar hues."[66] This section contains abbreviated versions Father Ripperger's book of minor exorcism and is what exorcists use "to determine the sin, vice or spirit involved" when dealing with cases of extraordinary diabolic affliction.[67] What follows are the most common, but you will find a full list in appendix C. As you read through these, ask your ranger buddy to identify the ones that you need to work on.

The Orphan Spirit

A common defect in many Christians today that exposes a soul to diabolic influences stems from what is referred to as an *orphan lifestyle*. This spirit exploits the lack of relationship with God the Father. The orphan spirit usually finds its root in an independent or counter-dependent lifestyle based on a lack of the experience of true divine filiation (that of one's true identity as a beloved son or daughter of God). This sense of fatherlessness and/or motherlessness can lead to a lack of true identity (i.e., a sense of "nowhere to call home"). This spirit manifests itself in an *inability to share negative feelings with others, overcompensating, depression, a general dissatisfaction, and a restlessness or unsettledness*. Other manifestations include *inconsistency, rebellion, isolation, disconnectedness, shrinking back, powerlessness, comparing, impatience, disordered comforting of oneself through food, drink, or busyness, searching, false self-image*, and *a lacking belief of a true inheritance with God*.

If this describes your situation, you should confess any sins related to these spirits and wounds and also renounce the traumas, curses, and sins of the orphan lifestyle of your father or mother, and ancestors. You should also seek God the

---

[66] Liber Christo, "Companion Guide," 55.
[67] Ripperger, *Minor Exorcisms*, 419.

Father's blessings, to include the blessing of being found and connected to the Father with the awareness of deep belonging, of knowing our true identity as a beloved son or daughter of God, of being accompanied, seen, and known, of calm, purpose, and of being deeply satisfied and of the sense of family and confident of my inheritance of God, a heavenly home.

Pride and the Self:
Spirits of Guilt, Shame, and Rejection

Guilt is the experience of remorse over having done something wrong. The more you focus on the past, ruminating over the memory of past wounds, the more demons can work in distorting your memory. There is a positive and a negative type of shame. Saint Thomas calls shame a virtue—that is, a positive interior movement. He refers to this *virtue of shame* as the physiological distress or physical discomfort at the perception of wrongdoing, either by someone else or more poignantly by yourself. The virtue of shame is, essentially, a prick of conscience at the realization that you have done something wrong. The prick of conscience can also lead to an unhealthy guilt where "the Accuser" (cf. Rv 12:10), the devil, distorts this virtue of shame through accusing and condemning by projecting a negative, self-condemnatory *shame*.

Common spirits which co-animate with this vice are *narcissism, self-contempt, self-love, self-seeking behavior, self-destruction, self-abandonment, self-aggrandizement, self-assumed heavy burdens,* and *feeling unloved or unwanted.* Of note here is that one must catch the subtleties of the emotions. Although these may be valid human emotions, when the self—and not Christ—becomes the center, then the demon can use them against you. He militates against your baptismal dignity as a child of God, beloved by the heavenly Father.

A negative shame can flow from pride. Saint Thomas Aquinas refers to *pride* as the first sin, the worst sin, and the source of all other sins. Thus, it is an "excessive desire for one's own excellence" without any submission to God.[68] This defect stems from a disordered esteem of oneself and is marked by a "willful disobedience that recoils against rightful authority."[69] In his rebellion, Satan desired his own greatness and excellence apart from God. Spirits that are attracted to pride include *envy, bragging, haughtiness and arrogance, detraction, rebelliousness, perfectionism, rigidity, entitlement, machismo, egoism, distortion of truth, agitation, religiosity/spiritual superiority, intemperance, minimalization of sin, workaholism.*

The orphan lifestyle can stem from deep feelings of *rejection* and a turning in on the self. Notably, a prideful response to an event often stems from a subjective response of *rejection*. The spiritual defect that first flows from pride is *vanity*, which can be seen as the disordered desire for the affirmation of creatures (or created things) over that of Creator. This seeking of the affirmation of others and not God is a subtle indicator of a lack of connection with God the Father, which precedes the rejection response. The demon heavily traffics in this area, and it leads to *fear of people and their opinions*, and *human respect*. This can lead to spirits of *disordered love or compassion, self-assumed heavy, pious,* or *false burdens,* an *inability to receive or give love, shame, guilt, self-reliance* and *self-sufficiency, feeling accused, blaming/critical and impulsive.* The primary antithesis to rejection, then, is humility and the bearing of unpleasant events with patience.

Sexual Spirits and Anger

Sexual abuse and sexual deviancy are common among those who are spiritually afflicted, as gravely evil acts will often have diabolic accompaniment. Sexual abuse and disordered sexuality frequently lead to spirits of *disordered love relationships, pornography and masturbation, sexual fantasy and perversion,*

---

[68] Thus, "the proud man subjects not his intellect to God, that he may receive the knowledge of truth from Him." Saint Thomas Aquinas, *Summa Theologica* II-II, q. 162, art. 3.
[69] Liber Christo, "Companion Guide," 55.

lust, fornication, promiscuity, contraception, adultery, homosexu-
ality (Baal), lesbianism (Ishtar), demons of incubus and succubus,
pedophilia, Jezebel/seduction, unnatural intercourse, lack of mod-
esty, and *incest.* Common psychological wounds are *depression*
which leads to *hopelessness* and *despair.*

Sexual abuse can lead to *deep anger* and *rage. Anger* is "an
emotional sense of displeasure and usually antagonism,
aroused by real or apparent injury."[70] Whether hot or cold, this
spirit of anger can lead to spirits of *resentment, unforgiveness,*
spite and *animosity, brooding over injuries, bitterness, a spirit of*
death, stubbornness, confusion, self-mutilation, marital discord,
foul language, lying, gossip, sarcasm, cynicism, and blasphemy.

Using Your Hatchet: Spiritual
Defects, Vices, and Spirits

Bear in mind that the demon sees you differently than your
unbaptized neighbor. He recognizes the indelible mark of
Baptism which conforms you to Christ and the Church. Any
behavior inconsistent with this mark can draw the demon to
you, particularly within one's vocational construct. For this
reason, he is "drawn to us by a pattern break in righteous
behavior. This is especially true of deviant behavior that presents a vulnerability to the construct of a sacrament through
which grace flows."[71] A married man who takes his family to
Mass every Sunday but looks at pornography presents a pattern break. A person bearing the indelible mark of Baptism
who has an abortion, or in any way participates in abortion,
likewise presents a pattern break. The priest who does not say
Mass on his day off and instead attends a punk rock concert
exhibits a pattern change from his vocational sacrament. Any
behavior inconsistent with the ordering of natural law, divine
positive law, vocation, and Christian dignity creates a vulnerability that attracts the demon.

---

[70] Hardon, *Modern Catholic Dictionary*, 26.
[71] Liber Christo, "Companion Guide," 150.

If you recognize any of these above defects, vices, and spirits active in you, use your hatchet and militate against them with virtue and sacramental confession. As I wrote elsewhere, "By developing the virtues that correspond to the vices associated with the spirit, the soul now grows in self-mastery. As the Scripture says, 'Resist the devil, and he will flee from you' (Jas 4:17)." When we do not counterattack with a virtue, the demon is further empowered by vices. Developing the virtues that correspond to the vices associated with the spirit assists the soul in self-mastery. Thus, "confessing these vices by name . . . helps to break their hold over us. To rebuke, renounce and reject, moreover, is a vital step to becoming free of these spirits and their effects."[72]

When Jesus exorcised the Gerasene demoniac, for example, He demanded the demon to reveal its name ("Legion is my name," Mk 5:9). In a similar manner, during the Solemn Rite of Exorcism, the priest demands that the demon reveal his name. Jesus was asserting His authority over the ancient enemy of man, and the priest acting *in persona Christi* continues the same activity of dominion over evil spirits. In the primordial garden, God gave Adam dominion over all creatures by giving him the authority to name them (see Gn 1:28, 2:19). Accordingly, when you name the spirit and vice, first in the confessional, and then reject, renounce, and rebuke it by name, you loosen its power over you.

The list of vices can be overwhelming, so begin with the main one that you see. For example, bird hunters know the importance of picking their target before shooting. Quail, for example, travel in ground cover and fly only in short bursts when evading danger. When a covey of quail is flushed by a hunter or his dogs, the entire covey floods the air together in a moment of chaos before quickly finding cover again. The window for the hunter to shoot opens and closes very quickly. The instinct the hunter must override is the tendency to shoot into the covey in the hopes of hitting one of them. This never

---

[72] Liber Christo, "Companion Guide," 56.

works. The experienced hunter knows he must pick one bird, take aim, and pull the trigger.

Like hunting birds, you must also flush out the demon and vice through prayer and then take aim. We refer to this process as *severing of spirits*. This is done by a priest in deliverance and minor exorcism but can also be done by individuals over themselves. Rogers's advice to his rangers to "kill 'em with your hatchet" can be applied here. Once you identify these enemies in your soul, first confess the spiritual defect and any related sins, and then use your "hatchet" (that is, your will) to sever them. List evil spirits and vices that you need to sever:

A simple **prayer of renunciation** is:
I completely and utterly reject, with the full force of my will N. (insert any disorder one is experiencing or any evil one has committed).
I do this in the Holy Names of Jesus and Mary and in the name of the Father and of the Son and of the Holy Spirit. Amen. (Thrice)[73]

Once you identify a spirit or vices, you can pray a **Perimeter Prayer**:
I adjure all you evil spirits, in the name of the spotless Lamb of God, Jesus of Nazareth, to depart from here. I cast you out, every unclean spirit, every phantom, every encroachment of the devil. Yield then to God! You are vanquished in your citadel, all you vile demons. The most Sovereign Queen

---

[73] N.B. The instruction to pray a prayer thrice, or three times, is to directly counter any curses which often are prayed with a threefold seal in a mockery of the thrice-holy God.

of Heaven, the glorious and ever Virgin Mary, through her immaculate purity drives you out; before her countenance you must flee. Give way, you evil spirits, to the Queen of Heaven. She is destined by Almighty God to crush your head with her heel.

Appendix A contains other prayers as well, and appendix C lists more sins, vices, or spirits.

From Slingstones to Milestones: Introduction and Renouncing Evil Influences

1. How do you understand the statement, "The demon responds to the imposition of order as much as to deliverance prayers themselves"?

2. Do you identify in your life any of the ways that King Saul allowed the demon to get "inside his perimeter"? In other words, are there interior dispositions that allow the enemy to influence your thoughts, words, and deeds?

3. What in this lesson caused an interior resistance, such as anxiety or something you just did not like?

4. What is your takeaway from the story of David and Goliath and the symbolism of the five smooth stones?

5. Can you explain "psychological compatibility"?

6. After reading this lesson, are there any injuries you may have suffered that evoke unforgiveness, regret, remorse, sadness, or some other emotion? (Perceptions, objective vs. subjective)

7. What strategies can you employ to control the "data storage" of the memory and imagination?

LESSON TWO: HOLY AND UNHOLY ALLIANCES

U pon seeing David armed not as a warrior but with the weapon of the common shepherd, Goliath asks, "'Am I dog? That you come to me with a staff?' Then the Philistine cursed David by his gods" (1 Sm 17:43). To this day, feral dogs roam the Middle Eastern deserts outside of cities, surviving off refuse. David would have often used his slingshot to defend his sheep against these pack animals. According to Scott Hahn, "The dog in the Old Testament is a scavenger, equated with impurity." A "dog" was also a derogatory term, for example, to describe a male prostitute (see Dt 23:18).[74] In addition, the cultic purity of ancient Israel held in disdain the ritualistic, cultic sexual practices of the surrounding Gentiles. Like feral dogs that copulate indiscriminately, so did the Gentiles in their unholy rituals. For these, and other reasons, the ancient Jews considered the Gentiles as impure, scavenging and unclean "dogs." To call someone a "dog," therefore, was a grave insult (cf. 2 Sm 3:8; 16:9; Ps 22:17).

Note the irony in Goliath's words. The Philistines' religious rituals to their false gods resembled that of a dog copulating indiscriminately. For this reason, God commanded the people, as they approached the Promised Land, to make a clean break form their past idolatry while in the slavery of Egypt: "No longer shall they [the Israelites] offer their sacrifices to the demons with whom they prostituted themselves. This shall be an everlasting statute for them and their descendants" (Lv 17:7). How does a people "prostitute themselves with demons"? They defiled themselves then as many still do today: through ritualistic and indiscriminate sex. For this reason, God commanded Israel, "You shall not do as they do in the land of Egypt, where you once lived, nor shall you do as they do in the land of Canaan, where I am bringing you; do not conform to their customs" (Lv 18:3). Notably, Goliath

---

[74] Hahn, *Catholic Bible Dictionary*, 222.

was from the Philistine region of southern Canaan.[75] Leviticus describes what their "customs" entailed, detailing the forbidden sexual acts of incest of all sorts as well as bestiality (see Lv 18:7–24). Only dogs mate so capriciously. David's answer, then, was "yes, you are a dog, like all of your people."

The Israelites were, at times, no different than the Philistines in their sexual behavior as they fell back into false worship. Today, as well, many Catholics have sexual practices no different than their non-Catholic neighbors. Sex is a spiritually imbued act which can either be holy or unholy. For this reason, the demon particularly seeks to defile the marital act and distort the generative principle. In this section, we discuss the bonds created through unholy actions.

Spiritual and Psychological Bonds

Standing before the enemy who taunts and ridicules both you and God while facing the prospect of slavery and death, you may have come to realize that you have been unfaithful to God in many areas of your life. Many who have done this protocol report that certain memories of past sins now plague them. This is often due to the formation of *unholy soul ties*.[76] In modern times, the concept of "soul ties" has been popularized by Christian psychologist James Dobson, and not often presented from a traditional Catholic point of view. Although not writing from a Christian perspective, psychologist Carla Maria Manly (rightly, in my estimation) defines a soul tie as an "emotional or spiritual cording . . . an inexplicable, powerful

---

[75] This is perhaps the backdrop of Jesus's seemingly harsh words to the Canaanite woman, "It is not right to take the food of the children and throw it to the dogs" (Mt 15:26).

[76] This section, affirmed also in the experience of Father Ripperger, builds upon a presentation by Kyle Clement at the Pope Leo Institute in 2015, and is also found in Liber Christo, "Companion Guide," 78–81. Their contribution to the discussion lies in the expanded, Catholic, view of the phenomena. This includes the concepts of psychological compatibility with the animating demon, soul ties as created in a multiplicity of ways, and the ligatures formed in generational (procreational) curses.

emotional bond to another person."[77] The broad appeal of the idea of soul ties suggests that they are part of the human experience. Our human experience teaches us that holy alliances are created between married couples, holy friendships, and the like.

Although interest in soul ties is seemingly a modern (and non-Catholic) phenomenon, our understanding of holy and unholy bonds which unite souls traces its roots to both Saint Paul and Pope Saint Leo the Great. Saint Leo alluded to holy alliances when he wrote of that peace of soul that "the most intimate bonds of friendship and the closest affinity of minds cannot truly lay claim to . . . if they are not in agreement with the will of God." Peace is the reward of holy acts done together because, as Clement explains, "holy alliances are formed by acting together for the good, such as in a vocation, in service to the Church, in pursuit of the virtues, or in the pursuit of holiness."[78] These, Pope Saint Leo writes, "are bound together in holy harmony and are rightly given the heavenly title of sons of God, co-heirs with Christ."[79] These holy bonds are formed between parents and children, spouses, friends, teachers and students, et cetera and lead souls closer to God.

The opposite, however, appears also to be true. As Saint Paul writes, "Do not be led astray: 'Bad company corrupts good morals'" (1 Cor 15:33). This means that (pace, Clement) "we adapt the attributes of those with whom we associate with, particularly the effect that immoral people can have on those who are moving closer to God."[80] Certain acts bind people together in an unholy way and, consequently, away from God because they are "formed in practices and associations which are a perversion and corruption of the above [and] are forged in the transgressions of the commandments."[81] Thus, Father Ripperger defines a soul tie as "a spiritual bond between two

[77] Manly, "Pros and Cons," 4.
[78] Liber Christo, "Companion Guide," 156.
[79] Pope Saint Leo, Sermon 95, 8–9.
[80] Liber Christo, "Companion Guide," 157.
[81] Liber Christo, "Companion Guide," 78.

individuals, normally as a result of a mutual sin committed together or the sin of one committed against the other."[82] Sexual sins, abortion, criminal activity, and other violations of the moral teachings of the Church have the opposite effect of holy bonds. In our prudential experience, certain acts are so gravely evil that they have diabolic accompaniment. That is, the demons present to the act both co-animate and accompany the sinful behavior. As Saint Leo affirms, "Alliances based on evil desires, covenants of crime and pacts of vice all lie outside the scope of this peace."[83] Thus, while holy alliances bring peace, unholy ligatures bind those who commit grave sins together, creating unrest. The very word *conspire* means to "breathe together," and when two people conspire to commit evil, a spiritual bond is created.

For purposes here, the demon can continue to operate along these psychological and emotional ligatures (the "inexplicable, powerful emotional bonds" of Manly) between persons due to the demon's access to what Father Ripperger refers to as the "data stored in the memory." They operate through the imagination where the ties created through certain unholy acts provide a pathway for the projection of manipulated and distorted emotionally charged memories. Thus, these unholy bonds must be broken through sacramental confession and certain prayers as part of the temporal punishment due to sin.

For this reason, we hold that all unholy alliances are defect driven. According to Father Ripperger, "the demons are always trying to incite people to the excess or the defect in behavior."[84] Shared defects in virtue can sometimes become the commonality of a relationship and can become a point of unholy fixation for a person. This is often the case in divorce, marital infidelity, and the like. This can also be seen in the desire to manipulate or control, which can become the source of the unholy alliance. Behind the scenes, as it were, a co-animation of spirits can occur which exploits the common

---

[82] Ripperger, *Dominion*, 555.
[83] Pope Saint Leo, *Sermon 95*, 8–9.
[84] Ripperger, *Dominion*, 111.

defects or excesses which lead to mortal sin and concomitant unholy alliances.

Thus, Father Ripperger defines a negative soul tie as a "spiritual bond between two individuals, normally as a result of a mutual sin committed together or the sin of one committed against the other."[85] To detect the presence of any unholy ties, one should first go to Our Lady of Sorrows. As the words of Simeon at the Presentation in the Temple suggest: "(and you yourself a sword will pierce) so that the thoughts of many hearts may be revealed" (Lk 2:35). Ask her to reveal any unholy alliances, unconfessed mortal sins, or any defects which bind you to your past and prevent you from getting closer to God. The most common sins which create unholy soul ties include:

- incest and rape,
- homosexual acts,
- physical and emotional abuse,
- unholy sex acts, even within marriage,
- vows and pacts in the occult such as Freemasonry and other witchcraft,
- tattoos,
- criminal acts,
- pornography,
- abortion, and
- participation in satanic rock music.

If you had an abortion, for example, what Father Ripperger refers to as a "spiritual bond between two individuals" resulting "mutual sins committed together" was formed between you and the father of the child, the abortionist, staff, and anyone who counselled you or drove you to the clinic.[86]

If you consulted a *curandera*, or palm reader, an unholy alliance was likewise formed. If you were a victim of abuse, an unholy bond was created between you and the abuser. Every

---

[85] Ripperger, 555.
[86] Ripperger, 555.

previous sexual partner outside of sacramental marriage has created an unholy alliance. Breaking soul ties includes getting rid of any artifacts (gifts, photos, freemasonic regalia, etc.) related to the person or event, especially evil objects. Any interior resistance to getting rid of the objects suggests that an unholy bond may exist.

Releasing the Stone

A slinger first swings his sling overhead to gain momentum. This increases the terminal velocity of his projectile and maximizes its impact. Like David's stone, which penetrated through the helmet of Goliath before embedding into his forehead (see 1 Sm 17:49), the force of this stone increases when the sacraments are combined with inner purity. While sacramental confession removes the guilt of any sin, the breaking of soul ties helps to purify the memory and emotions so that the demon can no longer manipulate you through the imagination. Thus, when the breaking of soul ties is combined with sacramental Penance, not only is the sin forgiven, but also the emotional and psychological ligatures severed. This helps to untie the psychological enmeshment which, in turn, assists in removing any psychological compatibility that binds your soul to another in an unhealthy way.

The military uses a strategy of *counter-battery* when assaulted with artillery or mortars. When the enemy fires upon a combat outpost (COP), our military technology can track the source of the projectile and immediately fire back at the enemy's source. The artillery can even have a round outbound before the enemy's inbound round impacts. Spiritual warfare works in a similar way. Your interior life is like a combat outpost which must be defended. The demon uses unconfessed sin and unholy soul ties as an unprotected flank to launch his projectiles into your interiority. While a soul in a state of mortal sin has no protection, the emotional and psychological vulnerabilities from common sins with others create a vulnerability to your COP. Once you have confessed the sin and broken any unholy soul tie, however, you close off that vulnerability. You can now *project back* prayers for the other person, like counter-battery, in a free and holy way.

When the demon tries to project images of past sins through this bond, you are now invited to pray for the other person. The "accuser" now has no merits by which he can accuse you because the sin has been removed sacramentally and you have broken the psychological and emotional ligatures of your past. Your prayers for the other person hold even more merit. By the grace of God, you are on the pathway to freedom, holiness, and salvation, but you may not know where the other person is. To silence the enemy's projections over your past sins, therefore, project prayers back for the person with whom you have severed unholy ties.

This should be done in conjunction with, and as supplementary to, the sacrament of Penance. Recite the prayer of breaking of soul ties three times, preferably before the Blessed Sacrament. This should be done for each person with whom you have committed grave sin: three times for every previous sexual partner, anyone with whom you committed a crime, et cetera. If you had an abortion, do the same for the sire of the child, the doctor and staff involved, and anyone who accompanied you to the clinic. If you participated in witchcraft, break ties with anyone involved. Our Lady of Sorrows will lead you through those painful memories and help in breaking their hold on you. Once you have completed this, the enemy may try to project into the memory again. When that happens, know that the sin is forgiven and the tie is broken. Take it as an opportunity to pray for the other people. God has given you the great grace of conversion, so pray that they also might be set free.

According to Clement, discerning whether an alliance is holy or unholy is "our experience of the love of God." That is, "alliances which bring us closer to God are likely to be holy, and those that bring us farther away from God are most likely unholy." He considers it a three-step process: "First, we need to reject the relationship and we need to forgive; both forgive ourselves and the person with whom we had the alliance. Second, we need to renounce any disordered behaviors that were associated with the relationship (excessive drinking, gossip, improper language, etc.). Finally, we need to rebuke any attitude, spirit, disposition, or personality trait associated with this relationship (people-pleasing, neglect of vocation, etc.)."[87]

We can discern an unholy alliance though behavior changes around certain people, generally some form of a lack of virtue. In addition, part of the process of severing soul ties is getting rid of any material objects that remind you of the unholy relationship (gifts, jewelry, photos, etc.). Often, the presence of some interior resistance (a spiritual, physical, or psychological attachment) to parting with the object(s) suggests some unholy connection.

Pornography, for example, creates a soul tie. We directly combat pornography through the mortification of the flesh. The practice of Christian ascetical practices—through fasting, vigils, and other disciplines—help to mortify (literally, "to put to death") sinful tendencies. As Clement states, we also fight against impurity "through the devotion to the five Sacred Wounds of Jesus, particularly the wounded feet of Jesus. The desecration and wounding of His flesh was the result to our own sins of the flesh and, therefore, meditating on His wounds makes satisfaction for our carnal sins. In so doing, we slowly purify the unholy images embedded in our memories by the holy images of Christ's wounds. Accordingly, when the demon tempts us to look at pornography, we can project back to him images of the wounds of Christ."[88]

Following the example of Saint Mary Magdalene, you can spiritually embrace the feet of Christ in atonement for your sins (cf. Lk 7:36–50; 8:2). Accordingly, when the demon tempts you to look at pornography, you can project back to him, like stones from a slingshot, images of the five wounds of Christ.

---

[87] Liber Christo, "Companion Guide," 156.
[88] Liber Christo, "Companion Guide," 158.

As you consider your past, bear in mind that "the demon is tertiary in Catholic liberation."[89] Look at your past first through the lens of Jesus Christ, and second on removing any obstacle that keeps you from union with Him. The demon will attempt to keep your focus either on him or on yourself and your past. In so doing, many seek only the cessation of suffering rather than the development of virtue and union with God. The goal of liberation is reconciliation with God, so focus on Christ first and then on removing the obstacles preventing deeper union with Him.

At this time, examine your life and your relationships for anything unholy and improper. Once identified, say the prayer below of breaking unholy alliances.

List anyone with whom you may have formed an unholy alliance:

The basic **Prayer to Break Soul Ties** is as follows:
Lord Jesus Christ, I recognize that an unholy soul tie was created between me and (n.), whenever we . . . (n.). In the name of Jesus Christ, I give back any spiritual thing of the interior self that I took from _____ and I take back anything of my interior self that I gave to _____ and hereby break any and all unholy soul tie(s) with_____.

A longer form is found in the appendix.

---

[89] Liber Christo, "Companion Guide," 157.

From Slingstones to Milestones:
Holy and Unholy Alliances

1.   Did you experience any interior resistance, such as
      anxiety or something you just did not like, when
      reading any part of this lesson?
2.   From whom do you seek approval? Who is
      influential in your life, and why?
3.   Are there any areas in your life where you need to
      "untie the psychological enmeshment" with the
      past?
4.   Did you discern any unholy soul ties? Any artifacts
      from unholy alliances that need to be discarded?
5.   Recall the statement, "the demon is tertiary in
      Catholic liberation." In your struggle for liberation,
      have you focused too much on the demon and not
      on Jesus Christ?
6.   Have you discovered any memories of past behavior
      where you may have been like the Philistines and
      "prostituted yourself with demons"?
7.   What are your best and worst childhood memories?
      What emotions arise when you recall them?
8.   What is your earliest sexual memory?
9.   Was there ever an event in your life after which your
      life was never the same?

LESSON THREE: THE OCCULT
AND GENERATIONAL SIN

When David was presented to King Saul after his victory over Goliath, the king asked him, "Whose son
are you, young man?" (1 Sm 17:58). His actions spoke not only
of his own bravery and cunning but also of his upbringing.
We are all a product of our upbringing—good or bad. As Cle-
ments states, "Although every one of us 'speaks Egyptian' in
how we have been enculturated into non-Christian elements

of society, we do not belong in the 'Egypt' of sin and oppression. Like the Israelites, we have been assimilated into a culture of oppression that militates against God's law and ultimately seeks to enslave us."[90] The "Egypt" of oppression worsens if you do not reevaluate your past and break free by removing any obstacle that stands between you and the living God.

David did not grab just any rock, therefore; he "chose" specifically "smooth" ones. Precision is key in any warfare. Those who go through the first phase of the protocol know that it is not a retreat but a time of battle preparation—like David alone among the sheep. The skills he acquired while defending the sheep against lions and bears enabled him to beat the giant of Gath. For you, this means a withdrawal from the things which enmesh you with the three-fold enemy—the flesh, the world, and the devil. Now we must go deeper in identifying the lingering effects of sin which continue to empower the demon.

You may be reading this manual to learn how to counter the effects of previous occult activity. As I explain, "*occult* comes from the Latin *occultus*, meaning secret or hidden. In normal usage, it refers to invoking superhuman, but not divine, powers in order to obtain results that are beyond the capacity of mere nature."[91] This includes "mystical knowledge, supernatural or magical powers, practices, or phenomena. Because these practices call upon powers other than the true God, the Church condemns all such practices as 'gravely contrary' to true religion (*CCC* 2117)."[92] According to Father Ripperger, a generational spirit is "the spirit that is passed from one generation to another as the result of the sin of one of the ancestors or the suffering of grave harm by one of one's ancestors."[93] Accordingly, any participation in the occult is a grave sin against the first commandment.

When this type of sin enters a family and is not eradicated and atoned for, it can linger in the familial line for generations.

---

[90] Liber Christo, "Companion Guide," 57.
[91] Hardon, *Modern Catholic Dictionary*, 387.
[92] Liber Christo, "Companion Guide," 81.
[93] Ripperger, *Dominion*, 554.

Sometimes this takes the form of a curse from occult practices and other times a familial sin that plagues each generation. *Interactive diabolic activity* is a phrase used to describe
the activities in which a person invokes—whether through
incantation, pledge, or bodily ritual—a power other than the
One, True God. The *interactive* component is meant that such
invocations involve an exchange between participants and the
demons. These can be seemingly innocuous things like the
Ouija board of a previous generation, tarot cards and fortune
tellers, or some (but not all) modern video games where real
curses and spells have been coded into the game's script. Thus,
"tarot cards and Ouija boards, for example, invoke evil spirits
for some favor and open the persons to diabolic affliction by
giving permissions to the demons called upon."[94] These can
also be overt, according to Fr. John Hardon and the *Modern
Catholic Dictionary*, as in "Satanism, fetishism, black and white
magic, spiritism, theosophy, divination, and witchcraft."[95]

Witchcraft works as an unholy inversion of the sacred,
be it verbal, gestural, or physical movements. That is, occult
practitioners use language, hand gestures, handshakes, et
cetera to communicate with each other and with the preternatural. This communication includes bodily positions such
as yoga poses, ritual dance, or other movements—all with
determined, fixed patterns—designed to create a pathway
between the practitioner and the preternatural world. Just as
Gregorian chant is intoned at precise, patterned notes, occultists also utilize singing, or chant-like invocation, intoned at
specific tonal frequencies. Just as Catholic priests wear sacred
vestments when offering Holy Mass or in the performance
of sacred ritual, occultists will perform their rituals wearing
symbolically imbued regalia (or wearing nothing at all). The
Catholic priest uses blessed objects, such as the Saint Benedict
crucifix or relics of saints, to invoke heavenly assistance when
blessing a person or when exorcising demons. In an unholy

---

[94] Liber Christo, "Companion Guide," 81.
[95] Hardon, *Modern Catholic Dictionary*, 387.

inversion of this, the witch holds cursed objects, uses drawn-out sigils in the open, or ornately made symbols in the ritual area to invoke dark powers.[96] In an inversion of Catholic liturgy and the liturgical calendar, witches also ritualize and sacralize space and time by means of specific locations, times of the day, and days/months as deemed sacred according to pre-Christian or other pagan calendars. Everything they do is exact and ritualistic, as if in mockery of traditional Catholic liturgy and liturgical calendar, but in an upside-down world. In addition, the occult practitioner can "level up" in a coven through increasingly dark ways, which we will not relate here.

Often, we discover that someone along a family line has practiced witchcraft of various kinds. This, in turn, opened the future generations to the effect of curses. Knowingly or unknowingly, pledges were made by either the words spoken or bodily actions. We know as Catholics that both words and bodily postures/gestures can be spiritually charged. Not only the prayers we pray, but also making the sign of the cross, kneeling in prayer, or a priestly blessing are all examples of bodily actions which invoke the spiritual. Curses and the occult are diabolical inversions of the sacred.

Many have fallen into the trap of the occult through curiosity.[97] The virtue opposed is studiosity, or the pursuit of knowledge and truth according to one's vocation and state of life.[98] Thus, seeking "results that are beyond the capacity of mere nature" (as defined above) is often driven by an unholy desire either for power (control over others) or for knowledge of future events or simply an unholy curiosity about the occult

---

[96] A sigil is a sign, word, or device held to have occult, or magical, power in astrology or magic.

[97] The term *curious* here is not being used in the colloquial sense but in the technical, philosophical, and theological sense. Saint Augustine identifies "the lust of the eyes" (1 Jn 2:16) as curiosity, a vice he called a "lust for experimenting and knowing." Thus, he notes the "outrageous sights in public" which "satisfy this diseased craving." Saint Augustine of Hippo, *Confessions*, 10.35.55.

[98] As Saint Thomas teaches, studiosity is a potential part of the virtue of temperance, which moderates the desire for knowledge. *Summa Theologica* II-II, q. 166, art. 2.

world. Participation in the occult violates the first commandment and also reveals a "lack of trust in God's providence."
Thus, we encourage that "any such past activity should be
immediately confessed and atoned for through acts of penance
. . . as to break any diabolic claims or unholy soul ties created."[99]

Of note, however, this process is not deterministic. That is,
the presence of such familial sins does not mean an automatic
spiritual affliction or possession of a person or family line.
Sometimes they skip generations, and sometimes God does
not allow their effects to continue. In our experience, when
a curse is allowed by God to plague a familial line, there is a
"one-two punch" that gives full access to the demon. We often
see the combination of violations of the first commandment
(invoking false gods contrary to Dt 5:6–10) and the sixth commandment (the committing of grave sin, usually one of deviant sexual behavior). If a curse is operant in a family, however,
this does not mean that the effects are inevitable or insurmountable. God often seeks a strong soul who will suffer as
Christ to break the hold the enemy has on the family. Recall
that *single combat* means that two warriors fight on behalf of
their respective people with "winner-take-all" stakes. Just
as David chose to fight in single combat to keep his brothers
from slavery, you may be that person God chooses to fight for
your family as Christ fought for the entire human family.

A state of grace protects against curses, and the demon will
attempt to draw you out of that protective armor. If a familial spirit is present due to previous occult behavior, a person
becomes vulnerable to its effects when he commits grave sins.
All witchcraft is mortal sin due its grave matter. That is, it is
an intentional violation of the first commandment and severs
the relationship with God. We often hear that someone only
"dabbled" in witchcraft, saying things like, "Well, I only read
the horoscopes for fun," or, "I only do the tarot cards recre-
ationally," or, "It's only 'white magic' not the dark stuff." The
implication is that if someone did not really mean to commit

---

[99] Liber Christo, "Companion Guide," 159.

this or that sin, they are not culpable for its effects. This is false. Any activity where someone invokes false idols is a violation of the first commandment (mortal sin) regardless of his subjective intentions.

Victory in spiritual combat lies in purity of thought, word, and deed. This means militating strongly against all sin, for, as the *Catechism* states, "deliberate and unrepentant venial sin disposes us little by little to commit mortal sin."[100] While humans tend to be led by emotions and the subjective, the demon *always works in the objective*. The interactive aspect of the occult means that this activity is a two-way street. Prayer begets what it signifies. That is, you get what you ask for in prayer, according to the words of the Lord, "Ask and you shall receive" (Mt 7:7). Make no mistake: incantations, rituals using inanimate objects such as feathers, hair, clothing items, love potions, crystals, et cetera are all forms of prayers of petition to the demon behind them. The reason we emphasize this is because a significant number of possessions and deep obsessions are a result of occult involvement.

Rather than entrusting their situation to God—whether it be infertility, loneliness, financial problems, health issues, and the like—many people turn to alternative sources such as *curanderas*, tarot, New Age, and the like. Ouija boards and tarot cards, for example, "invoke evil spirits for some favor and open the persons to diabolic affliction by giving permissions to the demons called upon."[101] The demon will happily respond, especially when he sees that the one petitioning bears the indelible mark of Baptism in his soul. Imagine one of Rogers's rangers showing up at the enemy camp asking for some favor in exchange for information on Rogers's battle plans. He would be called a traitor, and rightly so, but welcomed into the enemy's camp with open arms. You are a spiritual traitor to the living God when you seek favors from the infernal enemy. Once inside his camp, it is not easy to get out.

---

[100] *CCC* 1863.
[101] Liber Christo, "Companion Guide," 81.

In laying down your arms and freely walking into the enemy's encampment—and to be clear, regardless of your subjective intention for doing so—you have opened yourself to diabolic affliction in the exchange because you have given permissions to the demons invoked. For this reason, "the Church forbids all *divination*, such as conjuring the dead or other methods which 'unveil' the future (*CCC* 2116)." You should, therefore, "learn to trust God in all things, even in suffering or in uncertainty."[102]

The activities performed through occult practices to obtain favors or discover the future deeply offend God. According to the *Catechism*, such activities are "a recourse to Satan or demons."[103] These are depraved acts of spiritual infidelity which call upon a demon for some favor. As the psalmist writes, "All the gods of the Gentiles are demons" (Greek *daemonia*, Ps 96:5).[104] Of those Israelites who committed false worship in the desert, he says, "They sacrificed to demons (literally "to demons" as seen in the Hebrew *shedim*, and Greek *daemonia*) / their own sons and daughters, / Shedding innocent blood, / the blood of their own sons and daughters, / Whom they sacrificed to the idols of Canaan" (Ps 106:37–38). The demon takes any such interactive activity very seriously. Accordingly, to participate in occult activity is to give an overt *permission* for a demon to enter into your life.

God makes this very clear when He gave the Ten Commandments to Israel, as part of the first commandment includes the consequences for "having other gods besides me" by carving "idols for yourselves in the shape of anything in the sky above or the on the earth below in the waters of the beneath the earth" (Dt 5:8). To these, God clearly commands, "you shall not bow down before them or serve them" (v. 9). This forbids making graven images of the idols, including amulets, talisman as sigils to invoke their power, as still used in the occult. Obedience or disobedience to this commandment has

---

[102] Liber Christo, "Companion Guide," 82.
[103] *CCC* 2116.
[104] This is my own literal translation from the Greek Septuagint.

an effect on the family line: "For I, the LORD, your God, am a jealous God, bringing punishments for their parents' wickedness on the children of those who hate me, down to the third and fourth generation, but showing love down to the thousandth generation of those who love me and keep my commandments (Dt 5:9–10). Notice the context here is the first commandment, and to "hate" God is to "bow down" to false gods (which the Psalmist clearly noted were demons).

The social laws given to the newly formed community led out of Egypt show the seriousness of idolatry: "You shall not let a woman who practices sorcery live. Anyone who lies with an animal shall be put to death. Whoever sacrifices to any god, except to the LORD alone, shall be put under the ban" (Ex 22:19). Elsewhere, the Lord reiterates the severity of recourse to demon-gods: "Anyone, whether an Israelite or an alien residing in Israel, who gives any of his offspring to Molech shall be put to death. . . . For in giving his offspring to Molech, he has defiled my sanctuary and profaned my holy name" (Lv 20:1–3). Equally offensive in the eyes of God are those who entice others to such sin: "A man or a woman who acts as a medium or clairvoyant shall be put to death. They shall be stoned to death; their bloodguilt is on them" (Lv 20:27). And, "Let there not be found among you anyone who causes their son or daughter to pass through the fire, or practices divination, or is a soothsayer, augur, or sorcerer, or who casts spells, consults ghosts and spirits, or seeks oracles from the dead. Anyone who does such things is an abomination to the LORD" (Dt 18:10–12). Thus, God says through the prophet Baruch, "For you provoked your Maker / with sacrifices to demons and not to God; / You forgot the eternal God who nourished you" (Bar 4:7).

These condemnations are not limited to the Old Testament. In the New Testament, as I wrote,

> St. Paul condemns sorcery among a list of sins with, "I warn
> you, as I warned you before, that those who do such things
> will not inherit the kingdom of God (Gal 5:21). In Acts, he

addresses a magician named Elymas with, "you son of the devil, you enemy of all that is right, full of every deceit and fraud" (Acts 13:8). Elsewhere in Acts, when Simon the magician wants to make himself more powerful by purchasing the power of the Holy Spirit, St. Peter rebukes him with: "repent of this wickedness of yours and pray to the Lord that, if possible, your intention may be forgiven. For I see that you are filled with bitter gall and are in the bonds of iniquity" (Acts 8:22–23). Revelation condemns occult practices even more forcefully: "As for the cowards and traitors to the faith, the depraved and murderers, the fornicators and sorcerers, the idol-worshipers and deceivers of every sort—their lot is the fiery pool of burning sulphur—the second death" (Rev 21:8).[105]

For this reason, the *Catechism* is quite clear on the gravity of the occult: "All forms of divination are to be rejected: recourse to Satan or demons, conjuring up the dead or other practices falsely supposed to 'unveil' the future. Consulting horoscopes, astrology, palm reading, interpretation of omens and lots, the phenomena of clairvoyance, and recourse to mediums all conceal a desire for power over time, history, and, in the last analysis, other human beings, as well as a wish to conciliate hidden powers. They contradict the honor, respect, and loving fear that we owe to God alone."[106] This is because "idolatry consists in divinizing what is not God. Man commits idolatry whenever he honors and reveres a creature in the place of God, whether this be gods or demons" and in so doing, "rejects the unique Lordship of God."[107]

Therefore, whether you intended to hurt another person in vengeance, or you tried to bring about some seemingly good thing, any practice which calls upon false gods (demons) or utilizes occult powers are condemned by God. All witchcraft—even those claiming to be "white" and not "black" magic—is a grave sin against the first commandment.[108]

---

[105] Liber Christo, "Companion Guide," 82–83.
[106] *CCC* 2116.
[107] *CCC* 2114.
[108] Liber Christo, "Companion Guide," 83.

Types of Curses and How to Remove Them

The ramification of *interactive diabolic activity* is that someone along the family line can do something gravely evil, as is
found in the interactive and ritual elements of witchcraft, and
a malefice can enter a familial line. The concept of *generational
curses* is sometimes dismissed as non-Catholic in origin, but
the prudential experience of those who work in the field of
Catholic exorcism suggests otherwise. Evidence can be found,
for example, in the possession of an infant or young child
who manifests one of the preternatural signs of possession
consistent (such as shapeshifting or aversion to the sacred)
with those prescribed by Saint Charles Borromeo in the *Praenotanda* of the Rite of Exorcism.[109]

Both an exorcist's lived experience and scriptural evidence suggest the reality of generational curses as affecting
the bloodline (see the previous section and Dt 5:9).[110] The
healing of the boy possessed by a demon in Mark's Gospel is
one example. When Jesus asks the father, "How long has he
been this way?" the father answered, "since childhood" (Mk
9:21). The Greek word used here is *paidiothen*, meaning "from
infancy, since birth, or from early childhood," suggesting
that a familial curse is operant.[111] This is often found where
there are grave mortal sins, curses, and other occult activity.
God permits these effects to linger so as to end its ability to

---

[109] These classical signs are occult knowledge, superhuman strength, aversion to the sacred. See *Glossary*. For more details on the various forms that
these take, see Bamonte, *Diabolical Possession*, 80–98.

[110] For more, see Father Ripperger's "The Sixth Generation." And also, Ripperger, *Dominion*, 174–76. The subject of blood curses was also presented by
Kyle Clement as part of the curriculum of the Pope Leo Institute from 2014
to 2018, a summarized version is contained here. See also, Liber Christo,
"Companion Guide," 160–63.

[111] That the ancient Jewish mind saw the reality of sins of parents passing
on to their children is seen in the man born blind ("Rabbi, who sinned, this
man or his parents?" Jn 9:2) and the Jewish leaders who told Pilate, "May
his blood be upon us and our children" (Mt 27:25). See also Hosea 4:6: "Since
you have forgotten the law of your God, I will also forget your children."

influence a family's line by allowing a person in the family to clean up the lineage through their suffering and reparation.

Thus, a spirit can enter a familial line through grave sin. That is, through the grave sin of one person, a demon enters both that person and, through him/her, into the family. There are basically three types of generational spirits which afflict family lines. A *generational spirit* can enter through grave violations of the marital act. In this sense, *generational* means *procreational* in that it centers around abuses of the generative principle (disordered and gravely sinful sexual acts). Any deviant sexual behavior which profanes the marital act can allow a demon to be present to the act and, consequently, can create a vulnerability to the progeny.

The *zeitgeist*, or *spirit of the age*, is also generational spirit in that it can affect worldwide (e.g., the "hippy generation," etc.), nations/countries (e.g., Nazi Germany), races (such as those passed on via pre-Christian spirituality, if kept alive in family), regions, corporations, dioceses, and religious orders (seen in certain dysfunction). While we are made in God's image and likeness (see Gn 1:26), the demonic seeks the inverse—that is, to make us (whether family, nation, generation, etc.) into *their* image, taking on a mindset of an area.

The third type of generational spirit which can enter a family line is done through a *blood curse*. Blood curses fall into two categories. *Rosicrucianism* is any type of witchcraft which claims to possess secret knowledge, ancient mysticism, and brotherhood, so-called. These include Freemasonry and other secret societies, some New Age methodologies, Gnosticism, and other esoteric sects and practices such as alchemy, occult healing, and various para-liturgical rituals which seek to attain occult knowledge. A second type of blood curse is found in *pelican witchcraft*. In antiquity, the pelican was thought to pull the flesh and blood from her own breast to feed her young. Thus, this became an ancient symbol of Christ, the Great Pelican, who offered His Body and Blood both to save us and to feed us in the Holy Eucharist.[112] The occult mocks and inverts this primitive Christian symbol. In this type of witchcraft, the practitioner (a witch, *santero*, etc.) uses part of his own flesh or blood in the ritual. He may also use part of the body of the petitioner in the curse, or that of animals. Thus, these types of practices are also called *ex carne* curses. Through the shedding of blood and using certain incantations and rituals, a diabolic entity is invoked and conscripted.

These third types of generational curses are referred to as *blood curses* also because they lay claim to the blood line of the one who commits the grave violation against the first commandment. If the descendants affirm the sin through their own sinful behavior, the effects of the curse continue along. If not, then the curse passes away. Often, a curse of this type will be latent in a family only to become active where there may be a vocation to the priesthood or religious life, or where there is deep conversion.

Why does God allow generational spirits? Saint Alphonsus says that God allows such suffering to chastise someone for the evil he is doing. That is, if the person does not expiate sins voluntarily, God will allow it for his purification. Through struggle, a person grows in virtue against the curse and conquers

---

[112] This image of the pelican stems from a third- or fourth-century anonymous Christian work which allegorized various animals as symbols of Christ. Perhaps due the reddish tip of the pelican's beak and the manner in which she feeds her young from beneath her wing, this became a common symbol of Christ through the Middle Ages and is seen in iconography adorning both tabernacles and crucifixes. One section reads: "If the pelican brings forth young and the little ones grow, they take to striking their parents in the face. The parents, however, hitting back kill their young ones and then, moved by compassion, they weep over them for three days, lamenting over those whom they killed. On the third day, their mother strikes her side and spills her own blood over their dead bodies and the blood itself awakens them from death. This is what our Lord did. . . . The Maker of every creature brought us forth and we struck him when we served the creatures [i.e., in idolatry] and not the Creator. The Lord ascended the height of the cross and the impious ones struck his side and opened it and blood and water came forth for eternal life." The blood and water that flowed from the side of Christ (see Jn 19:34), he states, are symbols of Baptism and the Eucharist. Anonymous, *Physiologus*, 9–10.

the demon. In addition, the struggle helps sanctify the whole family, as God desires certain perfections to be manifest in the family itself, which the battle perfects. As God allows them to struggle, they gain virtue and, in the process, humiliate and crush the demon.

Notably, in the story of the boy possessed by a demon in Mark 9:24–29, *the father intercedes* for his son to Jesus through the disciples (see Mk 9:17). Jesus gives us clues as to how to drive this demon out of the family line: "This kind can only come out through prayer and through fasting" (Mk 9:29).[113] That the father approached Jesus suggests that the first step in ridding the family of the effects of such curses is best done by the head of the household.

Spiritual warfare is like trench warfare. This means that you should get the demon out of your life first before cleaning up the bloodline. That is, once you expel the demon, you have a certain power over him and can then help other family members. Begin with the principle that you cannot heal the family tree but you can heal family members. Demons perpetuate by wounding within the family, so work on yourself first to develop the virtues to counteract it, then your children. Thus:

Fear	→	hope and confidence
Depression	→	joy via charity, telling God you love Him, etc.
Despair	→	hope
Fear of suffering	→	fasting, penances, voluntary suffering

A priest should also say prayers to break the generational spirit over you and your children because the institutional nature of the sin is greatly combatted by an institutional response of the Church. Other tactics include:

---

[113] Ancient manuscript evidence contains both "through prayer" and "through prayer and through fasting."

- fasting and prayer,
- binding prayers to bind the demon's activity,
- Mass for reparation of the sins of your family and souls in purgatory,
- praying a daily Rosary,
- general prayers, asking Christ with deprecatory prayers to drive it out of our family and generational line,
- offering your Holy Communion for this intention,
- asking Our Lady and your guardian angels for protection and to block them,
- fostering devotion to the nemesis-saint for that demon (God always sends help from the Mystical Body with a saint whose charism perfectly counters the nature of the afflicting demon),
- use of sacramentals in the home, and
- confessing the sin associated with it to break it.

Since these spirits can be stubborn and difficult to drive out, one must chisel away at them. Prayers of reparation should be prayed for three things:

1. For the sin that introduced the demon into the generational line, as this loosens his ability to affect family
2. For the sins of others in the family line and the effects of the collateral damage in family
3. For your own sins

To Divide and Conquer

This begs the question: *What makes one open to a curse?* The most common vulnerability to a curse is not being in a state of grace. Mortal sin leaves you without a shield on the battlefield. A malefice is a diabolic inversion of a blessing. Being in state of grace opens you the goodness contained in a blessing, while being in mortal sin makes you vulnerable to the evil contained in a curse. Too often, however, people will focus on the breaking of curses while ignoring what makes them vulnerable to the curse itself. As Clement says, "A curse can be seen as a gift in as much as God is allowing it to show us vulnerabilities that arise from defects in virtue."[114] When in this situation, look first to remedy the defect in virtue that makes you susceptible to an attack. A state of grace and holiness, particularly when combined with formal prayers of a priest, work well together to break curses.

The military strategy of "to divide and conquer" has been applied by generals ranging from Sun Tzu (544 BC) to Phillip II of Macedonia (359 BC) to Julius Caesar (60 BC) to Napoleon (AD 1804). Also called "divide and rule," this strategy entails the breaking up of existing larger power structures into smaller pieces to cause rivalries and factions and any sort of discord. By encouraging division and fostering distrust among various factions, a clever general can more easily defeat his enemy by preventing any alliances that could challenge his sovereignty. In so doing, he can more easily subjugate the people and expand his territory.

The demon uses this strategy quite effectively. The very name *devil* comes from the Greek word *diaballo*, meaning "to divide, make a quarrel between, slander, calumniate, be filled with suspicion, to misrepresent, to deceive by false accounts." Thus, Jesus calls the devil "a murderer from the beginning and does not stand in truth, because there is no truth in him. When he tells a lie, he speaks in character because he is a liar and the father of lies" (Jn 8:44). As applied to spiritual combat, often the devil's primary target is to divide the married couple. Forgiving one another for past sins and praying together are essential to maintaining marital unity. That unity assists the flow of sacramental grace into the familial construct and counteracts the effects of familial curses.

Many people come to the Church for help thinking that they are "under attack." What is often under siege is the marriage

---

[114] Liber Christo, "Companion Guide," 162.

itself, and the principal object of the enemy is not merely the individual but the entire family—especially the children. Thus, "to divide" the husband and wife means the children under their authority have no protection, so the demon can then "rule" the children while they are vulnerable. As will be seen in a later chapter, God has established the authority structure to provide for and to protect (cf. Power and Authority, below) those under authority. When the demon fractures a marriage through his subterfuge and lies, the provision and protection are diminished and, like an earthly general, he can more easily subjugate the whole family and expand his territory.

This analysis is based upon the observation that our vocational sacrament provides our base armor against evil, as it orients us toward God. This orientation towards God means that, for a married person, sacramental grace flows through the spousal union and, through each other, to the children. Stop that flow of sacramental grace and the "power structure" is fractured such that grace is occluded from flowing into the family. Consequently, you must look for deficiencies in the sacramental marriage, to include the grave sins of contraception and fornication. If you are not married in the Church, then you (and your children) are vulnerable. If you have not confessed (and ceased) the use of artificial means of birth control, the same vulnerability exists. Remember, "the demon looks for the mouth who blesses and curses"—do you *bless* God by receiving Holy Communion while *cursing* Him with behavior that directly opposes the Church's moral teachings? An astute predator, the demon not only notices these pattern breaks and inconsistencies but also quickly exploits them.

The sacramental grace of Holy Matrimony is "intended to perfect the couple's love and to strengthen their indissoluble unity. By this grace they help one another to attain holiness in their married life and in welcoming and educating their children."[115] This is the enemy's target. Another name of the devil is "the divider." He constantly seeks to weaken the "indissolu-

---

[115] *CCC* 1641.

ble unity" of marriage though division and discord. When the couple is divided, grace is occluded, and the children can now be more easily attacked.

Witchcraft and the Occult— Permissions and Rights

The demon will often claim a right to be present to a person, as if saying, "Look, God, this one let me in whenever he did x. I have a right to be here!" Remember, he is called "the accuser" (Rv 12:10) for a reason, a "lawyer from hell." The word for *accuser* also means "prosecuting attorney." As I wrote elsewhere, however, "the demon has no 'rights' over us, only 'permissions' to be there granted by our sinful behavior. Confession and acts of penance, especially when combined with prayer and the pursuit of holiness, removes all of his claims."[116] To be clear, if your soul bears the indelible mark of Baptism, you *belong by right to God alone.*

Witchcraft is the practice of magic or sorcery in any form. At the root, witchcraft is an "anti-religion" that counterfeits true religion and true worship. It is based on the belief, according to Father Hardon, that "material objects or nonhuman living creatures possess preternatural powers that can be invoked or appeased by hidden or occult means."[117] This invoking of the preternatural and the exultation of creature and creation to convey some power through animate or inanimate agency are diabolic inversions of Catholicism. In the Catholic religion, liturgy, sacraments and sacramentals, blessings, and material objects such as water, oil, and salt are utilized to convey the power of God. Witchcraft mimics this sacramental economy.

Since the demon takes our words and deeds very seriously, specifically when we invoke him in a ritualistic way, the following occult activities should be avoided by Catholics. Some are direct violations of the first commandment, and others have

---

[116] Liber Christo, "Companion Guide," 86.
[117] Hardon, *Modern Catholic Dictionary*, 329.

ties with the diabolic and should likewise be confessed so that the demon can no longer use the permission granted against you.[118] A short list of forbidden practices is found in a binding prayer that priests use to sever the spirits associated with witchcraft. These include:

> astrologers, bohmos, channelers, charters, clairvoyants, crystals, crystal healers, fortune tellers, mediums, and the New Age movement, occult seers, palm, tea leaf or tarot card readers, psychics, santeros (Santería), satanic cults, spirit guides, witches, witch doctors, dungeon masters and voodoo . . . participation in seances, divination, Ouija boards, horoscopes, occult games of all sorts, and any form of worship that does not offer true honor to Jesus Christ.[119]

As Clement notes, moreover, "manipulation is the simplest form of witchcraft." That is, "in witchcraft we place ourselves at the center of the activity and use false powers to manipulate people and events to our own gain. Conforming to God's will, rather than imposing your will, is paramount to liberation. All manipulation of others must cease as prerequisite to a trustful surrender to God's will in your life."[120]

The interactive nature of all witchcraft deeply offends God and creates an entry point for the diabolic. In addition, those practices that do not "offer true honor to Jesus Christ" are often a subtle blending of Christian and pagan elements. Some assert that "white" magic seeks good ends and "black" magic seeks evil or harm, justifying the former. As Father Amorth writes, however, "there are no such things as 'white' or 'black' magic. Every form of magic is practiced with recourse to Satan."[121] Even if the intended end is good, such as bodily

---

[118] I expand here in summary form the field experience of Father Ripperger and presentations on witchcraft and the occult by Kyle Clement to the Pope Leo Institute in 2016. See also Liber Christo, "Companion Guide," 81–87, 159–63.

[119] Ripperger, *Minor Exorcisms*, 26.

[120] Liber Christo, "Companion Guide," 161.

[121] Amorth, *An Exorcist Tells His Story*, 60.

or psychological healing, the means can still be a "recourse to Satan." This includes the invoking or channeling of "energies" to open chakras or meridians to heal or cleanse the body, as with many popular methodologies today. Many Christians are lured into this subtle trap. Whether the practitioner invokes Saint Padre Pio, prays in tongues, lights a Saint Jude candle, or has an image of Our Lady of Guadalupe on the wall makes no difference. The demon works only in the objective, and he tricks many Christians today through a syncretic blending of the clean and the unclean in the name of healing.

Father Ripperger defines the sin of superstition as "the attributing to creature that which is proper to God." This can range from "idolatry" to "vain observance."[122] Thus, superstition is "a belief that a temporal effect may be brought about through the agency of a certain 'lucky' object" or special prayer form, et cetera.[123] Ultimately, it renders to creature the worship that is owed to God alone. Other practices include "yoga, tai chi, reiki, feng shui, transcendental meditation, crystals, reflexology, water witching, psychic hotline, pendulum, soul travel, Edgar Casey, Course in Miracles, dreamcatchers, hypnotism (where one enters a vulnerable 'in-between' state of consciousness), etc. In each of these, a foreign, or false power, is invoked."[124]

One such practice to be avoided is Reiki, whose practitioners seek to channel "universal life energy." As the USCCB cautioned, Reiki and Christian healing are incompatible. To wit, "Some practitioners attempt to Christianize Reiki by adding a prayer to Christ, but this does not affect the essential nature of Reiki." They conclude that "Reiki therapy is

---

[122] Ripperger, *Dominion*, 555.
[123] Liber Christo, "Companion Guide," 160–61. The *Catechism* states, "Superstition is the deviation of religious feeling and of the practices this feeling imposes. It can even affect the worship we offer the true God, e.g., when one attributes an importance in some way magical to certain practices otherwise lawful or necessary. To attribute the efficacy of prayers or of sacramental signs to their mere external performance, apart from the interior dispositions that they demand, is to fall into superstition." *CCC* 2111.
[124] Liber Christo, "Companion Guide," 85.

not compatible with either Christian teaching or scientific evidence" and that "a Catholic who puts his or her trust in Reiki would be operating in the realm of superstition, the no man's land that is neither faith nor science."[125] Again, note the pattern to watch for—namely, the invocation of something (power, energy, etc.) from outside of the body to act in agency for healing and wholeness inside of the body. Bearing in mind the psalm which states, "The gods of the nations are idols" (Ps 96:5), all superstitious practices (even if they are presented with a veneer of true religion) must be avoided.

As the practice of authentic Christian meditation has fallen into disuse, many look to Eastern forms of prayer, such as yoga and transcendental meditation, for peace, psychic balance, or well-being. The Church has warned against Eastern practices and prayer forms which "can degenerate into a cult of the body and can lead surreptitiously to considering all bodily sensations as spiritual experiences."[126] While many non-Christian prayer forms seek "superior knowledge" or "experience," the goal of Christian prayer is union with God. Citing a fourth-century charismatic group that equated "the grace of the Holy Spirit with the psychological experience of his presence in the soul," the Congregation for the Doctrine of the Faith (CDF) documents notes that "the Fathers insisted on the fact that the soul's union with God in prayer is realized in a mysterious way, and in particular through the sacraments of the Church. . . . Moreover, it can even be achieved through experiences of affliction or desolation. . . . They may be an authentic participation in the state of abandonment experienced on the cross by Our Lord, who always remains the model and mediator of prayer."[127] In fact, many who seek Eastern prayer forms wish to avoid the cross: infertility, aging, physical or psychological pain, et cetera.

Some have tried to Christianize Eastern prayer. In the attempt to "fuse Christian meditation with that which is non-Christian," however, there exists a "danger of falling into

---

[125] USCCB, *Evaluating Reiki*, 12, 11.
[126] CDF, *Christian Meditation*, 27.
[127] CDF, *Christian Meditation*, 9.

syncretism" as found in Yoga and other Eastern meditative practices.[128] As I wrote, "'yoga' is derived from the Latin *iugo*, meaning to unite or to yoke, as seen the English word conjugal (which literally means to be bound or yoked together). In a Hindu context, 'yoga' means union with the absolute or some form of divinity. As the best-known practice of Hindu spirituality, yoga is incompatible with Catholicism. In fact, the physical poses of yoga invoke (false) Hindu gods."[129]

The body positions in yoga cannot be separated from the incantations any more than the sign of the cross from its Christian context. Thus, "the body-soul invocations of yoga grant permissions to the demon and can expose the soul to deep affliction."[130] In so doing, the above discussion on "interactive diabolic activity" applies, as the body positions and incantations are spiritual permissions given to the demons of yoga. Thus, the CDF asserts that "such erroneous forms, having reappeared in history from time to time on the fringes of the Church's prayer, seem once more to impress many Christians, appealing to them as a kind of remedy, be it psychological or spiritual, or as a quick way of finding God."[131]

Pope Saint John Paul II also noted that Eastern prayer forms have "in some quarters become fashionable and are accepted rather uncritically." Nonetheless, he writes that "it is not inappropriate to caution those Christians who enthusiastically welcome certain ideas originating in the religious traditions of the Far East—for example, techniques and methods of meditations."[132] Learn first, he encouraged, your own rich spiritual heritage on prayer before embracing Eastern forms of prayer incompatible with the Christian faith.

Other bodily actions that can have occultic connections include cutting and tattoos.[133] In Leviticus, we find a verse con-

---

[128] CDF, *Christian Meditation*, 12.
[129] Liber Christo, "Companion Guide," 85.
[130] Liber Christo, "Companion Guide," 160.
[131] CDF, *Christian Meditation*, 10.
[132] Pope Saint John Paul II, *Crossing the Threshold of Hope*, 89–90.
[133] The relationship between piercing, cutting, and tattoos and the occult represents the developed thought and experience of Father Ripperger and

necting the two: "Do not lacerate your bodies for the dead, and do not tattoo yourselves. I am the LORD" (Lv 19:28). We see the occultic use of cutting, for example, in Elijah's battle with the prophets of Baal who ritualistically "called out louder and slashed themselves with swords and spears according to their ritual until blood gushed over them" (1 Kgs 18:28). Although cultural norms have shifted over time, in antiquity, cutting was a pagan practice and tattoos were marks of enslavement. As Livia Gershon writes, "What tattoos were apparently often used for in ancient Mesopotamia was marking enslaved people (and, in Egypt, as decorations for women of all social classes). Egyptian captives were branded with the name of a god, marking them as belongings of the priests or pharaoh. But devotees might also be branded with the name of the god they worshiped."[134]

Egypt and Mesopotamia (Babylon), recall, are the nations which conquered and enslaved Israel. Over time, tattoos also became associated with idolatry. According to John Huehnergard and Harold Liebowitz, "the meaning of tattoos ranges from mythology to tribal history, to Buddhist religious symbols, to statements about personal values and beliefs." They note that "tattoos send a message" and are "prevalent among gang members and prisoners . . . celebrate life-changing events . . . serve as a sign of status within a culture such as the tattoos on an elder shaman" or to mark the "mistress of a gang leader to identify her as the leader's property."[135] At best, they tie a person to a specific (and often unholy) time and place, and at worst, they contain pagan, ritualistic, and occultic elements. Traditionally, Christians have followed the biblical prohibition, although that is changing.

As actions which violate bodily integrity, they are very difficult to separate from their ancient connection to slavery and paganism. As such, these constitute a form of

---

Kyle Clement and was presented to the Pope Leo Institute from 2016 to 2018.

[134] Gershon, "Why Does the Bible Forbid Tattoos?"

[135] Huehnergard, "Biblical Prohibition Against Tattooing," 60.

self-mutilation, forbidden by the fifth commandment.[136] In addition, as Clement notes, because "these can be performed in a ritualistic manner," it can "enable the demon to be physically present to the individual." As it applies here, Clement relates:

> *Cutting* may be a form of ritualistic scarring, especially if patterned symmetrically. This occurs more commonly among females of Celtic origin, suggestive of Druidic practices in which the demon was pledged for the letting of blood. *Tattoos* are occultic in as much as the person who gets a tattoo becomes part of a confraternity of others who wear the same image, or who went to the same tattoo artist. The person's flesh has been marked with an unnatural and foreign (and sometimes Satanic) object and image. Often, sigils of demons may be hidden in the imagery of the tattoo, which acts as a calling card for the demon.[137]

To aid in removing any occult connection, tattoos and ritualistic scarring can be decommissioned by a priest.[138]

Modern entertainment is becoming increasingly overt in its connection with the occult, such as *Harry Potter* and *Twilight*. The primary objection to Harry Potter, for example, is the imposition of his will through the dark arts upon another. The ends cannot justify the means, nor can we oversimplify by saying he uses "good magic" to combat "bad magic." Furthermore, "many incantations and satanic rituals found in Harry Potter are based upon actual occult rituals. As such, they also expose the soul to the demons who animate the rituals they invoke. In addition, such books appeal to children at the age when they are most spiritually open to the supernatural (often in sacramental years) and pull them away from finding their fulfillment in the true God."[139]

---

[136] See *CCC* 2297.
[137] Liber Christo, "Companion Guide," 162.
[138] For the full ritual, see www.liberchristo.org.
[139] Liber Christo, "Companion Guide," 160.

Regarding these books, Father Amorth stated succinctly, "In Harry Potter the Devil acts in a crafty and covert manner, under the guise of extraordinary powers, magic spells and curses."[140] Other activities with direct or indirect occultic connections include:[141]

- satanic music, hard rock, heavy metal, black metal
- pornographic and horror movies
- games: Charley Charley, Bloody Mary, Kabala, etc.
- previous participation in non-Christian religions: Islam, Buddhism, Hinduism, Taoism, Confucianism, Shintoism Scientology, Jehovah Witness, Christian Science, Mormonism, Unitarianism, Baha'ism, etc.
- violent, sexually explicit or occultic video games: some use the names of real demons and feature real incantations which invoke them. Sexual violence and unholy "role playing" can be common features

What about Freemasonry? Many who come to us for help have freemasonry in their family line. Freemasonry is a secretive male fraternity that appeals to a man's need for fellowship and ritual. Popular forms of Freemasonry include Scottish Rite, York Rite, Knights of the Pythias, Odd Fellows, Shriners, and Blue Lodge. In each, members progress through various degrees through rituals.[142] Commonplace to freemasonry are seemingly innocuous initiation rituals. As discussed above, curses are the counterfeit of a blessing. One way to distinguish between the two is the ritual effect vis-à-vis the integrity of the corpus (body). The human person is a body-soul composite. A blessing always seeks to preserve the integrity of the body as united with the soul, while curses always militate against that body-soul integrity.

---

[140] Amorth, cited in *The Telegraph*, "World's Top Exorcist Saw the Devil in Harry Potter."
[141] Liber Christo, "Companion Guide," 86.
[142] Children and spouses of freemasons often become members of DeMolay, Eastern Star, Rainbow Girls, and Job's Daughters.

For example, the initiation rituals of freemasonry invoke penalties for revealing its secrets with such language as "May my body be dissected, and my vital organs cut into pieces and thrown to the beasts of the field;" or, "May my eye be put out, my body cut in two and exposing my bowels;" or, "May I have my heart eaten by venomous serpents." Notice the inversion of a blessing whereby curses work to separate the body from the soul. As Clement explains:

> Masonic members, knowingly or unknowingly, pledge their future generations in order to gain status and power (this is consistent with Exod 20.5 and Num 14.18). At the 18th degree, for example, lodge members begin pledging descendants and the ritualistic practices are openly anti-God and anti-Catholic (in some rituals they are instructed to stomp upon a papal tiara as symbolic of their casting off the authority of the Roman Catholic Church). In addition, their rituals and practices are a corruption of Catholic liturgy and other rituals. Between 1738 and 2004, the Catholic Church issued thirty-six documents that continue to forbid Catholics from becoming freemasons. Therefore, membership in a masonic lodge cannot be reconciled with Catholicism and can be a common entry point for the diabolic into a family line.[143]

Clement gives insight into why Catholic tradition has long forbidden membership in a Masonic lodge. Pope Clement XII first condemned it in 1738 and prohibited as "valid forever" with penalty of excommunication.[144] Father Rumble (of *Radio Replies* fame of a previous generation) wrote clearly on the dangers of Freemasonry at the turn of the century. Rumble reminded Catholics of the longstanding enmity between Freemasonry and Catholicism in stating that the Catholic who joins a Masonic lodge is "guilty in the sight of God and of the

---

[143] Liber Christo, "Companion Guide," 161. For a summary of ecclesial condemnations, see Rumble, *Catholics and Freemasonry*, 5–7. See also, Pope Leo Institute, "Resources on Freemasonry."
[144] Pope Clement XII, *In Eminenti*.

Church" and even commits "injury to his own soul." Thus, he concludes that the "duty of Catholics is clear. Under no circumstances may they become Freemasons."[145]

Recall the words of Father Amorth: "Every form of magic is practiced with recourse to Satan." Blessings are of God and curses are of Satan. Satan will always militate against the dignity of the human person, the wholeness of the human person, including his psychological wholeness and his physiological wholeness. In addition, Freemasonic curses follow a distinctive pattern, often manifesting in later generations as health problems, especially in respiration and stomach disorders, sins against the sixth commandment, seen in molestation, alcohol abuse, and fertility issues among women. Thus, even in modern times the Church has consistently forbidden membership in masonic associations. In addition to the condemnation in the current Code of Canon Law, in 1983 the Congregation for the Doctrine of the Faith affirmed that "the Church's negative judgment in regard to Masonic associations remains unchanged since their principles have always been considered irreconcilable with the doctrine of the Church; and therefore, membership in them remains forbidden. The faithful who enroll in Masonic associations are in a state of grave sin and may not receive Holy Communion."[146]

If you were a member of a Masonic organization, or a descendant of a freemason, we recommend that you pray prayers of renunciation to break their effects.[147] This is best done in front of a practicing Catholic as a witness, preferably on holy ground, and three times over the course of several days or weeks. Having Masses said for the deceased family member is also laudatory. If you were a Mason, be sure to confess this as a first commandment violation.

---

[145] Rumble, *Catholics and Freemasonry*, 7.
[146] CDF, *Masonic Associations*. See also Canon 1374: "A person who joins an association which plots against the Church is to be punished with a just penalty; one who promotes or takes office in such an association is to be punished with an interdict."
[147] These are found in Ripperger, *Deliverance Prayers for Use by the Laity*, 122–35, and www.liberchristo.org.

Destroying Occult Objects in the Home

By now, you should begin to see that everything that the demon does is an inversion of the sacred. If you understand how Catholic sacramentals work, for example, then you can see how cursed objects work in the occult world. Sacramentals, such as the Saint Benedict's medal or the Miraculous Medal, the scapular, holy water, blessed salt, or a rosary, all carry the blessing and power of the Jesus Christ through the prayer of the Church. They are used to bear a spiritual influence—blessing and protection—upon persons, objects, and places through the power of Jesus Christ. The spiritual effects are "obtained through the intercession of the Church" and even help the faithful to be "disposed to receive the chief effect of the sacraments, and various occasions in life are rendered holy."[148] The Rite of Exorcism itself is a sacramental, where the Church publicly and authoritatively invokes the name and power of Jesus Christ against evil present in a place, object, or person. Ideally, a Catholic home should be filled with crucifixes (and sacred art) and regularly blessed with holy water and blessed salt by the head of household.

Both sacramentals and cursed objects are inanimate agents of cosmic, or spiritual, power—one through the cosmic power of Christ and the Church, and the other through the "ruler of this world" (Jn 12:31), as Satan is called by Jesus. In an inversion of the blessed sacramental, cursed objects are also used to bear a spiritual influence—through malefice and subterfuge—upon places, objects, and people by the devil's power. A *malefice* comes from the Latin meaning "to do + evil." Just as a blessed object invokes what is signified by the prayer of the Church, so also do cursed items signify what the occult practitioner invoked in his incantation upon it. In addition, some items that have been used for grave evil—such as items used in black masses or occult rituals such as in Freemasonry or other witchcraft, or abortion tools—are of themselves cursed and must be destroyed. Other common objects include:

---

[148] *CCC* 1667.

- Images and items from other religions such as of Buddhas, Hindu, Native American religious items (dreamcatchers, kokapelli), pre-Christian objects like African tribal masks or other items used in pagan rituals
- Any items directly associated with the occult, such as Santa Muerte, Santería, voodoo, tarot cards, Ouija board, amulets
- Masonic regalia such as rings, swords, bibles, aprons, etc.

If you have any such objects in your possession, we recommend that you destroy them, specifically that they be "blessed, burned, and buried" by the head of the household, or the owner of the items.[149] After sprinkling the objects with holy water, pray the following:

> In the name of Jesus Christ and by the authority as head of household [or, as rightful owner of this object] given to me by God the Father Almighty through natural law, I ask Jesus Christ to bless this item and to decommission any evil from it.

These occult items give honor to false gods (demons) and gravely violate the first commandment. And therefore, "the item(s) should be burned. If they are made of a material that cannot burn, then the image and form should be destroyed either by crushing or melting. Finally, the remnants should be buried, or the ashes cast into deep running water. The object should be unrecognizable and unusable."[150] Confession is also important. According to Father Ripperger, confessing occult-related sins "can sometimes break a malefice."[151] We

---

[149] The concept of bless, burn, and bury is not unique to this protocol, but this manual contains information from presentations by Kyle Clement to the Pope Leo Institute in 2015.

[150] Liber Christo, "Companion Guide," 163.

[151] He points out, however, that this is not always the case, and more work may be needed to root out curses, as explained in this book. Ripperger, Dominion, 208.

also recommend the Act of Reparation to the Sacred Heart of Jesus, Fatima Prayer, Prayer of Breaking Curses, and a Prayer against Retaliation when you do this (see appendix C for these and other prayers).

After the threefold process of bless, burn, and bury, it is laudable to pray prayers of reparation for the offenses against the Sacred Heart of Jesus with a **Prayer of Reparation**:

> *Most loving Jesus, when I consider Thy tender Heart and see It full of mercy and tenderness towards sinners, my own heart is filled with joy and confidence that I shall be so kindly welcomed by Thee. Unfortunately, how many times have I sinned! But now, with St. Peter and with St. Mary Magdalene, I weep for my sins and detest them because they offend Thee, infinite goodness. Mercifully grant me pardon for them all; and let me die rather than offend Thee again; at least let me live only to love Thee in return. Amen.*[152]

Prayer to Remove Generational Spirits

If you have participated in any occult activities, a sacramental confession is vital to gaining freedom. "The ultimate antidote against the occult," says Clement, "is the practice of authentic Catholicism. The ordinary means of the sanctification of the soul to counteract any unholy desire for the occult include attending Mass, Christian prayer, rosary, and . . . reading the Bible."[153] These help to counteract any unholy desire for the occult. That desire often flows from the avoidance of suffering or the desire for power. These actions also atone for the sins of participating in such activity. In addition to sacramental confession, one should pray the renunciation prayers found in the appendix.

Father Ripperger encourages Catholics to seek the assistance of Our Lady of Sorrows in uncovering the nature of a generational spirit and how they may have entered the

---

[152] This prayer of reparation taken from Ripperger, *Holy Hour of Reparation*, 21.
[153] Liber Christo, "Companion Guide," 163.

generational line. This aids in praying specific binding prayers against them and in developing the virtues to combat them. It is also salutary to have Masses offered in reparation for any sin that may be the cause of the generational spirit as well as healing of the members who may still suffer the effects of the evil spirit and for the repose of any souls in purgatory that may still be there as a result of sins they committed at the behest of the evil spirit. You can also use this prayer as needed:

Lord Jesus Christ, Incarnate Son of God the Father, Thou who has chosen to enter into human history by being carried in the womb of Thy Blessed Mother Mary, grant I beseech Thee, that any demons that may have been introduced into my generational line by any one of my ancestors may be blocked from passing to the subsequent generations. I ask Thee that if the evil spirit entered the generational line by the sin of one or more of my ancestors, that Thou wouldst pardon the temporal punishment due to their sin and free us from the demon's involvement in our lives. Blessed Virgin, we ask Thee to offer the Precious Body, Blood, Soul, and Divinity of thy Son to God the Father in reparation for the sins of those ancestors who may have introduced any evil spirits into my generational line, as well as any subsequent sins that may have resulted from the evil spirits affecting those of the generational line. If any evil spirit has been introduced into my generational line as a result of a curse or malefice done by someone outside my family, I ask thee to give me the grace to forgive them wholeheartedly and I ask Thee, Jesus, to break the curse or malefice, if it is still in place. God the Father, I forgive them for any of the effects of their sin that they may have committed against my family line and for any damage it may have caused. Jesus, I ask Thee to forgive me of any sins that may be the result of any generational spirits in my family, and I ask Thee to block any power the evil spirits may have gained in my generational line as a result of my own sin. Heal any damage in the lives of the members of my family as a result of the generational spirit. I bind and completely and utterly reject, with the full force of my will any sin or spiritual defect of mine as well as any temptation, allurements, or power that any generational spirit may have over me as a result of my sin or the sin of any other person. I do this in the Holy Names of Jesus and Mary and in the Name of the Father and of the Son and of the Holy Spirit. Amen.

More specific prayers are found in the appendix.

From Slingstones to Milestones: The Occult and Generational Sin

1. Did you experience any interior resistance, such as anxiety or something you just did not like, when reading any part of this lesson?

2. Explain the connection between the psalm that states "The gods of the nations are idols" (Ps 96:5) and the concept of interactive demonic activity.

3. Have you been involved in any occult practices? Have you confessed this activity?

4. Recall the statement: "The activities performed through occult practices to obtain favors or discover the future deeply offend God not only because it reveals our lack of trust in Him, but also because such activities are 'a recourse to Satan or demons'." What in your past caused you to exhibit a lack of trust in God, which may have resulted in occult activity?

5. Have you identified any generational sins affecting your family? If so, what are the best means to root them out?

Chapter Two

Repentance, Metanoia, and Forgiveness

"As a youth he slew the giant / and wiped out the peoples' disgrace; / His hand let fly the slingstone / that shattered the pride of Goliath."

—SIRACH 47:4

Earlier we explained that *five* symbolized the Torah, or the Law, the first five books of the Old Testament. A Christian lens also recognizes the number five as an allusion to the five wounds of Jesus Christ. The reader should recall the words of Isaiah that foretold of the suffering of Christ— namely, "he was pierced for our sins, / crushed for our iniquity. / . . . by his wounds we were healed" (Is 53:5). The Greek word for *pierced* is *traumizo*, which means "to wound, hurt, or damage." Interestingly, the noun *traumatized* was also a military term in antiquity which referred to those wounded in battle. Considering the above discussion on the modern misuse of trauma, it is noteworthy here that the suffering of Jesus Christ, the trauma of violence done against His sacred Flesh, was perfectly accepted and made redemptive for all humanity. After His resurrection, He never again mentions His suffering, but only pointed to the five wounds—His hands, feet, and pierced side—as evidence of His love for us so that we may believe (cf. Jn 20:27–29).

Thus, the cross of Jesus Christ, where He received His five wounds, is not a sign of defeat but rather victory. By His wounds we are healed—and defeat the enemy. This is why many of the early Church Fathers referred to the cross as a "war memorial." Saint John Chrysostom exclaims, "Have you seen the wonderful victory? Have you seen the splendid deeds of the Cross? Shall I tell you something still more marvelous? Learn in what way the victory was gained, and you will be even more astonished. For by the very means by which the devil had conquered, by these Christ conquered him; and taking up the weapons with which he had fought, he defeated him."[154]

This Doctor of the Church connects the "wood" of the cross to the tree of Adam where man was defeated by the devil in the garden. Thus, the cross is "a war memorial erected against the demons, a sword against sin, the sword with which Christ slew the serpent."[155]

Soldiers to this day keep war trophies upon their return. Recall how after defeating Goliath, David kept his sword and armor (see 1 Sm 17:54) and eventually had it displayed in the temple at Nob (see 1 Sm 21:9–10). The Greek word that Saint John Chrysostom uses for war memorial is *trópaion*. This is where we get the word for trophy, deriving from the verb meaning "to turn." In antiquity, the *trópaion* marked the spot where the enemy turned and broke ranks and, consequently, where the battle was won. The victors would memorialize that spot by erecting a cross or large X and suspend the armaments of the enemy upon it—a shield, helmet, sword, et cetera. Many Church Fathers (as early as the second century) likewise recognized that the cross is a *trópaion*, noting even the very T-shape that the ancient victors would erect for their memorial foreshadowed the cross. From the earliest of times, the cross has been understood as where Satan and his demons were vanquished by Christ.

Recalling Revelation 12, which describes the defeat of the devil, how did Saint John the Apostle say that "the accuser"

---

154 Saint John Chrysostom, *De cœmeterio et de cruce*, 2.
155 Saint John Chrysostom, 2.

was beaten? Notably, "They conquered him by the blood of the Lamb / and by the word of their testimony; / love for life did not deter them from death" (Rv 12:11). Giving "the word of your testimony" does not mean you beat the devil by telling your past sins and conversion experience in front of a group of people at church. Literally, Saint John says that they defeated him by the *logos* of their *martyria*. And Saint Paul writes, "The message [*logos*] of the cross is foolishness to those who are perishing, but to us who are being saved it is the power of God" (1 Cor 1:18). The "logic" of the cross lies in its power to save—not a one-time past event, but to the present day.

Jesus tells us the three conditions of discipleship are self-denial, the carrying of the cross, and following Him; for "whoever loses his life for my sake will find it" (Mt 16:25). Thus, the Greek *martyreo* means "to bear witness, give evidence" of these three conditions. The ultimate *witness* to Christ is with one's very life, and therefore, the *martyr* is one who dies for his faith in Jesus Christ. To defeat the enemy, you must enter the path of martyrdom, of death to self, "love for life did not deter them from death" (Rv 12:11). For this reason, Saint Paul asserts that you must "put to death, then, the parts of you that are earthly: immorality, impurity, passion, evil desire, and the greed that is idolatry. Because of these the wrath of God is coming upon the disobedient" (Col 3:5–6). Elsewhere, he links death to baptism, stating, "We were indeed buried with him through baptism into death, so that, just as Christ was raised from the dead by the glory of the Father, we too might live in newness of life" (Rom 6:4). The "old self" must be put to death so that Christ may live and reign in you. Saint Paul thus says, "I have been crucified with Christ; yet I live, no longer I, but Christ lives in me" (Gal 2:19–20). And, "Death is swallowed up in victory. Where, O death, is your victory? / Where, O death, is your sting?" (1 Cor 15:55).

Are you willing to fight this battle for your loved ones, your spouse, and children? Are you willing to do whatever it takes to jettison the enemy so he no longer taunts and enslaves you and your family, like Goliath taunted David and Israel? If so, take up the cross of Jesus Christ and continue the march, or "Charlie Mike" as soldiers say. In this section, we will show you how to identify and remove the obstacles to grace in your life so you can return home victorious.

LESSON FOUR: THE IMPEDIMENT OF UNFORGIVENESS

The motto of the British special forces, or Special Air Service (SAS), is *Who Dares Wins.* David certainly exemplified this daring when he boldly raced *toward* Goliath on the field of battle. One thing that prevents boldness in the spiritual life, however, is the weightiness of past sins. When David put on Saul's armor, it was so heavy that he could hardly move. To describe how heavy and awkward the armor was, the narrative literally states that "he walked with difficulty" (1 Sm 17:39). Unforgiveness works in a similar way. It wears you down and makes you vulnerable. Unforgiving people may think holding onto their pain provides them protection from future wounds, but the opposite is true.

An *obex* is an obstacle, barrier, or blockage, and here it means anything that blocks the flow of grace to the soul. In an analogous way, sin weighs down the soul like the heavy weight of Saul's armor, inhibiting life, movement, and growth. An obex to grace, then, is anything that encumbers the soul by weighing down and restricting movement, thus making it "difficult to walk"—let alone engage in spiritual combat. In fact, persistence in sin and the failure to break both physical and spiritual ties to past sins are major impediments to your relationship with God. This spiritual baggage is like heavy armor blocking the flow of grace. A hardened unrepentance and a failure to see your own faults, therefore, are the first *obices* which must be removed.

Unforgiveness of others stands in direct opposition to the command of the Lord, who taught us to pray, according to Saint Luke: "Forgive us our sins for we ourselves forgive everyone in debt to us" (Lk 11:4). Accordingly, a lack of forgiveness is a major obex which burdens the soul and restricts the flow of grace. This means surrendering any claim, even rightful ones, over anyone who has hurt you. In fact, the more rightful the claim you may have, the more merit there is when you surrender it to God. Saint Matthew teaches how Jesus gave further instruction on His words in the Lord's Prayer of "forgive us our debts, *as we forgive* our debtors" (Mt 6:12, emphasis added). Specifically, Jesus speaks with a pointed realism of His command to forgive: "If you forgive others their transgressions," He says that "your heavenly Father will forgive you. But if you do not forgive others, neither will your Father forgive your transgressions" (Mt 6:14–15). The emotions of anger, brooding, and retaliation have weighed on you and impeded your movement like heavy armor. Forgiving others is a willful act that sheds the heavy burden and helps to reopen the flow of grace. Just as David shed the awkward and heavy armor (see 1 Sm 17:39), so must you shed these interior habits.

Unforgiveness presents psychological and emotional wounds by which the demon can induce emotions of unholy shame and fear in you. Fr. Antonio Royo Marín, for example, lists the awareness of "the necessity of forgiveness" that flows from "seeing how mercifully the Lord has pardoned us" as one of the effects of a good confession.[156] When left unchecked, other vices can follow in the trail of unforgiveness, such as lies and a distorted or unfounded belief in the lies of others; apathy, or a lack of emotion; extreme emotionality, particularly when disproportionate to the circumstances; and feelings of worthlessness or self-loathing. As I stated, "For someone who suffers diabolic affliction, the need to forgive is an essential and a vital first step toward liberation."[157] This is because the demon feeds upon the wounds that have yet to be sacramentally and interiorly (psychologically and emotionally) healed. Just as sin affects our relationship with God, self, and others, so also does the sin of unforgiveness.

---

[156] Marín, *The Theology of Christian Perfection*, 351.
[157] Liber Christo, "Companion Guide," 36.

The Importance of Forgiveness

Father Ripperger defines despair as "the vice in which one estimates falsely about God's ability to save someone."[158] Often, many people harbor unforgiveness towards God, who they perceive (wrongfully) as not being present to their suffering. A major psychological compatibility between the diabolical and the human is this accusation or unforgiveness toward God. The common ligature, moreover, is a distorted image of God. God does not need to be forgiven for anything. Too often, however, we see people harboring this anthropomorphic and modernistic projection upon Him, that somehow His plan has been thwarted in their lives. This includes the false accusation that God did not intend for them to be hurt and that the greatest good is that God wants them to be happy. As to the latter, there are many definitions of "happy," but those who accuse God usually define "happiness" as a lack of suffering of any kind (when, in reality, happiness is the ultimate end of the moral life). This is why many people who come to the Church for liberation are seeking, in reality, the cessation of suffering and not reconciliation and union with God.

Part of the fallen human condition is the reality of suffering, and too often people "project" upon God blame for the unpleasant things that happen to them. Whether you conform yourself to the will of the Father (which is always and everywhere our salvation) or instead focus narrowly on the events in your life will determine how long this affliction remains. To borrow language from tradition, you are either *ad orientem* or you are *ad hominem* (the Latin *ad* = to/towards). Until the modern period, churches were always built so that the altar faced *towards the east* (*ad orientem*) in anticipation of the second coming of Christ. This second coming, promised by Jesus after His resurrection which happened at or around sunrise (cf. Lk 24:1), is anticipated by the rising of the sun which also is in the east (*oriens* is the Latin word for east, deriving from

---

[158] Ripperger, *Introduction to the Science of Mental Health*, 370.

the word meaning "to rise"). When the priest (and people with him) face *ad orientem* at Holy Mass, the Body of Christ stands in hope filled anticipation of Christ's return. Conversely, to be *ad hominem* (to be to/towards man/human being) is a phrase used since Aristotle to describe an inward turning towards emotion rather than the intellect. That is, in the face of suffering, either you turn with hope and look towards Christ or you turn inward and are drawn into the lower emotions.

The emotional response centers upon the self and "often leads to a sense of entitlement and a hyper-sensitivity that leads one to be easily offended when others do not conform to meet our expectations. This, in turn, often leads to unforgiveness and resentment."[159] When a demon sees a person with an inward posture of *ad hominem* in the face of trial, he begins his work. Soon he will project emotions of blame towards God, others, or oneself. Why? Simply stated, the demon lives in this existential (and eternal) state of sadness, remorse, and despair over his fall and consequently blames God for his own suffering. Conversely, when the demon sees a person who turns *ad orientem* in the face of suffering, he is like Goliath seeing David running towards him with his sling circling over his head. The choice is yours. Focus not so much on the event as on your reaction to the event. What was your reaction then, and what would have it been today? Have you fallen into any negative patterns of sinful behavior since the event?

Too often, however, we blame others for our suffering. Accordingly, you must forgive anyone who has injured you. Bearing in mind the above discussion on trauma, a subjective response to events can flavor our memory of the actual events, requiring caution. There can be *perceived* offenses by others which the demon can exploit. Offering prayers and sacrifices for someone who has hurt you is a proven means of breaking the grip of unforgiveness. As Jesus warned in the parable of the

---

[159] Liber Christo, "Companion Guide," 147.

unforgiving servant, "So will my heavenly Father do to you [that is, 'hand . . . over to the torturers' until the debt is paid] unless each of you forgives his brother from his heart" (Mt 18:35).

Sometimes the person we need to forgive most is ourselves. By forgiving yourself, the demon cannot elicit an unholy shame or fear response in you by projecting a memory for your past sins. This is often regarding things involving actions from long ago. Because we tend to demand more of ourselves than others ("I should have *known* better!"), releasing ourselves from past sins and mistakes can be very challenging. Often, a *spirit of mockery* derides the person who cannot forgive himself. The demon will project things like "How did you let this happen to you?" Or, "What were you thinking? You are worthless." The perception of the event can be distorted by a self-love attached to the failure to forgive yourself, but it is purified when you surrender the event to God and link your suffering to the suffering of Jesus Christ.

Spiritual Judo

Vicarious suffering means making a spiritual offering for others by uniting your suffering with that of Jesus. This seemingly simple offering of your physical or emotional pain, minor inconveniences, is a powerful way to loosen the enemy's grip. Resist, therefore, the desire for revenge. As Saint Paul reminds us, "'Vengeance is mine, I will repay, says the Lord.' Rather, 'if your enemy is hungry feed him; if he is thirsty, give him something to drink; for by doing so you will heap burning coals upon his head.' Do not be conquered by evil but conquer evil with good" (Rom 12:19–21). As I stated, "Vengeance . . . poisons the human soul when we seek to avenge our pain. In fact, holding resentment and unforgiveness over past hurts is like drinking poison and waiting for the other person to die. We must free ourselves of both if we want to experience true inner freedom."[160]

---

[160] Liber Christo, "Companion Guide," 42.

Conversely, releasing whoever has hurt you opens your soul to graces that were previously blocked. Since the demon can manipulate your perception of people and events, particularly when you harbor resentment in the emotions, allowing Christ's light into the construct can be very helpful. This prayer is called the **Light of Christ Prayer**:

May the light of Christ be on (n.), so that they see themselves as the Heavenly Father sees them; and that I see them as the Heavenly Father sees them.

By inviting the light of the One who prayed "Father, forgive them" from the cross, you uncover the demon who is feeding from the memory. Cut off his source of supply. As Clement, who wrote this simple but effective prayer, explains, "This projects the love of Christ upon the person and enables us to grow in our loving trust of God."[161] This simple prayer also changes perceptions of the event, yourself, and others. Bear in mind also that the soul of the person you need to forgive may be in grave danger. They may need someone to pray and suffer for them. Surrendering your claim over them may be exactly what it takes to release a flood of graces from heaven into both of your lives.

The volitional act of forgiving another is deeply augmented by sacramental confession. Asking God for the grace to forgive may mean that you ask Him to change your heart towards the person that you need to forgive. That willful act will aid in the release of graces in confession. Thus, the "light of Christ" prayer can be modified and used as a form intercessory prayer as well:

May the light of Christ be upon me that I forgive (n.) as the Lord has forgiven me.

Sometimes, however, the enemy keeps targeting you and you need to change tactics. Whenever you experience any sort of pain—whether physical, psychological, or emotional—the "Judo Prayer" is also quite effective. In judo, you learn to use your opponent's force and momentum against him. In a similar

---

[161] Liber Christo, "Companion Guide," 167.

way, this prayer takes the force and momentum of the enemy and uses it for the salvation of souls. This prayer also shows the subtleties of how to use mental prayer as a projection and also the value of using suffering as a weapon in spiritual combat. When your opponent rushes you, use the **Judo Prayer**:

> *Lord, I am experiencing (n.). If this is not from you and is diabolic in origin, I ask you to send it back to its source with a tenfold blessing. If, however, you want me to carry this cross, I willfully accept it, I ask you for the grace to carry it, and I offer it for* (insert your intention here).

Whether you have something as simple as a headache or sleeplessness, or an intense diabolic affliction and attack, offer your affliction for the person you need to forgive, the purification of the Church, the souls in purgatory, a family member who has left the Church, or in atonement for a past sin which bothers you. If you begin to offer all the little crosses of your day to the Lord, especially for anyone who has hurt you, you will progress quickly towards freedom.

Remove the Heavy Armor of Saul

In this section, we focused on identifying and removing obstacles to grace so that God's divine life may purify your soul. Without grace, interior freedom is impossible. A major obex to the flow of grace is unforgiveness. Like the heavy armor of King Saul, it weighs you down and limits your mobility. When you release others, however, you free yourself of any attachments the enemy may use against you. Confess any unforgiveness and then work on forgiving them by an act of the will. List here those people that you need to forgive:

The following prayer may be used to help remove various obstacles as well as aid you in uncovering where the demon may be hiding:

By the power of Thy Holy Spirit, reveal to me, Father, any people I need to forgive and any areas of unconfessed sin. Reveal aspects of my life that are not pleasing to Thee, O Father, and ways that have given or could give Satan a foothold in my life. Father, I submit to Thee any unforgiveness; I submit to Thee my sins; and I submit to Thee all the ways that Satan has a hold on my life. Thank Thee, O Father for this knowledge; thank Thee, for Thy forgiveness and Thy love. Amen.

For other formulae and prayers, see the appendix.

From Slingstones to Milestones: The Impediment of Unforgiveness

1. Was there anything in the lesson that was difficult for you to read?

2. Recall the statement: "A hardened unrepentance and a failure to see your own faults is the first obex which must be removed." How prone are you to look for the faults in others while ignoring your own?

3. How can you use "spiritual judo" when experiencing an affliction? How does this connect to the old truism of "offer it up"?

4. The section on unforgiveness listed several emotional and psychological wounds that the demon can induce emotions of shame or fear when you do not obey the Lord's command to forgive ("Forgive us our trespasses as we forgive those who trespass against us." Mt 6:12). Which of the four applies most to you (lies and a distorted or unfounded belief in the lies of others; apathy, or a lack of emotion; extreme emotionality, particularly

when disproportionate to the circumstances; and
feelings of worthlessness or self-loathing)?

5.   Who are the three people who you find most
difficult to forgive and why?

Lesson Five: Repentance and Metanoia

Jesus begins His public ministry with a salvo of truth for all generations. As I explain, "Jesus' first words in the Gospel of Mark show precisely this necessity to both believe and make the necessary changes in behavior so as to live an authentic Christian life: 'Repent and believe in the gospel' (Mark 1:15). Saint Peter echoes this very thing in his first sermon, preached at Pentecost ('Repent and be baptized, every one of you, in the name of Jesus Christ for the forgiveness of your sins; and your will receive the gift of the Holy Spirit' (Acts 2:38)."[162] For the reader who has been baptized, this means three R's: *repent* (of your sins), *renew* (your baptismal promises), and *receive* the Holy Spirit (that is, restore sanctifying grace in your soul).

Conversion comes from the Latin *converso*, which means "to turn around, revolve, change, or transfer from one composition to another" and, therefore, "to make a moral change or make a conversion." In military usage, this is the command of "*About . . . Face!*" in which soldiers standing in rank make a 180 degree turn. That is, at the command of *converso*, they immediately place the tip of their right foot behind their left heel and snap around to face the opposite direction. Thus, I explain, "Conversion, then, is part of the growth toward spiritual maturity for the baptized Christian and is essential to liberation from the influence of demons."[163]

Remember, the demon always works in the objective but drives us to focus on the emotions, the subjective. As a result, many seek prayer forms that give an emotional release but

---

[162] Liber Christo, "Companion Guide," 17.
[163] Liber Christo, "Companion Guide," 74.

neglect the self-examination requisite to true contrition for the sins that block union with God. An authentic conversion involves *contrition,* which means not only sorrow for one's sins but also the willful detestation of sin and the commitment not to sin again. The contrite soul operates out of the will, not the emotions, in the desire to regain friendship with God, which was damaged or lost due to one's own sinful behavior. Thus, the contrite soul is, in a sense, *ad orientem* in his determination both not to commit the sins again and in his commitment to do whatever it takes to conquer them. While tears of compunction (remorse or regret resulting from one's actions) may result in a temporary feeling of remorse, contrition is an ongoing condition of the soul that recognizes sin as the greatest evil and commits in the will to avoid sin at all costs.

This "about face" means you were going in one direction and now go in the opposite direction. The impetus for the turnaround is an interior movement of repentance for one's sins *principally because they offend God.* Wanting to be liberated from demonic activity is not sufficient. According to the *Catechism,* repentance (metanoia) is first a movement of conversion and is the "radical reorientation of our whole life, our return, a conversion to God with all our heart, and end of sin, turning away from evil, with repugnance towards the evil actions we have committed."[164] By "radical" is implied the Latin *radix,* which means "root" (think: radish, a root vegetable). Thus, for liberation to occur, you must have a *radical reorientation of life* in the truest sense of the word. That is, at the deepest level, the foundation, the origin upon which one is fixed must be rooted in God alone, for God alone, and by God alone. All other goods must be reordered to that foundation and that which is unholy must be discarded. This means also a "desire and resolution to change one's life" to include "hope in God's mercy and trust in the help of his grace."[165]

---

[164] *CCC* 1431.
[165] *CCC* 1431.

Repentance, then, is the movement away from the subjective, emotional response to the events in your life towards the willful resolution (at the root of one's interior self) to never again offend God with one's actions. We distinguish, moreover, between repentance and metanoia. As I explain, *Repentance* comes "from the Latin *re+poenitire*, meaning "to regret" or "to be deeply sorry for." This intellectual and interior movement of sorrow for sin and self-condemnation leads a person to resolve not to offend God further. *Metanoia* "comes from the Greek word meaning to repent or, literally, change one's mind in the sense of changing one's purpose." That purposeful change means a movement from unbelief to belief and from sin and vice to the practice of virtue. To repent implies the commitment "to change for . . . good, one's thoughts, words and deeds," and metanoia flows from that commitment. Metanoia refers to "the tangible actions or movements in the will that are requisite with, and necessary for, perfect repentance."[166]

One may repent that they have fallen into a life of sin and slavery but still lack the deep inner conviction to do whatever is necessary to change and acquire true freedom. Metanoia, therefore, goes beyond just feeling sorry for your sins and gives impetus to the radical reorientation of one's life. This is to say, there should be an "about-face" in both the intellect and the will, a gathering up of the intellect in a willful desire to make a radical change. This *gathering up* means assenting to all that the Church teaches and seeking Christian perfection. Maintaining a state of grace and living the Catholic faith are essential to long-term liberation. Grace can be blocked, even rejected, to the extent doctrines and dogmas are discarded. Consequently, it is important to conform both your beliefs and practices to the truths of the Roman Catholic faith. The demon is always present wherever there are heresies (whether false beliefs or ignorance), and consequently, we emphasize the importance of living orthodoxy and orthopraxy.

---

[166] Liber Christo, "Companion Guide," 17.

This is akin to how a rock climber scales a mountain face by means of two types of handholds. Along the wall, there are either crevices into which he can place his hand or foot or there are protrusions which he can grab or step upon. In an analogous way, through ignorance (little crevices) or false beliefs (protrusions), the demon can hold in a soul. An important step towards dispossessing the demon from your soul, therefore, is to fill in the areas of ignorance with knowledge and grind down heresies with the truth. Make that wall a smooth face that cannot be scaled. You can bounce from exorcist to exorcist or from prayer meeting to prayer meeting in search of liberation, but to the extent your soul has ignorance or heresy, and attachment to mortal sin, the demon can still remain active.

While we have seen some liberations occur in souls who are not detached from mortal sin and have yet to conform their belief to the truths of the Roman Catholic faith, inevitably the words of Jesus ring true: "When an unclean spirit goes out of a person it roams through arid regions searching for rest but finds none. Then it says, 'I will return to my home from which I came.' But upon returning, it finds it empty and swept clean, and put in order. Then it goes and brings back with itself seven other spirits more evil than itself, and they move in and dwell there; and the last condition is worse than the first" (Mt 12:43–45).

In our experience, most people who live in mortal sin, almost 90 percent of cases, end up being possessed again because of the lack of detachment to sin and conformity of belief. Thus, if a person does not cleanse himself and grow in holiness of thought, word, and deed, he can end up in a worse condition.

Metanoia, therefore, involves both the intellect (viz., change of purpose) and demonstrative movements in the will. The fruit of metanoia is the gradual acquisition of holiness in thought, word, and deed. We emphasize this point for two reasons. One, many people seek prayers of liberation because of the emotional release that they experience, but they never examine the deeply embedded sinful behavior which, ultimately, allows the demon to remain present to them. Two, the holiness requisite to true contrition and metanoia is what is needed for long-term liberation. That is, many people never do an "about-face."

Diabolic Lies and Removing Obstacles to Grace

One of Rogers's rules is how to handle enemy prisoners. "If we take prisoners," he counsels, "we keep 'em separate 'til we have had time to examine them, so they can't cook up a story between 'em." One of the main stories that our spiritual enemy likes to "cook up" is to present a better way out of the problems we face than fidelity to the Church's teachings. An honest and close examination of your life may reveal precisely this. At some point, you were confronted with a cross or a difficult decision and let the demon convince you that his was an easier or quicker way out. For this reason, the Scriptures speak of the "snares" of the evil one (see Lk 21:35; 1 Tm 3:7; 6:9; 2 Tm 2:26) because the demon uses various schemes and traps to enmesh you. By this point, you are beginning to recognize the demon has been "cooking up a story."

The words that God spoke through the prophet Hosea may also apply to you: "When Israel was a child I loved him, / out of Egypt I called my son. / The more I called them, / the farther they went from me, / Sacrificing to the Baals / and burning incense to idols" (Hos 11:1–2). That is, the effects of the events of the past can linger and even block our return to God. And yet, God continues to call us into friendship. "I drew them with . . . band of love," He says through Hosea, "yet though I stooped to feed my child, they did now know that I was their healer" (Hos 11:4).

The enemy undoubtedly has "cooked up a story" convincing you that returning to God is impossible and that healing is impossible. Jesus, however, says the opposite: "I no longer call you slaves . . . I have called you friends" (Jn 15:15). Divine friendship is made possible through your baptismal dignity, but once this is forfeited through grave sin and heretical beliefs and practices, the demon lays claim (albeit false) to the soul and begins his destructive activity. You may have given him permission through sinful activity, but you belong—by right—to Christ through the seal of Holy Baptism. The release of baptismal graces, therefore, must be preceded by a penitential disposition (contrition, repentance, and metanoia) so as to unlock its salvific effects. The demons will not leave simply by the merits our baptism, as some falsely assert. He will, however, yield when forced to do so.

The challenge of Goliath to the men of Israel was clear: "Choose one of your men and have him come down to me. If he beats me in combat and kills me, we will be your vassals; but if I beat him and kill him, you shall be our vassals and serve us" (1 Sm 17:9). Slavery in Egypt was part of the ancestral memory of the Israelites, so this challenge must have been particularly difficult to hear. God called the Israelites out of Egypt (= sin and slavery) and into the desert (= solitude with the divine Healer). There, the Israelites complained against God and Moses and even expressed their desire to return to slavery rather than face the hardship it would take to receive the promises of God (see Ex 16:2–3). In the end, they were fearful and lacking trust in God—both products of their years of enslavement.

Goliath continued, "I defy the ranks of Israel today, give me a man and let us fight together" (1 Sm 17: 10). Not one man answered the challenge. In fact, we are told that "Saul and all the men of Israel, when they heard this challenge, were dismayed and terror-stricken" (1 Sm 17:11). Literally, they were "disordered, out of wits, astonished, deranged to the point of changing their minds and, thus, dismayed" and "exceedingly, violently afraid." Goliath continued his challenge the next day and, upon hearing him, the soldiers remained "very much afraid," and consequently, they "all retreated before him" (1 Sm 17:24). The demon uses similar tactics to keep you in fear, confusion, and dismay so that you will retreat before him as the Israelites before Goliath.

In spiritual battle, as in earthly battle, courage is needed. Courage moderates fear so that the man who has perfected the virtue of courage is not fearful in relation to those things which can be overcome. Rather, he has caution, which is part of prudence. Many obstacles can militate against courage, leading to a rashness which causes you to be "deeply afraid" and to "retreat" before the enemy. Learn to recognize the voice of Goliath as he shouts (or whispers) lies to you to keep you in fear and to make you retreat. Do not take the bait that he had laid into the trap to ensnare you. Goliath is like the serpent in the garden who enticed Eve, the "talking snake" always "cooking up a story" and even voicing your own fears to you. Recall the words of David when he tells Goliath, "Today the Lord will deliver you into my hands" (1 Sm 17:46). God will act if you trust Him. He will guide your stone.

Leaving Egypt

Even though the Israelites had left Egypt, Egypt had not left them. They had yet to make the "about-face" and conform completely to God's will. Admittedly, this is not an easy task. What Moses and Aaron reported to Pharaoh applies to you today: "Thus says the Lord, the God of Israel: Let my people go, that they may celebrate a feast with me in the desert" (Ex 5:1). Just as Israel's *freedom from* slavery was *freedom for* union with God through right worship, so also you must seek to be freed from spiritual bondage so that you can reconcile with God the Father through the sacramental and liturgical life of the Church. Do you want to leave Egypt? Do you grumble or do you trust God? Can you leave *all* of Egypt—all physical and emotional reminders—behind you?

When people approach their local church for assistance from affliction, they often lack interior peace and emotional and psychological self-control. They have not closed off interior portals to the demon who projects a barrage of emotions and memories. The first step towards interior freedom is the establishment of a monastic-type discipline, to include a withdrawal from the world and the ordering of your life to prayer. Sometimes, however, more is needed, and a second phase is introduced. As Moses exhorted the Israelites to "Fear not! Stand your ground," so you must engage your will to choose to be free. As Saint Augustine said, "God who created you without your consent will not save you without your consent."[167] Accordingly, you cannot be a passive recipient; rather, you must be an active agent in your own liberation.

In the early tradition of the Church, Egypt was seen as a type of slavery from which Christ saved us. Origen (185–253) stated that "you must not think that these events belong only to the past" because "you have recently abandoned the darkness of idolatry, and you now desire to come and hear the divine law. This is your departure from Egypt . . . when you became a catechumen and began to obey the laws of the Church." He states that "you passed through the Red Sea" when "you come to the baptismal font and, in the presence of the priests and deacons, are initiated into those sacred and august mysteries . . . then, through the ministry of the priests, you will cross the Jordan and enter the promised land. There Moses will hand you over to Jesus, and He himself will be your guide on your new journey."[168] Similarly, Saint Augustine said, "You too left Egypt when, at baptism, you renounced that world which is at enmity with God."[169]

You may have left Egypt in Baptism but returned to it through your sins. To "leave Egypt" means to cut all ties, physical and spiritual, with the enslavement of the past. Recall also how the Israelites used the jewelry and artifacts that they brought with them from Egypt and fashioned to a false idol (Ex 32:1–6). Thus, while they were physically freed from bondage, they were still very much spiritually enslaved by the demons of Egypt. Saint Paul refers to this time in Israel's past as a "type" for the Christian today, and is worth stating at length here: "I do not want you to be unaware, brothers, that our ancestors were all under the cloud and all passed through the sea, and all of them were baptized into

---

[167] Saint Augustine, *Sermon 169*.
[168] Origen, *Homily 4*,1.
[169] Cited in Laughlin, *The Almanac for Pastoral Liturgy*, 151.

Moses in the cloud and in the sea. All ate the same spiritual food, and all drank the same spiritual drink, for they drank from a spiritual rock that followed them, and the rock was the Christ. Yet God was not pleased with most of them, for they were struck down in the desert" (1 Cor 10:1–5).

Why were the Israelites struck down? Saint Paul continues:

> These things happened as examples for us, so that we might not desire evil things, as they did. And do not become idolaters, as some of them did, as it is written, "The people sat down to eat and drink, and rose up to revel." Let us not indulge in immorality as some of them did, and twenty-three thousand fell within a single day. Let us not test Christ as some of them did and suffered death by serpents. Do not grumble as some of them did and suffered death by the destroyer. These things happened to them as an example, and they have been written down as a warning to us, upon whom the end of the ages has come. (1 Cor 10:6–13)

Even though God delivered them from slavery and now dwelled in their midst, Saint Paul noted several things which attracted the serpents to them:

- Desiring/lusting after evil things
- Revelry/partying (here the implication of ritual intoxication and sex as the Apis ritual to a fertility god as before the golden bull, cf. Ex 32:2–6)
- Deviant sexual practices (the Greek word *porneo* is glossed as "immorality")
- Grumbling, complaining

Note the behaviors he lists that attract the serpents—deviant sexual behavior and unholy speech. Thus, there must be a turning away from these things (a spiritual "about-face") so you can discern the clean from the unclean.

At the Water's Edge

Although the enemy may be pursuing you like Pharaoh's army, the goal of liberation is your salvation. This is the true land of promise and God's will for you. See yourself at the Red Sea, at the water's edge waiting for a miracle, as you pray the following **Prayer of Healing**:

> *Holy Spirit, come down and reclaim my body which was consecrated to Thee at my baptism, filling my entire dimensive quantity, from the top of my head to the bottom of my feet. Fill my faculties with Thy presence; my senses, memory, imagination, cogitative power, commonsense power, intellect, will and appetites. Take up Thy residence in all aspects of my body and soul, leaving no place unfilled, closing off any doors, caves or portals to the demons, driving them to the foot of the Cross of Jesus Christ, never to return again. Heal my other wounds of (name the wounds). In the name of the Father, and of the Son, and of the Holy Spirit. Amen.*

Recall from the earlier discussion that a simple definition of grace is divine life, a holy vitality of the life and power of God, which purifies everything it touches. A life ordered to prayer will open you to that vitality, but unless you deeply repent and turn away from sin, the serpents will keep coming back. The appendix contains more prayers that may help this process.

From Slingstones to Milestones: Repentance and Metanoia

1. Since beginning this program, what personal changes have you seen and made in regards to repentance and metanoia? Have you made an "about-face" in any areas of your life?

2. What is your reaction to the statement, "Remember, the demon always works in the objective but drives us to focus on the emotions"?

3.   Is there any inner lie, wound, or "cooking up a story"
      that still goes on interiorly to you? Or between you
      and your family members?

4.   Have you noticed any disproportionate reactions
      such as anger, anxiety, defensiveness, isolation, or
      sadness in response to any people or events?

5.   What claims against me is the accuser still trying
      to make? Are there any areas where "Goliath" lies
      to you, thus keeping you afraid and making you
      retreat?

6.   Explain the meaning of standing at the water's edge
      in a "Red Sea moment."

LESSON SIX: THE VIRGIN MARY AND SPIRITUAL COMBAT

A marked characteristic of the Rangers is their adaptabil-
ity, even when facing a well-trained and larger force.
One of Rogers's rules simply stated, "Every night you'll be told
where to meet if surrounded by a superior force." Following
this rule helped a small contingency of rangers who encountered a much larger force along Lake Champlain in a snowy
and cold mid-January in 1757. With the superior-in-number
French force in hot pursuit behind them, the rangers slipped
into the woods and quickly donned snowshoes. With the
French detachment slogging through snow up to their knees,
the rangers easily outpaced the enemy and, by aid of the cover
of darkness, quietly disappeared.

In today's military terminology, the ingenuity of the use of
snowshoes would be called a "force multiplier." Force multiplier
refers to those operations other than combat which can affect
the fight but used generally more to shape the environment
(and thus effectively multiply the force). In spiritual combat, a
primary means by which you can neutralize the superior force
is by true devotion to the Blessed Virgin Mary. Simply stated, if
you lack both a proper understanding and true devotion to her

in the spiritual battle, you are losing grace (and spiritually slogging in snow up to your knees while your enemy gains ground on you). According to Saint Maximillian Kolbe, "Unfortunately, even among those who have received Holy Baptism and perhaps also deepened their religious knowledge, there is a significant number of people who can only with difficulty manage to access the Heart of the Immaculata, the Mother of God, the Mother of Jesus our Brother, the Mother of the supernatural life, the Mediatrix of all graces, our Queen, our Sovereign, our Leader, and the Vanquisher of Satan."[170]

The purpose of this chapter is to briefly examine who and how the Virgin Mary is a force multiplier that not only helps in evading the enemy but also is waiting to assist you in vanquishing him.[171]

The Lady in Blue

Make no mistake: we are surrounded by a superior force, but have a warrior Queen, a Twelve Star General on our side. A bishop recently recounted the story of his former training in exorcism by a renowned exorcist. During one session, the demon manifested and snarled at the exorcist: "I would absolutely destroy you if it weren't for the Lady in Blue standing behind you." This "Lady in Blue" is the Mother of God, the Virgin Mary. The *Catechism* states that she the "'splendor of an entirely unique holiness' by which Mary is 'enriched from the first instant of her conception' comes wholly from Christ: she is 'redeemed, in a more exalted fashion, by reason of the merits of her Son.' The Father blessed Mary more than any other created person 'in Christ with every spiritual blessing in the heavenly places' and chose her 'in Christ before the foundation of the world, to be holy and blameless before him in love.'"[172]

---

[170] Saint Maximillian Kolbe, *The Kolbe Reader*, no. 1210.
[171] This lesson on the Virgin Mary's role in spiritual combat contains reprints of, and expansions upon, my original work in Liber Christo, "Companion Guide," as well as Schneider, *Eve Was Named an Apostle.*
[172] *CCC* 492.

According to Blessed Pope Pius IX in his declaration of the dogma of the Assumption, her preservation from the effects of original sin, to include even venial sin, was the "unique privilege" that made her higher than the angels and saints. Flowing from this unique privilege of being preserved from any sin means that she possesses a holiness beyond any other human—and a power over the devil like no other.

For Saint John Henry Newman, the most common teaching in the writings of the early Church Fathers concerning the mother of Jesus is Mary as Second Eve. "This parallelism," states Newman, "is the doctrine of the Fathers from the earliest times" and "seems to me undeniable." Therefore, he catalogues the development of the doctrine of the New Eve, both linearly apostolic and geographically independent, into a larger picture: "First, then Justin Martyr (120–165), St. Irenaeus (120–200), and Tertullian (160–240). Of these, Tertullian represents Africa and Rome; Justin represents Palestine, for he had been taught by the martyr St. Polycarp, who was the intimate associate of St. John, so of the other Apostles."[173]

This is to say, long before Google searches and e-libraries, the greatest minds of the early Church in the second century all came to the same conclusion in every corner of the world: Mary is to Eve as Christ is to Adam.

According to the experience of many exorcists, this "Lady in Blue" not only protects them in their ministry but also is present at every extraction of an evil spirit. She was predestined by God to be with the Redeemer in the defeat of the infernal enemy. Saint Louis de Montfort, therefore, concludes, "Where Mary is, there the evil spirit is not."[174] Mary's uniqueness, moreover, has shaped the environment of humanity in light of the spiritual combat that ensued after the fall of our first parents. At the moment of her immaculate conception, she was preserved from any stain of sin so that she could give a perfectly sinless human nature to her Son. Why? She possesses a

---

[173] Saint John Henry Newman, *Second Eve*, 3. See also Schneider, *Eve Was Named an Apostle*, 3–4.

[174] Saint Louis de Montfort, *True Devotion*, no. 166.

holiness beyond all others. Accordingly, her role in the battle against the enemies of her spiritual children is singular.

Therefore, as Pope Saint John Paul II noted, when Jesus calls His mother "woman" from the cross, He is showing us that she is the "woman" whom God said would have total enmity with the seducer of mankind and be with the Redeemer. In what is called the *protevangelium* (or "first gospel" announcing our redemption), God tells the serpent in the Garden that He "will put enmity between you and the woman, and between your offspring and hers; he will strike at your head while you strike at his heel" (Gn 3:15). When Jesus gives Mary the title of Woman-Eve, according to Pope Saint John Paul II, this "indicates her unique place which she occupies in the whole economy of salvation."[175] She is inseparable from her Son.

Interestingly, the various ancient versions of this text are unclear as to who will strike (not just strike, but literally will "grind down") the head of the ancient serpent. The Hebrew version could be "he/she" or even "they" will crush his head. The Greek says "he," and the Latin reads that "she" will crush the head of the serpent. He, she, or they—what is implied is the unique participation of the woman-mother with her Son in the conquering of evil.

At the Foot of the Cross: Stabat Mater

Stabat Mater is Latin for "the Mother stood," referring to her place at the foot of the cross of Christ where the ancient enemy was defeated. As recounted in Saint John's Gospel (Jn 19:25), this refers to one of the seven sorrows of Our Lady of Sorrows. Furthermore, Saint John Chrysostom connected the parallelism between Adam-Christ and Eve-Mary in the same homily on the cross as a war memorial previously referenced. He writes:

A virgin, a tree and a death were the symbols of our defeat. The virgin was Eve: she had not yet known man; the tree was

---

[175] Pope Saint John Paul II, *Redemptoris Mater*, no. 24.

the tree of the knowledge of good and evil; the death was Adam's penalty. But behold again a Virgin and a tree and a death, those symbols of defeat, become the symbols of his victory. For in place of Eve there is Mary; in place of the tree of the knowledge of good and evil, the tree of the Cross; in place of the death of Adam, the death of Christ. Do you see him defeated by the very things through which he had conquered? At the foot of the tree the devil overcame Adam; at the foot of the tree Christ vanquished the devil. And that first tree sent men to Hades; this second one calls back even those who had already gone down there. Again, the former tree concealed man already despoiled and stripped; the second tree shows a naked victor on high for all to see. And that earlier death condemned those who were born after it; this second death gives life again to those who were born before it. Who can tell the Lord's mighty deeds? By death we were made immortal: these are the glorious deeds of the Cross.[176]

For this reason, a cross is displayed for veneration during the Good Friday liturgy.

As mentioned above, the ancient understanding of the cross is that of a sign of victory, a war memorial. For this reason, the demon is repelled by a blessed crucifix. The war memorial includes the weapons of the ancient enemy, which proved useless against his Conqueror and our Rescuer, Jesus Christ. Thus, this *trópaion* marks the greatest victory ever, and as the priest lifts high the cross, he is proclaiming that the greatest enemy was destroyed. Here, life met death, holiness met sin, light met darkness, and hope met despair in fearful and deadly combat. Here, all the dark forces which have ever sought to crush the human spirit and lead it into their own despair did themselves go down to their final defeat. Here, the New Adam defeated the serpent, with the New Eve in complete conformity of wills.

---

[176] Saint John Chrysostom, *De coemeterio et de cruce*, 2.

An ancient poem commemorating this reality is read on Good Friday. Fifteen hundred years ago, a Christian poet who was one of the last of the old Romans sang the tale this way:

> *Sing, tongue, [of] the battle of decisive conflict,*
> *and of the noble victory procession, too:*
> *tell how the world's redeemer was victorious*
> *when he was sacrificed on the trópaion of the cross.*[177]

Calvary was the setting of the "rematch" between the devil and the New Adam. The tradition of the Church is that Mary was not a passive bystander, but she *actively participated* with her Son in the defeat of the ancient enemy. Where Eve failed in disobedience, Mary triumphed through obedience. Thus, as early as second century, Saint Irenaeus exclaimed, "Death through Eve, life through Mary."

Vanquisher of Satan

The Virgin Mary holds a prominent role in Catholic liberation, as evidenced by the various invocations of her in commands and rituals used to drive out demons.[178] Because of her unique role in salvation history as mother of the Word of God, Mary plays a key role in spiritual warfare. The more you understand her powerful role, imitate her example, and invoke her intercession in crushing the head of Satan (as prophesied in the *protoevangelium* of Gn 3:15), the more quickly will you begin to drive the evil one back. Conversely, I wrote, "By not invoking her assistance . . . you neglect a most powerful weapon in liberation."[179]

Sacred Scripture affirms that Jesus Christ is the sole mediator before the Father (see 1 Tm 2:5). That is, Jesus (who is both fully God and fully man) obtained the objective graces of man's salvation as a unique mediator who offered Himself as

---

[177] With thanks to Fr. Michael Cotone, O.S.C.
[178] This is an expansion of my original work contained in "Companion Guide" under the previous title, *The Blessed Mother*, 65–68.
[179] Liber Christo, "Companion Guide," 65.

Priest and Victim for us. This does not mean, however, that we can stand by idly. In fact, Jesus invites our participation in the subjective distribution of Calvary's graces. We most approximate Christ as *co-redeemer* when we suffer for others as He suffered for us. Saint Paul told the Philippians, therefore, to "stand firm in one spirit . . . struggling together for the faith of the gospel" while not being "intimidated" (Phil 1:27–28). The secret to standing firm in the struggle and not being intimidated lies in union with the suffering Lord: "For to you has been granted, for the sake of Christ, not only to believe in him, but to suffer for him" (Phil 1:29). He allies this principle to himself elsewhere, when he states, "I rejoice in my sufferings for your sake, and in my flesh I am making up what is lacking in the afflictions of Christ on behalf of his body, which is the church" (Col 1:24). Our sufferings, therefore, help distribute the graces that Christ merited on Calvary. In so doing, we uncover a powerful weapon in defeating Satan; that is, we become co-redeemers with Christ in the salvation of souls.

All liberation comes by uniting ourselves to Jesus. From Christianity's infancy, invoking Jesus's name was used to drive out demons and liberate souls from the power of Satan (cf. Lk 19:17; Acts 19:13–20). We do not conduct the battle against Satan alone, however, but the battlefield also includes the saints and angels in the Mystical Body. In the Acts of the Apostles, for example, when "face cloths or aprons" belonging to Saint Paul (what we would call relics today) were applied to the sick, "the evil spirits came out of them" (Acts 19:12). Over time, the effectiveness of including the Blessed Virgin Mary, the angels, and the saints in militating against evil became known, and practiced, in the Church.

The Virgin Mary, moreover, plays a singular role in spiritual warfare precisely because she is Christ's mother and is completely sinless in her human nature. She cooperates as no other creature can with her Son, the Redeemer, in the mystery of redemption. Although Mary is also a redeemed creature (the first of the redeemed, and in the most sublime way), she nonetheless cooperates with Christ in a unique and unrepeatable way. Her participation in the acquisition and distribution of her Son's graces is unique and forms her special role in defeating the demon.

From the cross, Christ entrusted humanity to His mother with the command, "Behold, your mother" (Jn 19:26). In calling His mother "woman" (Jn 19:26; cf. 2:4), Jesus points to Mary's special mission of the New Eve, echoing the words of the first Adam ("This one shall be called 'woman,'" Gn 2:23). Significantly, God promised that a "woman" would accompany the promised redeemer and participate in the "crushing of the head" of the serpent (Gn 3:15). The cooperation of Mary is realized during the very event of redemption (i.e., during the earthly life of her Son), and her free consent was necessary for it to take place. Thus, Pope Saint John Paul II said that her suffering at the foot of the cross was "a contribution to the Redemption of all" and "was mysteriously and supernaturally fruitful for the redemption of the world."[180]

The Blessed Mother's role in salvation history has long been affirmed by the Church and continues today in her prolific, maternal mission as advocate for the people of God. Because of her special relationship with the Holy Trinity, her strategic position in the economy of grace uniquely and singularly impacts the redemption of humankind. Her motherly care for all is extended to all believers when Jesus commended her to the "Beloved Disciple" from the cross (see Jn 19:26). This is the foundation of her person and office (seen in the titles of "woman" and "mother" that Jesus gives her) within the Mystical Body. Her Immaculate Heart beats in perfect obedience to the Father's will, to the all-consuming love of the Son, and to the spousal fidelity of the Holy Spirit. To be a "beloved disciple" of Jesus, therefore, is to likewise "take her into" our "homes" (Jn 19:27)—that is, into the intimate interior of our spiritual selves.

Countless exorcists have affirmed the Virgin Mary's essential role in liberation. According to Father Gabriel

---

[180] Pope Saint John Paul II, *Redemptoris Mater*, no. 25.

Amorth, who spent his entire priesthood as the chief exorcist of the diocese of Rome, God has "chosen the Most Holy Virgin Mary as a permanent antidote to the enmity between mankind and Satan."[181] As the New Eve, Mary cooperated in a unique way in the redemptive graces that flow from the supreme sacrifice of Christ, the New Adam, on Calvary. According to the measure to which we appropriate this grace, we are capable of destroying the devil's artifices. This grace is particularly reinforced by our faithful recourse to the special intercession of the Virgin Mary. By virtue of her immaculate conception, Mary stands in clear and absolute contrast (or the "total enmity" of Genesis 3:15) to Satan's actions and the other rebellious angels. She extends herself totally (as no human or angelic being does) to repel demonic attacks and to expand the reign of the Son.

Experienced exorcists, moreover, affirm the presence and action of Mary during formal exorcisms. This teaches us the importance of true devotion to Our Lady in the fight against Satan. Father Bamonte further states, "The cooperation of Mary in the victory of her Son over the demons humiliates them more than if Christ defeated them alone. To be defeated by God through the cooperation of a human creature greatly humiliates their bloated pride. The impact of the dogma of the Immaculate Conception means that she has a perfectly sinless human nature. Thus, she is preserved from original sin and its effects by which the demons brought all humanity under their power. The holiness and splendor of Mary elevates her high above all human and angelic creatures."[182] Father Bamonte notes, moreover, that the demons are frequently forced to praise her for her greatness, as well as the power and divine splendor that shines in her.

But what is the theological basis for Mary's authority over demons? This can be found in the four Marian dogmas and the doctrine of Mary's universal maternity.[183] With regard

---

[181] Amorth, *An Exorcist Tells His Story*, 10.

[182] Bamonte, *Mary and the Devil*, 12.

[183] See, for example, *Lumen Gentium*, no. 25.

to the Church's teachings on the mother of Jesus, moreover, the dogmas tell us *who Mary is* (as she proclaimed to Saint Bernadette at Lourdes, "I am the Immaculate Conception"), and doctrine tells us *what she does* (as she said to Saint Juan Diego at Tepeyac, "I am the one who crushes the stone serpent [Guadalupe]. . . . I am your merciful mother.").[184] The former describes who she was on earth; the latter describes what she does from heaven. These reveal both her person (woman) and office (mother) seen in the titles given to her by Jesus. Both the dogmas and the doctrines find their roots in Sacred Scripture, but her instrumentality (what she does from heaven or what *Lumen Gentium* calls her "saving office")[185] is particularly operant in the dogmatic affirmations.

Exterminatrix of Heresies: The Four Marian Dogmas

The four Marian dogmas are as follows: Divine Motherhood, Perpetual Virginity, Immaculate Conception, and the Assumption. These will be explained in this section. Canon Law, which is the official law of the Catholic Church, states very clearly that each Christian should have devotion to Mary: "To foster the sanctification of the people of God, the Church commends the special and filial veneration of Christ's faithful to the Blessed Ever-Virgin Mary, Mother of God, whom Christ constituted the Mother of all. The Church also promotes the true and authentic cult of the other Saints, by whose example the faithful are edified and by whose intercession they are

---

[184] Dogmas are doctrines that have been elevated to a higher degree by means of a papal decree or conciliar pronouncement. Thus, a dogma is first a doctrine before being declared a dogma. Both, however, are to be adhered to with the "obedience of faith" as part of the deposit of faith.

[185] "Taken up to heaven, she did not lay aside this saving office but by her manifold intercession continues to bring us the gifts of eternal salvation. By her maternal charity she continues, she cares for the brethren of her Son, who still journey on earth surrounded by dangers and difficulties, until they are led into their blessed home. Therefore, the Blessed Virgin is invoked . . . under the titles of Advocate . . . Mediatrix." *Lumen Gentium,* no. 62.

supported."[186] This is to say, Mary is part of the ordinary path of salvation for the Christian.

In addition, theologians distinguish between *latria* (worship) and *dulia* (honor). Worship is owed to God alone due to some *divine excellence* (hence, we kneel before God alone). Honor is what is owed to a person due to some *human* excellence (hence, we stand before a judge, soldiers salute a higher-ranking officer, etc.). Mary is not divine and is not given *latria*. Nonetheless, she is given a special honor for two principal reasons according to Church Doctor Saint Alphonsus Liguori:[187]

1. Immaculate Conception (she is *Panagia*, or Holy)
2. Virginal, Mother of God (she is *Theotokos*, or the "*God-bearer*")

Thus, because Mary is sinless and also the Mother of God, the honor owed to her is greater than any other human being. Accordingly, the Church teaches that the filial devotion to her is *hyperdulia* (*hyper* is a prefix denoting "over and above, beyond, above measure"). This special honor to the Virgin Mary is due to her "unique privileges" seen in the dogmas relating to her.

Because the demon is an angelic being and pure (non-bodily) intellect, he knows Mariology far better than the best theologian. He knows well the "woman" who is to crush his head, and as a result, he seeks to convince you that the Church's teachings are wrong about this or that doctrine. Saint Bonaventure wrote that the Virgin Mary preserves the virtue of those who are devoted to her, and she keeps the demons from harming them. Thus, he states, "the devils enter a soul when it is darkened by ignorance. And if the dawn suddenly comes, namely the grace and mercy of Mary, they flee as everybody flees death."[188] According to Saint Bernardine of Siena, Mary is also queen over hell and the demons, that she

---

[186] *Code of Canon Law*, no. 1186.
[187] Saint Alphonsus Liguori, *Glories of Mary*, 179–88.
[188] Cited in Saint Alphonsus Liguori, *Glories of Mary*, 73.

incites terror among the demons, as "terrible as an army set in array" (Sg 6:3).[189]

Other saints echoed this understanding of Mary as a warrior queen. Saint Alphonsus Liguori likens her to a general who "knows how to deploy her forces . . . to the confusion of the enemy and for the benefit of those who call on her for defense in temptation."[190] Saint Louis de Montfort echoed this: "Mary must be terrible to the devil and his crew as an army ranged in battle, principally in these latter times, because the devil, knowing that he has but little time, and now less than ever, to destroy souls, will every day redouble his efforts and his combats." Also, that "Satan, being proud, suffers infinitely more from being beaten and punished by a little and humble handmade of God—and her humility humbles him more than the divine power" and also "because God has given Mary such great power against the devils that—as they have often been obliged to confess, in spite of themselves, by the mouths of the possessed—they fear one of her sighs for a soul than the prayers of all the saints, and one of her threats against them more than all other torments. What Lucifer has lost by pride Mary has gained by humility. What Eve has damned and lost by disobedience, Mary has saved by obedience."[191]

Saint Bruno said, "In Eve are darkness and death; and in Mary, life and light. He was conquered by the devil. Mary conquered and bound the devil." Saint Bridget of Sweden said that God made Mary so powerful against the devils that whenever they are attacking someone who has called upon her for help, they are immediately terrified and cease molesting that soul. They prefer to flee than to take a "double dose" of their torments and be subjected to her power.[192] Thus, Saint Alphonsus, following Saint Bernard, asserts that "the devils tremble at the mere mention of Mary's name." And that "just as men

---

[189] Cited in Saint Alphonsus Liguori, 72.

[190] Cited in Saint Alphonsus Liguori, 72.

[191] Saint Louis de Montfort, *True Devotion*, no. 53.

[192] Cited in Saint Alphonsus Liguori, *Glories of Mary*, 12.

fall to the ground when a bolt of lightning strikes near them, so the devils quake when they hear Mary's name."[193]

Saint Louis de Montfort, moreover, connects the demon and heresy by citing an ancient liturgical document: "As it is Mary alone, says the Church (and the Holy Ghost who guides the Church), who makes all heresies come to naught—'Thou alone hast destroyed all heresies in the world'—we may be sure that, however, critics may grumble, no faithful client of Mary will ever fall into heresy or illusions, at least formal ones."[194]

Pope Saint Pius X, in his 1904 encyclical on the fiftieth anniversary of the declaration of the dogma of the Immaculate Conception, explained the importance of clear truth in times of modernist heresy, echoes this ancient title, saying, "And thus once again is justified what the Church attributes to this august Virgin that she has exterminated all heresies in the world."[195] We have found that *the demon enters through sin and holds through heresy*. It follows, then, that she is key to exposing the lies of the evil one.

All heresy challenges the sovereignty of Christ. Heresy is an adherence to an untruth, or "the post-baptismal, obstinate denial of a truth that is to be believed with a divine and Catholic faith." Further, as Clement explains, "adherence to an untruth can be either an ignorance or a falsehood. Because the devil is 'a liar and the father of lies' (John 8:45), when a person obstinately denies or rejects, even out of ignorance, some element of the deposit of faith, he is vulnerable to the demon's influence. Thus, living in the truth is itself liberating. As Jesus, has said, his followers 'will know the truth and the truth will set you free' (John 8.32)."[196] Living in the truth and surrendering to the teachings of the Church (dogmas and doctrines) is self-liberating.

---

[193] Saint Alphonsus Liguori, 49.
[194] "The Office of the Blessed Virgin" (1st Antiphon, 3rd Nocturn). Notably the original *Little Office* likely dates to the eighth century. Saint Louis de Montfort, *True Devotion*, no. 167.
[195] Pope Saint Pius X, *Ad Diem Illum Laetissimum*, no. 22.
[196] Liber Christo, "Companion Guide," 151.

Just as David chose five smooth stones when he faced his enemy, you have five "Marian" stones ready for you. As the *Catechism* states, there is "an organic connection between the spiritual life and the dogmas." As such, "dogmas are lights along the path of faith [that] illumine it make it secure. Conversely, if our life is upright, our intellect and heart will be open to welcome the light shed by the dogmas of faith."[197] A dogma is a truth revealed by God (such as the Trinity, Christology, number of sacraments, infallibility of the pope, etc.) which the Magisterium has declared as binding, usually for clarity in time of need.[198] Also binding are Christian doctrines, which consist of the Church's teaching of faith and morals as handed down in Sacred Scripture and Sacred Tradition.[199] Thus, "the Church, in her doctrine, life, and worship perpetuates and transmits to every generation all that she herself is, all that she believes."[200] This is explored through the lens of the lived experience of Church—that is, ancient liturgies, sacred iconography and architecture, creedal formula/magisterial statements, lives of the saints, and writing of the Fathers of the Church.

Accordingly, there are four dogmas concerning Mary and a fifth Marian doctrine that help us to understand not only who she is but also what she does from heaven. The four Marian dogmas tell us who she is. The fifth doctrine reveals to us what she does from heaven. You may ask why this is relevant to spiritual combat. As Pope Saint Paul VI wrote, "Knowledge of the true Catholic doctrine regarding the Blessed Virgin Mary will always be a key to the exact understanding of the mystery of Christ and of the Church." That is to say, if you understand her "person and office" of her role in salvation history as "woman and mother," you will more clearly understand both Christ and His Church.

---

[197] *CCC* 89.
[198] See *CCC* 88.
[199] See *CCC* 185.
[200] *CCC* 97.

Her *divine motherhood* is seen in her ancient title *Theotokos*. As mother of the second Person of the Blessed Trinity, Jesus Christ, Mary has been called the "Mother of God" from antiquity. She did not give birth to a nature, notably, but rather to a Person—Jesus Christ who is both fully human and fully divine. The incarnation of God was affirmed in the Council of Chalcedon in AD 381 with the affirmation that in the person of Jesus are "two natures, without confusion, without change, without division, without separation."[201] Mary conceived and bore the God-man. Accordingly, the *Catechism* affirms, "Hence, the Church confesses that Mary is truly 'Mother of God.'"[202] The ancient title of *Theotokos* (literally, "God-bearer") was given to her dogmatically at the Council of Ephesus in AD 431.

While a true mother, she is also a *perpetual virgin*. As early as the first decade of the second century, the virginal conception of Jesus in the womb of Mary was affirmed. As Saint Luke tells us, the angel Gabriel appeared "to a *virgin* . . . and the *virgin's* name was Mary" (Lk 1:27). The expression *perpetual virginity*, however, means that she maintained her virginal purity before, during, and after the birth of Jesus. Thus, "at once virgin and mother, Mary is the symbol and most perfect realization of the Church."[203] From her unique virginal purity flows her unique power over demons.

To prepare her to be both Theotokos and Ever-Virgin, she received the special grace of being *immaculately conceived*. The dogmatic decree on the Immaculate Conception of Blessed Pope Pius IX in 1854 states, "The most Blessed Virgin Mary, from the first moment of her conception, by a singular grace and privilege from Almighty God and in view of the merits of Jesus Christ, was kept free of every stain of original sin." Mary's all-holiness, moreover, is the consequence of God preserving her from original sin. That she has not been tainted by original sin means that she lives intimately united to God

---

[201] Known as the "Chalcedon Formula." See Bettensen, *Documents of the Christian Church*, 73. And, Saint Louis de Montfort, *True Devotion*, no. 167.
[202] *CCC* 495.
[203] *CCC* 507.

in a wholly singular way. As such, her perfected human nature means that she is not under Satan's dominion, and therefore, from this space of immaculate purity, she defeats the demon.

The natural result of her immaculate purity is her *bodily assumption* into heaven at the end of her earthly life. The declaration on the assumption of Mary in 1950 by Pope Pius XII affirms the ancient belief that "Mary, Immaculate Mother of God ever Virgin, after finishing the course of her life on earth, was taken up in body and soul to heavenly glory."[204] This unique grace flows from the grace of the Immaculate Conception. As preserved from the effects of the Fall ("sin and death," according to Saint Paul in Rom 5:12), Mary enjoyed the unique privilege of escaping the corruption of bodily death. Thus, while Jesus ascended by His own divine power, she was taken up by the power of her Son, to whom she is perfectly conformed.

The Universal Queenship of Mary: Mary's Maternal Mediation

While the four dogmas tell us who she is, a fifth Marian doctrine teaches us what she does from heaven. Embedded in Tradition is the doctrine of the Universal Queenship of Mary, or her Spiritual Maternity, seen in her titles of Co-Redemptrix, Mediatrix of All Grace, and Advocate for the People of God.[205] In Saint Paul's one reference to Mary, he states, "But when the fullness of time had come, God sent his Son, born of a woman, born under the law, to ransom those under the law so, that we might receive adoption. As proof that you are children, God sent the spirit of his Son into our hearts, crying out, 'Abba, Father!' So you are no longer a slave but a child, and if a child then also an heir, through God" (Gal 4:4–6).

---

[204] Pope Pius XII, *Munificentissimus Deus*, no. 44.
[205] While the Church has not declared this a dogma, its place as doctrine is clear and is aptly shown in recent times by many theologians, such as Miravalle, Caulkins, O'Carroll, Most, de la Potterie, and Schug. For more, see Miravalle, ed., *Mary Coredemptrix, Mediatrix, Advocate*. On the distinction between dogma and doctrine, see fn. 171 above.

The *Catechism* similarly alludes to her unique relationship to the Blessed Trinity: "By her complete adherence to the Father's will, to his Son's redemptive work, and to every prompting of the Holy Spirit, the Virgin Mary is the Church's model of faith and charity. Thus, she is a 'preeminent and . . . wholly unique member of the Church'; indeed, she is the exemplary realization (*typos*) of the Church."[206]

As one scholastic theologian stated, the Blessed Virgin Mary has an "intrinsic relationship with the Blessed Trinity." This intrinsic relationship looks like this:

- Mother to the Son → Co-Redemptrix
- Spouse of the Holy Spirit → Mediatrix of All Graces
- Daughter to Father → Advocate for the People of God

This Trinitarian Mariology should leave us in awe. Saint Teresa of Calcutta expounds on this notion: "Mary is our Co-Redemptrix with Jesus. She gave Jesus his body and suffered with him at the foot of the cross. Mary is the Mediatrix of all grace. She gave Jesus to us, and as our Mother she obtains for us all his graces. Mary is our Advocate who prays to Jesus for us. It is only through the heart of Mary that we come to the Eucharistic heart of Jesus."[207]

***Theotokos* and Icon of the Church.**[208] The Council of Ephesus (AD 431) concluded with a syllogism which formulated the dogma of Mary as Mother of God, or *Theotokos*: Mary is the mother of Jesus; Jesus is God; therefore, Mary is the Mother of God. Mary's role in relation to the Church and to all humanity, however, extends beyond this dogma. She is also mother of the Church and has been given the title Queen Mother as descriptive of her relationship to her divine

---

[206] *CCC* 967.

[207] Miravalle, "Is Mary Co-Redemptrix A 'False Exaggeration'?" During his pontificate, Pope Saint John Paul II also used the title "Co-Redemptrix" in reference to Mary.

[208] This section is a reprint and expansion of what I wrote in Liber in the "Companion Guide" under the previous title, *Mary is the Mother of God and icon of the Church*, 27–28.

Son. She cooperated by her obedience, faith, hope, and charity in the work of salvation.[209] Thus, by her cooperation with the mystery of redemption, she has also become mother to all of us. We call her "Advocate" and "Helper,"[210] and great is her maternal care for those who offer special devotion to her in prayer and reverence. This is echoed in the Second Vatican Council, which states that the Church rightly honors "the Blessed Virgin with special devotion."[211]

With regard to spiritual warfare, Marian devotion is central to slaying the Goliath that stands before you. Because the Virgin Mary has been preserved from the effect of original sin, she participates in the liberation of souls in a unique way. Saint Bernard, who is a doctor of the Church, encourages us to adopt the practice of special devotion to Mary because "when Mary holds you up, you do not fall; when she protects you, you need not fear; when she leads you, you do not tire; when she is favorable to you, you arrive at the harbor of safety."[212] Thus, she assists souls—especially those souls beset by the storms of life—in arriving at "safe harbor" through her intercession to help conform the soul to her Son.

Mary's virginal purity extends beyond her body and into her very orientation toward God. Her docility to the Holy Spirit is well attested to in Scripture. By her willful obedience and her complete acceptance of the Father's will, Mary participates uniquely in the redemptive work of Jesus.[213] She models docility, attentive listening to God's voice, and responding with complete love. Mary gave to God her complete "fiat" (which means "Let it be done!")—the total and unconditional "yes" to the will of God (see Lk 1:26–38).

Mary's *yes* flows from her virginal purity and reflects her complete obedience to God's will. When the angel Gabriel appeared to her, she willingly proclaimed, "Behold, I am the

---

[209] Cf. *Lumen Gentium*, no. 53.
[210] Cf. *CCC* 968–69.
[211] *Lumen Gentium*, no. 66; also *CCC* 971.
[212] Cited in Saint Louis de Montfort, *True Devotion*, no. 174.
[213] See *CCC* 967.

handmaid of the Lord. May it be done to me according to your word" (Lk 1:38). Mary's fiat was the ultimate act of human free will. This total obedience to God's will, when combined with her virginal and immaculate purity, enables her to defeat the enemy in union with her Son in a singular way. Thus, Saint Louis de Montfort teaches, "In the heavens, Mary commands the angels and the blessed. As a recompense for her profound humility, God has empowered her and commissioned her to fill with saints the empty thrones from which the apostate angels fell by pride."[214] Saint Bonaventure also suggested this teaching, which explains why the demons hate humans and fear the Blessed Virgin so greatly. Thus, we should not neglect so great an ally in this spiritual battle.

Spouse of the Holy Spirit. After the annunciation of the angel Gabriel, Mary visited her cousin Elizabeth, who "cried out in a loud voice and said, 'Most Blessed are you among women, and blessed is the fruit of your womb'" (Lk 1:42). Elizabeth's unborn child, John the Baptist, was sanctified by the presence of Mary, who carried the Redeemer in her womb. Mary, in a similar way, mediates Jesus to us.

Interestingly, Elizabeth did not simply "cry out" upon seeing Mary, she "intoned"—the same word to describe the Levites before the Ark of God (1 Chr 15:28; 2 Chr 5:13). The Israelite army, recall, used to bring the Ark of the Covenant into battle with the cry: "Arise, O Lord, that your enemies may be scattered, and those who hate you may flee before you" (Nm 10:35).

David echoed this in a Psalm which is also read during the Rite of Exorcism: "May God arise; / may his enemies be scattered; / may those who hate him flee before him. / As the smoke is dispersed, disperse them; / as wax is melted by fire, / so may the wicked perish before God" (Ps 68:2–3). Mary's spousal union with the Holy Spirit means she bears God just as the Ark bore the Presence of God. Accordingly,

---

[214] Saint Louis de Montfort, *True Devotion*, no. 17.

Saint Louis de Montfort teaches that Mary is the "dear and inseparable spouse" of the Holy Spirit. So intimate is this union that "the more He finds Mary . . . in any soul, the more active and mighty He becomes in producing Jesus Christ in that soul, and the soul in Jesus Christ."[215] Have you brought the Ark of the New Covenant into your spiritual battles?

Like snowshoes for the rangers, a force multiplier is anything that affects the fight by shaping the environment and effectively multiplying the force. Due to her unique holiness, the Virgin Mary is your spiritual combat's force multiplier. As a result of Mary's holiness, Saint Louis de Montfort could declare that God has made her "sovereign of heaven and earth, general of His armies, treasurer of His treasuries, worker of His greatest marvels, restorer of the human race, Mediatrix of men, the exterminator of the enemies of God, and the faithful companion of His grandeurs and triumphs."[216] The *Hail Mary* is an excellent spiritual warfare prayer when prayed with love as it re-echoes the words of the angel Gabriel into the angelic realm.

Another ancient and very powerful, prayer is called the **Memorare**, which was probably written by Saint Bernard. This can be used at any time you suspect the diabolic at work, or need of a quick favor from Our Lady:

> *Remember, O most gracious Virgin Mary, that never was it known that anyone who fled to thy protection, implored thy help, or sought thy intercession was left unaided. Inspired by this confidence, I fly unto thee, O Virgin of virgins, my Mother. To thee do I come, before thee I stand, sinful and sorrowful. O Mother of the Word Incarnate, despise not my petitions, but in thy mercy hear and answer me. Amen.*

The appendix contains several prayers to help you to tap into this great resource that God has given you. Specifically, when

---

[215] Saint Louis de Montfort, no. 14.
[216] Saint Louis de Montfort, no. 28.

the demon oppresses your temporal goods, consecrate them to Mary and pray the prayer against oppression.

From Slingstones to Milestones: The Virgin Mary and Spiritual Combat

1. What is something new that you learned from this week's lesson?
2. What title of Mary are you most drawn to and why?
3. On a scale of 1 to 10, how would you rate your devotion to the Virgin Mary? How do you ask "the Lady in Blue" to help you in your struggles?
4. Did you experience any interior resistance, such as anxiety or something you just did not like, when reading any part of this lesson? If so, why?
5. Summarize each of the Marian dogmas. Why is the image of Mary as a "warrior queen" important in spiritual combat?
6. Who are your favorite three saints, and why? How could they be acting as the nemesis to the demons who may be afflicting you? What in their lives or charism could you most use right now?
7. Do you pray the Rosary every day? Do you have any sacred images of the Blessed Mother in your home? Why or why not?

Chapter Three

Examination of Conscience and Confession

"For he had called upon the Most High God, / who gave strength to his right arm / To defeat the skilled warrior / and establish the might of his people."

—SIRACH 47:5

The sling was a common weapon used both in hunting and in combat among the ancients. The improvised weapon essentially served as an extension of the human arm. The Roman historian Livy tells us that the most famous slingers in antiquity were the Numidians, a tribe of warriors from the Balearic Islands. He recounts that their mothers would not give their children so much as a piece of bread to eat unless they could first knock it off a wall from a distance.[217]

Two straps, or retention cords, made of sinew, rope, or leather were held together with a leather pad, which housed a projectile (a stone or piece of lead). A loop at the end of one retention cord allowed the slinger to insert his finger and cling to a knot on the other end. He would then swing the device several times over his head to gain momentum, releasing the projectile by letting go of the knotted end. This primitive weapon was deadly accurate

---

[217] Livy, *Geography*, III, 5.

(having a "kill radius") of up to six hundred yards and capable of piercing armor and shattering bone. In other words, the slingers were the first snipers. Every ancient army had its slingers, and among the tribes of Israel, the Benjaminites were these select troops. Scripture recounts that these men were all "picked men who were left-handed, every one of them able to sling a stone at a hair without missing" (1 Kgs 20:16; cf. 1 Chr 12:2).

The sling also had the biblical symbolism of deliverance from one's enemies. As Abigail told David, "If anyone rises to pursue you and to seek your life, may the life of my lord be bound in the bundle of the living in the care of the LORD your God; may God hurl out the lives of your enemies as from the hollow of a sling" (1 Sm 25:29). The prophet Zechariah uses the sling to describe the protection of God under the Messiah: "The Lord of Hosts will be a shield over them, they shall overcome sling stones and trample them underfoot" (Zec 9:15). That David used a sling suggests again the symbolism of God delivering His people from their oppressors.

The lesson of the sling and meticulous training to use it effectively on the battlefield is precision. Precision is key in combat. In this "stone," we will teach you the skills requisite to "sling a stone at a hair without missing" like a Benjaminite slinger. Rather than by sling, you will achieve precision by developing virtue and making a thorough confession of your sins. These are essential elements for spiritual victory.

LESSON SEVEN: THE DEVELOPMENT OF VIRTUE

If precision is key in physical combat, why would we think that this principle does not apply in spiritual combat? Think of the Numidian mothers who drilled the skill of slinging into their children as you read these words of Moses to the people of God just after the giving of the Law on Mount Horeb: "Hear, O Israel! The LORD is our God, the LORD alone! Therefore, you shall love the LORD, your God, with all your heart, and with all your soul, and with all your strength. Take to heart these words which I command you today. Keep repeating them to your children. Recite them when you are at home and when you are away, when you lie down and when you get up. Bind them on your arm as a sign and let them be as a pendant on your forehead. Write them on the doorposts of your houses and on your gates" (Dt 6:4–9).

This prayer is called the *Shema Yishrael* and was prayed morning and evening by the Israelites. Notably, Moses, just after giving the Ten Commandments to the people, commanded the people to *drill them into your children*. The word for "to drill" is the same used for a military unit at drill, practicing to precision various movements. To drill means to repeat over and over continually until it becomes second nature. Moses did not say to set aside an hour a week for this activity, moreover, but to *whether at home or abroad, whether busy or at rest*—literally, "whether sitting at home or on a journey or in bed or getting out of bed." That is, this drilling has a militaristic undertone and should happen all the time and impact every aspect of your life. The reorientation of life is the only way to attain the accuracy of a Numidian. The discipline of praying at set times is part of developing the habit of religiosity and the expression of faith through vocal prayer.

Virtue and vice share this common reality: both are habitual, repeated acts. A virtue is the "habitual and firm disposition to do the good," which means that the "virtuous person tends toward the good with all his sensory and spiritual powers [to] pursue the good and choose it in concrete actions."[218] Virtue is the patterned behavior that allows you to see and acquire the good. That ultimate good is God, and the pursuit of virtue, therefore, is the complete union with God. That is, "the goal of a virtuous life is to become like God."[219] Conversely, sin "engenders vice by repetition of the same acts" resulting in "perverse inclinations which cloud the conscience and corrupt

---

[218] *CCC* 1803.
[219] *CCC* 1803.

the concrete judgment of good and evil."[220] Thus, the habit of sin has the opposite effect, drawing us away from God by corrupting our "judgment of good and evil." The demon's goal, then, is to lead us to a life of vice so that we become like him.

Think, then, of this section as teaching you how to clear your vision so as to make precise judgments between good and evil, and between the clean and the unclean. The demon is always present to the unclean—from unclean speech to unclean sex and everything in between. The more unclean it is, the more the demonic is attracted to it. Accordingly, we will examine virtue and vices as they relate to spiritual combat. Just as a Numidian slinger perfected his skill by the repeated act of practice (to wit, *drilling*) for success in combat, so you must learn the importance of the development of virtue in spiritual combat. Simply stated, you must learn to hit your target with precision.

A Time of Affliction and Testing

Just after giving the *Shema* and greatest commandment, Moses told the people, "Remember how for *forty years* now the LORD, your God, has directed all your *journeying in the wilderness*, so as to test you by affliction, to know what was in your heart: to keep his commandments, or not" (Dt 8:2). This suggests that *desert* and the number *forty*—seen in the number of years that the Israelites wandered due to their infidelity—are symbolic of testing.

The number forty, then, is significant, as it is a penitential number. When Jesus went to the desert to fast and pray (and to defeat the devil in his temptations), he did not go for a week, or a month, but precisely *forty days* (see Mt 4:1; Mk 1:12; Lk 4:1). We follow this in the liturgical season of Lent, which is also a penitential forty days. The Israelites wandered for forty years precisely due to their infidelity. Although they had left the idolatry and slavery of Egypt, the idolatry and

---

[220] *CCC* 1865.

slavery of Egypt had not left them. Consequently, as if to undo the infidelity of Israel, Jesus Himself goes into the desert "to be tempted" by—and defeat—the devil before He begins His public ministry: "Jesus was led by the Spirit into the desert to be tempted by the devil. He fasted for forty days and forty nights, and afterwards he was hungry" (Mt 4:1–2).

Not until the reader is told that Jesus "was hungry" does "the tempter" approach Him (Mt 4:3). For purposes here, the *withdrawal into the desert* is the act of blocking out all worldly distractions by depriving your senses and ordering your life to prayer. In military language, to withdraw for a period of prayer and fasting is like "reconnaissance by fire." Ground forces will use this tactic to expose an enemy who is hiding and refusing to engage in battle. In this tactic, a military unit will briefly expose itself to draw fire from the enemy who reveals his position with his muzzle blast. By analogy, when a Christian follows Christ into the desert and picks up the ancient weapons of prayer and fasting, that same "tempter" is drawn out and exposed. This withdrawal into the desert is the logic behind the sensory deprivation of Phase One of the Liber Christo protocol (see appendix A).

Once the Israelites crossed the Red Sea, their battle went from exterior to interior. Their pursuers were no more. Pharaoh and his army were dead, but the effect of their cruelty still lingered as they crossed over. God had miraculously freed His people from physical oppression. Now they had to learn to live as free people. In a similar way, your battle will move from exterior to interior as you come to separate yourself more and more from your oppressor. You may have been freed from some carnal sin, but now the interior fight begins. Like the Israelites, you may still carry the wounds of your past slavery with you. For purposes here, a wound (stemming from a past traumatic experience) causes some "damage to one of the faculties in such a manner that vice becomes present and operant in the soul." The demons want you to carry the wounds of Egypt with you "because this empowers them to continue to afflict the soul." As the battle moves from the exterior to the interior, moreover, the demon both holds in those wounds and feeds off any vices. Healing, then, is the "reordering of the faculties and removal of all obstacles between the soul and God."[221] The development of virtue and the cessation of habitual sin are keys to keeping your Egypt forever behind you.

Clement refers to this as a "Red Sea moment," where some situation presents "a decision point" to a person. In response to some trauma, he says, you can move either "closer to God or away from God"—that is, you either grow in virtue or in vice, towards liberation or towards slavery. This is not necessarily a one-time event. These moments arise through the course of your life, particularly when you are confronted with various trials, temptations, and difficulties. When you are confronted with such trials, see yourself standing before the water's edge. God is calling you to trust, "just as Moses trusted, in His providence . . . [because] in those moments, God reveals Himself."[222]

The imposition of order, by design in this program, forces the enemy out of hiding. What will undoubtedly surface while withdrawing from the world (and praying three times a day, like the Israelites praying the *Shema*) are long-held vices in the soul. Like the Israelites who grumbled against Moses and longed for return to the slavery of Egypt because of the sensory satisfactions there (cf. Ex 16:2–3), you will likely find yourself grumbling and longing for past things. Part of the logic of Phase One, therefore, is to draw out the enemy so you can see where he is hiding. See yourself as engaging the enemy in this way.

After God's people crossed the Red Sea and were liberated from Pharoah, they immediately fell back into idolatry. As punishment for their *false worship* (the golden calf, Ex 32:2–6) and *lack of trust in God*, seen in their *grumbling and rebellion* (cf. Ex 16:12), God allowed a time of affliction. This would purify the Israelites. God tested their faith and their intention to serve Him. Rather than arriving in the Promised Land, they instead spent four hundred years in Egypt after the famine. Although

---

[221] Liber Christo, "Companion Guide," 148.
[222] Liber Christo, "Companion Guide," 166.

freed by God, they still longed to return to slavery rather than endure the march to the land of Promise. Their infidelity meant forty years in the desert—or 10 percent of their time of previous enslavement. The purpose of this time was for them to do penance and be cleansed of the *false worship, lack of trust in God, and grumbling and rebellion* which still remained within them.

A one-to-one ratio would have meant they would have to wander in the desert for four hundred years, but God in His mercy does a one-to-ten. We see here hints of the economy of grace—satisfaction for sin but also the promise of blessing. Clearly, God multiplies your efforts. Thus, regarding development of virtue, the flow of actual grace starts when we begin that practice. That is, offer Him the sacrifices and hardships of this cross you are carrying, and He will return to you a tenfold blessing of grace. He will take your efforts and multiply them back tenfold.

Growing in virtue and combating the evil one is as old as Christianity itself. In the Epistle of Barnabas—a letter attributed to Saint Barnabas and written as early as the first century when the Bible itself was also being composed—we discover the importance of the virtues in fighting the evil one. "When evil days are upon us and the worker of malice gains power," writes Saint Barnabas, "we must attend to our own souls and seek to know the ways of the Lord." Notice how he states that we counter the enemy's power first by safeguarding our souls and by growing in the knowledge of God's ways. He then describes how to guard the soul and the mind. He continues, "In those times, reverential fear and perseverance will sustain our faith, and we will find need of forbearance and self-restraint as well. Provided that we hold fast to these virtues and look to the Lord, then wisdom, understanding, knowledge and insight will make joyous company with them."[223]

Thus, this first-century Christian writer (and companion of Saint Paul according to Acts 14:14) urges that to defeat Satan, the Christian must develop virtue (reverential fear, perseverance, forbearance, self-restraint), which, in turn, will help the intellect

---

[223] *Epistle of Barnabas*, 1, 1-8; 2, 1-5.

to secure the requisite virtues for battle (wisdom, understanding, knowledge, and insight). This apostolic Father gives us the foundation of our assertion that "the demon enters through sin but holds through heresy." Sin lets him in, but he must be rooted out with both virtue and the right knowledge of God's truths.

Setting the Ambush: Virtue as Holiness in Thought, Word, and Deed

Rogers instructed his rangers that "if somebody's trailing you, make a circle, come back onto your own tracks, and ambush the folks that aim to ambush you." The development of virtue is a bit like this. It requires that you identify the vice that is "trailing you" so that you can set an "ambush" with the corresponding virtue. At a very basic level, the only way to correct a bad habit is to replace it with a good habit. Saint Jane Frances de Chantal, for example, gave this advice when confronting one's sins: "Should you fall even fifty times a day," she writes, "never on any account should that surprise or worry you. Instead, ever so gently set your heart back in the right direction and practice the opposite virtue."[224] To borrow Rogers's terms, you need to ambush the vice by circling back with virtue. That is, reorient of your life.

Vice is more than sinful behavior. In spiritual combat, a vice is a disposition or quality of the soul, a disordered inclination toward some evil. By definition, it is "a bad moral habit . . . the strong tendency to a gravely sinful act acquired through frequent repetition of the same act."[225] Virtue, on the contrary, is a "good habit that enables a person to act according to right reason enlightened by faith."[226] Both good and bad acts are patterned behaviors in which one displaces the other. Too often, however, we place the emphasis on the vice rather than the virtue. This modern and minimalist view is contrary to how the

---

[224] Saint Jane Frances de Chantal, *Selected Letters*, 18.
[225] Hardon, *Modern Catholic Dictionary*, 561.
[226] Hardon, 563–64.

tradition of the Church orders the two. Saint Thomas Aquinas states, "Vice is contrary to virtue" such that it militates against the good in the soul through evil inclinations. Thus, he states that when "a man is ill-disposed inwardly, through some inordinate affection, he is rendered thereby unfit for fulfilling his duties."[227] The natural state of man is a life ordered to virtue, therefore, so that you can fulfill the duties of your state in life. Saint Gregory of Nyssa describes what this looks like practically:

> The life of the Christian has three distinguishing aspects: deeds, words and thought. Thought comes first, then words, since our words express openly the interior conclusions of the mind. Finally, after thoughts and words, comes action, for our deeds carry out what the mind has conceived. So, when one of these results in our acting or speaking or thinking, we must make sure that all our thoughts, words and deeds are controlled by the divine ideal, the revelation of Christ. For then our thoughts, words and deeds will not fall short of the nobility of their implications. What then must we do, we who have been found worthy of the name of Christ? Each of us must examine his thoughts, words and deeds, to see whether they are directed towards Christ or are turned away from him. This examination is carried out in various ways. Our deeds or our thoughts or our words are not in harmony with Christ if they issue from passion. They then bear the mark of the enemy who smears the pearl of the heart with the slime of passion, dimming and even destroying the luster of the precious stone. On the other hand, if they are free from and untainted by every passionate inclination, they are directed towards Christ, the author and source of peace. He is like a pure, untainted stream. If you draw from him the thoughts in your mind and the inclinations of your heart, you will show a likeness to Christ, your source and origin, as the gleaming water in a jar resembles the flowing water from which it was obtained.[228]

---

[227] Saint Thomas Aquinas, *Summa Theologica*, I-II, q. 71 a. 1.
[228] Saint Gregory of Nyssa, *De Perfecta Christiana Forma*, 46.

Notice how this Doctor of the Church connects the growth of virtue with growing in holiness in thought, word, and deed. The lack of virtue means a person "bears the mark of the enemy" by the "slime of passion."

The repeated act of virtue or vice, then, is a movement either towards freedom or slavery. Thus, I affirm that "interior freedom is not static. Freedom *from* (disordered attachments that expose the soul to the diabolic) means also freedom *for* (a life of virtue which allows for a deeper life in Christ)."[229] Our Lady of Sorrows is particularly helpful in assisting souls in this area. Pray to her and ask her to reveal any sins and vices of which you are ignorant but are blocking God's grace in your life.

The remaining sections of this lesson contain lists of virtues and sins contrary to them so that you can confess them. In addition to confession, begin to work on a calm interiority which can withstand the assaults of the enemy. As Saint Thomas notes, our thoughts, words, and deeds are directed either towards or away from Christ. That is, you either are moving towards Christ (→ *ad orientem*) or away from Him (→ *ad hominem*). The following **Prayer to Protect Faculties** can be used to keep away the "slime of passion" and can help you to uncover hidden vices in the soul:

> *Lord Jesus Christ, let Thy Precious Blood flowing from Thy wounded Heart cover me, my cogitative power, memory, imagination, common sense power, sensitive appetites, my sight, hearing, taste, touch and smell, (and any part of your body they are affecting) driving the demons to the foot of thy Cross where they may be judged by Thee. In the Name of the Father, the Son and the Holy Spirit. Amen.*

This prayer (and others in the appendix) will help you to order your interiority with virtue.

---

[229] Liber Christo, "Companion Guide," 15.

The Queen of Sins and Her Daughters

Saint Thomas calls pride the "Queen of Sins" and refers to the seven deadly (or capital) sins as the "generals" of the enemy's forces. According to the *Catechism*, these sins "engender other sins, other vices."[230] These are (1) lust, (2) gluttony, (3) greed, (4) sloth/melancholy, (5) wrath, (6) envy, and (7) pride.[231] According to Saint Thomas, each "general" has an army of other vices working for him, to whom he refers as their "daughters." Thus, once one of the seven deadly sins enters, it calls forth its army of corresponding sins and vices. There is a ligature, so to speak, which connects you to both sides of the Red Sea—the carnal and the spiritual sin. When the capital sin of lust is allowed into the interiority, it opens the soul to other "daughter vices" which can now plague the soul like soldiers of an invading army.

Our experience is that most cases of diabolic affliction contain some element of sexual disorder, such as incest, same-sex ideation, sexual abuse, fornication, pornography addiction, contraception, and abortion. Let us analyze the connection between pride and lust. According to Pope Saint Gregory the Great, for example, when the "general" of lust is given ground in the soul, he brings with him eight companion vices:

1. Blindness of Mind
2. Thoughtlessness (inconsiderateness towards others)
3. Inconstancy (inability to control emotions, thoughts, etc. in relation to the events of life)
4. Rashness (precipitation, or behaving too quickly or rashly without thinking)
5. Self-Love
6. Hatred of God

---

[230] *CCC* 1866.

[231] Pope Saint Gregory the Great, *Moralia in Job*, XXXI, XLV. On pride, see Saint Thomas Aquinas, *Summa Theologica* II-II, q. 162. Evagrius Ponticus also speaks of the "eight evil thoughts" and gives strategies to overcome them in *The Praktikos*, 16–31.

7. Love of this World (affection for this present world
    and over attachment to worldly things and events,
    etc.)

8. Abhorrence or Despair of a Future World (dread or
    despair of the future, lack of hope in God)

The capital vice convinces the conquered heart to continue
to engorge itself on pleasurable goods, especially sexual pleasures. The demon, however, does not stop there. That same
spirit of lust creates a host of other defects in the soul, including thoughtlessness, affection for the world, dread of the
future, inconstancy, and even hatred of God.

Seeing how the "generals" and the "daughters" work can
help you to unmask the demon. To divert your attention, the
enemy will often drive you to focus on the obvious vice (the
carnal) when the real issue lies in the more subtle vice (the
spiritual). The latter, which is the deeper and more spiritual
defect, is usually the primary attachment point by which the
demon holds in your soul. Your anger, for example, may have
at its root an unwillingness to suffer. Accordingly, to borrow a
term from geology and gardening, you must unearth the "taproot" defect in the soul (a taproot is the principal root taper-
ing vertically downward from which all subsidiary rootlets
spring) to eliminate the secondary and tertiary vices behind
which the demon both holds and finds a source of strength.
Thus, if you remove the spiritual defect of a lack of willingness
to suffer and endure hardship for the Kingdom of God, the
carnal appetite toward anger will dissipate.

Combatants never show their weakness. Instead, they cun-
ningly always show their strength. Both the javelin and the
sling were range weapons in ancient warfare. While Goliath
mocked David's choice of weapon, David undoubtedly knew
that his shepherd's sling had a longer kill radius than that of
Goliath's javelin. As it applies to this ministry, the demon is
masterful at inciting us to habituate our inner dispositions to
lure us to sinful behavior, within range of his javelin. We, however, must take advantage of the longer reach of the spiritual

sling. Demons cannot habituate our behavior, but they can influence our decisions through a barrage of images in the imagination. That is, when we lack virtue, the demon prompts us with emotionally charged "projections" into our imagination which trigger some patterned psychological response within us. The demon knows which "buttons" to push, so to speak. He watches our response to persons, events, and places, and he patiently seeks to habituate our behaviors and reactions. He is especially present when we display a high emotionality.[232] To be clear, the demon cannot read our minds. He can, however, influence our thoughts by exploiting psychological wounds and vulnerabilities by manipulating images in our imagination. Thus, Clement calls the demon "the world's greatest actuary" because he "knows statistically what our predictable behavior is and exploits our weaknesses."[233]

By way of example, this is like the older brother who pins his younger sibling and uses the latter's fist to force the little brother to punch himself while asking, "Why are you hitting yourself?" The demon leads us to "hit ourselves" through sinful behavior by baiting the person with an emotionally charged memory. Do not take the bait. When a temptation arises in the mind, you must recognize and reject it with an act of the will. This means you must *disappropriate* (or separate) the image or emotion from the memory of the event. If the intellect does not direct the will to reject the image and emotion, then the enemy can then project more images and emotions more forcefully into the imagination. These sentiments proceed into the intellect and compromise the soul's self-mastery by blurring one's emotions and thoughts. Thus, when we lack interior discipline, sin frequently follows.

The best way, therefore, to keep someone from "pushing your buttons" is to eliminate the buttons. The focus cannot be on the vice and the demon; rather, it must be on becoming holy so that your prayers for liberation are more efficacious and the

---

[232] For more on the sensitive appetites and passions, see Ripperger, *Introduction to the Science of Mental Health*, 127–70.
[233] Liber Christo, "Companion Guide," 150.

pathway to freedom is more direct. The demon finds a pathway into the soul's interiority, however, through disordered inner dispositions and sinful acts. That is, the demon both fuels the inordinate affections of the soul and uses them to trigger the person into sinful behavior and, thereupon, makes a legal claim to be there. Therefore, it is not sufficient simply to set upon the overcoming of some vice so as to be "demon-free." If you only do that, your focus is still on the demon and the vice. Rather, you must prioritize fostering the virtue counter to that vice and reordering your interior life by the self-mastery that comes through holiness and the practice of virtue.

Moreover, the emphasis must be upon God because we owe it to Him in justice. In addition, the development of virtue both reflects and welcomes His presence. Saint Thomas (following Saint Augustine) shows that vice is contrary to virtue because it distorts that image of God in us and diminishes our supernatural merit (which, in turn, diminishes the effectiveness of our prayers). Hence, if you want the demon to leave you alone, you must make a total reorientation of your life to God and render to Him what is due. For those who have strayed far from the truth, minor adjustments in the spiritual life will not suffice. A disposition in which metanoia gives way to the primacy of virtue in the soul is the foundation that lasting liberation is built upon.

We're Surrounded. That Simplifies the Problem.

Father Amorth tells how his teacher, Fr. Candido Amantini, once asked a demon, "How many are you?" The demon replied, "We are so many that, if we were visible, we would darken the sun."[234] These are sobering words, to be sure, but should not make you lose heart any more than the people of God at their Red Sea moment. The virtue of courage is always needed in battle. The source of your courage is trust in God for, as

---

[234] Amorth, *An Exorcist Explains the Demonic*, 17.

Moses told the people, "the Lord himself will fight for you" (Ex 14:13–14).

The most decorated US marine was Chesty Puller, who fought in both World War II and Korea (among other places). He is known for both his bravery and wit. Once, when asked to give a report of his company's dire situation, he replied, "We're surrounded. That simplifies the problem." Chances are, you are also surrounded by sins, vices, or spirits, which make things simple. In explaining the situation to his men, Puller is reported to have said, "All right, they're on our left, they're on our right, they're in front of us, they're behind us. They can't get away this time. Now we can shoot at them from every direction." The good news is that no matter what direction you shoot, you also can hit one. The key here is to identify the vices one at a time.

In ancient times, in fact, *virtus* meant "manly courage and honor," specifically on the field of battle. When Julius Caesar prepared his legionaries for battle, for example, he would exhort them to be *virtus*—that is, to be courageous and manful in the face of the enemy. This inner disposition for success in physical combat is no less important for the spiritual battle. The Latin word for *man* is *vir*, and thus, to be *virtus* (or virtuous), implies that virtue is part of what it means to be fully human. The need for "manful" courage, moreover, does not only apply to men. Saint Teresa of Avila, for example, told her Carmelite daughters that they should not be "effeminate" (*de mujeres*, in the sense of soft and delicate) but rather be "manly" (*varoniles*) in their pursuit of virtue—so manly, she said, that their toughness should astonish or even "scare" men (*espanten a los hombres*).[235] Thus, she encourages her daughters to be spiritually courageous, tough, and rugged like soldiers coming off a long and successful campaign.[236] This is "momma bear" tough.

---

[235] Saint Teresa of Avila, *Obras Completas*, 486. Translation mine. Cf. Saint Teresa of Avila, *Way of Perfection*, 54–55.
[236] Cf. Saint Teresa of Avila, *Life*, 300.

Since the demon exploits our human weaknesses and effeminacy in the face of difficult tasks, we complete this section with the virtues and a detailed list of vices which militate against them. Admittedly, the following list (as was the list of clusters of spirits) can be intimidating, even overwhelming. The following examination of the theological and cardinal virtues was developed by Father Ripperger and Kyle Clement specifically for use in spiritual combat.[237] As you go through the list of virtues, first identify any vices that are most present to you or your family. Then, confess any sins related to the vice and begin to militate against it by praying for and practicing the related virtue. Make note of areas of weakness where the demon could exploit, or even neutralize, you in battle. Then militate against them, like a Numidian slinger perfecting his skills, through the development of virtue and sacramental confession.

Recall the previous discussion that King Saul exhibited vices and behavior patterns (proud, disobedient, angry, etc.) that led him to eventually become "tormented by an evil spirit sent by the Lord" (1 Sm 16:14). At some point, the scales tipped, and the demon exploited his vulnerabilities to become interior to him. This section is meant to help you see the defect first before it grows into something larger, as what happened to King Saul. The monastic tradition does something similar when reading the Psalms. The Psalms contain several "imprecatory psalms" which take on deeper meaning when read in light of the spiritual enemies of God's people. In one, David prays that God seize the children of his enemies and smash "them against the rock" (Ps 137:9). The desert Fathers read this as meaning that we should destroy any vices and sinful thoughts that militate against the soul by "smashing" them on the Rock, Christ, especially while they are "babies."[238]

---

[237] This use of the virtues in spiritual combat is based upon the work of Father Ripperger and was also presented by Clement to the Pope Leo Institute in 2016. This section includes as well an expansion of my own thoughts in Liber Christo, "Companion Guide," 10–12.

[238] For the monastic tradition on sinful thoughts and desires, see also fn. 205.

That is, vices must be destroyed while they are still small and before they mature and take root in the soul.

By way of modern analogy, in dealing with emotions, psychologist Daniel Seigel coined the phrase "if you can name it, you can tame it" in dealing with emotions and trauma.[239] That is, a person can better manage emotions by naming them before they rise and gain strength. The same principle can be applied to identifying sins, vices, or spirits. Name it and tame it—before it grows into something bigger.

Theological Virtues

We begin with the **theological** virtues of faith, hope, and charity. According to the *Catechism*, these are called "theological" because they are "infused by God" into the soul and "make [the faithful] capable of acting as his children and of meriting eternal life." In addition, these three virtues "are the pledge of the presence and action of the Holy Spirit *in the faculties of the human being*."[240]

Faith is the virtue by which one gives assent to the Deposit of Faith.[241] Sins against faith include:

- Infidelity: lack of belief in the deposit of faith
- Heresy: lack of belief in one or more of the doctrines of the Faith
- Apostasy: rejection of the Faith entirely by someone already baptized
- Blasphemy: denigration of something sacred by means of speech

---

[239] Seigel, *Mindsight*, 116.

[240] *CCC* 1813.

[241] The *despositum fidei* is the body of teachings handed down from Christ to the apostles, and to their successor bishops, which we are bound to believe. These are the revealed truths (dogmas and doctrines) found in Sacred Scripture and Sacred Tradition as taught by the Roman Catholic Church and safeguarded by her Magisterium, or supreme teaching office.

Hope is the virtue by which one awaits the beatitude and has confidence in God's aid. Sins against hope include:

- Desperation: lack of confidence in God's ability to save someone or to aid him
- Presumption: excessive confidence in one's own capacities beyond one's abilities to achieve some end

Charity is the virtue by which one loves God and one's neighbor for the sake of God. Vices that militate against charity include:

- Hatred of God
- Sloth: unwillingness to engage the arduous in order to achieve some excellence
- Envy: desire to have something possessed by another in such a manner that the other no longer possesses it
- Discord: the vice in which one knowingly and intentionally dissents from the divine Good and the good of his neighbor (a vice in which one does not seek union of wills)
- Contention: the habit of contrariety in speech
- Schism: lack of submission to the authority of the Church, especially the pope and bishops
- Unjust War: the waging of battle without due cause
- Quarreling (*Rixa*): contrariety in deeds (private warring, sometimes called feuding)
- Scandal: the drawing of another into sin or the placing of an impediment of the assent of faith on behalf of another

Cardinal Virtues

Because the theological virtues are infused into the soul at Baptism, they lay the foundation for the cardinal virtues and the moral life.[242] The cardinal virtues (also known as the moral virtues) also need to be developed by human effort assisted by grace. In addition, I wrote, "'Cardinal' comes from the Latin *cardo*, meaning 'hinge,' and the other virtues 'hinge' upon these four, namely, *prudence, justice, temperance,* and *fortitude.* These are 'acquired by human effort' (cf. *CCC* 1804) and are essential in spiritual warfare."[243] Part of the human effort, according to the Council of Trent, is to "manfully resist" and "wrestle against" the "inclination to sin" (known as concupiscence) which remains even after Baptism.[244] Tanquerey defines concupiscence as "the inordinate love of sensual pleasures."[245] The demon exploits these tendencies in inciting us to habituate our responses to the people and events in our lives and trigger us to commit sin. The effort-laden growth in the "hinge" virtues counters the momentum of the inordinate loves driven by concupiscence.

Prudence is knowing the means to attain the end. Elements of a developed virtue of prudence include:[246]

- Memory (*Memoria*): the ability to remember the right things pertaining to the action and its circumstances
- Understanding (*Intellectus*): the ability to grasp practical principles and the nature of various situations
- Docility (*Docilitas*): ability to be led and to take counsel from others

---

[242] See *CCC* 1813.
[243] Liber Christo, "Companion Guide," 14.
[244] See *CCC* 1264.
[245] Tanquerey, *The Spiritual Life*, no. 193.
[246] This list and definitions were compiled by Father Ripperger and Clement from *ST* II-II, 47-170 and is used with permission.

- Shrewdness (*Solertia*): quickness in arriving at the means to the end
- Reason (*Ratio*): ability to reason about practical matters; the ability to apply universal practical principles to particular situations
- Foresight (*Providentia*): ability to see future outcomes of actions based upon past experience
- Circumspection (*Circumspectio*): virtue by which one keeps track of one's circumstances
- Caution (*Cautio*): application of knowledge of the past to action in order to avoid impediments and evils

The potential parts of prudence include:

- Good Counsel (*Eubulia*): the habit of taking good counsel
- *Synesis*: the ability to know what to do when the common law applies
- *Ratio*: the ability to know what to do when the common law does not apply

Vices that militate against prudence include:

- Precipitation: the vice in which one does not take counsel (results in acting too quickly)
- Inconsideration: the vice in which one does not judge which means is the best among the various means arrived at during counsel
- Inconstancy: a vice in which one does not command or do the action which has been counseled and judged as the best
- Negligence: failure to take counsel or a failure to do what one should when one ought
- Carnal Prudence: the vice in which one applies one's reason to arrive at means to attain created goods which are seen as one's final end

- Craftiness (*Astutia*): industry in not using the right or true means to an end
- Guile (*Dolus*): the habit of deceit (usually in words)
- Fraud (*Fraus*): the habit of deceit (usually in deeds)

Justice is to render another his due. Elements of a developed virtue of justice include:

- Commutative: justice between individuals
- Legal: justice of the individual to the common good
- Distributive: justice of those in charge of the common good to the individual
- Restitution: the habit by which one pays back what one owes
- Religion: the virtue by which we render to God what is due to Him
- Devotion: the habit by which one has a prompt will to do those things pertaining to the service of God
- Adjuration: the swearing or taking of an oath, such as in a court of law
- Piety: the virtue by which one renders to one's parents due honor and reverence
- Patriotism: the sub-virtue to piety in which one renders to one's country the honor due
- Observances: making acts of religion
- *Dulia*: giving due honor to one's superiors
- Obedience: promptness of will to do the will of one's superior
- Diligence: fulfilling one's duty according to one's state in life
- Gratitude (Thankfulness): appreciation (normally expressed) to a benefactor for some gift given
- Just Vindication: the habit by which one puts an end to the harm caused by others
- Truthfulness (Honesty): the habit of telling the truth

- Friendship (Affability): the virtue by which one is able to be befriended
- Liberality: the use of one's surplus means to aid the poor
- *Epieikeia*: the virtue by which one knows the mind of the legislator

Vices that militate against justice include:

- Acception of Persons (Human Respect): excessive deference paid to someone
- Murder: unjust killing of the innocent
- Mutilation: physical harm or changes made to one's body aside from the order of nature
- Theft: occult taking of that which belongs to another
- Robbery: non-occult (usually violent) taking of that which belongs to another
- Judgment: judging another over whom one does not have authority or contrary to the truth
- False Accusation: accusing somebody of something that is false
- Perjury: lying under oath
- Contumely: attack on a person's reputation (usually done in their presence—normally it is the saying of something false to destroy someone's reputation)
- Detraction: saying something true in order to destroy someone's reputation
- Murmuring: occult detraction in order to separate the affections of one person from another
- Derision: laughing at another in order to lower him in the estimation of others
- Malediction (Cursing): calling down condemnation on something or someone
- Usury: the taking of (excessive) interest on a loan
- Illicit Adjuration: swearing an oath outside due circumstances

- Superstition: the rendering of some honor or practice to a creature that is due only to God
- Idolatry: worshiping some created thing as God
- Divination (and Witchcraft): the use of the demonic in order to achieve something, such as knowledge of the future, hidden knowledge, to gain power over something, etc.
- Tempting God
- Sacrilege: ill-use or abuse of something sacred
- Simony: the purchasing or selling of something sacred
- Disobedience: a lack of promptness to do the will of one's superiors
- Vengefulness: inordinate desire for vindication (inordinate desire to cause harm to another in order to put an end to the harm he is causing)
- Lying: saying the false in order to deceive
- Simulation (sometimes called Hypocrisy): doing the false in order to deceive
- Boasting: the drawing of attention to or the exaggeration of one's perfections
- Ingratitude: lack of appreciation for the benefit granted by a benefactor
- Irony: the lowering of oneself below one's state usually in speech
- Adulation: the use of speech whereby one flatters another
- Litigiousness: excessive desire or practice of taking someone to court
- Avarice: excessive desire to make and hold onto money or wealth
- Prodigality (Wastefulness) lack of sufficient desire to hold onto one's money or the excessive use of something outside what is necessary

Temperance is the virtue that moderates attraction and desire for pleasure and provides balance in the use of created goods. Elements of a developed virtue of temperance include:

- Shame: the fear of being perceived as lowly
- Honesty (may also be called integrity): the habit of always seeking to do what is virtuous in each situation
- Abstinence: refraining from eating of certain kinds of food
- Fasting: refraining from eating food in general
- Sobriety: the virtue by which one has moderated use of alcohol
- Continence: the virtue in the will by which one remains steadfast despite the tumult of the appetites
- Chastity: the virtue which moderates the pleasures of the senses in relation to those matters pertaining to the sixth commandment
- Virginity: the habit of mind or soul which always refrains from taking delight, even interiorly, from pleasures associated with the sixth commandment
- Clemency (Meekness): moderation of the delight of vindication (of anger)
- Modesty (proper): the virtue in which one's externals do not draw others into sins against the sixth and ninth commandments
- Humility: willingness to live in accordance with the truth; refrain in the irascible appetite from striving for excellence beyond one's state; not judging oneself greater than one is
- *Eutrapelia*: the virtue of right recreation
- Sportsmanship: the virtue in which one regulates the pleasures specifically in relation to play or games
- Decorum: the virtue in which one's externals suits person and circumstances
- Silence: the virtue by which one does not speak

unless necessary; also, the virtue in which one seeks
to have interior quiet of the appetites
- Studiosity: the virtue in which one pursues
knowledge according to one's state in life
- Simplicity: the virtue in which one moderates one's
externals as to quantity (having neither more nor
less than is necessary)

Vices that militate against temperance include:

- Gluttony: eating to excess
- Drunkenness: drinking alcohol to excess
- Lust: illicit desire for the pleasures pertaining to the
sixth commandment
- Fornication: conjugal relations by the unmarried
- Mutual Acts outside the Marriage State: foreplay by
those outside of marriage
- Rape: conjugal relations outside of marriage under
the duress of violence
- Adultery: conjugal relations between two people, of
which at least one is married to someone else
- Incest: conjugal relations between blood relatives
- Incontinence: lack of steadfastness because of the
tumult of the appetites
- Anger: a vice in which one does not moderate
the passion of anger; an inordinate desire for
vindication arising from unmoderated sorrow at
some offense
- Cruelty: unmoderated vindication with respect to
external actions
- Pride: unwillingness to live in accordance with the
truth; excessive striving for excellence beyond one's
state; judging oneself greater than he is
- Curiosity: inordinate desire for useless or profane
knowledge
- Crudity: lack of etiquette or manners
- Immodesty: lack of moderation regarding one's
externals

Fortitude is the willingness to engage the arduous. Elements of a developed virtue of fortitude include:

- Magnanimity: the virtue by which one seeks excellence in all things but especially great things
- Magnificence: the virtue by which one uses his wealth to do great things
- Patience: the ability to suffer evils well or the equanimity in the face of evils
- Perseverance: the virtue by which one persists in the arduous good until the end is achieved
- Longanimity: largess of soul; the ability to await the good
- Mortification: the willingness to suffer

Vices that militate against fortitude include:

- Fear: the vice in which one has an unmoderated passion arising from the perception of future evil
- Fearlessness: lack of moderated fear
- Audacity: excessive aggressiveness toward imminent danger without reasonable fear
- Presumption: thinking one can attain some end which is beyond him without aid, usually from God
- Ambition: striving for honor above one's excellence
- Inane Glory: seeking honor in those things unworthy of honor
- Pusillanimity: smallness of soul; the habit of not striving for excellence
- Parvificience (Stinginess): unwillingness to use one's wealth to do great things
- Mollities or Softness (Effeminacy): an unwillingness to put aside pleasure in order to engage the arduous
- Pertinacity: excessive clinging to one's assertions or intellectual convictions

Taking Aim at Your Target

This lesson focused on the importance of "drilling" the virtues so that you can hit your target when the time of battle arrives. Ultimately, God permits a demonic adversary so that you will grow in holiness by the development of virtue. This allows grace to flow not only to you but also into your entire familial construct. Thus, the demon becomes the instrument of sanctification for you and your family (and you the instrument of torment for the demon). Recall the words of Chesty Puller: "We're surrounded. That simplifies the problem." However, you cannot hit a target that you cannot see. Now is the time to ask your guardian angel, the "ranger buddy" who God has assigned to you, for help. Ask him to identify the enemies (defects and spirits) of your soul, and then calmly and methodically militate against them. Once you identify one, you can take aim. Rather than being overwhelmed by the task, pick one vice, sin, or spirit at a time and calmly, methodically militate against it.

After reviewing these vices that militate against virtue, list the ones you see first:

In addition, the following prayers are easy to pray and may help free up some interior space. The real work, however, is in the *practice of the virtue*. See the appendix for more prayers, but once you identify the vice or demon, a **Simple Binding Prayer** is very effective:[247]

In the Name of our Lord Jesus Christ and by the power of His Most Precious Blood, I bind, I chain, and I silence any demon(s) of (n.) and I send them to the foot of the Cross for

---

[247] For another form of binding prayer with suggested use, see appendix B.

*Jesus Christ to do with as He wills. In the Name of the Father,
and of the Son and of the Holy Spirit. Amen. (Thrice).*[248]

(By "any demon of n." insert emotion, passion, vice, condition,
or disposition you wish to militate against.)

The following prayer can be modified to sever any interior
attachments, such as unforgiveness, resentment, anxiety, or
other clinging spirits:

*I bind in the Blood of Jesus all of your hooks, lines and
tentacles, your roots, attachments and attenuations, and
I command you in the Name of Jesus to remove them now
completely and entirely: In the Name of Jesus, remove them
now. (Thrice)*

You will find other prayers in the appendix.

From Slingstones to Milestones: The Development of Virtue

1. What is the importance of "drilling" in the spiritual life? What spiritual practices do you practice consistently? What areas of your life lack discipline?

2. To which of the eight "companion vices" that accompany the "general" of lust are you most vulnerable?

3. What are the definitions of virtue and vice? What do they have in common?

4. What is the significance of the biblical number forty, and what does it mean to you?

5. Regarding the trap being set for the ranger described by Rogers, how does this relate to your pursuit of virtue?

6. According to Saint Gregory of Nyssa, to grow in virtue means holiness of thought, word, and deed. How do you understand this to be possible?

7. What is your understanding of the "Queen Vices

---

[248] Liber Christo, "Team Training Manual," 30.

and the Daughters"? Are you able to look beyond your carnal sins to identify the underlying spiritual vice, or taproot?

8. How do you understand the statement that "any behavior inconsistent with the indelible mark of Christ is what draws the demon to you?"

9. How do you understand "psychological compatibility" with the demon as it relates to vices?

LESSON EIGHT: THE SACRAMENTS AND THE FLOW OF GRACE

By now, you may understand that spiritual combat is akin to guerrilla warfare. Guerrilla warfare is best used when facing an enemy who is superior in number and weapons. These combat tactics can equalize the battlefield because it limits the combat effectiveness of conventional weapons and tactics. Accordingly, another nugget from Rogers's rules is: "Don't stand up when the enemy's coming against you. Kneel down, lie down, hide behind a tree." His style of fighting was the opposite of the British allies who fought a European style of combat by standing up in linear battle formation, uniformed in easily visible bright red coats. When the British would encamp for the winter and wait for spring, as was the custom of the day, Rogers and his men would continue to take the fight to the enemy. They engaged in long-range reconnaissance patrols to gain intelligence, conducted ambushes and raids, and in general disrupted the enemy.

Goliath confronted David with conventional weaponry: bronze helmet, scale armor, greaves, sword, javelin (see 1 Sm 17:4–7). These weapons in hand, he also had his shield and armor bearer ahead of him. David, meanwhile, had neither shield nor sword, but would later tell us why. In what is known as the Soldier's Psalm, David states, "[God's] faithfulness is a protecting shield" (Ps 91:4). Listen to the other shield imagery that David uses in the Psalms:

- "God is a **shield** above me" (Ps 7:11).
- "LORD, my rock, my fortress, my deliverer, / My God, my rock of refuge / **my shield**, my saving horn, my stronghold!" (Ps 18:3).
- "The LORD is my strength and **my shield**, / in whom my heart trusts" (Ps 28:7).
- "Our soul waits for the LORD; / he is our **help and shield**" (Ps 33:20).
- "May God **go before me** / and show me my fallen foes" (Ps 59:11).
- "The house of Israel trusts in the LORD / who is **their help and shield**. / The house of Aaron trusts in the LORD, / who is **their help and shield**" (Ps 115:9–10).
- "You are **my refuge and shield**; / in your word, I hope" (Ps 119:114).

In fact, David even states that God is his armor bearer, asking God to "take up the shield and buckler, / rise up in my defense. / Brandish lance and battle-ax / against my pursuers. / Say to my soul, / 'I am your salvation'" (Ps 35:2–3).

When reflecting back on his victory over Goliath, David says that God has "given me your protecting shield, / and your help has made me great" (2 Sm 22:36). In this section, we will briefly explore the sacraments of the Roman Catholic faith as the principle means through which God pours grace into the world. In a manner only described as mysterious, God *stoops to make us great* in allowing us to be partakers in His divinity. This is precisely the reality against which the demon militates. The sacraments are, by way of analogy, akin to a spiritual shield against evil.

Attack in a Different Direction: A Sacramental Orientation

Chesty Puller refused to use the phrase "retreat." He preferred, rather, to call it "attacking in a different direction." To attack from a different direction means to control the terms of engagement in a manner that both exploits the enemy's weakness and maximizes your strengths. For the Christian, this means capitalizing on the reality of the baptismal seal, or what Saint Paul describes as, "Christ in you, the hope for glory" (Col 1:27). Thus, when exhorting the Corinthians to avoid sexual immorality, he writes, "Do you not know that your body is a temple of the Holy Spirit within you, whom you have from God, and you are not your own? For you have been purchased at a price. Therefore, glorify God in your body" (1 Cor 6:19–20).

The price of our salvation came at the greatest cost, the cost of royal, divine blood. And the fruit Christ's redemption was Baptism, where we became temples of the Holy Spirit. If you are baptized, you are a living temple of God, which means that the living God dwells in you. In this section, we will explore how to attack from that position of strength, from a sacramental orientation.

According to the *Catechism*, "the sacraments are efficacious signs of grace, instituted by Christ and entrusted to the Church, by which divine life is dispensed to us." Each sacrament contains "graces proper to each" and "bears fruit in those who receive them with the required disposition."[249] In response to the Protestants, the Council of Trent affirmed the ancient tradition that "the sacraments of the new law were . . . all instituted by Jesus Christ our Lord." This is confirmed as found in "the teaching of the Holy Scriptures . . . the apostolic traditions, and to the consensus . . . of the Fathers."[250] Specifically, there are seven sacraments: "Baptism, Confirmation or Chrisma-

---

[249] *CCC* 1131.
[250] *CCC* 1114.

tion, Eucharist, Penance, Anointing of the Sick, Holy Orders, and Matrimony."[251] Quoting Pope Saint Leo the Great, the *Catechism* also states, "Sacraments are 'powers that come forth' from the Body of Christ, which is ever living and life-giving" because they "are actions of the Holy Spirit at work in his Body, the Church."[252] When battling against the forces of death and corruption, draw your opponent to the high ground of these *ever living and life-giving* weapons which *bring forth powers*.

Tapping into sanctifying grace, this divine vitality and the life and power of God, provides the armaments for spiritual combat.[253] On the reality of man's capacity to share in the life of God, Saint Augustine states, "The mind is the image of God, in that it is capable of Him and can be partaker of Him."[254] He states that man is *capax Dei*; that is, he is aptly suited to conceal and contain God within the depths of his inner being. *Capax* also has the meaning of "possessing the right to inheritance." Thus, a baptized Catholic has an indelible mark of Christ and possesses an inheritance as a child of God.[255] This dignity is precisely that which the demon militates against. Any behavior inconsistent with this indelible mark of Christ acts as a target.

In other words, what Christ assumed He also redeemed. When Jesus Christ took on human flesh, He radically transformed it. The new life in Christ begins at baptism, and this spiritual life is sustained through the sacraments, which "touch all the stages and all the important moments of Christian life."[256] You are oriented to Christ through your vocational sacrament and receive grace through that construct. For this reason, the demon routinely attacks the sacraments of

---

[251] *CCC* 1113.

[252] *CCC* 1116.

[253] This section on the sacraments expands upon my presentations at the 2018 and 2019 Liber Christo Conferences, as well as Liber Christo, "Companion Guide," 11–12.

[254] Saint Augustine of Hippo, *On the Trinity*, XIV.

[255] Thus, the *Catechism* affirms that in the sacraments, "the Church . . . receives the guarantee of her inheritance." *CCC* 1130.

[256] *CCC* 1210.

Matrimony and Holy Orders (and is attracted to any behavior contrary to the integrity of each). In addition, we have found that the demon is often more aggressive against families and individuals who are approaching sacramental years—children approaching their First Communion or Confirmation, a seminarian approaching ordination, et cetera. The devil attempts to block the flow of grace because he recognizes the power of the sacraments for what they are—*ever-living and life-giving* weapons which *bring forth powers* when dispensing their graces to us.

The sacraments, according to the *Catechism*, are the means "by which divine life is dispensed to us." In addition, the "visible rites . . . make present the graces proper to each sacrament" but "bear fruit in those who receive them with the required dispositions."[257] Being in a state of grace is an essential part of the "required dispositions" which sets a soul up so that the sacrament may "bear fruit" in the recipient's life. As stated above, by "state of grace," we mean being free from mortal sin and, therefore, pleasing to God. A soul in a state of grace has friendship with God, the necessary condition to attaining heaven. Even a possessed person who dies in a state of grace has this friendship and promise.

By definition, "grace is a participation in the life of God. It introduces us into intimacy of Trinitarian life,"[258] a reality which is "infused by the Holy Spirit into our soul to heal it of sin and to sanctify it."[259] The demon knows that the more we participate in God's life—by means of grace—the less he can entice us to a life of sin. Theologically, there are two principal kinds of grace:[260]

- *Sanctifying grace* is a divine vitality of supernatural life of God in the soul, "a stable and supernatural disposition" which "perfects the soul itself to

---

[257] *CCC* 1131.
[258] *CCC* 1997.
[259] *CCC* 1999.
[260] For more, see *CCC* 1996–2005.

enable it to live with God, to act by his love."[261] This is sometimes referred to as habitual grace (from the Latin *habere*, which means something had or possessed by the soul) and implies a permanency unless mortal sin causes God to retract His causing it in the soul.

- *Actual graces*, according to Father Hardon, are "temporary supernatural intervention by God to enlighten the mind or strengthen the will to perform supernatural actions that lead to heaven."[262] The *Catechism* calls them "God's interventions."[263]

Thus, God gives us grace through holy promptings ("God's interventions") so that we may secure the "stable and supernatural disposition" of the soul living in holy friendship with God.

The grace of each sacrament is objectively present regardless of the merits of the minister or the recipient. In the tradition of the Church, this is termed *ex opere operato* ("from the work performed"), meaning that the sacraments confer the grace that they signify.[264] There is, however, a *proviso* on the appropriation of sacramental grace. As stated by Father Hardon, "Provided that no obstacle (obex) is placed in the way, every sacrament properly administered confers the grace intended by the sacrament."[265] Thus, a worthy reception of the sacraments (referred to as *ex opere operantis*, or by virtue of the agent in whom the work is being done) is necessary. Accordingly, the soul must be properly disposed to receive the grace contained in the sacrament. Many who come to us for help, for example, attend Mass and receive Communion while

---

[261] *CCC* 2000.

[262] Hardon, *Modern Catholic Dictionary*, 11.

[263] *CCC* 2000.

[264] Council of Trent, Sess. VI, 1605-1608. See also Saint Thomas Aquinas, *Summa Theologica* III q. 68, art. 8.

[265] Hardon, *Modern Catholic Dictionary*, 201. See also *CCC* 1128.

having unconfessed mortal sin on the soul. Attack from a different direction. First, get sacramentally reconciled through confession before expecting true liberation. This will release the stone—and with lethal accuracy.

Not by Sword or Spear: Baptism and Confirmation

David's last words to Goliath before racing to meet him were a reminder to all present, "It is not by sword or spear that the Lord saves. For the battle belongs to the Lord, who shall deliver you into our hands" (1 Sm 17:47). You stepped onto the battlefield when you were baptized. Equipped to win "the Lord's battle," however, you are not alone. That David said God has delivered Goliath not into *his* but into *our* hands suggests that he is fighting for more than just himself. Even rangers fight as part of a greater force. When you were baptized, you were oriented to Christ through the Church, the Mystical Body. For Saint Augustine, the Head and members inseparably form the *Totus Christus*, or the Whole Christ. Your fight, therefore, has an ecclesial element. As David did battle as part of the people of God, so also you do as a member of the Church. This means that your union with Christ as *capax Dei* unites you not just to Christ but also to His Body, the Church. Witnesses at Baptism, therefore, should see themselves in a combat role as part of the Church Militant. By their words of rejecting Satan on behalf of the child, the witnesses are saying, "Hear this Satan, this is our lamb, and if you mess with this lamb, we are coming after you!"

Besides now fighting as a member of Christ's Body, another central feature of liberation is recognizing the reality of God's indwelling presence in the soul and your identity as a child of God. As Saint John writes, "See what love the Father has bestowed on us that we may be called children of God. Yet so we are" (1 Jn 3:1). Saint Paul says that God "saved us through the bath of rebirth and renewal by the Holy Spirit" (Ti 3:5).[266] Saint Peter echoes this when he says, "Baptism . . . saves you now. It is not a removal of dirt from the body but an appeal to God for a clear conscience, through the resurrection of Jesus Christ" (1 Pt 3:21). The *Catechism* affirms, "The two principal effects are purification from sins and a new birth in the Holy Spirit," and "through the Holy Spirit, baptism is a bath that purifies, justifies and sanctifies," which gives the Christian the "hope of resurrection."[267]

You were presented with a white garment at baptism to symbolize your new purity of soul. When you were baptized, an ontological change (that is, at the level of being) took place that is recognizable in the spiritual world. The demon sees that indelible mark of Jesus Christ in your soul (and makes note of, moreover, any actions contrary to that mark). You now belong to God's army, and you wear His uniform. Like a ranger who wears camouflage to blend into his surroundings, wear the uniform of Christ boldly. Hear the words of Saint Paul: "For all of you who were baptized into Christ have clothed yourselves with Christ" (Gal 3:27). Your camouflage is all white, symbolic of the purity of a soul restored in grace. And like a ranger, seek cover. Do not stand in the open, but "kneel down" in prayer and "hide behind a tree," which is the cross of Jesus Christ.

Recall how David chose stones that were smoothed in running water to increase their accuracy. The Fathers of the Church saw this as an allusion to the lustral waters of Baptism for the Christian. One of the rules of engagement in the spiritual life—something the enemy does not want you to know—is the authority of the baptized Christian over the evil one. Baptism is where you were truly "born again" because God took up residence in your soul. With this indwelling of God comes the power over the demons in relationship to yourself, your family, and temporal goods (cf. authority section, below). Sin both damages that relationship and compromises your authority over demons. A polished stone is more accurate—and lethal.

---

[266] See *CCC* 1215.
[267] *CCC* 1262, 1227, 1274.

The battle began in the original Garden, where our first parents committed the original sin by giving into the temptation of the serpent and eating from the "tree in the middle of the garden" from which they were commanded not to eat (Gn 3:1–7). This *original sin* was a "disobedience toward God and a lack of trust in his goodness"[268] and left humankind in a state of privation of our primordial state, which was a "state of holiness." Thus, while "man was destined to be fully divinized by God and glory," the first couple gave into the seduction of the devil.[269] This original disobedience also introduced disorder, and rebellion now entered the human family, a generational sin. Just as Adam and Eve suffered the effect of sin in the form of curses that befell them because of their disobedience (cf. Gn 3:16–18), so also our sins have lingering effects on us and our families.

Thus, we say that the demon enters through sin but holds through heresy. Saint Bonaventure taught that Baptism "releases" the neophyte "from the servitude of the devil and the power of the prince of darkness." This occurs through the exorcism contained in the ritual which, he says, "expunge[s] the opposing power." This "expunging," however, is also from "the darkness of error." This means the baptized must be taught the truths of the Faith "lest the sacrament of baptism be impeded by a human defect."[270] Thus, to realize the effects of Baptism, you must remedy all defects and conform yourself to the truth in thought, word, and deed.

The demons, recall, only work in the objective. They constantly militate against this ontological reality imparted in Baptism. Our vulnerability lies in the fact that although Baptism restores the likeness of God to the soul, the disordered inclination towards sin, called concupiscence, still remains.[271] Thus, I wrote elsewhere, "Baptism does not, however, restore the preternatural gifts lost by the sin of our first parents—

---

[268] *CCC* 397.
[269] *CCC* 398.
[270] Saint Bonaventure, *Breviloquium*, 193–94.
[271] See *CCC* 1264.

freedom from ignorance, freedom from the inordinate inclinations of the passions, and freedom from suffering and death. That is, while Baptism restores us to life with God, it does not abolish the frailty and weakness of our human nature, nor our inclination to sin."[272]

The demon attempts to counteract the effects of Baptism by leading you into sin and robbing you of eternal life. This single combat, like David meeting Goliath in the open field, means the demon's goal is to take you, and your family, to hell. We should find encouragement, however, because "no sin can erase this mark, even if sin prevents Baptism from bearing the fruits of salvation."[273] To do so, you must first arm your sling.

The sling is like Baptism and the stone is like *Confirmation*. The one makes possible the other, and the two together enable you to fight against evil with the confidence of David. According to the *Catechism*, Confirmation "brings an increase and deepening of baptismal grace" and "completes" Baptism by imprinting "on the soul an indelible spiritual mark."[274] This mark "is the sign that Jesus Christ has marked a Christian with the seal of his Spirit by clothing him with power from on high so that he may be his witness."[275] This means having the special grace of courage in the face of suffering and hardship for the name of Christ.

Our fallen human nature needs the spiritual help both to live the truth and to proclaim the Gospel in the face of trials and opposition. In the Saint Andrew Missal, Dom Gaspar Lefebvre uses militaristic imagery to describe the effects of Confirmation on the Christian. Namely, this sacrament "makes the Christian a soldier, and marks him with a new character which is, as it were, the military credentials of the souls in perpetual warfare with God's enemies."[276] At Baptism, God gives us our armor. At Confirmation, He gives us even more spiritual weap-

---

[272] Liber Christo, "Companion Guide," 32.

[273] *CCC* 1272.

[274] *CCC* 1303.

[275] *CCC* 1304.

[276] Lefebvre, *St. Andrew Missal*, 1867.

ons: the gifts of the Holy Spirit. These "military credentials" and "mark of the King" continue after death. Saint Thomas notes how this mark/character remains forever, "as the status of a solider remains after the victory, to the glory of the conquerors and the shame of the conquered."[277]

Saint Bonaventure uses similar language in stating that through Confirmation, "a person is strengthened to be *a fighter for Christ*, to confess his name courageously and publicly."[278] Specifically, he states that the effect of this sacrament means that "a person shall be, as it were, a true fighter anointed for battle; a strong soldier bearing the symbol of his King on his forehead and the triumphal standard of His cross with which he is prepared to penetrate the mighty strongholds of the enemy."[279] In fact, this Doctor of the Church likens the oils used in Confirmation as the oils used to "rub a true wrestler before the bout," as was custom in ancient combat sports. Even today boxers use Vaseline to protect their faces from their opponent's blows. Confirmation is the sacramental equivalent of combat sports in that it strengthens us for battle. For this reason, in the old Rite of Confirmation after the bishop anoints the forehead, he would lightly slap the *confirmand*, a gesture showing the need for courage henceforth in the spiritual life in both defending and spreading the Faith. As the boxing referee tells the fighters before they engage, "Defend yourself at all times!"

Catholic parents frequently come to the local church seeking help for an afflicted child. The demon tries to separate the child from his parents (and their authority over the demon), which renders the child acutely vulnerable to temptation. Once separated from the parents through rebellion, the child now becomes more isolated (or even tempted to same-sex and suicidal ideation) in the months leading up to Confirmation, especially if there are familial curses present. Simply stated, the demon knows what Catholics have understood about

---

[277] Lefebvre, 1876.
[278] Saint Bonaventure, *Breviloquium*, 195.
[279] Saint Bonaventure, 196.

the effects of Confirmation. He does not want another "true fighter and strong soldier for Christ" to be indelibly marked and sent onto the battlefield.

The bishop confirms with the words, "Be sealed with the gift of the Holy Spirit." Now is the time to open the gift. The devil seeks to keep you from understanding and accepting your true identity. He also tries to block the new fighter and soldier of Christ from using this "power from on high" and "special strength of the Holy Spirit" because these enable the confirmed Christian to militate more fiercely and effectively in the field of battle. Like David, you have the sling (Baptism) and the stone (Confirmation). Now you must arm the weapon with faith. Hold these truths firmly in mind as you spin the sling over your head and take aim.

Incendiary Weapons: Holy Eucharist, Holy Orders, and a Theology of Sacrifice

The use of fire as a weapon is ancient, and an *incendiary weapon* refers to anything utilized to ignite fires in battle. Archers would use pitch (a flammable tar resin) on the end of their arrows to set them aflame before launching at the opposing forces, or as part of sieging a fortification. Saint Paul alludes to this when he instructs that "in all circumstances" the Christian soldier should "hold faith as a shield, to quench all the flaming arrows of the evil one" (Eph 6:16). By the sixth century AD, the flaming arrow developed into a weapon used in naval battles, which projected a napalm-type substance in bursts of fire to burn enemy ships. Historians refer to this primitive flamethrower as "Greek fire" or "wild fire." In the history of combat, incendiary devices are considered *combat multipliers*.

A combat multiplier is anything which adds to the combat effectiveness of the ground force. Sacrifice is a spiritual incendiary weapon that greatly enhances the effectiveness of one's prayers. The religious system of ancient Israel was built upon various sacrificial offerings; the primary one was the *olah*, or burnt offering. The Hebrew *olah* means "that which rises or goes up," and the priest would first lay hands on the sacrificial victim, sacrifice the animal, pour its blood upon the altar, and then burn the animal in a fire which consumes it completely (see Lv 1.17). In the ancient mindset, the blood represented the life-force of the animal and the smoke of the holocaust rose like incense to heaven—both actions in atonement for the sins of the people. Thus, "the priest shall then burn the whole offering on the altar as a holocaust, a sweet-smelling oblation to the Lord" (Lv 1:9). Saint Paul links this to Christ when he said that "Christ loved us and handed himself over for us as a sacrificial offering to God for a fragrant aroma" (Eph 5:2).

Fire purifies and blood atones for sins. The author of Hebrews writes, "According to the law almost everything is purified by blood, and without the shedding of blood there is no forgiveness" (Heb 9:22). He is referring to the sacrificial cult of ancient Israel by which animal sacrifice was used for expiatory (the remission of sins) and unitive (all the people were united under the same law and cult) purposes. In the new dispensation, the unbloody representation of the sacrifice of Christ on Calvary replaces the bloody sacrifices of the old sacrificial system of the Levitical priesthood. Thus, rather than making daily and annual bloody sacrifices of animals, Jesus Christ "offered himself once to take away the sins of many" (Heb 9:28) and this He did "once for all" (Heb 9:26). His sacrifice is eternal, and by His perfect obedience, He "offered one single sacrifice for sins, and has taken his place forever at the right hand of God (Heb 10:2–13).

Saint John recounts in Revelation that Jesus is "the lamb who was slain" (Rv 5:6), an allusion to the new Passover Lamb of God. As the Council of Trent affirmed against the errors of the Reformers, Jesus Christ offered Himself "on the altar of the cross [to] God the Father" for our eternal redemption. This self-offering is an ongoing reality continued to this day through the ministerial priesthood. As the council affirms: "Declaring Himself constituted a priest forever, according to the order of Melchizedek, He offered up to God the Father His own body and blood under the species of bread and wine; and, under the symbols of those same things, He delivered (His own body and blood) to be received by His apostles, whom He then constituted priests of the New Testament; and by those words, 'Do this in commemoration of me,' He commanded them and their successors in the priesthood, to offer (them); even as the Catholic Church has always understood and taught."[280]

Thus, His death did not end the sacrificial system and the priesthood but rather transformed it. Jesus left "to His own beloved Spouse the Church, a visible sacrifice" which is to "be applied to the remission of those sins which we daily commit."[281] That "visible sacrifice" is the Holy Eucharist and is central to the Catholic faith. The "new priesthood" is now conferred to the apostles, and through them to their successor-bishops. Every validly ordained Catholic priest, therefore, shares in this reality. As the Second Vatican Council states, priests are "made sharers in a special way in Christ's priesthood" whose every action is "bound up with the Eucharist and directed toward it."[282]

Saint Bonaventure cites Peter Lombard stating the uniqueness of the priesthood: "[holy] orders is a certain sign by which spiritual power is given through ordination." Thus, the "one ordained is completely set aside for the service of God" and has a unique orientation to "the restorative Principle, namely, the incarnate Word." Christ Himself "instituted the remedies of the sacraments" which the priest administers and brings forth the spiritual powers contained within.[283]

The essence of priesthood, moreover, is to offer sacrifices in union with Christ who is "priest, victim, and altar of sacrifice,"

---

[280] Council of Trent, Sess. XII.
[281] Council of Trent, Sess. XII. The Second Vatican Council echoes Trent: "The liturgy, then, is rightly seen as an exercise of the priestly office of Jesus Christ." *Sacrosanctum Concilium*, no. 7.
[282] *Presbyterorum Ordinis*, 5.
[283] Saint Bonaventure, *Breviloquium*, 208.

as is prayed in the Good Friday Canon of the Holy Mass.[284] One of the Scriptures read at priestly ordination is: "you are a priest forever, according to the order of Melchizedek" (Heb 7:17; Ps 110:4). Like the seal of Baptism that marks an ontological change in the soul of the baptized, so also the soul of a priest is indelibly marked and ontologically changed. Now conformed to Christ to dispense "spiritual power," the priest has a unique jurisdictional authority over demons. Just as the old sacrificial cult has expiative and unitive purposes, so now does the new sacrifice because Christ "did not come to abolish the law but to fulfill it" (Mt 5:17). Thus, the Council of Trent affirms that Jesus constituted the apostles as "priests of the New Testament" who will continue to offer an unbloody re-presentation of Christ's sacrifice on Calvary. The priest not only acts *in the person of Christ* but also stands as *another Christ*.[285] This sacrificial theology imbues every aspect of the ministerial priesthood. The priest has a unique, ontological (that is, at the level of being through the sacramental grace of Holy Orders) orientation to Christ. His duty is to offer sacrifice.

Saint Paul also applies the sacrificial theology of "aroma" to every Christian in stating that "we are the aroma of Christ for God" (2 Cor 2:14). While the priest shares in the *ministerial* priesthood of Jesus Christ, all of the baptized share in the *universal* priesthood of Jesus Christ. Although the commonality is the offering of sacrifices, the two differ both in essence and in degree. That is, all Christians are called to "fill up what is lacking in the afflictions of Christ on behalf of his body, which is the church" (Col 1:24) and to "offer your bodies as a living sacrifice, holy and pleasing to God, your spiritual worship" (Rom 12:1). As discussed above, this sacrificial

---

[284] For more on the sacrificial nature of the priesthood, see Hardon, *Modern Catholic Dictionary*, 339.

[285] According to Pope Saint John Paul II, "The priest offers the holy Sacrifice in persona Christi." Pope John Paul II, *Dominicae Cenae*, 8. In Augustinian terms of the Church as the *Totus Christus* comprised in the unicity of Head and Members, the priest can also be seen as *in persona Christi capitis* (or "in the person of Christ, the Head").

theology is what breaks the diabolic hold as it makes present and effective the perpetual sacrifice of Jesus Christ. While the priest offers an unbloody sacrifice for the remission of sins, we share in that by offering spiritual sacrifices for others in union with the sacrifice of the priest.

Thus, a sacrificial theology means that you must begin to offer your suffering in union with Christ's suffering. This can be either done in reparation for your sins or for the sins of others. As Saint Peter wrote, "Let yourselves be built into a spiritual house to be a holy priesthood to offer spiritual sacrifices acceptable to God through Jesus Christ" (1 Pt 2:5). According to Pope Pius XII, although Christ needs nothing from us, He nonetheless "require[s] the help of the Body." That is,

> He wills to be helped by the members of His Body in carrying out the work of redemption. That is not because He is indigent and weak, but rather because He has so willed it for the greater glory of His spotless Spouse. Dying on the Cross He left to His Church the immense treasury of the Redemption, towards which she contributed nothing. But when those graces come to be distributed, not only does He share this work of sanctification with His Church, but He wills that in some way it be due to her action. This is a deep mystery, and an inexhaustible subject of meditation, that the salvation of many depends on the prayers and voluntary penances which the members of the Mystical Body of Jesus Christ offer for this intention and on the cooperation of pastors of souls and of the faithful, especially of fathers and mothers of families, a cooperation which they must offer to our Divine Savior as though they were His associates.[286]

A sacrificial theology means that you must begin to see yourself as an "associate" of Christ in the distribution of the graces of redemption. You must learn to echo the words of Christ who said, "This is my body which I give up for you." That is,

---

[286] Pope Pius XII, *Mystici Corporis*, no. 44.

develop a Eucharistic spirituality that offers your body (all of your physical, emotional, spiritual, and psychological affliction) for Him and for others.

Saint Bonaventure states clearly that "in this sacrament not only is the true Body and Blood of Christ signified but it is actually contained under the double species, namely, bread and wine." That is, although "the sensible species remain" (what we see with our senses), nonetheless "each element is transubstantiated in substance into the body and blood of Jesus Christ."[287] According to the *Catechism*, this has various effects on the one who receives the Holy Eucharist in a worthy manner: a renewed intimacy with Jesus Christ,[288] it "preserves, increases, and renews the life of grace received at Baptism,"[289], it "cleans[es] our past sins and preserve[s] us from future sins,"[290] a "wiping away of venial sins,"[291] it "preserves us from future mortal sins,"[292] and increases our bond with the Church.[293] Thus, Saint Ignatius of Antioch, who was a first-generation disciple of the apostle John, calls the Eucharist "the medicine of immortality, the antidote against death, enabling us to live forever in Christ."[294]

How does this apply to spiritual warfare? From the earliest of times, the Eucharist received in a state of grace was seen as a weapon against the demon because it brings down heavenly fire. Saint John Chrysostom, roughly in the year AD 350, asked, "When you see the Lord immolated and lying on the altar, and the priest bent over that sacrifice praying, and all the people empurpled by that precious blood, can you think that you are still among men on earth? Or are you not lifted up to heaven?" He goes on to say, "If the devil merely sees you returning from the Master's banquet, he flees faster than any wind, as if he had

---

[287] Saint Bonaventure, *Breviloquium*, 197.
[288] See *CCC* 1301.
[289] *CCC* 1392.
[290] *CCC* 1393.
[291] *CCC* 1394.
[292] *CCC* 1395.
[293] See *CCC* 1396.
[294] Saint Ignatius of Antioch, *Letter to the Ephesians*, 20.2.

seen a lion breathing forth flames from his mouth. . . . If you show him a tongue stained with the precious blood, he will not be able to make a stand; if you show him your mouth all crimsoned and ruddy, cowardly beast that he is, he will run away."[295]

In military terms, this Doctor of the Church is saying that the Eucharist is an incendiary weapon. In recent times, rangers and marines effectively used modern versions of the flamethrower against machinegun nests and pillboxes, and to flush out a hiding enemy. The next time you receive the Holy Eucharist, picture yourself raining fire down from heaven upon the enemy of your soul. Breathe heavenly fire from your crimson lips that have kissed and consumed the body, blood, soul, and divinity of Our Lord.

Since the last thing the demon wants is to face a lion who breathes fire, he will try to get you to receive Communion in a state of mortal sin. He knows well the teaching of Saint Paul that anyone who receives Communion unworthily "eats and drinks judgment on himself" (1 Cor 12:28). That phrase of "liable to judgment" is used elsewhere to denote "guilty of murder" (cf. Mt 5:21; 26:66), of the death penalty. Make no mistake; you must be in a state of grace to receive Our Lord in the Holy Eucharist. This mortal sin, even if not done intentionally, should be confessed lest it attract the demon closer to you. When received worthily, however, you breathe fire in the spiritual realm. Bear these realities in mind as you prepare to receive Holy Communion.

Posting Sentinels: Penance and Reconciliation

Rogers instructed, "When we camp, half the party stays awake while the other half sleeps." These are the sentinels, or night guards, who keep vigil for enemy attacks. The best way to "post guards" around the soul is by going to confession. The *Catechism* states, "Individual and integral confession of grave sins followed

---

[295] Saint John Chrysostom, *On the Priesthood*, 3.4.

by absolution remains *the only ordinary means of reconciliation* with God and with the Church."[296] Accordingly, Penance is the gateway to the right reception of the other sacraments and is the first step toward opening the flow of grace into your life and your home—and providing guard against diabolic attack.

We confess our sins to a priest because Jesus gave jurisdictional authority over sins to the twelve apostles when He "breathed" on them and said, "Receive the Holy Spirit. Whose sins you forgive are forgiven them, and whose sin you retain are retained" (Jn 20:22–23). This echoes the special authority Jesus gave to Peter (symbolized by the "keys of the kingdom") with the command, "Whatever you bind on earth shall be bound in heaven and whatever you loose on earth shall be loosed in heaven" (Mt 16:18–19). The *Catechism* affirms, "Reconciliation with the Church is inseparable from reconciliation with God."[297] Accordingly, Saint Bonaventure said that "man is absolved from sin . . . through the medium of the priestly key" and "the jurisdiction" over sin given specifically to the local bishop.[298] This jurisdictional authority is shared with the priest who hears your confession, who receives the "power of absolution . . . from the bishop as the spouse of the Church."

Most people seeking our help from evil spirits are in mortal sin. That is, although their soul bears the mark of Jesus Christ from Baptism, they have long given themselves over to the demon through grave and habitual sinful behavior. Mortal sin destroys the life of God in the soul.[299] Those who have committed grave sins have a "privation of sanctifying grace" which "causes exclusion from Christ's kingdom and the eternal death of hell."[300] *This is the "end game" for the demon: to lead you to mortal sin; deprive you of heaven; and take you to hell.* Although uncommon, one mortal sin is sufficient to open the soul to diabolic possession.

---

[296] *CCC* 1497.
[297] *CCC* 1445.
[298] Saint Bonaventure, *Breviloquium*, 201.
[299] See *CCC* 1855.
[300] *CCC* 1861.

Because sin provides an entryway for the evil one, sacramental confession is essential to victory and freedom in Christ. Confession also systematically removes the demon's claims against you. According to *Catechism*: "Christ instituted the sacrament of Penance for all sinful members of his Church: above all for those who, since Baptism, have fallen into grave sin, and have thus lost their baptismal grace and wounded ecclesial communion. It is to them that the sacrament of Penance offers a new possibility to convert and to recover the grace of justification."[301]

Thus, I assert that "sacramental confession and deliverance, moreover, compenetrate in the pastoral practice of the Church" who has been charged with the "ministry of reconciliation" (2 Cor 5:18–21).[302] While all sin disfigures the soul, mortal sin removes the ability to merit supernatural grace entirely.

Many spiritually afflicted people contact the local church seeking an exorcism. What they really need is a priest to hear their confession so they can return to the life of grace. The demon has little sway over the person who possesses holiness in thought, word, and deed. Father Amorth said that "one good confession is worth a hundred exorcisms." He affirmed that "the best exorcism is confession" and "is the most direct means to fight Satan because it is the sacrament that tears souls from the demon's grasp, strengthens against sin, unites us more closely to God, and helps to conform our souls increasingly to the divine will. I advise frequent confession, possibly weekly, to all victims of evil activities."[303]

---

[301] *CCC* 1446.

[302] Liber Christo, "Companion Guide," 25. As stated by the USCCB: "Jesus entrusted the *ministry of reconciliation* to the Church (2 Cor 5:18–21). The Sacrament of Penance is God's gift to us so that any sin committed after Baptism can be forgiven. In confession we have the opportunity to repent and recover the *grace of friendship with God*. It is a holy moment in which we place ourselves in his presence and honestly acknowledge our sins, especially mortal sins. With absolution, we are *reconciled to God and the Church*. The sacrament helps us stay close to the truth that we cannot live without God." USCCB, *Catholic Catechism*, 242.

[303] Amorth, *An Exorcist: More Stories*, 195.

"Confession," therefore, "is a *sacrament* where special graces are conferred, while exorcism is a *sacramental*, that is, part of the Church's liturgical prayer."[304] For those engaged in a spiritual battle, weekly confession will help keep a sharp edge on your spiritual "hatchet."

Each sacrament brings forth the reality that it signifies. Saint Bonaventure gives the "integral parts of this sacrament" on the side of the penitent as:

1.   Contrition in the soul
2.   Oral confession of sins
3.   Actual satisfaction

"Out of these," he says, "penance is integrated when the sinner, after having perpetuated mortal sin, deserves the same by deed, accused himself by word, and detests his sin within his soul, proposing never to repeat the sin."[305] That is, "since one sins against God with delight, consent, and perpetration, namely, in the heart, mouth, and deed," he says, our reconciliation must also involve thought (contrition), word (confession of sins), and deed (making satisfaction to God).

Saint Bonaventure calls the sacrament of Penance "the second plank after the shipwreck by which he who has been wrecked through mortal sin can return as long as he is in the present life, when and as often as he wished to invoke divine mercy."[306] We refer to this as "the *de profundis* privilege" from the first words of Psalm 130, which is a prayer for pardon and mercy:

Out of the depths (*de profundis*) I call to you, LORD;
    Lord, hear my cry!
May your ears be attentive
    to my cry for mercy.
If you, LORD, keep account of sins,
    Lord, who can stand?

---

[304] Liber Christo, "Companion Guide," 35.
[305] Saint Bonaventure, *Breviloquium*, 201. See also *CCC* 1490–91.
[306] Saint Bonaventure, *Breviloquium*, 201.

But with you is forgiveness
>and so you are revered.
I wait for the LORD,
>my soul waits
>and I hope for his word.
My soul looks for the Lord,
>more than sentinels for daybreak.
More than sentinels for daybreak,
>let Israel hope in the LORD,
For with the LORD is mercy,
>with him is plenteous redemption,
And he will redeem Israel
>from all its sins. (Ps 130)

Like Goliath, who used threats of violence to discourage anyone from accepting his challenge, the demon will try to discourage you from invoking the *de profundis* privilege, reaching for "the second plank" and sacramentally confessing your sins. The "demon Goliath" will incite you to despair for what you have done or has happened to you. Ignore it! Be like David and trust in the Lord. This stone will pass through the helmet and penetrate the head of your accuser if you have the courage to launch it. Additionally, the demon will attempt to block you from recalling specific sins, especially those beneath which he hides and holds, so post sentries and stay alert. In a later section, we will go into further detail on the mechanics of a good confession.

The First Target of Opportunity: Holy Matrimony

In the original garden, God observed that "it is not good for man to be alone," so he made "a suitable partner for him" (Gn 2:18). His first command to Adam and Eve, moreover, was that they "be fruitful and multiply," giving them "dominion" over the earth (Gn 1:28). Christian marriage, then, is ordered towards two principal ends—namely, the *unitive* and the *procreative*, what the *Catechism* affirms as "the good of the spouses and the procreation and education of offspring."[307] Thus, the graces of this sacrament aid the couple in "welcoming and educating their children" as well as perfecting their love for one another by "strengthening their indissoluble unity."[308] By holding together these twofold ends, moreover, the goal of a sacramental marriage is to help each grow in holiness and get each other to heaven.

Matrimony is like the Holy Eucharist in that marriage is both a sacrifice and a sacrament. In fact, Dom Lefebvre calls marriage "a double sacrifice" because in this sacrament are "two chalices" of suffering which correspond to the two ends of marriage. One chalice (*unitive*), he writes, is the "unselfish affection . . . unwearying devotion [and] generosity on both sides." The other chalice (*procreative*) contains the "pains and sufferings of a whole existence passed together . . . the sorrows and cares of father and mother" which "the bridal pair" should together "offer to God."[309] "Moreover," he says, "the Church counsels the bride and bridegroom to offer their cup of gold all full of the blood, we may say, of their soul, in union with the offering of the golden chalice filled with the Blood of Jesus, from which they derive all strength and grace." Thus, like an incendiary weapon, Catholic couples have a combat multiplier when they offer their sufferings and trials for each other and their children.

The devil always looks for what military tacticians call a *target of opportunity*, which is an unplanned, but opportune target that arises suddenly and unexpectedly in the course of combat operations. Since the sin of the first couple, the demon looks to marriage for any target of opportunity to exploit. Once Adam and Eve fell, marriage "has always been threatened by discord, a spirit of domination, infidelity, jealousy, and the conflicts that can escalate into hatred and

---

[307] *CCC* 1601.
[308] *CCC* 1641.
[309] Lefebvre, *St. Andrew Missal*, 1876.

separation."[310] These things draw the demon's attention to the marriage and home. Dominion becomes domination, therefore, when Christ is not the *spiritual and sacramental* center of the marriage.

The demon specifically hates what the unity of Christian marriage symbolizes. As the Nuptial Blessing states, "God has . . . consecrated the union of spouses by a mystery so excellent that the nuptial bond is the figure of the sacred union of Christ with His Church."[311] Because of the sublime dignity of marriage as reflecting the "nuptial bond" between Christ and the Church, the demon works tirelessly against marriage. Thus, the demon looks for every opportunity to block the graces of Matrimony from flowing into the family.

Venerable Sister Lúcia de Jesus Rosa dos Santos, OCD, one of the visionaries of Fatima, is reported to have said that "the final battle between the Lord and the reign of Satan will be about marriage and the family." She calls this "the decisive issue" in the struggle against evil.[312] In military parlance, marriage and family is where "decisive battle"—a strategic engagement which determines the outcome of the war—takes place. To achieve his end, the demon will often attack the perception of one's spouse and prod each toward unforgiveness. When you fight with your spouse (especially in front of your children), you offer the demon a clear target. To combat this, a couple must regularly pray with and for each other. Any unforgiveness, quarrelling, brooding over injury, and the like also acts to block the flow of sacramental grace.

When serious sin is present in a home, the effects are not just upon the individual who perpetrated it. The demonic entity requisite with that sin becomes present to the marriage and to the entire home. For example, when a father

---

[310] *CCC* 1606.

[311] Lefebvre, *St. Andrew Missal*, 1877.

[312] In addition, she stated that "this is the decisive issue" and "anyone who works for the sanctity of marriage and the family will always be fought and opposed in every way. Nonetheless, she added, "Don't be afraid . . . Our Lady has already crushed its head." *Catholic News Agency*, "Fatima Visionary," 3.

views pornography, that spirit is now in the house. While the father's job is to keep the family spiritually and physically pure, the lustful man lowers the familial shield. When he allows impurity in, the entire family is now vulnerable to spirits of lust, fornication, infidelity, et cetera. The tempter will often suggest to the father that he should hide the impurity and tell no one of it. Meanwhile, the demon begins to work on the children now unprotected by the father. The father must regain purity and chastity by bringing this sin into the light and raise his shield over the family.

The contracepting couple presents another target for the enemy to exploit. Pope Saint Paul VI defines contraception as "any action which, either in anticipation of the conjugal act [sexual intercourse], or in its accomplishment, or in the development of its natural consequences, proposes, whether as an end or as a means, to render procreation impossible."[313] Such actions include the pill, condoms and other barrier methods, withdrawal (or, *coitus interruptus*, cf. Gn 38:6–10), spermicides, and all other methods, including misuse of Natural Family Planning (NFP). This includes the self-mutilation of sterilization (vasectomy or tubal ligations). The couple who contracepts denies this moral teaching in the Church which protects the marriage and, as a consequence, expose themselves to the diabolic. In our prudential experience, sexual deviancy is often present in cases of diabolic affliction.

As the first couple was fashioned "in the image and likeness" of God (Gn 1:26), so now the demon militates to refashion the home through disorder and disunity by closing off the openness to life. According to the 1917 Code Canon Law (no. 1013), "the primary end of marriage is the procreation and education of children; its secondary end is the mutual help and the allaying of concupiscence." The new code echoes this in defining marriage as being "ordered to the good of the spouses and the procreation and education of children."[314] The demon's attack

---

[313] Pope Paul VI, *Humanae Vitae*, no. 14.

[314] *Code of Canon Law*, no. 1055. For a full and comparative commentary, see Beal, ed. *New Commentary*, 124–47.

is always to disrupt the ordering of these two ends of marriage, specifically through sexual deviancy. A recent Pew Research survey, for example, reveals the modern diminution of marriage through the widespread acceptance of artificial means of contraception among Catholics. In this study, only 8 percent of Catholics, and 13 percent who attend Mass every Sunday, say that contraception is morally wrong. Additionally, 41 percent think it is morally acceptable and 45 percent do not even think it is a moral issue at all.[315] Part of the sacrificial nature of marriage, however, is the cross of living the Church's moral teaching on sexuality, to include the openness to life.

The demon's plan is working in this decisive battle in part due to sexual immorality. Saint Alphonsus Liguori refers to impurity and sexual sins as "hell's widest gate" because "it is by this gate that the greater number of the damned enter." His words are sobering:

> Some will say that it is a trifling sin. Is it a trifling sin? It is a mortal sin. St. Antoninus writes that such is the nauseousness of this sin that the devils themselves cannot endure it. Moreover, the Doctors of the Church say that certain demons, who have been superior to the rest, remembering their ancient dignity, disdain tempting to so loathsome a sin. Consider then how disgusting he must be to God, [when the impure person], like a dog, is ever returning to his vomit, or wallowing like a pig in the stinking mire of this accursed vice (2 Pet 2.22).

Recalling that the great flood was the result of the sexual immorality of Sodom and Gomorrah (see Gn 18–19), Saint Alphonsus reminds us that "the most horrible chastisements with which God has ever visited the earth have been drawn down by this vice." He notes that impurity "is a sin which God punishes, not only in the other life, but in this also."[316]

---

[315] Pew Research, "Very Few Americans."
[316] Saint Alphonsus Liguori, *Six Discourses*, 33.

Thus, the enemy seeks to walk you down this path and into an ambush which traps not only you but your family.

As Hebrews says very clearly, "Let marriage be honored among all and the marriage bed be kept undefiled, for God will judge the immoral and the adulterers" (Heb 13:4). The *Catechism* also lists the following as offenses against chastity: lust, masturbation, fornication, pornography, prostitution, and rape.[317] In addition, it describes homosexuality as a "grave depravity" and "intrinsically disordered."[318] Some couples are united only civilly and not sacramentally married in the Church. The *Catechism* notes such unions (sometimes referred to as "irregular marriages") are gravely sinful. It also defines fornication as the "carnal union between an unmarried man and an unmarried woman."[319] Many couples simply cohabitate. In our prudential experience, many who suffer spiritual affliction have some of these unconfessed sins.

We also have seen a pattern where a cohabiting couple presents a child for a sacrament only to find the child become the target of diabolic affliction. At times, a generational curse is operant as well. Even after the reception of the sacrament, the child may still be vulnerable because the parents are not in a state of grace since they are not married in the Church. The target of the enemy is always the marriage, but specifically so that the demon can gain access to the children. In our experience, moreover, we have discovered that the demon's strategy is to fracture the marriage by dividing the couple, making the children acutely vulnerable. The sacraments and the state of grace, recall from the discussion above, are a shield against evil. When a couple practices grave sin together, they enable the enemy to set his sights on the children before they attain spiritual and sacramental maturity. This is to say, if you will not clean up your life for your own or your spouse's sake, do it for the sake of your children.

---

[317] See *CCC* 2351–56.
[318] *CCC* 2357–59.
[319] *CCC* 2353.

If the demon manifests in a family, however, it is because God is forcing him to show himself for a greater salvific reason. In our experience, when a child is afflicted, it is often a wake-up call by God for the parents to convert more deeply and return to Church. Living out the Church's teachings helps restore the flow of grace into the family. In such cases of fornication, the couple should confess their sin, practice a Josephite marriage (named after Saint Joseph who lived as "brother and sister" with the Virgin Mary), and see their parish priest for sacramental preparation. The suffering they endure in a renewed state of grace will help restore the flow of grace to the home.

Another common situation is a "mixed" marriage, where a Catholic person marries a non-Catholic (or a "disparity of cult," where a Catholic marries a non-Christian). The *Catechism* notes the inherent difficulties of such unions and how these couples "risk experiencing the tragedy of Christian disunity even in the heart of their own home." This is because "differences about faith and the very notion of marriage, but also different religious mentalities, can become sources of tension in marriage, especially with regards to the education of children." As a result, the "temptation to religious indifference can then arise."[320] That is, such marriages have an inherent vulnerability by nature of the disparity in belief structures. In such cases, the Catholic should offer his suffering for the conversion of the spouse.

Couples should pray with and for each other every day. This includes simple things like the **Perimeter Prayer**:

Lord Jesus Christ, in thy love and mercy establish a perimeter of protection around N. and myself and all our loved ones, those who pray for us and their loved ones. May the Holy Angels guard him/her/us and all our possessions, establishing a perimeter of protection around N., rendering him/her/us immune from any kind of demonic influence. I ask that no demonic bondage, door, demonic entity, portal, astral projection, or disembodied spirit may enter the space

---

[320] *CCC* 1634.

of 100 yards in all directions of him/her/us. I ask that any demons within this vicinity or any that should try to enter here be rendered deaf, dumb, and blind; that Thou would strip them of all weapons, armor, power, illusions, and authority; that Thou would bind, rebuke and disable them from communicating or interacting with each other in any way. Remove them, sending them directly to the foot of Thy Cross. Jesus, Son of the Most High, I ask this in Thy Glorious and Most Holy Name. Amen.

Another simple, but effective, prayer is called the **Divine Praises**. This prayer was written to be prayed as reparation for the sins of blasphemy and the use of profane language. A couple can pray this together as their final prayer before falling asleep. This prayer projects the praise of Jesus and Mary into the cosmos as the last act of the day.

Blessed be God.
Blessed be His Holy Name.
Blessed be Jesus Christ, true God and true Man.
Blessed be the Name of Jesus.
Blessed be His Most Sacred Heart.
Blessed be His Most Precious Blood.
Blessed be Jesus in the Most Holy Sacrament of the Altar.
Blessed be the Holy Spirit, the Paraclete.
Blessed be the great Mother of God, Mary most Holy.
Blessed be her Holy and Immaculate Conception.
Blessed be her Glorious Assumption.
Blessed be the name of Mary, Virgin and Mother.
Blessed be St. Joseph, her most chaste spouse.
Blessed be God in His Angels and in His Saints. Amen.

May the heart of Jesus, in the Most Blessed Sacrament, be praised, adored, and loved with grateful affection, at every moment, in all the tabernacles of the world, even to the end of time. Amen.

Other prayers to pray for one another and your family can be found in the appendix.

From Slingstones to Milestones: The Sacraments and the Flow of Grace

1. How does the shield imagery help you? Where have you lowered your shield, and what was the result? How did you get it back up?

2. Why are the sacraments so important in the spiritual battle, and why does the demon militate against them?

3. How do you understand "capax Dei" as it relates to your core identity as a child of God?

4. When are these sanctifying graces given to us? When is actual grace given to us?

5. What is the "ontological" reality imparted in Baptism, and why does the demon militate against this reality?

6. What is "concupiscence," and why are we affected by it?

7. What is the most effective weapon in breaking the "diabolic matrix"?

8. What does the *Catechism* say is the purpose of special strength of the Holy Spirit received in Confirmation?

9. What are some specific features to the orders of the priest?

10. What did you learn from the section on Matrimony? How can you tighten the "perimeter" around your marriage?

LESSON NINE: MAKING A GOOD CONFESSION

Being afflicted by a demon can be seen as an avenue for grace, as God allows it for you and your family's purification and salvation. For this reason, we prefer to replace the phrase "spiritual attack" (which places the emphasis on the devil) with "spiritual formation" (which places the emphasis on identifying the obstacles which keep us from becoming holy). See your suffering as your own incendiary weapon and use it as a means to become holy and to rain down a holy fire of purifying grace into your family. In the language of Saint Paul, God sometimes allows a "momentary light affliction" so as to produce "an eternal weight of glory beyond comparison" in our lives (2 Cor 4:17–18). You are not under attack; you are experiencing spiritual formation. Now is not the time to lower your shield.

How did an ancient combatant lower his opponent's shield? Samuel tells us that Goliath had a spear that weighed "over six hundred shekels," or about fifteen pounds, and was likely two inches in diameter and twelve feet long (1 Sm 17:7). This weapon could be used for close fighting, but more commonly, it was launched as a missile weapon, a precursor to modern artillery or mortars. The Romans perfected this weapon (theirs was called a *pilum*) and would launch it before engaging the enemy hand-to-hand. The only way to defend oneself against this indirect fire was to hide behind one's shield. If thrown accurately, the *pilum* would embed into the shield, effectively disabling the combatant's defense. Imagine trying to hold up your shield with a twelve-foot-long shaft weighing about the same as a bowling ball embedded into it. The choice was either to fight with a lowered shield or sheath the sword and use your strength to hold up the shield. Neither option had a good outcome.

The *Catechism* states in no uncertain terms the "dramatic situation" in which we find ourselves. This is because "the whole world is in the power of the evil one [making] man's life a battle." This situation, however, is not new: "The whole of man's history has been the story of dour combat with the powers of evil, stretching, so our Lord tells us, from the very dawn of history until the last day. Finding himself in the midst of the battlefield man has to struggle to do what is right, and it is at great cost to himself, and aided by God's grace, that he succeeds in achieving his own inner integrity."[321]

---

[321] *CCC* 409.

Thus, Clement notes how the "stark language of spiritual combat used by the Church reminds us that we are members of the Church Militant who are engaged in the "dour combat" of spiritual warfare and not "spiritual negotiation." For this reason, he encourages you to "not be surprised" that you are "confronted with a Goliath of some sort standing before" you as you prepare to do your own dour combat with him in the confessional.[322] David did not engage in ecumenical dialogue with Goliath. He confronted him, even raced toward him. So, arm yourself and race him to the confessional.

The spiritual enemy knows that he must first get you to lower your shield before attacking. Your spiritual shield is the protection provided by the sacraments. As David wrote, "God is a shield above me" (Ps 7:11). This is your base armor. The enemy, meanwhile, will look for any opening in your armor. This means that we must take serious not only mortal sin but also the venial (or common) sins that make us vulnerable. In this section, we will show you how to keep your shield up by making a good confession.

Either Come Back With Your Shield or On It

In an ancient hand-to-hand battle, at some point in battle one side would sense that their defeat was near, and panic would quickly set in. Then, their ranks would break, and dropping their shields, they turned and ran (recall the *trópaion* discussion above). This, however, did not help many in their attempts to save their lives. In fact, it only increased their chances of dying an ignoble death. One mission of the mounted cavalry was to chase down the fleeing infantrymen, now entirely defenseless with backs turned, and cut them down with their longer sabers. For this reason, the Spartan wives were said to have encouraged their husbands as they went off to war: "Spartan, either come back with your shield or on it." That is, "if you return home without your shield, I will know that you

---

[322] Liber Christo, "Companion Guide," 11–12.

ran in battle. I would prefer that you die with honor and be carried back on top of your shield than to live with the shame of cowardice."

Like the *pilum* which lowers the shield to set up the sword, a common "one-two punch" that opens many people to heavy diabolic influence is the combination of violations of the first and sixth commandments. That is, a person participates in occult activity in some way while also practicing deviant sexual behavior. In addition, these grave sins are often committed to avoid the cross and suffering (going to a *curandero* for a love potion, or practicing yoga for infertility, etc.). Although a single mortal sin is sufficient to allow a soul to be possessed, this is very rare. When someone actively participates in grave evil, however, he discards his spiritual armor and becomes easy prey to the enemy's sword. For this reason, Penance is needed as it restores a pathway to true and lasting freedom.

In spiritual battle, mortal sin immediately lowers your shield, rendering you virtually defenseless on the battlefield. In the words of Saint John, "There is such a thing as deadly sin" (1 Jn 5:16). According to Father Hardon, a sin is called *mortal* (also used to describe this are *deadly*, *grave*, and *serious*) because "it destroys sanctifying grace and causes the supernatural death of the soul [and] deprives the sinner of a right to heaven."[323] As I explained what the *Catechism* (CCC 1857) states, "For a sin to be 'deadly' there is **grave matter**, **sufficient knowledge** and **willful consent**. If these conditions are not fulfilled, then a sin is venial. Either way, however, the demon will claim permissions to the soul and begin to torment where grave sins have been committed." That is, when the three conditions are met, mortal sin "causes a death blow to the life of God in the soul" which leaves it exposed.[324] As Saint Alphonsus writes concerning the sinner, "They know that God cannot remain with sin in the soul: and, in violating the divine commands, they feel that God must depart; and, by

---

[323] Hardon, *Modern Catholic Dictionary*, 362.
[324] Liber Christo, "Companion Guide," 89.

their acts they say to him: since you cannot remain any longer with us, depart farewell. *And through the very door by which God departs from the soul, the Devil enters to take possession of her.*"[325]

Thus, while venial sin defaces, or damages, the soul and offends God, mortal sin effaces, or erases, the soul of sanctifying grace, thereby destroying friendship with God. In battle terms, venial sins wound you and restrict your combat effectiveness, and mortal sins leave you lying dead on the battlefield.

And through the very door by which God departs from the soul, the devil enters to take possession of her. According to Saint Alphonsus, that door by which God entered the soul was Baptism: "When the priest baptizes an infant, he commands the demon to depart from the soul: 'Go out from him, unclean spirits, and make room for the Holy Ghost.' But when a Christian consents to mortal sin, he says to God: Depart from me; make room for the Devil, whom I wish to serve."[326]

Saint Alphonsus also draws imagery from Job to describe the stubbornness of the person who commits mortal sin: "He hath run against him with his neck raised up and is armed with a fat neck" (Job 15:26, DV). "The sinner," he says, "raises his neck" particularly when his pride swells up, and he runs to insult his God, and because he contends with a powerful antagonist, "he is armed with a fat neck." This "fat neck" is "the symbol of ignorance, of that ignorance which makes the sinner say: This is not a great sin; God is merciful; we are flesh; the Lord will have pity on us. O temerity! O illusion! which brings so many Christians to Hell." Saint Alphonsus concludes, "When the soul consents to mortal sin she ungratefully says to God: Depart from me. . . . Sinners, as St. Gregory observes, say the same, not in words, but by their conduct."[327] Thus, the *Catechism* teaches, "Unrepented [mortal sins] brings eternal death" and renders "eternal beatitude impossible."[328]

---

[325] Saint Alphonsus Liguori, *Sermons*, 69.
[326] Saint Alphonsus Liguori, 69
[327] Saint Alphonsus Liguori, 70.
[328] *CCC* 1875.

Little Sins: A Big Deal Often Overlooked

Before going to confession, remember that every sin is an offense to God, no matter how small. Therefore, you must confess and make satisfaction for all sins, but especially grave sins, so that you can return to the life of grace. Just as a soldier can hide behind a brick wall or a bush, the demon can obfuscate behind the smallest of disordered attachments. He can also block, obscure, or distort your memory of an event—anything he can to keep you from bringing the sin into the light. Accordingly, we recommend that as part of a thorough examination of conscience, you write down the sins you wish to confess. Since sin has the twofold effect of darkening the intellect and weakening the will, deliberate venial sin can blind you to mortal sin. It numbs you. Bear in mind also that the demon has access to our memory and can block the memory of those sins—even the common sins, so called—which empower him in your life.

When you commit a sin, therefore, you cannot claim that "the devil made me do it." If the devil is present to you, it is because somewhere along the way, you have denied your baptismal dignity and let the demon in through sinful patterns of thought, word, and deed. Thus, the "essence of liberation" can be described as "the soul as free to pursue God, its greatest Good." This means the soul "must first be free of sin, however, before it can be free of the demon. The first step in liberation is to stop the sin or cease the habitual mortal (and venial) sin. True liberation, therefore, is *freedom from* sin and the tyranny of the devil and *freedom for* union with God.[329] Liberation means breaking free from even the "common sins" because they "become big things" in spiritual combat. The demon will take any foothold you give him, however small.

As Dom Lefebvre counsels, "If you go to confession frequently, you will have little difficulty in discovering the sins you have committed." Thus, he cites the Council of Trent and says

---

[329] Liber Christo, "Companion Guide," 165.

that you should "tell your sins as they are in your mind, that is, as they appear to you according to your own feeling about them." To aid in examining your conscience, he suggests using the Ten Commandments or the capital sins, as we have listed here. He suggests also meditating on the *Confiteor* (which is part of the Liber Christo prayer regimen) because in that prayer, he says, "we call on the court of heaven to bear witness to our faults and implore them to come to our aid."[330] In the language of the Church, the penitent effectively says, "I accuse myself" of these offenses against God. Accuse yourself often and the accuser (see Rv 12:10) will have little left with which to accuse you.

The demon, however, will try to get you to *excuse*—rather than to *accuse*—yourself and hold back certain sins (which is, itself, a grave sin). Not only can the demon distort our memory of past sins, but he can also obscure his holding place in the soul (where he entered via sin and now from which he operates). As a result, our (distorted) memory of the events is often merely our most recent memory, and not the truth, of the events themselves. Accordingly, as you progress toward deeper interior freedom through a monastic discipline and the practice of mental prayer, you may have discovered a freeing up of such memories. You may also have a new clarity and a new perception of past sins and events. As part of your examination of conscience, then, consider the following:

- Has something ever happened to you after which you were never the same?
- What is your earliest sexual memory?
- Is there anyone in your life that you find it difficult to forgive?
- Are there any of the daily *Auxilium Christianorum* prayers—or times of the day or days of the week—that you find harder to pray?[331]

---

[330] Lefebvre, *St. Andrew Missal*, 1872–73.

[331] The *Auxilium Christianorum* (named after Mary's title of "Help of Christians") is an association of the faithful who pray for priests and lay associates working in the ministry of exorcism. The daily regimen of prayers is

- Are there any mysteries of the Rosary that are more difficult to pray than others?

By answering these questions, you can better identify any areas of unconfessed mortal sin, unforgiveness, and wounds to which the demon has access.

In addition, these will help you to track any interior movements in the soul as you grow in prayer. The little stirrings of interior resistance also help you identify obstacles to grace. The imposition of order assists in purifying the memory and re-ordering the spiritual faculties so that you can more clearly discern your thoughts from your emotions and your emotions from the diabolic projections into the imagination. Clement refers to these areas of vulnerability to diabolic projection as the "low spot in our wall." These "low spots" (picture a broken-down fence that various critters can now easily breach) are "defects in virtue or those areas of our lives we have not fully surrendered to the Lord." Thus, if virtue is a "defensive wall," then "the demon will attack at the point at which we are lacking in virtue. We must work, therefore, to build up the virtues in which we are weak, in order to defend ourselves against the demon."[332] For this reason, you must grow in mental prayer so you can repair the "wall" of the interior life. The more proficient you become in mental prayer, the less the demon can affect your interiority.

Saint James warns against sins of the tongue in saying, "From the same mouth come blessing and cursing" (Jas 3:10). The *Catechism* gives a valuable teaching on the importance of clean speech in a section called "Offenses Against the Truth."[333] As the demon is drawn to inconsistent behaviors, he is also attracted to the mouth that blesses and curses—that is, one

---

very efficacious in driving out demons, is part of a spiritual discipline, and provides protection for anyone engaging in the apostolate of deliverance. These prayers are part of the Liber Christo protocol as well. For information on how to become a member, see Ripperger, *Deliverance Prayers for Use by the Laity*, 89–90.

[332] Liber Christo, "Companion Guide," 167.

[333] See *CCC* 2475–87.

who professes belief in the living God while cursing his neighbor though detraction, gossip, and the like. Simply stated, are you who you say you are?

The impediment of unforgiveness is often seen in one's speech. The word *diaballos* means slanderer and divider, and we are like him when we do the same. According to the *Catechism*, we must respect the reputation of others and are guilty of sin when we injure others through both "attitude and word." A person is guilty of (1) *rash judgment* who, even tacitly, assumes as true, without sufficient foundation, the moral fault of a neighbor; (2) *detraction* who, without objectively valid reason, discloses another's faults and failings to persons who did not know them; (3) *calumny* who, by remarks contrary to the truth, harms the reputation of others and gives occasion for false judgments concerning them[334] The *Catechism* also warns against flattery, adulation, or complaisance, boasting or bragging, and lying.[335] It also emphasizes that "every offense committed against justice and truth entails the duty of reparation, even if its author has been forgiven." This includes any "offenses against another's reputation."[336]

To raise your shield for spiritual battle through sacramental confession means acts of faith and will—that is, to keep our shield up in defense and at the ready when the hand-to-hand begins. This is done through an examination of conscience. Accordingly, the *Catechism* instructs, "The reception of the Sacrament of Penance . . . ought to be prepared for by an examination of conscience made in the light of the Word of God. The passages best suited to this can be found in the moral catechesis of the Gospels and the apostolic Letters, such as the Sermon on the Mount and the apostolic teachings."[337] When we imbue our thoughts with images of Our Lord in Sacred Scripture, we develop the ability to judge more clearly the clean from the unclean.

---

[334] See *CCC* 2477.
[335] See *CCC* 2479, 2481, 2482.
[336] *CCC* 2487.
[337] *CCC* 1454.

In examining your conscience, "accuse yourself" not only of the big sins but also of the little sins which you are inclined to overlook. Like Rogers demanded of his men, "have your musket clean as a whistle, hatchet scoured" so that you are ready to march at a moment's notice. As you go through the following examination of conscience, recall that you should confess all mortal sins by name and number. In addition, "if you are not conscious of any mortal sins, you should confess venial sins, especially the predominant venial sins [to wit, the 'common sins'] with which you struggle." This is because "regular confession . . . helps to fight temptation and loosens the enemy's grip on the soul.[338] The *Catechism* states that "regular confession of our venial sins helps form our conscience, fight against evil tendencies, let ourselves be healed by Christ, and progress in the life of the Spirit."[339] As you work through this protocol and your memory grows in clarity, weekly confession can be quite fruitful.

Absolution and the Proper Disposition

Concerning confessing of all of one's sins in Penance, Jesus had stern words to Saint Faustina Kowalska. "If you hide your sins from the confessor," Jesus told her, "I will hide from you."[340] As the devil seeks to hold you in fear and shame, therefore, recall the words of Saint James who says that "mercy triumphs over justice" (Jas 2:13). To maximize the effects of the mercy contained in this sacrament, however, you must have the *proper disposition*, which includes (1) sufficient contrition for your sins and (2) the firm resolve not to commit them again. Thus, after you confess, you will make an Act of Contrition:

> O my God, I am heartily sorry for having offended Thee, and I detest all my sins because I dread the loss of Heaven and the pains of Hell; but most of all because they offend Thee, my God, Who art all good and deserving of all my love. I firmly

---

[338] Liber Christo, "Companion Guide," 89.
[339] *CCC* 1458.
[340] Kowalska, *Diary of Saint Maria Faustina Kowalska*, 71.

resolve, with the help of Thy grace, to confess my sins, to do
penance, and to amend my life. Amen.

According to the *Catechism,* "Contrition is 'sorrow of the soul
and detestation for the sin committed, together with the resolution not to sin again.'"[341] Therefore, accuse—not excuse—
yourself with heartfelt contrition and the commitment to sin
no more.

While these two elements mark a proper disposition
for absolution, Catholics often present themselves with an
improper disposition. As Clement notes, "a common *improper
disposition* is seen in a penitent who confesses a sin that they
have no intention of ceasing to commit, such as a couple who
is cohabitating outside the sacrament of Matrimony who have
no intention of remedying their irregular arrangement or cease
fornication. It is important, therefore, to be completely honest and thorough when confessing one's sins." Accordingly, he
soberly warns, "If a penitent goes into confession with three
mortal sins and purposely conceals one, he leaves the confessional with four mortal sins: the original three that were not
forgiven, plus an additional mortal sin of sacrilege for profaning the sacrament."[342] Thus, Dom Lefebvre succinctly defines
contrition as "a ready sorrow for our sins, because by them we
have offended so good a God, together with a firm purpose of
amendment."[343] The improper disposition lacks one or both of
these elements.

Part of the proper disposition and firm purpose of amendment is making satisfaction for sins which offend "so good
a God." Voluntary acts of penance assist in spiritual warfare
because, according to the *Catechism,* while "absolution takes
away sin . . . it does not remedy all the disorders sin has
caused."[344] Wherever there is disorder, there is the demon.
The disorder created by sin means that although communion
with God is restored by the sacramental forgiveness of sin,

---

[341] *CCC* 1451.
[342] Liber Christo, "Companion Guide," 110.
[343] Lefebvre, *Saint Andrew Missal,* 1873.
[344] *CCC* 1459.

nonetheless "the temporal punishment of sin remains."[345] The satisfaction for past sins, made by voluntary penances and offering of suffering, can be done either on earth or in purgatory. Thus, the more a person atones for past sins— also called expiation, making satisfaction for, or making amends—and grows in virtue, the more he limits the demon's ability to be active against the soul. Thus, the "Christian must strive to accept this temporal punishment of sin as a grace," as it purifies the faculties through virtue and restores friendship with God.[346]

Pope Saint John Paul II wrote, "It is suffering, more than anything else, which clears the way for the grace which transforms human souls."[347] You should hold nothing back, therefore, so that you can hear the words and experience the effects of the prayer of the Church through the ministry of the priest. The priest then prays the following prayer of absolution:[348]

> *May Almighty God have mercy on you, forgive you your sins, and bring you to life everlasting. Amen. May Almighty and Merciful God grant you forgiveness, absolution, and remission of your sins. Amen. May our Lord Jesus Christ absolve you; and by His authority I absolve you from every bond of excommunication (suspension) and interdict, so far as my power allows and your needs require. + Thereupon, I absolve you from your sins in the name of the Father, and of the Son, and of the Holy Ghost. Amen.*

And also:

> *May the passion of our Lord Jesus Christ, the merits of the blessed Virgin Mary and the saints, and all the good you do*

---

[345] *CCC* 1473.

[346] *CCC* 1473.

[347] Pope Saint John Paul II, *Salvifici Doloris*, no. 27.

[348] *CCC* 1449 gives the Ordinary Form: "God the Father of mercies, through the death and resurrection of His Son has reconciled the world to Himself and sent the Holy Spirit among us for the forgiveness of sins; through the ministry of the Church may God give you pardon and peace, and I absolve you from your sins in the name of the Father, and the Son, and the Holy Spirit. Amen."

and the suffering you endure, gain for you the remission of your sins, increase of grace, and the reward of everlasting life. Amen.

Absolution from sin is no small matter. As I wrote:

> In this sacrament, the properly disposed penitent receives "absolution." To "absolve" comes from the Latin *absolvo* which has a wide array of meaning, all of which flavor what happens when the priest prays the words of absolution ("I absolve you of your sins..."). *Absolvo* means to loosen, set free, detach, or untie; to dismiss by paying off; to release from a long journey, to dismiss or release, to free from; thus, to acquit or declare innocent, to bring to a conclusion, finish or complete; an unconditional release. Packed into this word uttered by the priest [*I absolve you from your sins*] is the very act of God who loosens the devil's hold over us through our sin, frees us from its effects, and declares us now innocent and released from the long journey of slavery to sin.[349]

Being in a state of grace is your shield and your armor against Goliath. Do not lower it. In the sacraments, we discover not only how He made us capable of receiving His divinity but that He also adopted us as His children, sons and daughters whom He feeds, heals, and nourishes. The demon seethes at this reality, so wear it well. Do whatever it takes to maintain a state of grace and live out your filial dignity. Now is the time to raise your shield, scour your hatchet, clean your musket, and end the long journey of slavery to sin.

Examining Your Conscience and Making a Thorough Confession

If sin is like lowering your shield, a good confession raises it back up. There are many ways to do an examination of

---

[349] Lewis, *An Elementary Latin Dictionary*, 11.

conscience in preparation for a good confession. Your parish priest will also be able to walk you through it, especially if you have not been to confession for many years. Father Ripperger has created the following checklist for preparing for sacramental confession, which follows the Ten Commandments and the Five Precepts of the Church.[350]

Sins Contrary to the First Commandment

I am the Lord thy God. Thou shall not have strange gods before me.

- Neglect of prayer
- Ingratitude toward God
- Spiritual sloth (having no interest in prayer, sacraments, living a spiritual life)
- Hatred of God or of the Catholic Church/ Christianity
- Tempting God (explicitly or implicitly—e.g., by exposing oneself to danger of soul, life, or health without grave cause)
- Not behaving reverently when in church (e.g., not genuflecting to the Blessed Sacrament when entering or leaving the church, etc.)
- Excessive attraction to things/creatures as more important than God (e.g., over-affection to animals, being a sports-fanatic, having movie star/music/tv idols, love for money, pleasure or power)
- Idolatry (worshiping false gods such as giving honor to a creature in place of God—e.g., Satan, science, ancestors, country)
- Superstition (ascribing powers to a created thing which it does not have)
- Hypnotism

---

[350] This list is compiled from Ripperger, *Deliverance Prayers for Use by the Laity*, 112–21. Used with permission. See also, Liber Christo, "Companion Guide," 90–105.

- Divination (communication with Satan, demons, the dead or other false practices in order to discover the unknown; to wit, consulting horoscopes, astrology, palm reading, fortune telling)
- Attaching undue importance to dreams, omens, or lots
- All practices of magic or sorcery (e.g., witchcraft, voodoo)
- Wearing charms or other occult items
- Playing with Ouija boards or rotating tables
- Spiritism (talking with the spirits)
- Sacrilege (profaning or treating unworthily the sacraments, especially the Holy Eucharist, and other liturgical actions, as well as religious persons, blessed things such as sacred vessels or statues, or places consecrated to God)
- Sacrilege by receiving a sacrament, especially the Holy Eucharist, in the state of mortal sin
- Simony (buying or selling of spiritual things)
- Profane or superstitious use of blessed objects
- Practical materialism (desiring only material things); atheistic humanism (falsely considering man to be an end in himself, and the sole maker with supreme control of his own history/destiny)
- Atheism in general (reject, deny, or doubt the existence of God, either in theory or practice—i.e., ignoring God in the daily living of one's life)
- Agnosticism (belief in the existence of a transcendent being which is incapable of revealing itself, and about which nothing can be said or known—i.e., holding that no judgment about God's existence is knowable and, thus, declaring it impossible to prove or even to affirm or deny God's existence)

Sins against Faith

- Willful doubt of any article of faith
- Deliberate ignorance of the truths of faith which ought to be known
- Neglect of instructing oneself in the Faith according to one's state in life
- Rash credulity (e.g., giving credence to private revelation too easily or believing in a private revelation which has been condemned by lawful Church authority)
- Apostasy (renouncing or abandoning the Faith)
- Heresy
- Indifferentism (to believe that one religion is as good as another, and that all religions are equally true and pleasing to God, or that one is free to accept or reject any or all religions)
- Reading or circulating books or writings against the Catholic belief or practice so as to jeopardize one's own faith or that of another
- To remain silent when asked about one's faith
- Engaging in schismatic or heretical worship
- Joining or supporting masonic groups or other forbidden societies

Sins against Hope

- Despair of God's mercy (to give up all hope of salvation and the means necessary to be saved); or the lack of confidence in the power of God's grace to support us in trouble or temptation
- A lack of desire to possess eternal happiness in heaven after this earthly life
- Presumption (to hope for salvation without help from God, or to assume God's forgiveness without conversion; to hope to obtain heavenly glory without merit)

- Presuming on God's mercy or on the supposed efficacy of certain pious practices in order to continue in sin
- Refusing any dependence on God

Sins against Charity

- Not making an act of charity at regular intervals during life, especially during times of necessity
- Egoism (caring only about oneself, love of self/self-praise, selfish, enjoy receiving praise)
- Willfully rebellious thoughts against God
- Boasting of sin
- Violating God's law, or omitting good works out of human respect

Sins Contrary to the Second Commandment

Thou shall not take the name of the Lord thy God in vain.

- Dishonoring of God by profane or disrespectful use of the Holy Name of God, the blasphemous use of the name of Jesus Christ, or the names of the Blessed Virgin Mary and the saints
- Blasphemy (speech or gestures that have contempt for or express insult to God, Jesus Christ, the Catholic Church, the Blessed Virgin Mary, or the saints)
- Perjury (to promise something under oath with no intention of keeping it, or breaking a promise made under oath)
- Taking false or unnecessary oaths (to call on God to be witness to a lie); breaking vows or promises to God
- Talking during Mass and in a Church without sufficient reason or to the distraction of others

Sins Contrary to the Third Commandment

Remember that thou shall keep holy the Lord's Day.

* Omission of prayer and divine worship (not attending Mass on Sundays and Holy Days of Obligation)
* Unnecessary servile work on Sundays and Holy Days of Obligations
* Activities that hinder the keeping of the Lord's Day holy (engaging in unnecessary commerce—i.e., buying and selling on Sundays and Holy Days of Obligation)

Sins Contrary to the Fourth Commandment

Honor thy father and mother.

For Parents and Their Relationship with Their Children

* Hating their children
* Cursing one's children
* Giving scandal by cursing, drinking, etc.
* Allowing them to grow up in ignorance, idleness, or sin
* Showing habitual partiality without cause
* Deferring a child's baptism
* Neglecting to watch over their bodily health, their religious instruction, the company they keep, the books they read, etc.
* Failing to correct them when needful
* Being harsh or cruel in correction
* Sending children to Protestant and other dangerous schools
* Neglect of taking/directing them to attend Holy

Mass on Sundays and Holy Days and to practice frequent reception of the sacraments

For Children and Their Relationship with Parents

- All manner of anger or hatred against parents and other lawful superiors
- Provoking one's parents to anger; grieving them; insulting them; neglecting them in their necessity; contempt or disobedience to their lawful commands
- Disobedience or disrespect to parents

Husbands and Wives

- Ill-usage (i.e., using them without consideration for their own welfare and without regard to charity)
- Putting obstacles to the fulfilment of religious duties
- Want of gentleness and consideration in regard to each other's faults
- Unreasonable jealousy
- Neglect of household duties
- Sulkiness, brooding over injury
- Injurious words
- Neglect of attempting to secure means of supporting the family due to laziness or timidity

For Employers

- Not allowing one's employees reasonable time for religious duties and instruction
- Giving bad example to them or allowing others to do so
- Withholding their lawful wages
- Not caring for them in sickness
- Dismissing them arbitrarily and without cause
- Imposing unreasonable policies

For Employees

- Disrespect to employers
- Lack of obedience in matters wherein one has bound oneself to obey (e.g., by fulfilling a contract); waste of time; neglect of work
- Waste of employer's property by dishonesty, carelessness, or neglect
- Violating company policies without sufficient reason

For Professionals and Civil Servants

- Culpable lack of knowledge relating to the duties of office or profession
- Neglect in discharging those duties
- Injustice or partiality
- Exorbitant fees (this sin may also be included under the seventh commandment)

For Teachers

- Neglecting the progress of those confided to their care
- Unjust, indiscreet, or excessive punishment
- Partiality
- Bad example
- Loose or false maxims (i.e., teaching them things which are untrue as being true)

For Students

- Disrespect
- Disobedience
- Stubbornness
- Idleness
- Wasting of time

- Giving in to idle distractions (e.g., partying and undue recreation)

For All

- Contempt for the laws of state and country as well as of the Church
- Disobedience to lawful authority
- Not abiding by civil laws when there is no just cause to do so

Sins Contrary to the Fifth Commandment

Thou shall not kill.

- Murder
- Performing an abortion
- Having an abortion
- Aiding in someone procuring an abortion (having or aiding in an abortion causes one to be excommunicated)
- Euthanasia
- Withholding ordinary means to a dying or terminally ill patient
- Suicide
- Attempts of suicide
- Serious thoughts about committing suicide
- Fighting, quarreling
- Anger, hatred
- Desires of revenge
- Human torture
- Gluttony (excessive eating or drinking)
- Drunkenness
- Abuse of alcohol, medicine, or drugs
- Endangering another's life (e.g., by drinking and driving, by driving too fast, etc.)

- Risking one's own life or limb without a sufficient reason (e.g., daredevil stunts, Russian roulette, etc.)
- Carelessness in leaving about poisons, dangerous drugs, weapons, etc.
- Mutilation of the body, such as castration or hysterectomy when organs are not diseased
- Tattooing of the body (images that are Satanic or contrary to Christian faith, with ink that has had spells placed on it, excessive tattooing)
- Immoral scientific research and its applications
- Bad example or scandal; inducing others to sin by word or example
- Disrespect for the dying or the dead
- Showing aversion or contempt for others
- Refusing to speak to others when addressed
- Ignoring offers of reconciliation, especially between relatives
- Cherishing/harboring an unforgiving spirit
- Raillery and ridicule
- Insults, irritating words and actions
- Sadness at another's prosperity
- Rejoicing over another's misfortune
- Envy at attention shown to others
- Tyrannical behavior
- Injury to health by overindulgence
- Giving drink to others knowing they will abuse it
- Taking contraceptive pills which may or may not be abortifacient
- Use of prophylactic or barrier methods to avoid pregnancy
- Using licit means of avoiding conception while fostering a contraceptive mentality
- Direct sterilization (vasectomy, tubal ligation)
- Causing unnecessary suffering or death to animals
- In-vitro fertilization or other artificial means of conceiving a child (donating sperm/ova; manual insemination; surrogate motherhood; etc.)

Sins Contrary to the Sixth Commandment
Thou shall not commit adultery.

- Impurity and immodesty in words, looks (deliberately not practicing custody of the eyes), and gestures/actions, whether alone or with others
- Telling and listening to dirty jokes
- Deliberate vulgar, impure language
- Wearing immodest clothing
- Buying, renting, or watching indecent movies, television, or books
- Pornography, as well as books which contain descriptions of impurity (e.g., "romance" novels that are descriptive of sexual acts)
- Masturbation
- Fornication (sometimes called premarital sex)
- Marriage outside of the Catholic Church of a baptized Catholic such as before a civil official or non-Catholic minister, and the sexual relations that take place in this invalid union
- Prostitution
- Homosexual sodomy and other homosexual practices
- Heterosexual sodomy
- Adultery
- Swinging/spouse-swapping; adultery with consent of spouse
- Divorce
- Polygamy
- Incest
- Sexual harassment
- Sexual abuse
- Rape
- Prolonged and sensual kissing between persons who are not spouses
- Petting or foreplay outside the context of marriage

- Petting or foreplay within the context of marriage whereby foreplay does not end up in the consummation of the natural conjugal act
- Immodest dancing
- Dating without taking the necessary precautions to safeguard purity or one's faith
- Unnatural sexual act (such as with an animal, object, etc.)

Sins Contrary to the Seventh Commandment

Thou shall not steal.

- Stealing
- Petty thefts (e.g., taking things from one's employer or family member to which one is not entitled and without permission)
- Cheating
- Plagiarizing
- Breaking copyright regulations, (e.g., photocopying without permission)
- Keeping borrowed or lost objects without making a reasonable attempt to restore the other's property
- Possession of ill-gotten goods
- Counseling or commanding someone to do injury to another person or to his goods
- Careless or malicious injury to the property of others
- Concealment of fraud, theft, or damage when in duty bound to give the information
- Tax evasion by not paying just taxes
- Business fraud
- Dishonesty in politics, business, etc.
- Not paying just debts at scheduled time and neglecting to make reasonable efforts and sacrifices in this matter—e.g., by gradually laying up the amount required

- Not making reparation or compensation to someone suffering from unjust damages
- Forcing up prices by taking advantage of the ignorance or hardship of another
- Usury (lending money at high interest rates to someone in financial difficulty)
- Speculation in which one contrives to manipulate the price of goods artificially in order to gain an advantage to the detriment of others
- Corruption in which one influences the judgment of those who must decide in legal matters
- Accepting bribes
- Appropriation and use for private purposes of the common goods of an enterprise; work poorly done
- Paying unjust wages or depriving an employee of due benefits
- Forgery of checks and invoices
- Writing checks knowing that there are not enough funds to cover them
- Excessive expenses and waste
- Not keeping promises or contractual agreements (if the commitments were morally just)
- Gambling and betting (if they deprive someone of basic living needs for himself or others)
- Excessive and unnecessary waste of goods, resources, money, or funds

Sins Contrary to the Eighth Commandment

Thou shall not bear false witness against thy neighbor.

- Lying
- Boasting or bragging
- Flattery
- Hypocrisy
- Exaggerating

- Sarcasm
- Unjust injury to another's good name either by revealing true and hidden faults (detraction) or by telling false defects (slander or calumny)
- Tale-bearing, spreading rumors, or gossip
- Criticizing others
- To listen with pleasure to others being criticized
- Unjustly dishonoring another person in his presence (contumely)
- Rash judgment (firmly believing, without sufficient reason, that someone has some moral defect)
- Revealing secrets
- Publishing discreditable secrets about others, even if true
- Refusing or delaying to restore the good name one has blackened
- Baseless accusations
- Groundless suspicions

Sins Contrary to the Ninth Commandment

Thou shall not covet they neighbor's wife.

The ninth commandment forbids all impure thoughts and desires that we take deliberate pleasure in so thinking, or to which we willingly consent whenever these unchaste thoughts or passions come into our mind. The penitent should keep in mind that any sin listed under the sixth commandment, in which one willing or deliberately entertains the desire, may have the same degree of gravity (i.e., either mortal or venial sin). In other words, this commandment refers to any deliberate impure thoughts: any deliberate desiring, undue thinking about, or mentally consenting to any of the sins against the sixth commandment. If consent is not given to these thoughts, then, these thoughts are temptations. Our effectiveness in spiritual battle is dependent on our purity of thought, word, and deed. Therefore, *sins against this commandment include* the deliberate thinking or fantasizing about:

- Thoughts of vulgar, impure language
- Attention to those wearing immodest clothing
- Recalling (fantasizing about) what one has seen in watching indecent movies or television or in reading impure books
- Recalling (fantasizing about) what one has seen in pornography, as well as what one has read in books which contain descriptions of impurity (e.g., "romance" novels that are descriptive of sexual acts)
- Thinking about/fantasizing about masturbation
- Thinking about/fantasizing about fornication (sometimes called premarital sex)
- Thinking about/fantasizing about prostitution
- Thinking about/fantasizing about heterosexual sodomy
- Thinking about/fantasizing about adultery ("committing adultery in one's heart")
- Thinking about/fantasizing about incest
- Thinking about/fantasizing about sexual harassment
- Thinking about/fantasizing about sexual abuse
- Thinking about/fantasizing about rape
- Thinking about/fantasizing about prolonged and sensual kissing between persons who are not spouses
- Thinking about/fantasizing about petting or foreplay outside the context of marriage
- Thinking about/fantasizing about petting or foreplay within the context of marriage whereby foreplay does not end up in the consummation of the natural conjugal act
- Deliberate thinking about/fantasizing about immodest dancing

Sins Contrary to the Tenth Commandment
Thou shall not covet thy neighbor's goods.

- Envy (desire of another's goods)
- Jealousy (a zealous vigilance in keeping a good enjoyed by oneself from others)
- Greed and the desire to have material goods without limit (avarice)
- The desire to become rich at all costs
- Businesses or professions which hope for unfavorable circumstances for others so that they may personally profit from it
- Being envious of someone else's success, talents, temporal or spiritual goods
- The desire to commit injustice by harming someone in order to get his temporal goods

Five Precepts of the Church

Many Catholics are ignorant of the fact that attending Sunday Mass is an obligation and that to miss Sunday Mass ("unless excused for a serious reason . . . or dispensed by their own pastor," as per *CCC* 2181 and Canon 1245) is a mortal sin. Other areas of examination of conscience for confession include whether you have violated this or any of the **Five Precepts of the Church**. As the *Catechism* states, "The precepts of the Church are set in the context of a moral life bound to and nourished by liturgical life. The obligatory character of these positive laws decreed by the pastoral authorities is meant to guarantee to the faithful the very necessary minimum in the spirit of prayer and moral effort, in the growth in love of God and neighbor."[351]

The following five precepts are found in the *Catechism*:[352]

---

[351] *CCC* 2041.
[352] *CCC* 2042–43.

1. You shall attend Mass on Sundays and holy days of obligation and rest from servile labor. In addition to Sunday, the days to be observed as holy days of obligation are as follows:[353]
   - January 1, the solemnity of Mary, Mother of God
   - Thursday of the Sixth Week of Easter, the solemnity of the Ascension
   - August 15, the solemnity of the Assumption of the Blessed Virgin Mary
   - November 1, the solemnity of All Saints
   - December 8, the solemnity of the Immaculate Conception
   - December 25, the solemnity of the Nativity of Our Lord Jesus Christ
2. You shall confess your sins at least once a year.[354]
3. You shall receive the sacrament of the Eucharist at least during the Easter season.[355]
4. You shall observe the days of fasting and abstinence established by the Church.[356]
5. You shall help to provide for the needs of the Church.

From Slingstones to Milestones: Making a Good Confession

1. While the sacraments are a spiritual shield against evil, the devil looks for any opening in your armor.

---

[353] Holy Days of Obligation may vary slightly depending on diocesan regulations, as determined by the USCCB or the local ordinary in conformity with Canon 1246, para. 2.

[354] Confession once a year is the bare minimum. We recommend that anyone who is in the process of deliverance should to go to confession weekly.

[355] This also is a minimum. Attending daily Mass greatly helps in growing in sanctity and liberation.

[356] Abstaining from meat on Fridays throughout the year is highly recommended. The Church allows other substitutions so long as some form of fasting takes place on Fridays.

Which venial sin have you overlooked which has now made you spiritually blind to its effects?

2. What does a good sacramental confession involve?

3. What are the three elements that deem a sin mortal?

4. When was the last time you went to the sacrament of Penance?

5. Did you write down your sins and take that list with you into the confessional?

6. Did you confess them all in addition to any others that came to mind while in the confessional?

7. Discuss what is meant by being properly disposed to receive absolution.

Chapter Four

Power and Authority

"When he received the royal crown, he battled and subdued the enemy on every side. He campaigned against the hostile Philistines and shattered their power till our own day."

—SIRACH 47:6–7

<hr>

Thus far we have focused on David's use of the slingshot and the stones. The narrative mentions, however, an often-overlooked detail. After shedding Saul's armor and before he reached for his sling, David rather unceremoniously first grabbed his staff: "Then, *staff in hand*, David selected five smooth stones" (1 Sm 17:40). In this section, we will explain a similarly often-overlooked element of spiritual combat: the importance of power and authority.

Like a ranger's hatchet, which could be used as both an implement and a weapon in hand-to-hand fighting, a shepherd's staff was a multi-use instrument. He would use it for assistance in climbing hills, but also to beat the bush to help pull straying sheep out of low brush and to defend them from snakes and other dangerous animals.[357] A staff was used for similar purposes by travelers as well. At the first Passover, when God led the Israelites out of slavery in Egypt, He commanded the people, with the exact same phrase, to be "staff in hand" as they began their sojourn:

<hr>

[357] Unger, *The New Unger's Bible Dictionary*, 1644.

"This is how you are to eat it: with your loins girt, sandals on your feet and your *staff in hand*, you shall eat like those in flight" (Ex 12:11). That David was said also to have "staff in hand" is likely not coincidental. The subtle allusion to the Exodus suggests the protection of God who is about to deliver His people again.

In ancient Israel, a staff acted like a seal in the sense that it symbolized one's office and authority, as was conferred upon Moses (see Ex 4:1–5). When God called Moses to lead the people out of slavery, He commanded Moses to use the staff (again, "staff in hand") as a sign of his authority (see Ex 4:5). When God parted the waters of the Red Sea, He commanded Moses to "lift up your staff" and "with hand outstretched over the sea" so that the waters would part (Ex 14:16). In Numbers, for example, God told Moses to collect a staff from each "ancestral house, twelve staffs in all, one from each of their tribal princes," and "mark each man's name on his staff" (Nm 17:16–17). From these, Aaron's sprouted "shoots and blossoms and even bore a ripe almond" as signifying his distinct, priestly authority.

Elsewhere, David makes the same connection. The former shepherd, who knew how to defend sheep and eventually became a warrior-king, writes, "The LORD is my shepherd, / there is nothing I lack" (Ps 23:1). He lacks nothing because "even though I walk through the valley of the shadow of death, / I will fear no evil, for you are with me; / your rod and your staff comfort me" (Ps 23:4). Thus, while the slingshot yields the power of the Law of God, the staff is symbolic of the protection provided by being under God's authority. This distinction is crucial for spiritual combat.

LESSON TEN: DEMONIC COMPLIANCE AND THE RULES OF ENGAGEMENT

We are often told after a mistake that "It's okay, God knows your intention." Indeed, He does. Nowhere in the natural realm, however, does our ignorance of a rule or law mean we are not subject to the penalty of its violation.

This is seen in the legal phrase, "Ignorance of the law is no excuse." In (ironic) military language, "friendly fire isn't." That is, regardless of the subjective intention of the shooter, the bullet carries an objective and lethal reality with it. The demon works according to the rules God has established while also obscuring those rules so that he can mitigate our prayer.

The demon, therefore, always works in the objective (what *is*) and not the subjective (such as our intentions or feelings). He is pure intellect, a crafty and powerful predator who strictly follows the rules established by God (hence, a "lawyer from hell"). These rules are found in natural law and divine positive law.[358] Natural law is the structure put into our minds so that we can grasp right from wrong. Saint Thomas states that natural law is "nothing else than the rational creature's participation in the eternal law."[359] God has established natural law in the rule of creation which can be grasped by the light of human reason. That is, there are behaviors and morals intrinsic to human nature, and things work best when they operate according to the nature and structure established by the Creator.

Although the precepts of natural law are embedded into us, so to speak, these inclinations can be silenced through sin. There is a connection, moreover, between law and obedience. As C. S. Lewis explains, "As an organism, man is subjected to various biological laws which he cannot disobey any more than an animal can. That is, he cannot disobey the laws which he shares with other things." No creature can choose to disobey, for example, the law of gravity (even birds must use lift to overcome gravity). Man can, however, choose to disobey laws specific to him, such as right and wrong and human sexuality. Man knows certain actions to be wrong in and of themselves, and everyone is expected to know, and follow, such laws. Check, for example, your inner response when someone cuts in front of you in line. Natural law is evidence of a shared

---

[358] Saint Thomas speaks of divine law, and "positive" comes from the Latin *positus*, meaning "placed," so divine positive law are those things "placed" by God that are over and above the natural law, such as the Ten Commandments, Church Law, etc.

[359] Saint Thomas Aquinas, *Summa Theologica* I-II, q. 91, art. 2.

set of rules that guide behavior. Thus, Lewis states that the law "which is particular to his human nature . . . he does not share with animals or vegetables or inorganic things, is the one he can disobey if he chooses."[360] This, Lewis states, is related to the specific quality of human obedience.

Accordingly, within natural law is embedded the obligation of human obedience. *Oboediens* is the Latin word meaning "to obey, yield, be subject to" and derives from the verb meaning "to listen to, harken" (and, therefore, be subject to). When a drill instructor walks into the barracks and yells out, "Listen up!" what follows is not open to discussion or debate. The office that the sergeant holds carries with it an authority which requires those under him to listen and obey. Father Ripperger defines an *office* as "the duty binding on or assigned to someone as part of his authority, position, or work; position of authority or trust, in state, church, banking, etc."[361] Thus, the first word of the monastic Rule of Saint Benedict is "Listen." Likewise, when Moses spoke the greatest commandment to His people in the *Shema*, He said to them "Hear, O Israel!" (Dt 6:4). What followed was also not open to debate. The greatest commandment (love of God) contains the blessings that comes with fidelity: "The LORD commanded us to observe all these statutes in fear of the LORD, our God, that we may always have a prosperous and happy life as we have today. This is our justice before the Lord, our God: to observe carefully this whole commandment he has enjoined on us" (Dt 6:24–25).

And: "As your reward for heeding these ordinances and keeping them carefully, the Lord, your God, will keep with you the covenant mercy he promised on oath to your ancestors. . . . You will be blessed above all peoples" (Dt 7:12, 14). Man can choose to yield or not yield to the commands of natural law and divine law—to his benefit or to his detriment.

God gradually revealed Himself to the Israelites through the Ten Commandments, et cetera, and penultimately "through

---

[360] Lewis, *Mere Christianity*, 6.
[361] Ripperger, *Dominion*, 34.

the prophets." In the fullness of time, however, His ultimate self-revelation is "through His Son" (Heb 1:1) who handed His authority over to the Church (see Mt 28:18; Jn 21:21–23). Divine positive law can be seen, for example, in the moral teachings of the Church. As a divinely revealed law, it binds us in conscience and obedience. The Church has the responsibility to safeguard, for our salvation, the teachings that Christ handed over to the apostles. We have the duty to "listen up" to those precepts. We respond, with the help of God's grace, to the divinely revealed truth contained in the doctrinal and moral precepts of the Church.

You may ask what a discussion on natural law has to do with spiritual warfare. As stated above, authority flows through office and not charism. When Israel rebelled in the desert, the people voiced complaints against Moses and their desire to return to slavery (Egypt) rather than endure the hardships of the journey to liberation (the Promised Land that awaited). They protested, "Why did you lead us out of Egypt only to bring us to this wretched place which has neither grain nor figs nor vines nor pomegranates? Here there is not even water to drink!" (Nm 20:5). In response, Moses and Aaron prostrated themselves before the Lord in reparation (v. 6). God then commanded Moses to "take the staff and assemble the people" (v. 8). God then commanded Moses, staff in hand, to "order the rock to yield its waters" (v. 9). The waters of grace flow through the right use of authority within one's office. By analogy, the first principle of spiritual warfare is that the demon, like the rock, will either yield or not yield based upon the authority of the petitioner.

Combustible Prayer: Calling Down Fire from Heaven

Every special-ops team has a demolitions expert who understands that chemistry, like any science, also works in the objective. For combustion to occur, three chemical elements must be present: oxygen, heat (an ignition source such as a spark), and fuel. If only two of the three are present, there remain only two inert substances. Whether you intend to start a fire or not, objectively speaking, combustion occurs only when those three elements are present in the right proportions. This is referred to in chemistry as the "fire triangle." By analogy, to ignite your prayer such that it burns and purifies like fire from heaven, there must also be three objective elements present. When you pray a spiritual warfare prayer, the demon goes down a checklist, as it were, in determining whether or not he will yield. His decision is not based upon our intentions or our emotions (subjective) but upon three principle (objective) factors. Namely, (1) Does this person have requisite authority? (2) What is the state of merit of the person praying? (3) What are the words themselves?

The prophet Elijah is considered the founder of the Carmelite order whose adherents retreat from the world and live a life of prayer and solitude. On multiple occasions, Elijah called down fire from heaven. Elijah was commanded by God to "leave here, go east, and hide in the Wadi Cherith, east of the Jordan. You shall drink of the stream, and I have commanded the ravens to feed you there" (1 Kgs 17:3–4). Strengthened by a time of prayer and solitude, nourished by God, Elijah does battle with the false prophets of Baal on Mount Carmel, *calling down fire from heaven* upon the enemies of God (see 1 Kgs 18:21–39) and even slaughtering them (see 1 Kgs 18:40). His challenge to Israel should echo in the ears of everyone who seeks liberation: "How long will you straddle the issue? If the Lord is God, follow him; if Baal, follow him" (1 Kgs 18:21). In spiritual warfare, there is no middle ground. To this day, this manner of radical Christianity is still found in monastic life and should form part of your own spirituality and prayer discipline moving forward. You may not be called to be a monk or nun, but you are being called to "straddle the issue no longer" and, like Elijah, to call down fire and even chase down your spiritual enemy and defeat him.

Not only did Elijah defeat the followers of Baal by fire, but he also used fire to defeat the followers of Beelzebub. The king of Israel, who had abandoned the true God and sought the help of Beelzebub, sent a cohort of fifty soldiers to retrieve the prophet: "Then the king sent a captain with his company of fifty men after Elijah. The prophet was seated on a hilltop when he found him. He said, 'Man of God, the king commands you, "Come down."'" Elijah answered the captain, 'Well, if I am a man of God, may fire come down from heaven and consume you and your fifty men.' And fire came down from heaven and consumed him and his fifty men" (2 Kgs 1:9–12).

Whether Baal, Beelzebub, or any other demon has afflicted you, you can become "a man or woman of God" and pray in such a way that fire consumes your spiritual enemies. But first, you must now learn the rules of engagement. In this section, we will explain the importance of power and authority as essential to spiritual combat.

Power and Authority in the Catholic Tradition

Now that you have taken up your shield through confession and have opened the flow of sacramental grace, you are ready to engage the enemy in a more direct way. In ancient warfare, the shield was not only a defensive protection against projectiles like arrows and slingstones but also used as a strike weapon. The heavy infantryman's shield was equipped with a large brass ball and spike (called a boss, or *umbo*) in the center, which was used offensively to ram one's opponent. This surprise tactic would throw the opponent off-balance and expose him to the sword. Like the spiked boss at the center of a soldier's shield, the right use of power and authority works in a similar way in spiritual combat. It can be used to both protect and attack.

Father Ripperger affirms that the longstanding "practice of the saints and the Church from the beginning has been one in which strict lines of authority, rights and duties are observed." That is, the Catholic Church "in her wisdom and experience has always known that authority is one of the primary requisites in order to drive out a demon."[362] After the Resurrection, Jesus sends the apostles forth in what is called "the great commissioning." There, before ascending into heaven, Jesus tells the apostles ("the Eleven" are the twelve apostles minus Judas): "All power [literally, the Greek is *exousia*, or authority] in heaven and on earth has been given to me." He extends jurisdictional authority to the apostles with the command to "make disciples of all nations" (Mt 28:19). In Mark's account, this includes the authority to "drive out demons in my name" as part of the "signs that accompany" the Eleven (Mk 16:17).

This mirrors the sending out of "the Twelve" as part of the missionary activity while Jesus instructed His disciples. Jesus gave them jurisdictional authority over evil spirits as part of the threefold *munera* (cf. "Overview" above) of the ordained priesthood: "He summoned the Twelve and gave them *power* and *authority* over all demons and to cure diseases, and he sent them to proclaim the kingdom of God and to heal [the sick]" (Lk 9:1). Likewise, when He sent out "seventy-two" with the same mission of evangelization, they returned with joy saying, "Lord, even the demons are subject to us because of your name" (Lk 10:17).[363] According to Saint Hippolytus of Rome, who was born within a generation of the death of Saint John the Evangelist, these seventy-two men were all made bishops of nascent (newly born) churches in first-century Christianity.[364] In addition, in Catholic doctrine this means that Christ gave authority to the apostles when He sent them forth with His power and authority.[365]

Many mistakenly collapse power and authority as a single reality. As I previously wrote, however, "power and authority

---

[362] Ripperger, *Deliverance Prayers for Use by the Laity*, 7.

[363] In refuting Lozano's claim (*Unbound*, 103) that this passage is proof that any Christian can drive out any demon, Father Ripperger notes simply, "While all Apostles are disciples, not all disciples are Apostles." That is, there is a "certain authority that is given only to them and not to all the disciples." Ripperger, *Dominion*, 127. That Hippolytus in the second century notes that those seventy-two were all given jurisdictional (episcopal) authority as bishop-apostles further supports Father Ripperger's assertions.

[364] Saint Hippolytus of Rome, *On the Twelve Apostles of Christ* and *On the Seventy Apostles of Christ*, 13.

[365] Ott, *Fundamentals of Catholic Dogma*, 276.

are two different things. *Power* is the ability to cause change. *Authority* is the right to use the power to cause the change."[366] While Baptism gives power over demons, jurisdictional authority over demons is conditioned by natural law and one's state in life. One may have the power to effect change, but this does not give a person the right to use the power. We know this instinctively through human experience. Father Ripperger uses the example of a misbehaving child in public to show the distinction between power and authority: "For example, if an individual encountered a misbehaving child in a supermarket that is not the parent of the child, he has the physical power to take the child and spank the child. That does not give him the right to spank him. What gives him the right to spank him is the authority over the child (that is, the moral claim in relationship to the disposition of the child)." The same thing, he says, "can be said of demons" and our right to command them as according to the distinction between power and authority.[367]

The Greek word for power is *dunamis*, which means "power, might, strength, the ability to do a thing, faculty, capacity." The word derives from the verb meaning "to be able to do x" and, thus, the acting upon something else to effect change. We get the words *dynamite* and *dynamo* from the Greek *dunamis*. In New Testament parlance, it is often the word used for "mighty deeds"—those things Christians are "enabled" to do in the name Jesus. In the early Church, as the praxis developed, driving out demons by invoking the name of Jesus gave witness as proof to the claim of Christ's divinity over (against) pagan religions.[368]

The Greek word for authority is *exousia* (literally, "out of or from the being, nature, or substance"), which means "authority, power over, license, office, magistracy." A part of the divine positive law is the jurisdiction given to the successors of the apostles. According to Ludwig Ott, "Hierarchical magisterial

---

[366] Liber Christo, "Companion Guide," 57.

[367] Ripperger, *Dominion*, 122.

[368] For a summary of the development of the Rite of Exorcism and its limitation to the priestly charism in the early Church, see Grob, "A Major Revision of the Discipline on Exorcism," 60–103.

powers of the church embrace the *teaching* power, the *pastoral* power (=legislative, juridical and punitive power), and the *sacerdotal* power. They correspond to the threefold office laid on Christ as man for the purpose of the redemption of mankind: the office of prophet or the teaching office, the pastoral or royal office, and the priestly office. Christ transferred this threefold office, with the corresponding powers, to His Apostles." This office (and concomitant power and authority that He sent them out with) was given to the apostles immediately, affirms Ott, and not gradually as "the result of historical development."[369]

This authority was "handed down" (the Latin *traditio* comes from the verb meaning "to hand down, deliver, entrust, or transmit") to their successor-bishops in a seamless line extending even to today's bishops who are descendants of "the Twelve." Thus, the Twelve became the Eleven when Judas killed himself, but he was immediately replaced after the resurrection of Jesus. Peter commanded that "may another take his office" (in Greek, his *episcope*) at the beginning of the Acts of the Apostles (see Acts 1:15–26) while they awaited the Holy Spirit at Pentecost. The demon knows this fact far better than we do: the local bishop is a prince of the apostles and has jurisdictional authority in his diocese. The bishop shares that power and authority, by the laying of hands in ordination, with his priests.

Authority is not attained by charism or special training but rather by office, such as priest, head of household, property owner, et cetera. The person with "staff in hand" has the moral (*viz.* grasped by human reason) power to command and enforce obedience—that is, to impose an obligation. The Latin *ligare* means "to bind, ratify an oath." To *obligare* means, then, to bind up, to tie around, put under obligation, make liable. Thus, the right to command, the binding (placing an obligation upon) of another person flows from one's office. As applied to spiritual warfare, "to bind" means to oblige a demon to do something. Like the ancient warrior's shield, the authority structure is given by God as a layering

---

[369] Ott, *Fundamentals of Catholic Dogma*, 276.

of protection and a bulwark against the diabolic and spiritual attack. Authority, however, is never something claimed or earned. For example, a police officer may have the power (=his weapon and uniform) to pull you over, but the ability to punish you is based on his jurisdictional authority (=his badge). Having a charism may give one the power, but having power is not the same as having the authority to do so. As I wrote, "Authority is never something claimed but is given by God either by the natural law (such as in the case of the authority that the parents have over their children) or by the divine positive law (such as the authority that a priest has over the faithful by virtue of his priesthood). Authority is a right possessed by those who have an office or delegated jurisdiction by which they are able to command those under their authority to perform a specific action."[370]

Recall Rogers's first rule: "All Rangers are to be subject to the rules and articles of war." These two laws—natural and divine—determine the authority structure which, in turn, establishes this key (and often overlooked) principle in spiritual warfare.[371]

A warrior's shield is first a defensive weapon. By analogy, the authority structure imposes an obligation on those with authority to rightly use their authority to *provide* and *protect*.[372] With regard to the interplay between power and authority, the tension is always between *dereliction* (not to deploy) and *usurpation* (take an authority that is not yours). For example, when the head of household chooses not to engage, the entire familial construct is vulnerable. This does not mean the wife can take charge and disregard the husband. God gave the shield to him, so he must pick it up and deploy it. Her prayers should first be directed toward her husband, that he deploy his shield on behalf of the family.

---

[370] Liber Christo, "Companion Guide," 58.

[371] For a detailed explanation of the authority structure, see Ripperger, *Dominion*, 148–65.

[372] As Father Ripperger writes, these two are "the final cause of authority." *Dominion*, 156. For an in-depth explanation of the structure of authority within the various offices (husband, wife, mother, father, owner, etc.), see *Dominion*, 154–72.

The implication, then, is that one does not "take" authority, as is the common language of Charismatic and Protestant-based deliverance, such as *Unbound*. Nor can you "grow" in authority, as Neal Lozano asserts (incorrectly), "We gain more authority as we bring more areas of our lives under His authority."[373] Your prayers may grow in merit as you grow in holiness, but your authority over a person, place, or object is tethered to your office as in relation to the same.[374] You do not "take" authority; rather, you claim what is yours by right given through natural or divine law by God the Father.

When someone steps outside of his authority structure, the demon can (and often does) retaliate for the violation of the rules of engagement. We see an example of demonic retaliation in the Acts of the Apostles. The seven sons of Sceva were Jewish exorcists who performed an exorcism by invoking the name of Jesus. Although not Christians, they nonetheless attempted to drive out demons. As a result, the demon assaulted and tormented them: "He so overpowered them that they fled wounded and naked" (Acts 19:16). Why? They had no authority by natural law or divine positive law over this possessed person. This is a classic case of retaliation that serves as a warning to the rest of us. This is what "demonic retaliation" looks like, and with the most common forms seen in a spiritual oppression which often includes "chronic physical ailments, children leaving the Catholic faith or failing to baptize the grandchildren, legal or financial difficulties, etc."[375]

---

[373] Lozano, *Unbound*, 103. For a thorough examination of *Unbound* and the authority structure, see Ripperger, *Dominion*, 126–34.

[374] For example, we read in the *Book of Blessings*: "The ministry of blessing involves a particular exercise of the priesthood of Christ and [is exercised] *in keeping with the place and office within the people of God belonging to each person.*" It explains that "laypersons exercise this ministry [of blessing] *in virtue of their office,*" citing as an example "parents on behalf of their children" (emphasis mine). Elsewhere, the document lists those individuals in the Old Testament who administered an office from which they blessed (or prayed over) others: "patriarchs, kings, priests, Levites, and parents—by allowing them to offer blessings in praise of His name and to invoke His name." *Book of Blessings*, 26, 22.

[375] Liber Christo, "Companion Guide," 155.

This is particularly acute when the person praying spiritual warfare prayers is not in a state of grace, which is why avoiding all sin and growing in holiness is the primary way to withstand evil. This is to say, the barometer of the right use of authority in driving out demons is retaliation, which usually comes in the form of an attack against one's vocation. Those structures differ between priests and the laity.

Priestly Authority

Just as the seal of Baptism is recognizable to the spiritual world, so also is the permanent mark of Holy Orders.[376] The one able to confer both permanent seals is the local bishop. Thus, we can assert: "The principal spiritual authority in the diocese is the local bishop who 'in an imminent and visible manner, takes the place of Christ himself, teacher, shepherd, and priest and acts as his representative.'[377] In union with the local bishop, a priest likewise has unique power and authority over demons."[378] Thus, the *Catechism* teaches, "In the ecclesial service of the ordained minister, it is Christ himself who is present to his Church as Head of his Body, Shepherd of his flock, high priest of the redemptive sacrifice, Teacher of Truth. This is what the Church means by saying that the priest, by virtue of the sacrament of Holy Orders, acts in persona Christi."[379]

Acting *in persona Christi*, the Catholic priest "exercise[s] the authority to forgive or retain sins, as was given to the apostles by Jesus in the upper room (cf. John 20:21–22)." He also has the authority to baptize, preach and drive out demons as commanded in the great commissioning (Matt 28:16–20)." Thus, "this same authority that Jesus gave to the Apostles to drive out demons, moreover, has been handed down to the

---

[376] The understanding of the authority structure presented here represents the developed thought of Father Ripperger, which is summarized in the following sections. See Ripperger, *Dominion*, 115–86. See also, Liber Christo, "Companion Guide," 57–65.

[377] *CCC* 1558.

[378] Liber Christo, "Companion Guide," 76.

[379] *CCC* 1548.

priests of today and is a vital part of their responsibility to sanctify and govern the people of God. Additionally, part of the faculties given to a priest include the right to pray the prayers of minor exorcisms including imprecatory forms and deprecatory forms. The efficacy of these prayers, which are part of his liturgical service to the Church, flow from the priest's unique, sacramental ordering to Christ through his local bishop."[380]

Notably, this authority flows from his office, not a special charism or training. The demon knows this objective reality. He sees the Catholic priest as another Christ and trembles before the bishop as Christ's full representative on earth, a prince of the Church and successor to the apostles possessing full authority over him. Much smarter than Goliath, who mocked the sling which David used to kill him, the demon trembles before the bishop as he does the crucifix, the weapon Christ used to humiliate and defeat him. He trembles also before the Catholic priest, who stands both *in persona Christi* and as *alter Christus*.

In modern times, much has been spoken about the "priesthood of the laity." Indeed, the Greek word *christos* means "anointed," and those who were anointed in the Old Testament were commissioned with the office of priest, prophet, or king. Thus, a "Christian" is marked by an anointing and union with Christ who is Priest, Prophet, and King. A layman shares in the "universal" priesthood of Christ. There is a difference, however, both in essence and in degree between this universal priesthood of the laity and the ministerial, hierarchical priesthood of the ordained.[381] Lozano, for example, collapses these when he states that in a deliverance session, "when someone comes to you for prayer, telling you secrets, you are invited in as a representative of Christ, an instrument of the love and mercy of God."[382] While this may be true at one level, the demon knows the difference between the ontological reality

---

[380] Liber Christo, "Companion Guide," 76.

[381] *Lumen Gentium*, no. 10.

[382] Lozano, *Unbound*, 103.

of the priest and the baptized lay person—and he responds accordingly. The priest uniquely acts *in persona Christi* as the true "representative of Christ," and only he can hear the "secrets" of past sins *and absolve them.*

This is because the indelible mark of Baptism, according to Father Ripperger, "is not the same as the indelible mark of the sacerdotal priesthood."[383] Thus, I wrote that "the rite of exorcism, inasmuch as it is an extension of the liturgical life of the Church, is thereby also reserved to the ordained priest due to his unique, ontological orientation toward Christ. Moreover, the Church affirms that ministerial priesthood and the common priesthood of the laity 'differ essentially and not only in degree' (cf. *LG* 10). Thus, the validly ordained priest is central not only to the sacramental life of the Church, but in the exercising the ministry of exorcism."[384]

The effects of ordination are (1) an increase of sanctifying grace, (2) a sacramental grace through which the priest has God's constant help in his sacred ministry, and (3) a character, lasting forever, which is a special sharing in the priesthood of Christ, and which gives special supernatural powers.[385] This is what is meant by the "universality" of the ministerial priesthood. That is, "the duly ordained priest has the authority to exercise his priestly gifts of teaching, sanctifying, and ruling over anyone. This is also why he can say binding prayers or prayers of command over any soul, whereas lay authority is limited to one's familial construct. His priesthood and authority derive from his bishop, who has supreme spiritual authority in his diocese."[386]

---

[383] Ripperger, *Dominion,* 131.

[384] Liber Christo, "Companion Guide," 25. Thus, the CDF affirms that "Canon 1172 of the Code of Canon Law states that no one can legitimately perform exorcisms over the possessed unless he has obtained special and express permission from the local Ordinary (§ 1), and states that this permission should be granted by the local Ordinary only to priests who are endowed with piety, knowledge, prudence and integrity of life (§ 2). Bishops are therefore strongly advised to stipulate that these norms be observed." CDF, *Letter to Ordinaries Regarding Norms on Exorcism,* no. 1.

[385] See *Baltimore Catechism,* 213.

[386] Liber Christo, "Companion Guide," 152.

The priest is the dispenser of the mysteries of God, and he brings forth the kingdom of God through preaching, healing, and exorcism. His ecclesial authority stems from a unique and ontological orientation towards Christ, through the bishop, received in the sacrament of Holy Orders. The inner logic of this structure flows from the inner logic of the Levitical priesthood, seen in the chart below:[387]

Old Testament	New Testament
The High Priest See Lv 21:10; Mt 26:57	→ **Jesus Christ** Our "eternal High Priest" (see Heb 7:1–3)
Types of Sacrifice Offered The chief priest was designated to enter the Holy of Holies and perform the religious rites on the annual Day of Atonement (see Lv 16).	→ **Types of Sacrifice Offered** Jesus gave His Body and Blood on the cross for the atonement of the sins of humanity (see Lk 23:46).
Ordained, Full-Time Ministerial Priests Pre-Levitical (see Ex 19:21–22) Levitical (see Ex 19ff)	→ **Ordained, Full-Time Ministerial Priests** See Lk 22:7–20; Rom 15:15–16
Types of Sacrifice Offered Animal (see Ex 29:10ff), drink (see Nm 15:10), grain (see Lv 2:14ff), etc.	→ **Types of Sacrifice Offered** All the sacrifices offered by the members of the common priesthood of all Christians plus the Holy Sacrifice of the Mass, which makes available to individual Christian souls, throughout the course of history, the merits of the once-for-all Sacrifice of Jesus Christ (see 1 Cor 10:16; 11:23–30)
The Common Priesthood Shared by All Jews See Ex 19:6	→ **The Common Priesthood Shared by All Christians** See 1 Pt 2:5; Rv 1:6

---

[387] Adapted from Romero, *Unabridged Christianity*, 111–12.

Old Testament	*New Testament*
Types of Sacrifices Offered Spiritual sacrifices to God (see Hos 14:2); also commissioned ordained, full-time ministerial priests to offer ritual sacrifice to God on their behalf in the Temple (see 2 Mc 12:43)	**→ Types of Sacrifices Offered** Spiritual (see 1 Pt 2:5), bodies (see Rom 12:1), donations (see Phil 4:18), praise, good deeds, generosity (see Heb 13:15–16); also commissioned ordained full-time ministerial Christian priests to offer the Sacrifice of the Mass to God for their needs and intentions

Thus, in the New Covenant, we see a unique ordering toward sacrifice in the office of ordained priest as fulfilling the Levitical priesthood of the Old Covenant.

Lay Authority

While the traditional Catholic approach to deliverance recognizes and maximizes priestly authority, it does *not* mean that lay people cannot engage in spiritual combat. Nonetheless, *all rangers are to be subject to the rules and articles of war.* As in all warfare, structure, order, and right execution are essentials to victory. Rogers also cautioned his rangers, "Don't never take a chance you don't have to." In spiritual warfare, this means taking calculated risks. Paddy Mayne, one of the highest decorated soldiers of the elite SAS (the British Special Forces called the Special Air Service) was known for his bravery and cunning in battle. When asked about his ability to act in the face of danger, he is reported to have said, "People think I'm a big, mad Irishman. But I'm not. I calculate the risks for and against and then have a go." In a similar way, spiritual warfare has "risks for and against." Learn these rules so you know the risks, and then grab your shield and weapons and "have a go."

The emphasis here on priestly authority is not to deny that lay charisms exist in the Church (we have seen them quite actively at work) but rather to assert that the demon follows the lines of authority perfectly and will yield to rightly asserted authority, ecclesial or lay. Some people wrongly think that if one person allows another person to pray for them, they can, and should, be able to drive a demon out. According to Father Ripperger, "a key distinction" that is often misunderstood in many modern deliverance models used today is that "permission is not the same thing as authority." This is something, he says, that "the demons understand" and respond accordingly.[388] This structure, in turn, determines both *what* we are responsible for and *how* we respond to those responsibilities.

Ownership is a right of disposition toward a thing and shapes the way spiritual battle is conducted. Father Ripperger summarizes the parameters of lay authority. Which bears repeating at length:

> This is also true in relation to rights which grant authority in relation to the object of the right. By this we mean that spouses, who by virtue of the marital contract . . . have rights over each other's bodies by virtue of the conceding of those rights to each other on the day of their marriage. For this reason, wives may command the demons to leave their husband's bodies and the husbands their wives' bodies. For the husband it is a two-fold authority; the one as head of the household and the other by virtue of the rights over his wife's body.

As for other familial relationships, he further explains:

> From experience, most exorcists concede that there is an ability to command the demons to depart . . . in relation to those of one's immediate family. It appears due to the nature of the obligations of the Fourth Commandment, that children, when saying binding prayers and other prayers of this sort for the parents, do not seem to be affected. This may flow from

---

[388] Ripperger, *Dominion*, 131.

the fact that they have the obligation to take care of them in their need as a result of the natural law. For this same reason, exorcists have noted a lack of retaliation when the prayers are said for one's siblings. This does not appear to be the case for godparents or grandparents since they do not have the same obligations under the Fourth Commandment.[389]

Thus, as stated above, authority is the right to use power (as opposed to the notion of "might equals right"). By "right" is meant something granted by moral law (that is, natural law grasped by human reason).

In explaining how the principle of "ask and it shall be given to you" applies to spiritual warfare, Father Ripperger states, "What one asked for is precisely what one gets. That means that prayer by its very nature has a spiritual force." He further explains the nuances of why the demon sometimes responds and sometime does not. This is because "Christ Himself said, 'By my name you will cast out demons. However, He did not say, 'By My name you will cast out *all* demons.' This is due to the fact that some demons actually require a legitimate moral claim on the side of the one commanding them in order to cast them out."[390] By "legitimate moral claim" is meant that an individual has a right over the person, place, or object which others "have an obligation to allow or observe."[391] If you have a statue, for example, you have the right to determine where and how it is placed in the home. You have a moral claim to the object which others are obliged to respect. Accordingly, when a person binds and commands, he must have a moral claim over the person, place, or the thing that the demon is afflicting.

As stated above, the barometer for the right use of imprecatory authority over a demon is retaliation. That is, "acting contrary to the authority structure that God has established

[389] Ripperger, *Deliverance Prayers for Use by the Laity*, 8.
[390] Ripperger, *Dominion*, 122.
[391] Ripperger, 121.

leaves one open to diabolic attack."[392] Recall how Rogers warned that "if somebody's trailing you, make a circle, come back onto your own tracks, and ambush the folks that aim to ambush you." The enemy will lure you into an ambush by enticing you to use imprecatory fire outside of your authority structure. In fact, the demon will gladly take a beating to draw a person out of this protective bulwark. That is, he also utilizes "reconnaissance by fire" and will try to draw you out of your protective cover.

Baptism does not grant a person authority over all things; rather, it confers sanctifying grace and the authority over demons within your own authority structure. This structure is where the human and demon interact and determines whether a demon responds; that is, they know and follow the natural law perfectly and must obey when rightly "obliged." That is, the demon must follow the legitimate commands made under legitimate authority over a person, place, or thing/object. If power is not exercised within one's authority structure (that is, outside of the bounds of the office of one's state in life), that person is vulnerable to demonic retaliation. For this reason, we recommend that if you "stay in your lane," you will be protected—and more effective in your engagement.

Authority is a protective shield. This is to say, you must have your *shield up* and *staff in hand* when you drive out demons. In the language of deliverance, to drive out demons usually means a twofold process of binding and casting or driving out (i.e., raise your shield and hit your enemy with the boss). The Latin *ligo* means "to bind, fix, or fasten," as in the English word *ligament*. To *obligo* (where we get the English word *obligation*) means "to bind around," but in the sense of to put under an obligation or make liable. One is under obligation to perform an act if one is under the authority of another. By virtue of the filial piety owed to parents, for example, a parent can "oblige" a child to do this or that. *Mutatis mutandis*, parents can "oblige" (*viz.*, bind) demons and command them

---

[392] Ripperger, 139.

to leave their children. Father Ripperger affirms that a father holds imprecatory authority and "has a right to command the demons to leave his children or to stop afflicting them."[393] Demons, he notes, respond to prayers of binding based on the level of authority (over an object, place, or person) of the person who prays.

How do you use your shield also as an offensive weapon? Just as the boss provided weight and balance for ramming into one's opponent, so the Christian can use binding prayers before striking his enemy. Binding prayers take two forms: *imprecatory* and *deprecatory*. The Latin word *precor* means "to entreat, request, or ask," and to *deprecor* means "to implore on behalf of, or to ward off by earnest prayers." Thus, the use of deprecatory prayer means specifically to avert, ward off, or intercede on behalf of. The deprecatory form usually begins with, *In your name, Lord Jesus Christ, I ask you to bind any demon afflicting (n). Or, May the Lord bind the spirit of x.* The deprecatory form also can invoke Our Lady, Saint Joseph, Saint Michael, your guardian angel, et cetera. Thus, *May Saint Michael unsheathe his sword and bind any demon present to (n.).* Or, *May the Holy Virgin Mary, Virgin Most Powerful, and Saint Joseph, terror of demons, bind, rebuke, and disable the demon of (x.) afflicting so-and-so.* This is the formula to be used when you do not have authority over a person, place, or object.

The boss strikes with more force, however, when the imprecatory form is deployed. Imprecatory authority flows through office and should only be used when (1) a person has requisite authority and (2) is in a state of grace. The Latin *imprecor* means "to call down, invoke upon." Thus, imprecatory prayer means to invoke or command and implies the one commanding must have an office. With that office of authority is implied an obligation to satisfy the two ends of authority (namely, provide and protect). The command usually begins with, *In the name of Jesus Christ, and by the authority given to me by natural law by God the Father Almighty, I bind (x.).* Or simply,

---

[393] Ripperger, 158.

In the name of Jesus Christ, I bind the demon of (x). If unsure of what is afflicting you within your authority structure, you can ask for help from the Mystical Body:

> *In the name of Jesus Christ [and by the authority given to me by natural law by God the Father Almighty], I bind any demon present to (n.) that is known to Saint Michael, his/her guardian angel, and the Virgin Most Powerful, and I command them to leave immediately, quietly, and permanently and go to the foot of the cross of Jesus Christ to receive their sentence.*

Another binding prayer that can be used when you have legitimate authority by office as per above, can be as follows:

> *In the name of Jesus Christ, and by the authority given to me through natural law by God the Father Almighty, I bind any evil spirit (of x., or afflicting my son or daughter, etc. that is present to this home, that is afflicting my wife, that is harassing my husband's body, etc.), and I send them to the foot of the cross of Jesus Christ to receive their sentence.*

When baptismal power is exercised according to one's vocation (that is, over those people and things under one's legitimate authority) *and in a state of grace,* then the shield can be safely and effectively deployed. Whether to utilize the imprecatory or deprecatory form is shown in more detail in the authority diagram below. You are the demolitions expert on your fire team. When you have met the first two conditions of "combustible" prayer, you can deploy the full imprecatory authority over yourself and your temporal goods and, depending on your sacramental configuration, over others. Within that structure, you are protected. Note the lines of authority in *Figure 01* on the pages below.

This chart shows that the laity are not to be passive in the spiritual battle. Quite the contrary, they have the weapons—whether shield, staff, sword, or slingshot—needed to engage the enemy with all power and authority. Thus, Father Ripperger states, "Some assert that the Church has only passed down to the laity the deprecatory prayers for their use and not imprecatory prayers. However, as we have already seen, St. Alphonsus and St. Thomas show that anyone has a right in private to adjurations, that is, commanding demons to depart or to do certain things."[394] The laity have always been able to do prayers of deliverance over themselves. They can, and should, "fire for effect," as they say in the artillery, against the demons afflicting them. As Clement aptly summarizes:

> One may only use the imprecatory form when one has authority over the person he is praying for. For example, a layman may use the imprecatory form over his minor children or his wife because of his office as father or husband. A mother can command based on the office of motherhood. She can command in relation to the husband due to the right to his body due to the marital contract. One does not have authority over another individual or demon purely by virtue of one's baptism. Baptism gives us authority over the demons in relationship to ourselves. In order to determine if one has the right to command the demons in relationship to a particular individual, it is simply required to ask whether one has the right to command the individual from the natural law in other matters. For example, a father has a right to tell his son to clean out the garage and, therefore, has the authority to use the imprecatory form in relationship to demons that afflict his son because of his rights over his son.[395]

When done correctly according to the rules of engagement, every Christian should be driving the evil from their families, homes, and temporal goods on a regular basis when he has a legitimate moral claim. This helps you, in the words of Paddy Mayne, calculate the risks for and against striking, before having a go.

---

[394] Ripperger, 167.
[395] Liber Christo, "Companion Guide," 58–59.

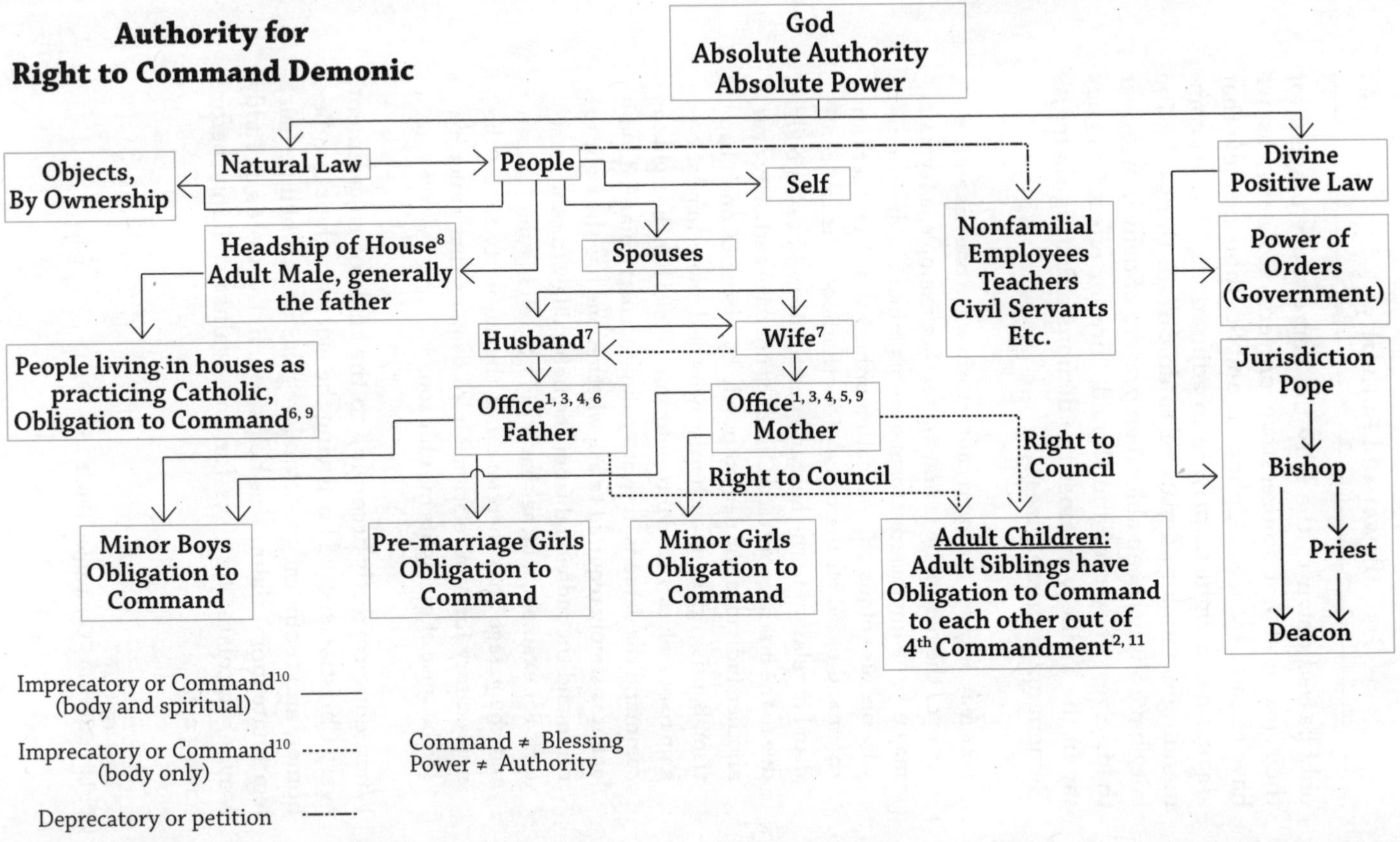

Authority for Right to Command Demonic

God
Absolute Authority
Absolute Power

Divine Positive Law

Power of Orders (Government)

Jurisdiction
Pope
Bishop → Priest → Deacon

Natural Law

People

Self

Objects, By Ownership

Headship of House[8]
Adult Male, generally the father.

People living in houses as practicing Catholic, Obligation to Command[6, 9]

Nonfamilial Employees Teachers Civil Servants Etc.

Spouses

Husband[7]

Wife[7]

Office[1, 3, 4, 6]
Father

Office[1, 3, 4, 5, 9]
Mother

Adult Children:
Adult Siblings have Obligation to Command to each other out of 4th Commandment[2, 11]

Right to Council

Right to Council

Pre-marriage Girls Obligation to Command

Minor Girls Obligation to Command

Minor Boys Obligation to Command

Imprecatory or Command[10] (body and spiritual) ———

Imprecatory or Command[10] (body only) ·········

Deprecatory or petition — · — · —

Command ≠ Blessing
Power ≠ Authority

Copyright 2019 Chad Ripperger

Figure 01

1. Biological Father or Legally Adopted
2. 4ᵗʰ Commandment, Subjection out of piety, giving honor to their parents.
3. Office of Father primarily to protect and provide; Mother, household/children
4. Office gives a right and a duty to command
5. Natural right to command however Father can counter command Mother with reason.
6. Obligation to Command through Office as head of household, (a house divided is an open door to demonic so all in house should be participating in the Sacraments and submit to authority of head of household).
7. Solemn contract is more than an oath or a vow, (Both parties of a solemn contract are bound to the contract even if other party does not abide by it.) This gives the right to give a command over the body, physical healing, not spiritual commands other than in retaliation to demons.
8. If the Father dies then the oldest adult son's obligation of support for the other siblings until age of majority, includes the obligation to command, according to Natural Law.
9. Office of Mother acts as Head of House when Father is absent unless the Father commands otherwise, (absence is different than death).
10. Without Authority may allow demonic affliction
11. Piety is made manifest toward the aged and infirmed patents by the discharge of the obligation to offer and provide temporal and spiritual support including the obligation to command evil spirits.

Blessing and the Imposition of Hands

As the above shows, we must be mindful that demons try to get us to disregard (or not learn) the rules of engagement when it comes to spiritual warfare. Thus, Clement refers to the demon as "the most tightly restricted creature in the universe." This is because, "in the demon's fallen nature, he is relegated only to what God will allow him to do. He has no autonomy and acts strictly according to his fallen (and distorted) angelic nature. The demons do not speculate or debate. Rather, they will yield as the result of being bound by truth, power, and authority, or they will not yield because of some permission granted to them by the soul."[396]

As Father Ripperger also states, "They work off of the objective criteria which God has established in relationship to the natural law and the divine positive law in relationship to human beings." That is, they do not act "according to theological speculation but according to the objective law of God."[397]

Praying with a person is not the same as praying over a person. The rules for blessings and the laying of hands generally follow the same "objective criteria" as the imprecatory and deprecatory forms of prayer. The laying (or imposition) of hands is a powerful, non-verbal sign of authority, and one which invokes dominion over a demon. Like the yoga postures which contain religious signifiers imbued with spiritual significance that are inseparable from the body, so also the imposition of hands.

According to Father Hardon, the purpose of laying of hands is "to convey the communication of some favor, power, duty, or blessing." Notably, in the Old Testament, this was used by the patriarchs to bless their children, in the consecration of priests, and in blessing an animal before sacrifice.[398] Thus, as I wrote elsewhere, the conveyance of a blessing through the imposition of hands "had a twofold purpose in the Old

---

[396] Liber Christo, "Companion Guide," 155.

[397] Ripperger, *Dominion*, 158.

[398] Hardon, *Modern Catholic Dictionary*, 223. See also fn. 296 above.

Testament." The first "was the customary Jewish way of designating someone for the special duty of priest, prophet or king." In this usage, the one who blesses invokes upon another "both the divine blessing and the special power to perform the duty signified by the transmission of authority." Accordingly:

> When Joshua received the office from Moses, for example, God told Moses, "Take Joshua, son of Nun, a man of spirit, and lay your hand upon him. Have him stand before Eleazar the priest and the whole community, and commission him in their sight. Invest him with some of your own power, that the whole Israelite community may obey him" (Num 27:18–20). The result? Elsewhere the Bible states that, "Now Joshua, son of Nun, was filled with the spirit of wisdom, since Moses had laid his hands upon him; and so the Israelites gave him their obedience, just as the Lord had commanded Moses" (Deut 34:9).[399]

The second usage was patriarchal, as seen "where the head of household imparts a blessing by laying of hands." Thus, "before the patriarch Israel died, he 'put out his right hand and laid it on the head of Ephraim . . . and his left hand on the head of Manasseh' and blessed them (Gen 48:14)."[400]

Jesus blessed the children by the imposition of hands (see Mt 19:15). Father Hardon notes how the gesture is also seen in the New Testament "with Christ performing miracles and with the apostles conferring sacraments, especially the priesthood."[401] Thus, I wrote how the same "twofold practice continued in the early Church, as the early Christian community used it as a symbol of installation into an office." This is seen in the Acts of the Apostles, where the first deacons were ordained with the same gesture. As I explained, "'They presented these men to the apostles who prayed and laid hands on them' (Acts 6:6) Elsewhere, and while the community was 'in liturgy' (leitourgeo, Acts 13:2),

---

[399] Liber Christo, "Companion Guide," 60–61.
[400] Liber Christo, "Companion Guide," 60-1. For more scriptural references, see Unger, *Dictionary*, 731-32.
[401] Hardon, *Modern Catholic Dictionary*, 223.

Paul and Barnabas were commissioned in the same way as was seen in the Old Testament: 'Then, completing their fasting and prayer, they laid hands on them and sent them off' (Acts 13:3)."[402]

The priestly office is conferred by Paul to Timothy, as seen in his exhortation: "Do not neglect the gift you have through the prophetic word with the imposition of hands of the presbyterate" (1 Tm 4:14). This practice then continued into Catholic liturgy in the various sacraments (specifically, Baptism, Confirmation, Anointing of the Sick, and Holy Orders all utilize the priestly gesture). Father Hardon also notes how it is used "in other rites and blessings such as exorcisms and before the consecration of the Mass when the Priest extends his hands over the bread and wine."[403]

Thus, Father Hardon shows how in the Old Testament, the "laying on of hands" is either a priestly action or an action from an Israelite father to his son.[404] This custom carries into the New Testament tradition and the practice of the Church where you will find fathers blessing their sons by praying over them and laying their hands on them. In addition, notice how the right to bless runs parallel with the right to command in the discussion above. Father Ripperger likewise states that "the ability of a specific layman to bless is essentially shown in the Old Testament in which parents, especially the father, has the right to bless his children by virtue of his office as father. The husband also has the ability to bless his wife by virtue of his spiritual headship over his wife. The wife has the right to bless the children, but not the husband because she does not have authority over him since she is not his head."

Thus, the right to bless "proceeds from an office by which one commands the blessing over the person." From the perspective of the diabolic, Father Ripperger states, if a person does not have the authority to command another (i.e., "who are not under them by virtue of an office or obligation"), then

---

[402] Liber Christo, "Companion Guide," 61.
[403] Hardon, *Modern Catholic Dictionary*, 223.
[404] Unger, *The New Unger's Bible Dictionary*, 1402–9.

"they do not have the authority to command blessings."[405] He concludes that outside the familial construct, "it is not normally conceded that a layman has the ability to bless another layman."[406] In other words, a father can bless his wife and children, but he should not bless anyone outside of his authority.[407] Rather, he should pray, "May the Lord bless (n)."

Interestingly, in the Bible, there is not a single verse where lay people impose hands over other lay people to drive out demons. As applied for laity today, Clement states:

> The imposition of hands or the laying on of hands is a manifestation of authority over the person by which one is conferring some good thing. The hands of the laypeople are not anointed as are those of the priest. The laypeople do not have authority over each other except as explained above. Even if the laying of hands is not intended as an assertion of authority (as in, for example, in prayers of healing), the gesture itself is priestly and, therefore, reserved for the ordained. Since they do not have the authority to command those people who are not under them by virtue of an office, lay people do not have the authority to command blessings. They can, however, petition our Lord to bless people in the deprecatory prayer such as "May our Lord bless you in the name of our Lord Jesus Christ" instead of "I bless you . . ."[408]

As in grace before meals ("Bless us, O Lord, and these thy gifts . . .") deprecatory blessings are quite efficient.

Conversely, when a priest raises his hands in a blessing, the power of Christ is invoked. When a father (or mother) blesses his children and lays hands on them, he invokes his

---

[405] Ripperger, *Dominion*, 166.

[406] Ripperger, 166.

[407] For example, he can lay hands upon his wife and children in a blessing, trace the sign of the cross on their foreheads, sprinkle with holy water, and the like. A mother can bless her children in the same manner. Since godparents do not have the right to command (but rather, counsel), their blessings should be deprecatory ("May the Lord bless my godchild.").

[408] Liber Christo, "Companion Guide," 59.

paternal blessing on them. When he lays hands on his wife and invokes a prayer or blessing (or command) over her, his gesture and words are also religious signifiers imbued with spiritual significance—and heard loudly in the spiritual realm. Likewise, when a father leads his family by invoking the Epiphany Blessing on the home or goes through the house or business sprinkling with holy water, the message is clearly sent. He strikes his opponent with his shield and says clearly, "Back off. This place, this family, these sheep all belong to Jesus Christ, and by His authority I plant the flag of Christ here." *Figure 02*, shown on following page, delineates the authority to bless.

With regards to deliverance ministry, we hold that the laying of hands can be done by lay people within the parameters described here. When Father Ripperger says that demons "are lawyers from hell," however, this means that they "know exactly the structure and demands of the law and use this to accuse and condemn us before God (cf. Rev 12:10). They also know the structure of authority that must be obeyed, and that they themselves must obey God."[409] When asked why demons obey someone who does not have authority, Clement explains:

> They are not actually obeying the person who is commanding them. Instead, they recognize and yield to the power of the Name of Jesus. They are not obeying the person who is saying the prayer but submitting to the authority of Jesus Christ. Thus, demons are bound by the authority of Christ's Name, not the authority of the individual. The demon also recognizes the disorder present when a person prays over someone with whom they do not have proper authority. That disorder can result in an open door to retaliation and, therefore, highlights the necessity to work within one's authority structure.[410]

---

[409] Liber Christo, "Companion Guide," 151–52.
[410] Liber Christo, "Companion Guide," 151–52.

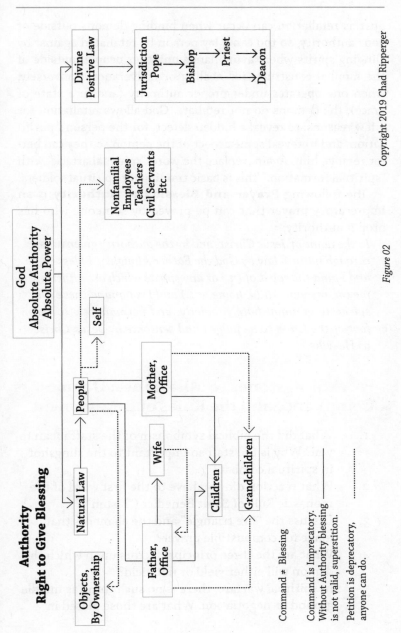

Figure 02

Just as retaliation can occur when binding demons outside of your authority, so too can a lay person be retaliated against by clinging spirits when laying hands on other people (outside of the familial construct) for healing or deliverance. Conversely, when one operates under proper authority (and in a state of grace), the demons do not retaliate. God allows retaliation for a few reasons: to reveal a hidden defect, for the person's purification, and to reveal some aspect of the demon so they can better remove him. Again, replace the word "spiritual attack" with "spiritual formation." This is basic training for spiritual soldiers.

The following **Prayer and Blessing of Authority** is an imprecatory prayer that can be prayed by someone who has proper authority:

> In the name of Jesus Christ, and by the authority given to me through natural law by God the Father Almighty, I bless (n.) and I bind the spirit of (n.) or any spirits which are afflicting me (or, my wife, child, home, etc.) and I command these evil spirits to go immediately, quietly, and permanently to the foot of the Cross to be judged and sentence by Jesus Christ as He wills.

From Slingstones to Milestones: Demonic Compliance and the Rules of Engagement

1. What did the biblical symbolism of the staff mean to you? Why is the staff so important to the slingshot in spiritual combat?
2. What reaction did you have to the first word of the monastic Rule of Saint Benedict ("Listen")?
3. Discuss the "fire triangle" and the elements that make for combustible prayer?
4. What are the three principal factors upon which the demon will either yield or not yield?
5. In spiritual warfare, there is no such thing as middle ground or negotiation. What are those placed in

authority, such as head-of-household, obliged to do? Is this based on merit or office?

6. Discuss the statement: "When someone steps outside of his authority structure, the demon can (and often does) retaliate for the violation of the rules of engagement. This is to say, the barometer of the right use of authority in driving out demons is retaliation, which usually comes in the form of an attack against one's vocation."

Chapter Five

Prayer, Weapons, and Tactics

"David answered [the Philistine]: 'You come against me with sword and spear and scimitar, but I come against you in the name of the LORD of hosts, the God of the armies of Israel that you have insulted.'"

—1 SAMUEL 17:45

On the cover of the Ranger handbook is a simple disclaimer: "Not for the weak or fainthearted." The ancients would prefer the phrase "Gird your loins"—although both communicate the same message. That David *raced toward* Goliath with staff and slingshot implies that he had tied up his tunic around his waist, as is customary for soldiers. To "gird your loins" meant tying your tunic around your waist and crotch area to be more mobile (and be protected by the extra padding of layered material). Accordingly, it means to prepare for battle, or to "man up" in modern parlance. God commanded Jeremiah to "gird your loins" and be fearless in proclaiming the truth (Jer 1:17). Likewise, God "addressed Job out of the storm" and commanded him, "Gird up your loins now, like a man" (Job 38:3).

You will need to gird your loins and be courageous and bold if you want to win this fight. By no means does this imply that only men can "grid their loins"—recall the discussion on Saint Teresa and the importance of moral courage. Saint Peter uses this phrase for all Christians to teach the importance of obedience and reverence. He uses the phrase "gird your loins" in the context of "sojourning" and allusions to Passover:

> Therefore, *gird up the loins of your mind*, live soberly, and set your hopes completely on the grace to be brought to you at the revelation of Jesus Christ. Like obedient children, do not act in compliance with the desires of your former ignorance but, as he who called you is holy, *be holy yourselves in every aspect of your conduct*, for it is written, "Be holy because I [am] holy." Now if you invoke as Father him who judges impartially according to each one's works, conduct yourselves with reverence during *the time of your sojourning*, realizing that you were ransomed from your futile conduct, handed on by your ancestors, not with perishable things like silver or gold but with the precious blood of Christ as of a spotless unblemished lamb. (1 Pt 1:13–19)

You have all you need to win this battle, so *be holy in every aspect of your conduct* and the Lord will guide your stone. You have a sling, a bag of five stones, and a staff. Now, gird your loins and let us turn to how to identify enemy tactics.

Lesson Eleven: Demonic Tactics

By now you recognize that David beat Goliath not with conventional weapons and tactics but by using guerrilla warfare. Rogers's rangers were successful because they rejected the traditional European style of fighting—formations of troops lined up in the open with bright jackets, fighting at set times and seasons under conventional rules of engagement. Rogers counselled his men to fight more covertly: "When you're on the march, act the way you would if you was sneaking up on a deer. See the enemy first." In spiritual combat, to "see the enemy first" requires sanctified vision that only comes through spiritual purity. In this section, we will then teach you the tactics that make for good spiritual ranging. That is, how to maintain interior silence on the march so as not to draw the demon's attention and how to "sneak up" in stealth. To "see the enemy first," you need to understand what his patrol teams and tactics look like. This means you must understand how your own spiritual faculties work because this is how the enemy sees you and sizes you up. After that, we will discuss the second element of "combustible" prayer and the importance of supernatural merit as it relates to spiritual warfare. First, you must first know how your enemy finds your vulnerabilities.

Thomistic Psychology: A Spiritual Remedy in the Face of "Diabolic Disorientation"

This section describes the basic Catholic understanding of the human person's faculties according to Saint Thomas Aquinas and forms the basis for what is known as Thomistic Psychology.[411] Recall the previous discussion on Saint Augustine and the human person as *capax Dei*, meaning that you not only are capable to receive the divine but also can share in divinity as your rightful inheritance through Baptism. He states that it was appropriate that God, who is Three-but-One, made man in His own image as one (person) but with three (spiritual faculties). Thus, God is three divine Persons—Father, Son, and Holy Spirit—but is one God. Man has three spiritual faculties—what here we refer to as the higher, intermediate, and lower—but he is one person. In that spiritual reality, we reflect the mystery of the Blessed Trinity. This is precisely what the demon militates against, and we expand on it briefly here because this is how the demon sees us. The human person can be seen as having three "faculties" or interior powers/capacities:

---

[411] This is an adapted version of Saint Thomas's teachings on human faculties. For more on Thomistic psychology, see Ripperger, *Introduction to the Science of Mental Health*, 1–307. Also, Brennan, *Thomistic Psychology*.

Higher faculties → Intellect and Will
Intermediate or Transitional faculties → Memory
and Emotion[412]
Lower faculties → Appetite and Instinct

Understanding the inner movements of thoughts and emotions helps to identify areas of vulnerability that the demon exploits. Unchecked, the demon even finds his own nourishment in your interior defects.

Towards the end of her life, Venerable Sister Lúcia of Fatima stated that we are living in a time of "diabolic disorientation." What we see in the socio-political realm, however, is a large-scale manifestation of what is at work in countless souls today. The right ordering of the instincts and appetites, for example, means that the flesh must be ordered to the soul, while a diabolic disorientation of the interior faculties means that the intellect and will are slaves of the instincts and appetites, as the following charts indicate.[413]

As the chart shows, the faculties include lower, intermediate, and higher powers. The descending order lists each faculty—*higher faculties* of intellect and will, *intermediate faculties* of memory and emotion, and *lower faculties* of appetite and instinct. The chart begins with an event and how each faculty is understood in response to that event. The upper right edge of the chart asserts what is understood by the term "to be properly ordered." The proper order is the flesh as servant of the soul, but this is damaged in the effects of the

---

[412] In medieval philosophy, these are referred to as the "internal senses" which are defined as "a class of cognitive faculties that were posited to exist between external sense perception and the intellectual soul." We simplify here by referring to the memory and emotions as "transitional" or "intermediate" in that these senses (including the imagination) mediate the external world to the higher self. In our prudential judgment and experience, this internal, intermediate sense is where the spiritual battle takes place. For more, see Kärkkäinen, "Internal Senses," in *Encyclopedia of Medieval Philosophy*, 564–67.

[413] Clement presented these slides in team training sessions in 2018 and also at the Liber Christo annual conference in 2019. See also, Liber Christo, "2019 Conference Manual," 77–140. Used with permission.

Faculties of Human Person

Proper—Flesh is Servant to Soul
Improper—Soul is Hostage to Flesh

Intellect—Truth/Reality

Will—Response to Event

Catholic

Memory—Recollection of Event

Emotion—Reaction to Event

Appetite—Desires

Instinct—Preservation of Corpus

Pagan

Figure 03

Fall and driven to "disorientation." The lower faculties, if left unchecked, seek to invert the right order due to concupiscence (see previous discussion on Baptism and the lingering effects of disordering of passions). We distinguish between the story and the event. Because the story is often filled with emotion, it can differ from the actual facts of the event itself. Thus, as we note, "the meaning and salvific purpose embedded in the event is often clouded or hidden. When you purify your faculties and grow in virtue, the event becomes imbued with meaning and ordered to Christ."[414]

In Catholic anthropology, the faculties of the human person operate with the help of grace and virtue to avoid vice. C. S. Lewis stated simply what a rightly ordered soul looks like: "The head," he says, "rules the belly through the chest."[415] That is, the intellect (the "head" or the seat of intellection) chooses the good and governs the lower faculties of instincts and appetites (the "belly" or the seat of our lowest natural movements most accessible to the demon) by instructing the will (the "chest" or the seat of volition) to govern by in accord with the good. To be improperly ordered (or to be "diabolic disoriented") is to place the soul as hostage (or even slave) to the flesh. When the "chest" mortifies of the "belly" in the flesh, the result is an increase in temperance. As Clement states, temperance is key because "when we have an immoderate behavior, such as overeating or even excessive devotion [that works against vocation], the will must be engaged to fast from this behavior for some period of time. The result is moderation and increased self-control."[416]

Conversely, diabolic disorientation of the interior self means that the belly rules the head through the chest. This inversion is counter to a Catholic, sacramental-orientated life where Christ is center of the soul. In the chart, the vertical arrows on the left side indicate this. The Catholic interiority is re-ordered through sacramental Baptism which removes the effects of original sin. This re-ordering means a special

---

[414] Liber Christo, "Companion Guide," 146.
[415] Lewis, *Abolition of Man*, 8.
[416] Liber Christo, "Companion Guide," 144.

infusion of sanctifying grace by the ontological (at the level of being and not merely symbolic) presence of the Blessed Trinity now residing in the soul. Thus, the intellect receives an infusion of the theological virtues of faith, hope, and charity, providing special assistance to choose the good.

Likewise, the effect upon the will in the state of grace means an orientation toward doing the will of the Father. Specifically, what Adam and Eve possessed in their original state was *original justice* (sanctifying grace) and preternatural gifts of *original integrity* (freedom from disordered desires, or the right ordering of the spiritual faculties), *original innocence* (freedom from concupiscence), and *original immortality* (freedom from death). The Fall, however, introduced a disordering of the human interiority. The effect of the Fall means a disordering of the faculties and necessitates the mortification of the lower faculties so as to experience freedom (and conformity to God) in the higher. According to Saint Thomas and Saint Bede, there are four "wounds" resulting from the Fall:

1. Original sin (loss of sanctifying grace)
2. Ignorance (lack of knowledge)
3. Concupiscence (disordering of passions)
4. Sickness and mortality (corruption of bodily death)

Thus, in God's creative design, the human person is ordered towards God as his highest good in the garden before the Fall. The intellect and will, the higher faculties, are what man has in common with the angels. You must, therefore, order all lower faculties by subjecting them to higher (thus the Catholic arrow descending to the lower and base faculty, which is most concerned with preservation of one's mortal life or flesh). The pagan, conversely, operates with a primacy in the lower instinct and his life choices begin with the thought of what is good for his own life, the flesh, and preservation of my bodily needs, seeking what brings pleasure and self-gratification. Survival by instinct and disordered appetites are what man has most in common with the base or lower faculties found in animals.

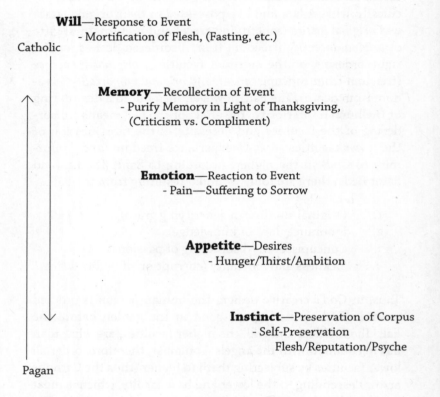

Faculties of Human Person

Proper—Flesh is Servant to Soul
Improper—Soul is Hostage to Flesh

Intellect—Truth/Reality
  - Dogmas, Catholic

Will—Response to Event
    - Mortification of Flesh, (Fasting, etc.)
Catholic

Memory—Recollection of Event
      - Purify Memory in Light of Thanksgiving,
        (Criticism vs. Compliment)

Emotion—Reaction to Event
        - Pain—Suffering to Sorrow

Appetite—Desires
          - Hunger/Thirst/Ambition

Instinct—Preservation of Corpus
            - Self-Preservation
              Flesh/Reputation/Psyche

Pagan

Figure 04

The next layer shows that under each faculty lies a specific human response necessary to strengthen that faculty. For instance, if there is a defect or weakness in the intellect, then it typically manifests itself in heresy or ignorance of a Church dogma or doctrine (what the Catholic Church teaches about man and God, life and death, sin, and grace). In addition, a

weakened will is strengthened by mortification or deprivation of the flesh, specifically of the five senses. Accordingly,
the prayer prescription is intended to strengthen your intellect and will through obedience, discipline, and the imposition of order. In cutting off stimulation to the senses through
the eyes and ears and the insatiable desire for information or
stimulation, the media fast draws the soul to a "desert" experience, which opens the soul to encounter God. This also helps
to bring the instinct into right order under the soul.

According to Clement, "God's will, always and everywhere, is
our salvation, and we must come to see everything in the light
of salvation. Everything that happens to us, therefore, has salvific potential."[417] In the recollection of the event, emotions tend
toward either criticism (fault-finding and negative) or compliment (thankful and positive). When asked how someone can
order the memory to the intellect, Clement explained, "We must
order our memory to salvation, recognizing that every event in
our past has a salvific purpose. This means to take our memory
and ask, how could this event be used for my/our salvation? This
requires a willingness to suffer for those who cannot or will not.
In order to do this, God—not the self—must be the center of
our focus. Our memories can drive us to sin and despair, or they
can increase in us a thirst for the salvation of souls."[418]

To do this requires a willingness to suffer. Ask yourself:
Does this emotion represent the proper response in light of
what is happening to what is happening? Do I turn inward,
or do I look upward to find the salvific potential in the event?
A disordered memory is seen in a person who only recalls a
memory or event with an unholy shame, by blaming, finding
fault, or criticizing others in the memory events. Conversely, a
memory is strengthened by forgiving and finding the good in
the event. This is done by inserting an act of thanksgiving to
God and by asserting the will to unite the suffering to the suffering of Jesus Christ. Thus, purifying the memory is achieved
through thanksgiving for the "good" and not harboring resentment or self-justification in holding on to the "just claim."

---

[417] Liber Christo, "Companion Guide," 144.
[418] Liber Christo, "Companion Guide," 144.

You must move from *why* to *how*. The reaction in the emotions and memory is strengthened by looking at one's reactions to the pain of the event. This implies an act of the will that seeks no longer to ask, *Why is this happening to me?* Rather, we must ask: *How can I use this for the salvation of souls?* Left unchecked, the reaction in the appetites will crowd out the higher faculties and grasp at that which will never satisfy. It can seduce the flesh into striving for the elevation of self, pleasure, control, asking: *What's in it for me?* The reaction in the instinct is concerned with survival and the preservation of one's mortal life to the disregard or denial that there is anything or anyone more significant than one's own well-being.

The chart on the following page shows what needs to happen in each faculty to facilitate proper ordering in response to the event. In the intellect, one must order his thinking to absolute Truth. This means an assent to what the Church teaches even if you do not yet understand. This assent is in an act of faith in God, His infinite wisdom and truth. By an act of the will, you must choose to order your life to prayer—and not the opposite. This means not giving into excuses that you are too busy to pray, or that God does not hear your prayers. He hears your prayers whether you feel it (in the emotions) or not. In fact, nowhere in the tradition of the Church do feelings dictate the certitude of one's relationship with God. Think, choose, and act.

The memory must be ordered to the intellect. You must stop and think: What is the salvific opportunity here? What is true, good, holy, and pure? What will bring me closer to God? This will help order the emotions and make them subject to the intellect through the memory. This means choosing (by an act of the will) to see the salvific value in this or that event rather than focusing on the pain. In the appetites, you must desire the good for the salvation of your soul, even if it is difficult and does not bring pleasure or emotional satisfaction. Desire this good because God wants it, and for no other reason. To subdue the appetites, then, you must choose virtue over vice for the salvation of your soul. This means the denial of fleshly desires. The lowest faculty, the instincts, must be directed by

Faculties of Human Person

Proper—Flesh is Servant to Soul
Improper—Soul is Hostage to Flesh

Intellect—Truth/Reality
- Dogmas, Catholic
- Order to Absolute Truth

Will—Response to Event
- Mortification of Flesh, (Fasting, etc.)
- Order Life to Prayer

Catholic

Memory—Recollection of Event
- Purify Memory in Light of Thanksgiving,
  (Criticism vs. Compliment)
- Ordering to Intellect, (Order to Salvation)

Emotion—Reaction to Event
- Pain—Suffering to Sorrow
- Order Emotion to Intellect Through Memory

Appetite—Desires
- Hunger/Thirst/Ambition
- Order to Adversity—Betrayal

Instinct—Preservation of Corpus
- Self-Preservation
  Flesh/Reputation/Psyche
- Order Flesh to Soul

Pagan

Figure 05

the will to order the flesh to the soul. Recognize that your body is a temple of the Holy Spirit and the works of your flesh have an effect on your soul (which will last eternally). Choose to serve your soul by acts of sacrifice, redemptive suffering, and virtuous living. That is, as Saint Peter wrote, "Gird up the loins of your mind, live soberly, and set your hopes completely on the grace to be brought to you at the revelation of Jesus Christ. Like obedient children, do not act in compliance with the desires of your former ignorance but, as he who called you is holy, be holy yourselves in every aspect of your conduct, for it is written, 'Be holy because I [am] holy'" (1 Pt 1:13–16).

This final chart reflects how Christ's life permeates each of the three spiritual faculties. Specifically, His passion and death analogously reveal the perfection of each human faculty. Christ's faith perfects the intellect by His total trust in the Father. His faith also drives Him to reconcile and to heal man's relationship with the Father, achieved through His passion, death, and resurrection for the salvation of souls. Yet, this requires an act of the will. Christ reveals the hope He possesses in the divine and sovereign will of the Father. He wants what the Father wants because the Father wants it.

Thus, while *faith* perfects the intellect and *hope* perfects the will, *love* perfects the memory. Christ reveals the love of the Father at the Last Supper when He instituted the Eucharist: "Do this in remembrance of me" (Lk 22:19) and offered Himself to the world for the fulfillment of the New Covenant and salvation of souls. "Remember," He says in effect, "that when you see me broken and poured out from the cross, this Eucharist prefigures the crucifixion." In effect, He attempts to purify the apostles' memory prior to His horrifying death. Christ was fully human: He wept at the death of Lazarus (see Jn 11:5), knew fatigue (see Jn 4:6) and hunger (see Lk 4:2), and agonized in the garden (see Lk 22:44). Nonetheless, He willfully ordered His emotions through the memory to the intellect. Just as He knew Lazarus's death was meant to glorify the Father (see Jn 11:4), so also His own death would glorify the Father (see Jn 12:27–28).

Faculties of Human Person

Proper—Flesh is Servant to Soul
Improper—Soul is Hostage to Flesh

Intellect—Truth/Reality
- Dogmas, Catholic
- Order to Absolute Truth
- Christ—On the Cross

Will—Response to Event
- Mortification of Flesh, (Fasting, etc.)
- Order Life to Prayer
- Christ—In Garden

Memory—Recollection of Event
- Purify Memory in Light of Thanksgiving,
  (Criticism vs. Compliment)
- Ordering to Intellect, (Order to Salvation)
- Christ—Last Supper

Emotion—Reaction to Event
- Pain—Suffering to Sorrow
- Order Emotion to Intellect Through Memory
- Christ—Wept at Lazarus's Death

Appetite—Desires
- Hunger/Thirst/Ambition
- Order to Adversity—Betrayal
- Christ—Wedding at Cana

Instinct—Preservation of Corpus
- Self-Preservation
  Flesh/Reputation/Psyche
- Order Flesh to Soul
- Christ—Days in Desert

Catholic

Pagan

Figure 06

At the wedding feast of Cana, we see the right ordering of the appetites, where Jesus meets the needs for more wine at the request of His mother (see Jn 2:4). This miracle reveals His power and initiates His public ministry. Likewise, through the temptations of the devil in the desert (see Mt 4:1–11), Jesus responded with the truth and reality found in His intellect, confounding the enemy and ultimately defeating him.

Why does *Liber Christo* discourage the reliance on the emotions in the spiritual life? Engaging in spiritual combat with a high emotionality is like trying to "sneak up on a deer" with a jackhammer. Simply stated, you cannot trust your emotions or the images in your imagination as true indicators of the objective reality of your relationship with God. In addition, a high emotionality gives access to the demons. Accordingly, we draw from a simplified version of how Saint Thomas Aquinas understood the human person's interior life (faculties). In each faculty, we find examples in Christ's life that highlight its perfection. Also, at each stage, there is marked the proper ordering of that faculty.

Demonic Tactics and Threats

When we speak of a "talking snake," we refer to the subtle temptations, the seductive voice which seduced Eve into disobedience. The surrender to the deception of the serpent lead to the breakdown of relationships, as I explain:

> Recall that in the creation story, everything that God created was called either "good" or "very good" (as mentioned at least six times in Genesis 1). Adam and Eve lived in a "garden in Eden" (Gen 2:8,15), that is, in a paradisal state of right relationship with God, each other and creation itself. They lived and walked in God's actual presence. Despite this idyllic state, however, Adam and Eve abused their freedom and their relationship with God by disobeying God's command (cf. Gen 2:17; 3:11-12). We refer to the fall of our first parents as

the first or "original" sin. This primordial choice of rebellion against God by our first parents has several lasting effects upon us. Not only did it separate mankind from God, but it has also 1) darkened the human intellect, 2) weakened the human will, and 3) introduced into human nature an inclination toward sin.[419]

Thus, not only did the first sin break the relationship with God, "in the rebellion of Adam and Eve against God, but our relationship with God also became fractured while our relationship with each other became disordered. Even our relationship with ourselves, our interior life, became disordered such that the lower spiritual faculties now militate against our higher self, the intellect and the will."[420] As Saint Paul writes, "I take delight in the law of God in my inner self, but I see in my members another principle at war with the law of my mind, taking me captive to the law of sin that dwells in my members. Miserable one that I am! Who will deliver me from this mortal body? Thanks be to God through Jesus Christ our Lord. Therefore, I myself, with my mind, serve the law of God but, with my flesh, the law of sin" (Rom 7:22–25).

This is our common struggle. Accordingly, the original sin means not only separation from God but also a lack of grace that results in a disordering of appetites. The demon exploits this tendency by appealing to our lower faculties.

Through emotionally charged memories and images, the "talking snake" seeks to influence intellection (what you think) and manipulate volition (what you choose). In so doing, he seeks to habituate your responses and perception of your past, daily events, and of God, self, and others. The demon will often glean from your emotions and speech to tempt you with your own fears. Listen to how he taunted David as the shepherd broke ranks from the Israelite army and approached the giant: "Come here to me, and I will feed your flesh to the birds of the air and the beasts of the field" (1 Sm 17:44). This

---

[419] Liber Christo, "Companion Guide," 9.
[420] Liber Christo, "Companion Guide," 9.

was not a random threat or mere trash-talk. He was mocking Israel's infidelity to the covenant and speaking their own fears to them. As part of the curses for disobedience, Moses used this same language in exhorting the people of God to be faithful to the Law. As punishment for unfaithfulness to the Law, Moses told the people, "Your corpses will become food for all the birds of the air and for the beasts of the field" (Dt 28:26).

The demon similarly will try to mock you, remind you of your past sins and infidelity to the covenantal seal of your Baptism. Just as Goliath held the entire army of Israel in fear, so also the "demon Goliath" seeks to neutralize you. Recall that he has access to the "data set" of memories and images in your imagination. He will distort those memories and images and voice your own fears, your own hurts, and your own vulnerabilities to you to keep you from fighting. If you have looked at pornography, for example, he can access the images and project them to you in order to tempt you or evoke a shame response. Thus, the purification of the memory and emotional constancy are essential in augmenting the will to choose the good.

"Seeing the enemy first" means to recognize his patterns. Do not take the bait. The demon knows our fallen human nature and, in our prudential experience, understands the human vulnerabilities according to Saint Thomas's description of the human person. Moreover, he is attracted by moral defects and psychological woundedness—both of which are signaled by high emotionality. In fact, there is an often-symbiotic attraction between the fallen angel who militates contrary to his original mission given by God and the broken or wounded human intellect and any concomitant lack of virtue. Thus, outbursts of anger attract a spirit of anger. Rebellion against authority attracts a spirit of rebellion, lust attracts a demon of lust, and so on. In addition, a psychological obsession over a divorce, a child who has left the Faith, loneliness, et cetera can also present a spiritual vulnerability. You must be careful, therefore, not to allow a psychological obsession to overtake your interior life because a psychological obsession can expose the soul to a spiritual oppression or even obsession.

Emotions such as worry, fear, regret, and anger crowd out, and even neutralize, your prayers. The sound of the dying rabbit attracts the coyote. These emotions cannot coexist in the same interior space. With an act of the will, you must eliminate them so that your wounded psychological state does not overtake your interior life and attract an evil spirit to you.[421] As Father Ripperger notes, this is particularly dangerous with psychological obsession. The more a person continues in an obsession, "he not only empowers the demon who is driving the obsession, but he also increases the strength of his psychological habits, resulting in it being extraordinarily hard to climb out."[422] Thus, seek a ranger's interiority "the way you would if you was sneaking up on a deer."

Recognize the enemy's pattern. He waits for an opportune time to project distorted images into the imagination. He strives to darken the intellect with doubt/unbelief and weaken the will through temptation to entice you to choose some evil. Although he can manipulate the intermediate faculties (memory and emotions) through the imagination, the demon does not have access to your higher faculties. He also cannot read your mind. He will, however, set traps to probe your reactions and test your resolve.

No one is a passive recipient in the spiritual life, and at some level, all liberation is self-liberation. For this reason, elsewhere I state that you "must willfully choose to follow God unreservedly, and often courageously, in the face of fear (as David did before Goliath)." Accordingly, the "willful choice in the face of the 'giants' that confront you is essential to liberation. You were created for God, your ultimate Good. All of your choices either draw you closer to, or further away, from

---

[421] Here I refer to unholy and disordered emotions which must be eliminated by a willful act, as opposed to neutral human emotions which must be regulated through virtue.

[422] Ripperger, *Dominion*, 294.

Him."[423] The *Catechism* defines freedom as "the power rooted in reason and will, to act or not to act, to do this or that, and so to perform deliberate actions on one's own responsibility."[424] Thus, I conclude, "Freedom, then, is a choice." Because freedom means choosing to be free and by resisting the devil—"For freedom Christ set us free; so stand firm and do not submit again to the yoke of slavery (Gal 5:1)—part of the "deliberate actions of personal "responsibility" is the choice *to do whatever it takes to attain and maintain freedom.* The enemy, meanwhile, knows the primacy of the human will and "works diligently . . . to habituate you into making poor choices (or, personal sins) so as to weaken your will and, thus, to elicit the emotions of shame or fear in you. These emotions distort your image of God and yourself as a child of God."[425] The demon, like Goliath, wants to break your will. You must be courageous, like David, and engage your enemy with faith, echoing David's words for all to hear: "All this multitude, too, shall learn that it is not by sword or spear that the Lord saves. For the battle is the Lord's, and he shall deliver you into our hands" (1 Sm 17:48). Thus, I state:

> The significance here lies in the fact that to the extent that you participate in a life of sin, you further alienate yourself from God, the inner self, and others—all of which the demon exploits. We speak of this as granting "permissions" to the demon. The demon has no "rights," properly speaking, over a soul (although he might claim as much). Part of the importance of this discussion on the human will, the effect of the Fall and liberation is so as to teach you how to identify where you are granting, or have granted in the past, permissions to the demon through personal sins. We should not despair, however, for this inclination toward sin does not mean we cannot achieve victory.[426]

---

[423] Liber Christo, "Companion Guide," 9.
[424] *CCC* 1731.
[425] Liber Christo, "Companion Guide," 8–9.
[426] Liber Christo, "Companion Guide," 10.

While permissions can create "targets of opportunity" for the enemy to exploit, you must not be discouraged. As Saint James writes, "Submit yourselves to God. Resist the devil, and he will flee from you" (Jas 4:7).

Unchecked Emotions and Spiritual "Odors"

David saw Goliath first. The narrative tells us that he "hastened to the battle line . . . [and] the Philistine champion . . . came up from the ranks and spoke as before, and David listened" (1 Sm 17:22–23). The intermediate faculty (the memory and emotions) is the battle line where Goliath stands, threatens, accuses, and rants. Memory and emotion, in turn, are affected by the appetites (concupiscible and irascible). *Concupiscible* powers (*cupio* is Latin for "desire") incline us toward bodily goods—that is, food, sex, et cetera—while the *irascible* powers (*ira* is Latin for "anger") are those which motivate us physically in order to get those bodily goods that are desired in the concupiscible appetite. A football player, for example, must have a moderated use of the irascible powers to attain the goods desired in the concupiscible appetite (touchdowns, a paycheck, et cetera). We are inclined toward bodily goods by the one and driven to do what is necessary to attain them in the other. The virtues are what moderates both. Accordingly, when there is a dissonance between the two, through a spiritual/moral and psychological disordering or defect, then a disharmony between their cooperation is introduced. Thus, there can arise a fear that expresses itself in anxiety in the concupiscible appetite. This fear-anxiety is a form of sorrow and stems from the thought of a task that is weighing over a person, which they do not think they are capable of overcoming.

Anger, rightly ordered, is the human emotion that drives a person to attain what they desire as good and pleasing. A rightly ordered anger gives a person daring or audacity, says Saint Thomas, to persevere and overcome the obstacles presented to the attainment of the good (and in your case, the good is free-dom from affliction and freedom for union with God). Fortitude is the virtue which makes one willing to engage the arduous. Conversely, unholy anger is an inordinate desire arising from unmoderated sorrow at some offense. Hence, a common holding point for the demon is unforgiveness and results in the lack of will power to do the arduous tasks required for self-deliverance.

Emotions affect the images presented to the imagination, which show the importance of using right reason to order the appetites. When emotions are allowed a higher place than rea-son, then the intellect and the will can modify an image and a person can desire something that is not natural. The operant virtue in question during spiritual combat is often hope, for hope is the virtue which imbues the irascible appetite (the moti-vation to do what it takes to get free) to know it can accomplish the task presented in the concupiscible appetite (the desire for liberation). Without hope, one experiences sorrow—the fear-induced anxiety that comes from shrinking in the face of the task at hand. Here, the irascible power of anger in the form of audacity (part of the virtue of fortitude) must engage. This gives a person the strength and motivation to accomplish something they are otherwise incapable of doing but do it anyway (trusting God to complete the task). The experience of fear (like the expe-rience of sorrow) says that there is some evil coming (or present, in the case of sorrow) which you cannot overcome or avoid. The demons very much play on this fear and sorrow. In fact, disor-dered emotions are an elixir to them, and they are drawn to it. Once in, the demons can lead a person to all sorts of disordered desires and projected emotions and images.

Anger, Saint Thomas says, is the perception of injury with a desire for vindication. Unholy anger arises when one lets the sorrow (fear in the face of great task) go unchecked. The wounds become the fount for the elixir that attracts the demon to you. Deep rage often flows from the deep sorrow over the perceived inability to attain the good (here, liberation). A wound still fes-tering (that is, not completely offered in reparation) is like an odor that draws the demon. In the words of Saint Paul, "We are the aroma of Christ for God among those who are saved and among those who are perishing, to the latter an odor of death that leads to death, to the former an odor of life that leads to life" (2 Cor 2:15). This is possible because "Christ loves us and handed himself over for us as a sacrificial offering to God for a fragrant aroma" (Eph 5:2). Our offerings in union with His makes us "'a fragrant aroma,' an acceptable sacrifice, pleasing to God" (Phil 4:18). Like Mary of Bethany who anointed the feet of Jesus, the aroma of our offering can "fill the house with the fragrance of the oil" when our self-suffering is in union with Jesus (cf. Jn 12:3). Conversely, the interior defects and wounds that fester in the emotions and memory are an "odor of death," a stench which is highly attractive to the demon.

Thus, by an act of the will and by means of reason, you must reject the emotions of anger or fear as they arise. This means that the emotion of (unholy) sorrow, when grasped and appropriated by the mind with no resistance of audacity or hope, leads to a vulnerability to projections by the diabolic. Remember, angels are pure spirits who communicate through illumination. This means that they project images and concepts through our imagination. In the case of the angels, they project good images so that we may use the light of human reason and choose the good. In the case of the fallen angel, who may be present to an afflicted person, those projections can be amplifications of your present (wounded and sinful) condition to entice you to choose evil. Significantly, they can also be the demon's own existential angst over his fixed state of damnation and the pain he is experiencing through this whole process. Either way, these emotionally charged images must be rejected. Therefore, an afflicted person can experience the sorrow-that-leads-to-rage simply from the woundedness of the evil spirit who is always present to the person. That is, sometimes it is *his* eternal sorrow that is projecting *his* existential rage over *his* eternal loss of the beatific vision. So, if it is his problem—the sorrow and the rage—let him own it. When it arises, remind him that this is his problem, not yours, and move on.

According to Saint Thomas, disordered anger is an inordinate desire for vindication arising from unmoderated sorrow at some offense. Bearing in mind the above discussion on trauma, you may be deeply wounded by some past hurt (such as your mother, father, spouse, your own past disordered and deviant behaviors). Remember also that the demon is deeply offended and wounded by the Incarnation, the Father's plan of salvation history, the glories of the Blessed Mother, her unique privileges, and the like. He is also deeply wounded by his own past (fall from grace), but the difference is *he has no hope* (his rebellion is permanent and irreversible) but *you always have hope* in the mercy of God. Accordingly, when the emotions (sorrow, anger, anxiety) arise, keep uniting them with Christ's passion and Our Lady's sorrows and trust in His infinite mercy. The more spiritually and morally healthy you become, the less the demon can feed off your wounds. When those lower emotions project upward, give them right back to the demon and remind him of his most pitiable state, as he is truly without hope. You, however, are a beloved child of God whose salvation is near at hand.

Modern psychology is discovering a twofold movement which, when slowed down, helps those with emotional disorders: (1) one must learn the nature of the underlying disorders, and therefore, (2) one must have an awareness of what triggers the emotion. To undo the "diabolic disordering" of the interiority, you must work on these two: the main causes and the triggers. This is the spiritual equivalent of "acting the way you would if you was sneaking up on a deer" and so "seeing the enemy first."

Supernatural Merit: "Without Me You Can Do Nothing"

Holiness is key to spiritual combat. The depth of your state of grace will affect your effectiveness in battle. Therefore, you must be completely free of past sins and attachments, living a life of great purity. The second condition, therefore, that makes your prayer more combustible, or efficacious, is the merit of the one who prays. The foundation of a theology of merit comes from Jesus who counsels His followers how to attain "recompense from your heavenly father . . . who sees in secret [and] will repay you" (Mt 6:14; see also Mt 20:1–16; 25:14–23; 1 Cor 3:8). By *merit*, we mean "a work completed for the benefit of another person on whom it established a claim for a reward founded on the work."[427] We must avoid, however, any juridical understanding of merit that suggests that any spiritual goods are earned or due to us by God in strict justice. As Jesus states, "Without me you can do nothing" (Jn 15:5). Saint Augustine teaches that "we need grace to merit grace," and all grace (as defined above as divine life) comes from God.

Modern warfare experts suggest that the ancient slingshot was as deadly as a .44 magnum round. This predicates, however, the accuracy of the shooter, which is a byproduct of both skill and the quality of the weapon. Hence, Rogers insisted that his rangers' muskets be "as clean as a whistle." He knew that a dirty rifle, especially one covered with black powder residue, is not accurate. David did not grab any five stones, he "selected five smooth stones" (1 Sm 17:40). Smoothness allows the projectile to have less wind resistance and increases accuracy. You are only as "accurate" in battle as you are interiorly clean and to the extent that you choose "smooth" stones for hurling at the enemy. The earlier lessons on developing virtue and making a good confession are all part of growing in merit so that your stone will hit its target.

In this lesson, then, we will discuss the concept of merit as it relates to spiritual warfare. When we spoke earlier of "sharing in divinity" we recall the teachings of Saint Peter: "His divine power has bestowed on us everything that makes for life and devotion, through the knowledge of him who called us by his own glory and power. Through these, he has bestowed on us the precious and very great promises, so that through them you may come to share in the divine nature, after escaping from the corruption that is in the world because of evil desire" (2 Pt 1:3–4).

---

[427] Ott, *Fundamentals of Catholic Dogma*, 189.

In the Christian West, this "sharing in the divine nature" is referred to as *sanctification* (growing in holiness and separation from the world, the flesh, and the devil). In the East, they call this process *divinization*, part of the process of divine condescension whereby God stoops to lower Himself to where we are to raise us up to where He is. Both terms allude to the same reality: in taking on human flesh, God made it possible for us to become like Him. This means that when we pray from this reality, our prayers are more meritorious.

"Our actions," states Father Jordan Aumann, "are meritorious in the measure that they proceed from grace and are motivated by charity."[428] Thus, the more the soul is filled with an intense charity (the perfection of which "casts out all fear" according to 1 John 4:18), the less lukewarm and susceptible to temptation is the soul. With respect to prayer, how does our prayer merit the response of God? Why should He answer it? Mindful that God owes us nothing in the order of justice, our prayers are meritorious according to three things:[429]

1. The prayer itself must be a good act, in accordance with moral law.
2. The person must be in a state of grace.
3. There is supernatural intention, accompanied by actual grace and proceeding from the person's surrender of his will to the will of God.

As Saint Thomas teaches, grace builds on nature by a threefold action of healing, perfecting, and elevating. Grace *heals* nature of the effects of sin; *perfects* nature so that it is more human, whole, and truly natural than ever before; and *elevates* nature to share in the very life of God. Thus, we emphasize here the definition of "healing" within the panorama of liberation, as the ultimate end being reconciliation and divine friendship with God the Father. Father Ripperger states, therefore, "It is

---

[428] Aumann, *Spiritual Theology*, 232.
[429] For a further discussion on merit, see Ott, *Fundamentals of Catholic Dogma*, 264–69.

always inadvisable to say prayers to help another in his spiritual combat when one's own spiritual life is not in order. In other words, we ought to fight our own spiritual battles first and only after we have attained a spiritual life of habitual sanctifying grace (i.e., never falling into mortal sin) and are sufficiently proficient in our prayer lives (especially meditation), that one ought to say the petition form of these prayers for another over whom one does not have authority."[430]

Accordingly, all supernatural merit comes not from our virtue but from the merits of Jesus Christ. As Blessed John Duns Scotus emphasizes, however, there is an essential need for the right disposition in receiving the reward of our prayers and acts.[431]

As seen in the discussion above, the sacraments work objectively (they confer the grace they signify), but one can receive more, or less, grace depending upon the subjectivity of the recipient. What Father Hardon says of the effectiveness of the sacraments can be applied to the meritorious nature of prayer. "Provided no obstacle (obex) is placed in the way, every sacrament properly administered confers the grace intended by the sacrament. In a true sense the sacraments are instrumental causes of grace."[432] The most common obstacles are "a lack of faith, or not being in a state of grace, or of a worthy intention."[433]

Thus, one's deep friendship with God fuels the efficaciousness of one's prayer. As Jesus states, "This is my commandment: love one another as I love you. No one has greater love than this, to lay down one's life for one's friends. You are my friends if you do what I command you" (Jn 15:12–14). How do we deepen our friendship with God? We must live with purity of thought, word, and deed. As stated in the

---

[430] Ripperger, *Deliverance Prayers for Use by the Laity*, 8–9.
[431] See Cross, *Scotus*, 105. A basic understanding is Scotus's notion that congruous merit (that is, not by one's own virtue but by the merit and virtues of Christ) is a *disposition* for the reception of a reward.
[432] Hardon, *Modern Catholic Dictionary*, 201.
[433] Hardon, 384.

Confiteor, "I have greatly sinned in my thoughts and in my words, in what I have done and in what I have failed to do." That inner purity is shown in a life of holiness and detachment, the reward of promises of blessings by God, as seen in the Beatitudes (see Mt 5:3–12) and to those who make sacrifices for the Kingdom of God (see Mt 19:29). This is why Father Aumann affirms that "since grace does serve as the basis for merit, those souls who are in state a grace may, by their prayers and good works, and by reason of a certain fittingness because they are friends of God . . . merit grace" not just for themselves but specifically for others. They especially should intensely pray "for the conversion of sinners" that they may obtain "whatever is necessary for the salvation of souls."[434]

Jesus warns, "Unless your righteousness surpasses that of the scribes and Pharisees, you will not enter the kingdom of heaven" (Mt 5:20). "Righteousness" is a centerpiece of blessedness and the meritorious nature of prayer. As Jesus taught, "Blessed are they who hunger and thirst for righteousness, for they will be satisfied" (Mt 5:6). And, "Blessed are they who are persecuted for the sake of righteousness, for theirs is the kingdom of heaven" (Mt 5:10). The Greek word for "justice" or "righteousness" is *dikaiosune*, which means not just observant of the law but also well-ordered, balanced, genuine. In ancient Greek society, when a crime was committed, there was not only an injustice but a rupture of civic order, an imbalance introduced into society. "Justice" is a restoration of balance (as seen in the common legal symbol of the scales). In a similar way, a "righteous person" has a well-ordered, balanced, and genuine relationship with God and others.

Our holiness, therefore, affects the power of our prayers. Thus, Saint James states, "The fervent prayer of a righteous person is very powerful" (Jas 5:16). The state of grace and the depth of purity of thought, word, and deed create an "inner

---

[434] Aumann, *Spiritual Theology*, 233.

equivalence" or harmony between the intentions of one's prayer and the promises of Jesus. You also grow in merit in resisting temptation. Father Aumann's insights are worth mentioning:

> Sometimes the temptation does not immediately disappear, and the devil may attack again with great tenacity. One should not become discouraged at this. The insistence of the devil is one of the best proofs that the soul has not succumb to the temptation. The soul should resist the attacks as often as necessary but always with great serenity and interior peace, being careful to avoid any kind of anxiety or disturbance. Every assault repulsed is a source of new merit before God and greater strength for the soul. Far from becoming weakened, the soul gained new energies. Seeing that he has lost, the devil will finally leave the soul in peace, especially when he sees that he has not been able to disturb the interior peace of the soul, which sometimes is the only reason he has caused the temptation in the first place.[435]

God owes us nothing by our merits but does answer our prayers according to His mercy and free ordinances. As Saint Augustine says, "The Lord has made Himself a debtor, not by receiving, but by promising." You can conform your faculties to Christ with the *Anima Christi* (see appendix), and also use this **Deliverance Prayer** as needed:

> *In the name of the Lord Jesus Christ, by the power of His cross, His Blood, and His resurrection, I bind you Satan, the spirits, powers and forces of darkness, the nether world, and the evil forces of nature. I reclaim the authority over all curses, hexes, demonic activity, and spells directed against me, my relationships, ministry, air space, finances, and the work of my hands; and I break them by the power and authority of Our Lord Jesus Christ. I bind all demonic interaction, interplay, and communications between spirits sent*

---

[435] Aumann, 161.

*against me, and send them directly to Jesus Christ for Him
to deal with as He wills. I ask forgiveness for and denounce
all negative inner vows that I have made with the enemy,
and ask that Jesus Christ release me from these vows and
from any bondage they may have held in me. I claim the shed
blood of Jesus Christ, the Son of the living God, over every
aspect of my life for my protection. I pray all these things in
the precious name of my Lord and Savior, Jesus Christ.*

From Slingstones to Milestones: Demonic Tactics

1. Why is it important to understand the inner movements of thoughts and emotions?

2. What are the three spiritual faculties (higher, intermediate, and lower)? Where does the spiritual battle take place?

3. How does sacramental Baptism reorder the interiority of a person and how is the intellect strengthened?

4. What did Adam and Eve possess in their original state? What are the four wounds of the Fall?

5. How does one strengthen the memory? How do you know when a memory is afflicted?

6. Recall the statement: "Unholy anger is an inordinate desire arising from unmoderated sorrow at some offense." How have you dealt with sorrow?

7. Our prayers are meritorious when these three conditions are present—what are they?

8. What is a wound, and why does the demon want us wounded?

LESSON TWELVE: THE
WEAPON OF PRAYER

For this final lesson, let us heed the words of Rogers: "Let the enemy come 'till he's almost close enough to touch. Then let him have it and jump out and finish him up with your hatchet." David followed this principle of guerrilla warfare. He had five stones and could have taken his chances from a distance. He chose instead to bring Goliath into an accurate range for his slingshot before firing. In warfare, precision is everything. In this final lesson, we will explain the principle that prayer begets what it signifies and the need for specificity in prayer.

The final element of the "fire triangle" of effective spiritual warfare prayer is specificity in prayer. Hopefully, by now you are getting more proficient with the sling as you pray the prayers at the end of each section. Jesus Himself assures us that we must petition should we expect to receive: "Ask and it will be given to you; seek and you will find; knock and the door will be opened to you. For everyone who asks, receives; and the one who seeks, finds; and to the one who knocks, the door will be opened (Mt 7:7–8). Elsewhere, he assures us, "Whatever you ask for in prayer with faith, you will receive" (Mt 21:22); and, "If you ask anything of me in my name, I will do it" (Jn 14:14).

Precision is essential for success on any battlefield, including the spiritual. Thus, we must remember that prayer begets what it signifies. This is to say, you must be specific in your prayers. In fact, in Saint John's Gospel, Jesus commands us to "ask" in prayer nine times. Supplication and petitionary prayer are not just a result of our personal needs but what the Father expects from His children. The Lord wants us to ask Him for certain things, and Sacred Scripture tells us what the Lord wishes us to pray for. Recall how God spoke to Solomon: "Whatever you ask I shall give you. Solomon answered: . . . 'Give your servant, therefore, a listening heart to judge your people and to distinguish between good and evil.' . . . The Lord was pleased by Solomon's request. . . . I now do as you request" (1 Kgs 3:5–6, 9, 10, 12).

A century ago, a Bernardine sister was shown the vast desolation caused by the devil throughout the world. The Blessed Virgin Mary requested to be invoked under the title Queen of the Angels and to seek her intercession and those of the legions of angels against the evil one and his minions. "But my good Mother," the sister replied, "you who are so kind, could you not send them without our asking?" Our Lady answered, "No, because prayer is one of the conditions required by God Himself in obtaining favors." Our Lady then gave to her a prayer to be prayed to this end, which is the conclusion of the daily *Auxilium Christianorum* prayers.[436]

> *August Queen of the Heavens, heavenly Sovereign of the Angels, Thou who from the beginning hast received from God the power and the mission to crush the head of Satan, we humbly beseech Thee to send Thy holy legions, so that under Thy command and through Thy power, they may pursue the demons and combat them everywhere, suppress their boldness, and drive them back into the abyss. O good and tender Mother, Thou wilt always be our love and hope! O Divine Mother, send Thy Holy Angels to defend us and to drive far away from us the cruel enemy. Holy Angels and Archangels, defend us, guard us. Amen.*

Thus, you must ask if you wish to receive. In a similar way, the Virgin Mary appeared to Saint Catherine Labouré and requested a medal be made. Designed by the Blessed Mother herself, the Miraculous Medal has an image of Mary with rays of light coming from some of her fingers. This, she explained to Saint Catherine, demonstrates *the graces that God gives through her to those who ask.* There are some fingers on her hands, however, from which no rays are shown. These, Our Lady explained, are *the graces that are not given because they were not requested of her.* This is another reminder of the words of Jesus: "Ask and it shall be given to you" (Mt 7:7).

---

[436] Tradition in Action, "A Prayer to Our Lady."

We must ask, however, with trust and detachment. A woman once said to me, "My daughter was in a very bad place. I was so worried that all I did was pray." I explained, however, "fear and trust cannot occupy the same space." This is because, as I note, "fear and worry directly militate against a loving trust of God and, therefore, neutralize the effectiveness of our prayers. As such, the negatively charged emotions of fear and worry are not from God and serve to attract the demon to us, even if our intentions are good. Saint Padre Pio, therefore, counselled to, 'Pray and don't worry.' If we pray *and* worry, we allow our lack of trust to negate the merit of our prayer."[437]

Mental Prayer, Ascesis, and Growth in Virtue

Up to this point, you have been shown the value of vocal prayer, which involves set formulas and invocations of God, the Virgin Mary, and the angels and saints. As Saint Teresa Benedicta of the Cross teaches, however, vocal prayer is not "simply saying words." Thus, "if the mere words of a prayer alone are said without the soul's raising itself to God, this is only an outward show and not real prayer. The designated words, however, support the spirit and prescribe it to a fixed path."[438] Vocal prayer is the first step upon the "fixed path" which leads to holiness and liberation, and such conversational prayer should always be part of your prayer life. Unless your vocal prayer includes the heart, however, you run the risk of merely reading to God. Vocal prayer should engage God with an act of the will. Project the words of the prayer over the person for whom you are praying.

The spiritual writers of the Church speak of the "three ways" of the interior life: the purgative, the illuminative, and the transformative way. Implied in the three ways are the steps a soul must take to be transformed; namely, it must first be purified, then grow in understanding before deep union with God is

---

[437] Liber Christo. "Companion Guide," 167.
[438] Saint Teresa Benedicta of the Cross, *Essential Writings*, 119.

possible. Accordingly, this program walks you along this traditional path by focusing on *asceticism*, which is spiritual exercise in the pursuit of virtue and holiness. *Ascesis* derives from the Greek verb meaning to acquire skills through practice and training, as do athletes and soldiers. A secondary meaning is to adorn or decorate, the byproduct of those who train diligently (the victor is adorned with a crown symbolizing his merit). Hence, the adornment, or fruit, of your spiritual labors and training is a soul filled with virtue. Virtue, in turn, helps you attain the goal of the spiritual struggle—namely, holiness and the presence of sanctifying grace. This is the crown which adorns the victor.

To perfect this, you should add to your vocal prayer by developing the habit of mental prayer, or meditation. The reasons for restricting all reading in phase one of the protocol to only the daily Mass readings are two-fold: (1) to teach you the power of meditation, which not only helps you to grow in union with God but also assists in your ability to focus your mind and control your thoughts; and (2) to teach you how to read the Bible from the heart of the Church. The monastic way to engage in mental prayer is called *lectio divina*, or the spiritual reading of the Bible. As I wrote elsewhere, "Monastic *lectio* is a mind-heart rumination of the sacred text that leads to prayer, guides to holiness and, ultimately, an encounter with God."[439]

Pope Benedict XVI said that this "prayerful approach to the sacred text [is] a fundamental element in the spiritual life of every believer."[440] According to Benedictine monk Fr. Luke Dysinger, *lectio divina* was once practiced by all Christians and is a "slow, contemplative praying of the Scriptures which enables the Bible, the Word of God, to become a means of union with God."[441] *Lectio divina* follow the rabbinic principle that "scripture is best interpreted with scripture"—that is, read the Bible in light of the Bible, as the revelation of God in Jesus Christ.[442] The four

---

[439] Schneider, *Eve Was Named an Apostle*, 20.
[440] Pope Benedict XVI, *Verbum Domini*, no. 86.
[441] Shultz, *Caring for People in Pain*, 150.
[442] Schneider, *Eve Was Named an Apostle*, 21.

stages of monastic *lectio* are read, meditate, pray, contemplate. Father Dysinger aptly describes the four steps of *lectio divina*:[443]

Read—choose a text and slowly read it, not the speed reading like a newspaper, but a reverential listening in a spirit of silence and awe; slowly, attentively, gently listening to hear a word or phrase that God's word has for you today.

Meditate—once a passage speaks to you, take it in and ruminate on it, like an animal quietly chewing the cud, so you ponder on the Word of God; let it interact and affect you at your deepest levels, your thoughts, hopes, memories, and desires; seek Him in silence.

Pray—dialogue with God in a loving conversation; a priestly offering of the things we have not previously thought that He wanted; hold up, like Eucharistic bread, your most difficult and pain-filled experiences to Him; be vulnerable and let the Word touch and change your deepest self; speak to Him, with words or with your imagination.

Contemplate—rest in the presence of Him who invites you to His transforming embrace; here, words are no longer necessary, but a quiet rest in His presence in a loving relationship, in a wordless exchange.

In so doing, Father Dysinger says, *lectio divina* is not a method of prayer but "serves as a training-ground for the contemplation of God."[444] As Pope Benedict XVI notes, the process asks four questions:

1.   What does the biblical text say in itself? (read)
2.   What does the biblical text say to us? (meditate)
3.   What do we say to the Lord in response to his word? (pray)
4.   What conversion of mind, heart and life is the Lord asking of us? (contemplate)[445]

---

[443] Shultz, *Caring for People in Pain*, 98–110.
[444] Shultz, 154.
[445] Pope Benedict XVI, *Verbum Domini*, no. 87.

The fruit of your *lectio*, therefore, will depend on the discipline with which you put into its daily practice, as well as your receptivity in offering yourself to God. "We must remember," Pope Benedict XVI teaches, "that the process of *lectio divina* is not concluded until it arrives at action (*actio*) which moves the believer to make his or her life a gift for others in charity."[446]

By training you in meditation, *lectio divina* also assists in the right ordering of spiritual faculties, a key element of spiritual warfare. According to Saint Bernard, the meditation on the life of Christ is perfecting one's vision by looking through "five windows" of "His incarnation, way of life, teaching, resurrection, and ascension." The effects of meditation, he says, are many: it purifies the mind, controls the affections, guides our action, corrects excesses, introduces order and dignity into our lives, and illumines our minds.[447] How can this be? Christian meditation is not a technique but an encounter with Jesus Christ. As I stated earlier, "The purification of the memory and emotional constancy are essential in augmenting the will to choose the good." Mental prayer is the means to this end because it leads you to encounter the incarnate Truth.

Thus, Saint Teresa of Avila defines mental prayer as "nothing else than an intimate sharing between friends; it means taking time frequently to be alone with Him who we know loves us."[448] Mental prayer is an interior, loving, and discursive meditation upon a mystery of the Faith or some religious truth. The spiritual faculties of intellect, will, and memory all engage in authentic meditation. Babbling and high emotionality that engages only the lower faculties is not mental prayer (nor does it aid you in spiritual growth). As stated above, in mental prayer, the virtues of faith, hope, and love imbue and perfect those faculties. Athletes develop "muscle memory" by repeatedly using the same muscular mechanics in their training. Soldiers likewise repeatedly practice with the same mechanics, and with the same rifle, to perfect the skill of marksmanship. Prayer as an ascetical act

---

[446] Pope Benedict XVI, no. 87.
[447] Sommerfeldt, "Meditation as the Path to Humility," 180.
[448] Saint Teresa of Avila, *Life*, 96.

is similar in that it aids in perfecting the faculties with the virtues and trains the intellect, memory, and will to be wielded in a disciplined, and loving, manner towards God.

Accordingly, just as an athlete or soldier uses mechanics to perfect his craft, so also the spiritual soldier. The mechanics of mental prayer are threefold:

1. *Consideration*: ponder the events and examine the subject in question.
2. *Application*: apply certain truths of the meditation to your life.
3. *Resolution*: make some practical resolve based on the fruit of 1 and 2.

That is, the intellect engages with the memory some mystery of the Faith or truth (consideration). Then, by use of the imagination and cognition, the mind connects the fruits of what is meditated upon to one's own life and situation (application). Finally, the will engages in resolving (resolution) to make this or that change in one's life. This process is sometimes termed *lectio divina*, or the holy reading of Scripture used by monks, which follows four steps: read, meditate, pray, contemplate.

Saint Thérèse of Lisieux had her own "five smooth stones" in defeating the devil, which was the fruit of her meditation upon the life of Jesus. What is known as her "little way" of holiness has five key elements: humility, trust, living in the present moment, love, and gratitude. She described mental prayers as "an uplifting of the heart; a glance towards heaven; a cry of gratitude and love." This upsurge towards God, she says, is "uttered equally in sorrow and in joy."[449] The fruit of mental prayer, then, is not spiritual or emotional consolation. Rather, authentic prayer can be gauged by asking the following:

*   Does it increase my virtue and holiness?
*   Am I experiencing growth in charity?

---

[449] Saint Thérèse of Lisieux, *Autobiography*, 242.

- Am I increasing in self-denial and the ability to sacrifice?
- Am I growing in my performance of my specific vocation—that is, a better husband/wife, father/ mother, priest, or religious?
- Do I have an increased capacity to suffer with Christ?

Simply stated, if the mechanics of your prayer can be summarized as "Our Father, Hail Mary . . . then gimme, gimme, gimme," you pray like a toddler and are bringing a Nerf gun, not a weapon, to the battlefield.

The reason why prayers are often not answered, moreover, is because we have conditions attached to them. Saint James again says succinctly, "You ask and do not receive, because you ask wrongly, to spend it on your passions" (Jas 4:3). Many Christians ask God to give them favors first and then promise Him their love in return. For example, "Take away this affliction and I promise I will go back to church." These foxhole-type prayers are rarely honored. The habitual practice of Christian meditation counters these tendencies, however, because it sharpens the interiority like a ranger's weapon. A soldier knows that a clean weapon has a better chance of striking its target, while a dirty weapon, even if wielded with perfect mechanics, is inaccurate and can even jam entirely. By analogy, a clean soul and habitual prayer makes for a spiritual sharpshooter.

Prayer Is the Best Weapon We Have

Now that you understand the mechanics of prayer and have cleaned your spiritual weapon, you are ready to engage the enemy through mental prayer. Implied in the deadly accuracy of David's stone and his recalling of defeating lions and bears in defense of his sheep is that David perfected the mechanics of the projectile weapon. That means he did not wait until something bad was happening to pull out his sling and reach for a stone. Rather, he practiced and perfected the craft in the solitude of the grazing fields. Prayer and virtue work in a similar way. Notably, Saint Paul concludes his famous teaching on spiritual warfare—"Put on the armor of God, for our battle is not with flesh and blood . . . [but] with the evil spirits in the heavens" (see Eph 6:10–20)—with a simple instruction to "pray without ceasing" (Eph 6:18). This is how you perfect the mechanics of mental prayer. Pray continually.

The first fruit of mental prayer is an interior stillness, which comes from a sanctified vision—that is, a view of your situation through the eyes of Sacred Scripture. Habitual prayer trains the interior faculties with a spiritual discipline like a soldier on the march who, when needed, can draw and fire with accuracy. The fruit of meditation over time is an inner stillness and peace. Spiritual writer Father Jean Pierre de Caussade said, "The great principle of the interior life is peace of the soul, and it must be preserved with such care that the moment that it is attacked all else must be put aside and every effort made to try and regain this holy peace, just as, in an outbreak of fire, everything else is neglected to hasten to extinguish the flames."[450]

The right ordering of the interior is accomplished through a disciplined prayer life and the pursuit of virtue. This, in turn, will help you to discern the Lord's voice, who speaks through peace of soul, from the voice of the demon, who projects his screeches through fear, dread, anxiety, and turmoil. Again, in the words of Rogers, "see the enemy first."

Once you see the enemy, you can engage. This is done by taking the fruit of mental prayer and projecting it back into the cosmos, calling down images from the life of the Lord or Our Lady in Scripture. As Saint Padre Pio said, "Prayer is the best weapon we have."[451] Specifically, Saint Padre Pio reminds us that the Christian soldier should have no fear because "Jesus is more powerful than all hell. At the invocation of his

---

[450] De Caussade, *Abandonment to Divine Providence*, 135.
[451] Francis Mary, *Padre Pio*, 182.

name every knee in heaven, on earth and in hell must bend
before Jesus; this is a consolation for the good and terror for
evil."[452] When we meditate on the words and deeds of Jesus in
Scripture, we make present the realities they symbolize.

Prayer is the best weapon we have because through it, we
invoke the One who defeated the devil definitively on the cross.
Isaiah spoke of the Warrior-God who sends His Word to "strike
the ruthless with the rod of his mouth, and with the breath
of his lips . . . shall slay the wicked" (Is 11:4). Notably, God's
Word projects forth like a sword into the cosmos. Elsewhere,
the Lord states, "By myself I have sworn, from my mouth has
gone forth in righteousness a word that shall not return: 'To
me every knee shall bow, every tongue shall swear'" (Is 45:23).
And, "So shall my word be that goes forth from my mouth; It
shall not return to me empty, but shall do what pleases me,
achieving the end for which I sent it" (Is 55:11). Thus, Saint
Paul echoes Isaiah that the proclamation of the holy name of
Jesus echoes into the cosmos: "At the name of Jesus, every
knee should bend, of those in heaven and on earth and under
the earth, and every tongue confess that Jesus Christ is Lord,
to the glory of the Father" (Phil 2:10–11).

Prayer has an effect, therefore, and it begets what you ask
for. To reiterate, demons respond to (1) the authority of the
person who prays, (2) the merit of your prayer (state of grace,
purity of life) and, (3) the precision of the prayer (prayer begets
what it signifies). With regard to the merit of your prayer, it
is like shooting a bullet from a dirty weapon. Just as dirt and
grime will jam the weapon and the bullet will not project, so
also when your soul is dirty, your prayers are ineffective. Likewise, even the most perfect weapon will not hit its target if
it is not aimed correctly. As Saint Paul says, "For though we
live in the world, we are not carrying on a worldly war, for the
weapons of our warfare are not worldly, but have divine power
to destroy strongholds" (2 Cor 10:4); or, as the prophet Jeremiah says, "Therefore, thus says the LORD, the God of hosts,

---

[452] Francis Mary, 70.

because you have said this—See! I make my words a fire in your mouth, and this people the wood that it shall devour!" (Jer 5:14).

Blaise Pascal said, "God instituted prayer in order to give His creatures the dignity of causality."[453] You become an instrumental cause of divine power and make present the Word made flesh when you pray mental prayer. You plant the war memorial of the cross into the cosmos, for example, when you meditate upon the wounds of Jesus. When you place yourself at His feet with Saint Mary Magdalene, you project His wounded feet like a hatchet against the spirit of lust. You call down the intercession of the Blessed Mother when you place yourself at the wedding feast of Cana and beg Him for more wine of charity in the face of evil. This is to say, Christian meditation takes on a dimensionality when united with the Word by making present the saving power of God in time and space. You become a cause of scourging to the demon when you meditate upon the scourging of Jesus and evoke the words of Isaiah, "By his wounds I am healed" (Is 53:5). Mental prayer, then, is a spiritual projection that wounds the devil when done correctly. You have experienced how the accuser projects his lies. Now you know how to project back with the Truth by uniting your interior faculties in prayer to Jesus Christ, who is "the way, the truth and the life" (Jn 14:6). In so doing, you experience the dignity of being a cause for the salvation of souls.

An Applied Sacrificial Theology: Scoot-and-Shoot Tactic

Like the ancient shield, which is both a protective and a strike weapon, discursive meditation also has a defensive and an offensive purpose. By means of mental prayer, not only do you shore up your interior perimeter, you can also learn the power of prayer as projection. In modern combat, the artillery

---

[453] Pascal, *Pensées*, 148.

utilizes a tactic called "counter battery" when dealing with enemy indirect (artillery) fire. Using radar technology, artillery soldiers can detect incoming indirect fire and immediately calculate its source location. Friendly forces then quickly move from that location and return fire to the point of origin of the enemy artillery. With this technology, the enemy's location can have a round incoming before their round impacts its target. Hence, the tactic of counter-battery is referred to as "scoot-and-shoot." When an enemy round is detected, the friendly forces quickly move (scoot) and return fire (shoot).

The "scoot-and-shoot tactic" can be used in spiritual combat. Recall how mental prayer is important for spiritual combat because it provides custody of the mind and purifies the imagination. Because the demon has access to the "data set" of images embedded into your memories, he often projects distortions of these images to you. Once you learn to recognize the voice of the temper and accuser, you can fire back prayers of reparation, love of God, and images from the life of Christ. If he projects an image of someone who hurt you, for example, *scoot* (recognize the temptation and disappropriate the emotion) and *shoot* (offer a prayer for the person instead).

Eucharistic Adoration is a powerful weapon in spiritual warfare. Adoration is where we render God His due and develop the virtue of prayer. Saint Padre Pio counselled souls to "keep close to the Catholic Church at all times" because "the Church alone can give you true peace, since she alone possesses Jesus, the true Prince of Peace, in the Blessed Sacrament."[454] Here is where one learns to wield the mind and imagination in meditation. According to the *Catechism*, "Adoration is the first act of the virtue of religion. To adore God is to acknowledge him as God, as the Creator and Savior, the Lord and Master of everything that exists, and infinite and merciful Love."[455]

When the devil tempted Jesus, moreover, Our Lord quoted the commandment to fidelity which Moses gave in the context of

---

[454] Assaf, *Essential Teachings*, 170.
[455] *CCC* 2096.

the *Shema*: "You shall worship the Lord your God, and him only shall you serve" (Lk 4:8; Dt 6:13). Frequent recourse to Eucharistic Adoration is a great gift most Catholics neglect. Listen to the words Jesus spoke to Saint Margaret Mary Alacoque: "Behold this Heart which has so loved men that it has spared nothing, even to exhausting and consuming itself in order to testify to its love. In return, I have received from the greater part only ingratitude, by their irreverence and their sacrilege, and by the coldness and contempt they have for Me in this sacrament of Love."[456]

Eucharistic Adoration, therefore, is the place where we focus our adoration by using our imagination and applying our intellect upon the words and deeds of Jesus Christ. If the Eucharist is not a symbol of Jesus but mysteriously is Jesus—truly, really, and substantially present—which Jesus are you looking at? Which Jesus do you most need to conform your life to in that given moment? Are you adoring the infant Christ? Are you adoring the condescension of God to man, the Word who "became flesh" (Jn 1:14)? Are you contemplating Christ's broken body in the tomb? What exactly are you contemplating? In meditation before the Eucharistic Lord, project one of those images of Christ and then focus on that mystery.

By the practice of mental prayer, we order our faculties better to detect the incoming projections of the enemy and apply this spiritual "scoot-and-shoot tactic." When beset with a temptation, therefore, apply your imagination to a particular aspect of Christ's life, especially one that you struggle embracing. Look somewhere along the Sacred Triduum of Holy Thursday, Good Friday, and Holy Saturday. Are you feeling abandoned and alone? Join your suffering to Christ who was abandoned by His friends in the Garden of Gethsemane. Does your suffering seem too much to bear? Join hands with Our Lady of Sorrows at the foot of the cross and offer them with hers. Do you feel mocked and ridiculed? So was Jesus—unjustly, no less. Do you think you are all alone? Link these feelings to Christ who said, "My God, my God, why have you

---

[456] Saint Margaret Mary Alacoque, *Autobiography*, 95.

abandoned me?" (Mt 27:46). This is the place to worship, adore, appeal, intercede, and conform your will to His. The practical aspect of a sacrificial theology is uniting your suffering to Christ's suffering through mental prayer.

The Holy Rosary: The Spiritual Battering Ram

Saint Padre Pio was a spiritual warrior and stigmatist who prayed the Rosary fervently every day. He even slept with a Rosary beneath his pillow just in case he needed one at a moment's notice. On one occasion, he could not find his rosary, so he called to a younger friar in his community. "Young man," he said, "get me my weapon; give me my weapon."[457] He also said, "Some people are so foolish that they think they can go through life without the help of the Blessed Mother. Love the Madonna and pray the Rosary, for her Rosary is the weapon against the evils of the world today. All graces given by God pass through the Blessed Mother."[458]

He undoubtedly knew the history of the Rosary. When the Blessed Mother first gave the Rosary to Saint Dominic, she herself referred to it as a weapon. "Dear Dominic," she said, "do you know what weapon the Most Holy Trinity wants to use to reform the world?" She then explained, "I want you to know that in this kind of warfare the 'battering ram' has always been the Angelic Psalter, which is the corner stone of the New Testament. So, if you want to reach these hardened souls and win them to God, preach my Psalter!"[459] The "cornerstone of the New Testament" is the Incarnation. God took on human flesh when Mary said "Let it be done" (Lk 1:38) to the Lord through the angel Gabriel at the Annunciation. The recitation of the Rosary, like the Angelus, echoes the salvation of humankind and the defeat of his infernal enemy.

---

[457] Francis Mary, *Padre Pio*, 68.
[458] Snyder, *Light of an Angel*, 88.
[459] Saint Louis de Montfort, *True Devotion*, no. 249.

Notably, when done properly, the Rosary combines both mental and vocal prayer. While the lips pray the set prayers, the intellect, imagination, and will meditate (with consideration, application, and resolution) upon the lives of Jesus and Mary. Thus, it is a deeply scriptural and Christological (Christ-centered) prayer, with each mystery focusing on some aspect of the Incarnation and its impact. Accordingly, as I wrote, "the rosary is a powerful prayer that helps the soul to learn how to meditate and pray the mysteries of our faith. It contains the story of our salvation by recalling the major events in the life of Jesus Christ—His birth, His earthly ministry, His suffering and death, and ultimate resurrection and glory."[460] As Saint Bernard notes, the effects of meditating on the mysteries of the Rosary are a purification of the mind, self-mastery over the affections, corrects and brings order, and illumines understanding. Thus, I conclude that "by meditating on the life of Jesus Christ, we begin to develop a sanctified vision in our own lives. We now have a template to daily live out our faith."[461]

The Hail Mary, says Saint Louis de Montfort, is "a heavenly dew for watering the earth, which is the soul, to make it bring forth its fruit in due season."[462] By "heavenly dew," he means that meditation on the events of the life of Christ through the Rosary brings fecundity, or life, to the soul. He further cautions that the soul "not watered by that prayer bears no fruit and brings only thorns and brambles."[463] According to Saint Teresa Benedicta, in meditative prayer on the Joyful Mysteries of the Rosary,

> the spirit moves more freely without being bound to specific words. It immerses itself, for example, in the mystery of the birth of Jesus. The spirit's imagination transports it to the grotto in Bethlehem, seeing the child in the manger, the holy parents, the shepherds, and the kings. The intellect ponders

---

[460] Liber Christo, "Companion Guide," 122.
[461] Liber Christo, "Companion Guide," 122.
[462] Saint Louis de Montfort, *True Devotion*, no. 157.
[463] Saint Louis de Montfort, no. 157

the greatness of divine mercy, the emotions are seized by love and thankfulness, the will decides to make itself more worthy of divine love. This is how meditative prayer involves all the soul's powers and, when practiced with faithful persistence, can gradually remake the whole person.[464]

Thus, the prayer of meditation on the events of the life of Christ helps to purify the faculties so that the interior life may produce fruit.

In addition to watering the soul, it also trains the mind to master the "scoot-and-shoot" tactic. Building on Saint Padre Pio's words that the Rosary is a weapon, Clement calls the Rosary a claymore, the massive and destructive broad sword used by Scottish warriors. By taking up the Word of God in meditation with the rosary beads, you hold in your hand a powerful offensive weapon against the evils that confront you. As God says through the prophet, "Is not my word like fire, says the LORD, and like a hammer which breaks the rock in pieces?" (Jer 23:29).

The Rosary is also like a ranger's hatchet in that it has two sides; namely, it has both a sharpened edge for cutting and chopping and a solid end to be used as a blunt instrument. Thus, Saint Louis de Montfort also says, "The Hail Mary well said—that is, with attention, devotion, and modesty—is, according to the saints, the enemy of the devil which puts him to flight, and the hammer which crushes him. It is the sanctification of the soul, the joy of the angels, the melody of the predestinate, the canticle of the New Testament, the pleasure of Mary, and the glory of the most Holy Trinity."[465] In addition, Saint Louis de Montfort list seven effects of praying the Rosary, which is consistent with what Saint Bernard lists as the positive effects of mental prayer on the spiritual faculties:

1. Gradually gives us a perfect knowledge of Jesus Christ.
2. Purifies our souls, washing away sin.

---

[464] Saint Teresa Benedicta of the Cross, *Essential Writings*, 119–20.
[465] Saint Louis de Montfort, *True Devotion*, no. 159.

3.   Gives us victory over our enemies.
4.   Makes it easy for us to practice virtue.
5.   Sets us on fire with love for our Lord.
6.   Enriches us with graces and merits.
7.   Helps us to pay our debt to God and others and
     obtains all kinds of graces from Almighty God.[466]

Thus, the Rosary prayed with devotion is like a battering ram
or broad sword to clear out obstacles in the battle against evil.
Like the young children of Numidia who had to knock down a
piece of bread with their slingshot before they could eat, you
should pray the Rosary daily as part of your spiritual discipline and nourishment.

Angels and Saints: A Spiritual Army

Another powerful weapon in spiritual battle is devotion to
the saints. God always sends help from the Mystical Body,
like Calvary, to help His children in their struggles. You may
have developed a new devotion to a particular saint, one who
has seemingly cycled into your spiritual life. Perhaps you have
a longstanding devotion to a certain saint. Each demon will
have a nemesis in the Mystical Body who will be sent to you at
the appropriate time. Ask for this heavenly assistance.

Prayers to Saint Michael and the angels are also very
helpful in spiritual combat, including the Chaplet of Saint
Michael.[467] In addition, as stated previously, angels go where
they are asked, and demons go where they are not resisted.
Thus, Saint Padre Pio says, "Invoke your Guardian Angel who
will enlighten you. God gave you your Guardian Angel for this
reason. So, make use of your Angel's service." Saint Padre Pio,
who is a great ally in spiritual combat, notes how effective

---

[466] Saint Louis de Montfort, *Secrets of the Rosary*, 50–53.
[467] This devotional is not reprinted here, but it is highly recommended for
the faithful to pray, particularly when needing to break through diabolic resistance or to unmask the enemy's movements.

the Guardian Angel prayer is for combatting the enemy as he assaults your interior peace:

> *Angel of God, my guardian dear, to whom His love commits me here; ever this day (or night) be at my side, to light and guard, to rule and guide. Amen.*[468]

At a time when the patrimony of the Church was under attack, Pope Boniface IV (AD 608–15) gathered up almost thirty wagonloads of the bones of saints and re-buried them beneath the Pantheon. The Pantheon was a pagan temple built to all-gods (hence, *pan-theon*), but the pope re-dedicated it to the greatest warriors in the Catholic Church, those who gave their lives for the Faith. This temple, which once honored the demon-gods, now became the Basilica of Saint Mary and the Martyrs. Thus, according to Venerable Bede, the pope intended "that the memory of all the saints might in the future be honored in the place which had formerly been dedicated to the worship not of gods but of demons." For this reason, the demons are acutely sensitive to the saints. This weapon also needs to be in your shepherd's bag of stones.

The Use of Sacramentals in Spiritual Combat

In ancient times, when a fortress was assaulted, the inhabitants would station archers on top of the high walls surrounding the city. Upon seeing the enemy approaching, the archers would launch volleys of arrows at their enemy. The Psalmist uses this imagery when he writes, "God shoots an arrow at them; / in a moment they are struck down" (Ps 64:8). A soldier has various weapons and tools in his rucksack. Rogers also taught, "Don't use your musket if you can kill 'em with your hatchet." In other words, do it quietly and save your ammo. A way of conserving ammo in battle is the use of sacramentals. In prayer, we have been given "the dignity of being causes"—that

---

468 Pasquale, *Padre Pio*, 243.

is, agents of divine grace. Besides human agents of grace, God also uses certain inanimate objects, when blessed by a priest, to convey grace.

As I wrote, "sacramentals are physical objects or observances, which are similar to, but not equal to, the sacraments."[469] The *Catechism* states that they "do not confer the grace of the Holy Spirit in the way that the sacraments do, but by the Church's prayer, they prepare us to receive grace and dispose us to cooperate with it."[470] Common examples of the sacramentals you should have in your spiritual rucksack are holy water, exorcised salt, the Saint Benedict medal (which has prayers of exorcism on it), the scapular of Our Lady of Mt. Carmel, the Miraculous Medal, and statues, icons, and sacred images. Some sacramental observances include litanies, the sign of the cross, Eucharistic processions, pilgrimages, and other devotions. The Rite of Exorcism itself is a sacramental, where "the Church asks publicly and authoritatively in the name of Jesus Christ that a person or object be protected against the power of the Evil One and withdrawn from his dominion."[471] Jesus Christ, who entrusted the care of souls to His Church, is the power behind the sacramentals.

Sacramentals employ the principle that material objects can convey divine power. Cursed objects work in an inverted manner where inanimate agency conveys the dark power of the curse that was placed upon it. Holy objects convey Christ's power and blessing. Accordingly, "for well-disposed members of the faithful, the liturgy of the Sacraments and sacramentals sanctifies almost every event of their lives with the divine grace which flows from the Paschal mystery of the Passion, Death, and Resurrection of Christ. From this source of all sacraments and sacramentals draw their power. There is scarcely any proper use of material things which cannot be thus directed toward the sanctification of men and the praise

---

[469] Liber Christo, "Companion Guide," 121.
[470] *CCC* 1620.
[471] *CCC* 1673.

of God."[472] Bear in mind the principle that "prayer begets what it signifies" as you read excerpts from the blessing of salt and water by a priest. He exorcises the salt and prays:

> Life-giving powers might be restored . . . a means of salvation for believers, that you may bring health of soul and body to all who make use of you, and that you may put to flight and drive away from the places where you are sprinkled; every apparition, villainy, turn of devilish deceit, and every unclean spirit; [that it] become a source of health for the minds and bodies . . . [and] it rid whatever it touches or sprinkles of all uncleanness, and protect it from every assault of evil spirits . . . so that you may put to flight all the power of the enemy, and be able to root out and supplant that enemy with his apostate angels, through the power of our Lord Jesus Christ; to drive away evil spirits and dispel sickness, so that everything in the homes and other buildings of the faithful that is sprinkled with this water, may be rid of all uncleanness and freed from every harm; so that everything in the homes and other buildings of the faithful that is sprinkled with this water, may be rid of all uncleanness and freed from every harm. Let no breath of infection and no disease-bearing air remain in these places. May the wiles of the lurking enemy prove of no avail. Let whatever might menace the safety and peace of those who live here be put to flight by the sprinkling of this water, so that the health obtained by calling upon your holy name, may be made secure against all attack. Through Christ our Lord.

The demon recognizes the blessing of the Church, the specificity of the prayer, and responds accordingly by fleeing. From these words of blessing, you may see why Saint Teresa of Avila was so fond of the use of holy water as a weapon in spiritual warfare. She says, "I often experience that there is nothing the devils flee from more—without returning—than holy

---

[472] *Sacrosanctum Concilium*, no. 61.

water."[473] You should sprinkle holy water or blessed salt regularly in your home or office. You should also regularly bless yourself and your family, particularly before bedtime or travel.

Gaining Proficiency with the Sling

While vocal prayer is essential in spiritual warfare, you must learn to use your imagination to engage the intellect and will in prayer. This means becoming more confident when you take aim. The Rosary is the best way to gain proficiency with the "slingshot" of mental prayer. One prayer that also teaches this skill is called the **Punishing Prayer**. This is designed to ward off evil spirits who try to afflict you while you sleep. Besides keeping a blessed candle lit and playing Gregorian chant at low volume in the home, this prayer can be prayed before going to bed. This prayer may be modified for any form of temptation or diabolic attack throughout the day:

> *Lord Jesus Christ, I ask Thee that from now and until I fall asleep, while I sleep and during my dreams, that if any evil spirit tries to affect me that Thou wouldst punish him by making him focus on the thing that causes the most pain during the entire time he tries to affect me and for ten minutes more. I also ask Thee to not allow him to retaliate.*

Other prayers are found in the appendix.

From Slingstones to Milestones: The Weapon of Prayer

1. Have any saints cycled into your life lately?
2. How do you understand the applied sacrificial theology of the "scoot-and-shoot tactic" in the spiritual battle?

---

[473] Saint Teresa of Avila, *Life*, 265.

3.   Do you spend time in Eucharist Adoration? How often, and what have been the effects in your life?

4.   What did you learn that was new about the Rosary? Which of the seven effects of praying the Rosary were new to you?

5.   Why must the heart be engaged in vocal prayer? How is the imagination used in mental prayer, and how can mental prayer be a spiritual weapon?

6.   According to Saint Teresa, how does praying the Rosary help us in meditative prayer?

7.   What is the difference between a sacrament and a sacramental? Do you use sacramentals?

Conclusion

Warriors Now, Fighting on the Battlefield of Faith

"There—anoint him, for this is the one!"

—1 SAMUEL 16:12

W e return to Saint Augustine, a man who himself lived a life of impurity and false belief before slaying his own Goliath. Augustine wrote this homily on Psalm 144, a psalm which David himself composed after he defeated Goliath:

The title of this Psalm is brief in number of words, but heavy in the weight of its mysteries: "To David himself against Goliath." This battle was fought in the time of our fathers, and you, beloved, remember it with me from Holy Scripture. David put five stones in his scrip, he hurled but one. The five Books were chosen, but unity conquered. Then, having smitten and overthrown him, he took the enemy's sword, and with it cut off his head. This our David also did, He overthrew the devil with his own weapons: and when his great ones, whom he had in his power, by means of whom he slew other souls, believe, they turn their tongues against the devil, and so Goliath's head is cut off with his own sword. 'Blessed be the Lord my God, who teaches my hands for battle, my fingers for war' (Ps 143:1). These are our words if we be the Body of Christ.

He goes on to say that we defeat the devil by the pursuit of holiness and virtue through mortifying the flesh, the profession of the Catholic faith, and by living a life of charity.

In this manual, we have tried to show that lasting liberation comes through the ordinary means of the Catholic Church. You are not going to beat Goliath by facing him with armor that does not fit and will slow you down. David did it by using the smallest of things with the greatest of faith. Live your faith—in thought, word, and deed—and God will give you the courage to race toward your enemy. He will guide your stone when you perfect the mechanics of prayer. He will train your hands for battle through the Church's ordinary means: her sacramental and prayer life. As you spend more time before Christ's Eucharistic Presence, Christ will instruct you and give you His peace, "that surpasses all understanding" (Phil 4:7).

Saint Padre Pio adds, "When you are exposed to any trial, be it physical or moral, bodily or spiritual, the best remedy is the thought of Him who is our Life, and not think of the one without joining to it the thought of the other."[474] Thus, the greater the trial, the greater the reward. As Saint Padre Pio recounts the words of Jesus to him, "In reward for your victory over him [the devil] I will give you a shining crown to adorn your brow."[475] As Saint James says, "Blessed is the man who perseveres in temptation, for when he has been proved he will receive the crown of life that he promised to those who love him" (Jas 1:12). Saint Paul writes, "The one who began a good work in you will continue to complete it until the day of Christ Jesus" (Phil 1:6). Elsewhere, he exhorts you to "put on the armor of God, that you may be able to resist on the evil day and, having done everything, to hold your ground" (Eph 6:13). Resist and make a stand, as soldier for Christ. Remember always that this is warfare, not negotiation, and engage

---

[474] Francis Mary, *Padre Pio*, 74.
[475] Francis Mary, 12.

in your single combat in this no-man's land with courage and faith. You are not alone. The *Responsory* in the *Office of Readings, Common of Martyrs* bespeaks of this reality:

> We are warriors now, fighting on the battlefield of faith,
> and God sees all we do;
> the angels watch and so does Christ.
> – *What honor and glory and joy, to do battle in the presence of God,*
> *and to have Christ approve our victory.*
>
> Let us arm ourselves in full strength
> and prepare ourselves for the ultimate struggle
> with blameless hearts, true faith and unyielding courage.
> – *What honor and glory and joy, to do battle in the presence of God,*
> *and to have Christ approve our victory.*[476]

Fight for What Stands Behind You

"The true soldier," says G. K. Chesterton, "fights not because he hates what is in front of him, but because he loves what is behind him." Do not fight because you hate the evil that is in front of you, but because you have something greater behind you worth fighting for. Fight because you love who and what stands behind you—your family, your Church, your marriage, your priesthood, your fellow Catholics. God has put you on the pathway to salvation, so offer Him a heart of thanksgiving that tells Him often of your love for Him. Do this in thought, word, and deed. Show your love for Him through your fidelity to the teachings of the Church and a life that is ordered to prayer and the sacraments. Take the counsel of Saint Padre Pio to heart: "Have courage and do not fear the assaults of the devil. Remember this forever; it is a healthy sign if the devil shouts and roars around your conscience, since this shows that he is not inside your will."[477] He may howl, but he is outside of your

---

[476] *Liturgy of the Hours*, 1986–87.
[477] Cited in Tassone, *Jesus Speaks*, 18.

perimeter. Now, stand guard, like a sentry, over yourself and your loved ones.

In combat, there are attacks and counterattacks, ground taken and ground lost. To prevent giving up ground that you have newly retaken, develop a robust prayer life and an interior discipline becoming of a true soldier for Christ, particularly when you suspect that the demon is probing your "wire." This includes changing how you see yourself. No longer a victim or bystander, you are a warrior for Christ—trained and ready for battle, joyful but vigilant. This means that you must endure on the field of battle to win the crown that awaits the victor. The Syriac Father Saint John of Dalyatha echoes the words of Saint Bonaventure that the Catholic is a "true fighter and strong soldier for Christ" when he wrote:

> The athlete who looks at the crown is not disheartened by the intensity of the struggles. And the crown, which Christ crowns the one who loves Him, at the end of his strife, is the vision of the Holy Trinity. Blessed are you, O combatant, if you look on this goal and you do not turn back. If you are struck with arrows by your enemies, behold, your King observes your struggle and He Himself will heal your wounds. He will anoint you with sweet oil, the oil of joy, and He will refresh your weary limbs which have been afflicted for his sake.[478]

The enemy will shoot, but you now know how to shoot back. Thus, when pressed by our enemy, the saint says, "Let us not be deserters from the battle . . . but let us call on the Chief of our army to help us and He Himself will give us victory. Let us declare our weakness before Him, and He Himself will be the strength of our limbs."[479] That is, keep your eye on the prize promised to the victory.

The Bible recounts how Judas Maccabeus and his brothers waged war after a pagan king who claimed to be god

---

[478] Saint John of Dalyatha, in Hansbury, *The Letters of John of Dalyatha*, 48.
[479] Saint John of Dalyatha, in Hansbury, 48

desecrated the Temple of the Lord (1 Mc 12–24; 2 Mc 8:2–7), while many of his fellow Israelites abandoned their faith and took on pagan practices. Your temple has been cleansed of its desecration, so now you must be vigilant. Like Judas and his brothers, you must "carry on Israel's war joyfully" (1 Mc 3:2) by "fighting with [your] hands and praying to God with [your] hearts" (2 Mc 15:27). This ancient warrior for God knew that "victory in war does not depend on the size of the army, but the strength that comes from heaven" for God Himself "will crush them before us, so do not be afraid of them" (1 Mc 3:9, 22).

The Benedictines' ancient monastic motto is *ora et labora*—pray and work. Listen to the words of a modern Carthusian monk as he describes his experience of prayer and solitude. The poem is entitled, *The Iron Bow*:

> Here in this lonely outpost
> (Silent beneath the silent stars,)
> On the edge of life,
> (A muffled rumbling I sometimes hear)
> I am at home.
> Here are the stark frontiers:
> Time and Eternity,
> Life and Death,
> Satan and my Savior.
> All is reduced to simple terms:
> A vast choice, a vast rejection.
> The choice involves ceaseless
> Labor, the rejection ceaseless
> Vigilance;
> The victory is in my Savior's hands.
> He alone can bend the Bow
> of Iron.
> Hidden in his quiver I wait.
> One day he'll bend the Bow,
> Fire me beyond the frontiers of time,
> Death and Satan's chasm.

In eager expectations
I wait
(Silent beneath the silent stars),
Here in this lonely outpost.[480]

You have been equipped with the weapons to defeat your enemy, and now the Lord, who alone has the strength to bend the iron bow, will pull you from His quiver and use you as He sees fit.

We fight an ancient enemy, and the best weapons and tactics are those tried and tested by the Church's greatest warriors, her saints, who have fought victoriously before us. We give the last word to Doctor of the Church Saint Peter Damian:

> If you wish to be a knight of Christ and to fight manfully for him, as a renowned warrior take up arms against the vices of the flesh, against the stratagems of the devil— enemies, indeed, who never die. Now therefore, put off the garb of your old self and accept the sacrament of new grace. Follow the path to the truth of evangelical grace. May the God of your fathers remove the ancient veil of ignorance from your heart and, dispelling the darkness of error, flood you with the new light of his knowledge. May almighty God in his mercy protect you from the hidden snares of the enemy and bring you safely through the battles of this world to his heavenly kingdom. Amen.[481]

"For freedom Christ set us free; so stand firm and do not submit again to the yoke of slavery."

—Galatians 5:1

---

[480] Carthusian, *Silence*, 20.
[481] Saint Peter Damian, *Letters*, 82.

Appendix A

The Four-Phase Diocesan Protocol

The foundation for our system is the four-phase diocesan protocol—a methodology meant to apply objectivity and standardization in addressing the high number of inquiries coming into both the society and many dioceses each year. The Liber Christo method was produced for training parish priests and the laity who assist and support exorcists in the ministry of liberation where there is suspected extraordinary diabolical activity.

This method follows Catholic liberation practices which focus on the petitioner's return to the sacraments. The goal is reconciliation to God the Father through Jesus Christ by means of the sacraments of the Catholic Church and continual deepening of the practice of the Catholic faith. Thus, the focus is not simply to alleviate a person's suffering but to lead the soul to a sustainable state of grace where lasting, spiritual healing is much more important than the cessation of temporal affliction. On the contrary, this methodology teaches souls to use suffering as a spiritual weapon. A low recidivism rate among the souls who are healed and minimal diabolic retaliation among those who help them are two key markers of success reported by teams throughout the country. As you go through the thirty consecutive days, note your general response and pattern to the prayers and any inner resistance, as these may be indicators of what is happening at an objective level.

A Medical Model

This method follows a medical model whereby the exorcist can be seen as the surgeon/specialist and the parish priest as the general practitioner, or family doctor. In this model, the lay team members serve as intake personnel, nurses, triage, case administrators, and surgical theatre staff. In our prudential experience, most people do not need to see an exorcist and can be cleaned up through the imposition of order, prayer, catechesis, confession, and a general return to living the Catholic faith. Part of the success of this model is that it relies not on individual charisms but on the imposition of order and the authority which comes through office and vocation. This ordering of spiritual life focuses on the healing power of the sacraments. In this model, liturgical prayer is given priority over charismatic or ecstatic prayers. By observing the ministerial hierarchy and authoritative structure established by Christ through both natural law and divine positive law, we open ourselves to greater graces of healing and liberation.

The medical model has other advantages. When all practitioners in a diocese follow the same protocol, they work under the authority of the local bishop. This ensures minimal spiritual and temporal risk to the one who seeks help from the Church (the petitioner) as well as the priests and team members. Thus, to borrow a term from the military, each of the members in this model learns what it means to "stay in your lane." This allows for a greater outpouring of grace, for it invites the *auctoritas* of the Church, and not our own creativity, to come to bear on the enemy who afflicts one of our own.

The protocol also helps to distinguish causality. That is, the team and the petitioner alike can more clearly identify whether the psychological or the spiritual is more operant in the reported afflictions. The process involves the implementation of four distinct phases and, hence, the name "four-phase protocol." In the *first phase*, the petitioner who is seeking help from the Church is placed on a strict prayer regimen for thirty consecutive days. Although this phase is diagnostic and not curative, many people who have done the set prayers as a private devotion report great spiritual benefit. We have found that the demon responds to the imposition of order as much as to the prayers themselves. Additionally, many who come to us are spiritually "flabby" with vices, spiritual excesses, and defects, as well as heresies which negatively influence both their cognition and volition. When combined with a withdrawal from the world and worldly concerns, the prayer discipline is like the self-correction of physical therapy, diet, and exercise for the soul.

Accordingly, the protocol is built upon a monastic-type foundation. In the first phase, by means of prayer and discipline, the *petitioner* learns to engage his will as an essential aspect of liberation. Invariably, memories of patterned sinful behavior, unconfessed mortal sins, deep psychological wounds, and other obstacles to grace emerge as a result of the newly imposed prayer discipline. Sometimes, after this order is established, a good confession can clean up the matter and the person need simply to maintain good spiritual and mental health habits moving forward.

In the *second phase*, the petitioner becomes a *penitent*, and that penitential disposition is key to liberation. This book is the catechetical component of phase two, where the penitent is guided to identify the obstacles to grace. These obstacles impair the free flow of grace into the soul and are best addressed in what Saint Thomas called "the medicine box"—the confessional—where the Divine Physician dispenses the medicine which heals the soul. This phase also helps to uncover areas of trauma and interior defects which create a vulnerability to the demon. Some people have even experienced spiritual oppression, and even low-level obsession, being lifted simply by the imposition of order, a deeper commitment to holiness through prayer, and a more honest and thorough confession.

After going through the *first phase* and *second phase*—the thirty consecutive day prayer regimen and expanded catechesis contained here, to include sacramental confession—some individuals may require formal deliverance prayers by a priest. Although the latter is beyond this book's scope, the first two phases prepare those individuals for formal prayer by the Church. For those cases, Liber Christo provides consultation to the local parish priest on how to assist these individuals during the *third phase*. This includes how to deploy deliverance and severing prayers and minor exorcisms. Many souls who suffered higher levels of diabolic affliction find liberation through the institutional, sacerdotal ministry of the Catholic Church, particularly when combined with a return to the sacramental life.

The *fourth phase*, which is very rare, involves formal exorcism by the diocesan exorcist or the society. The penitent now becomes an *energumen*, a technical term for one possessed by a demon. Again, in those rare cases of possession, the groundwork is laid by the first three phases and greatly assists the possessed person to attain lasting liberation.

This book contains insights on how to use one's spiritual authority as well as how to safely and effectively pray spiritual warfare prayers. These prayers greatly aid all four phases. Quite frankly, when this protocol is followed, we have found that most people are liberated by the ordinary means of the sacraments when combined with catechesis and the development of mental prayer. Those who seek help must learn to engage their will and actively participate in their own liberation. In that sense, all liberation—even solemn exorcism—is self-liberation. A person is normally freed when he finally pushes back with his will and fully embraces the teachings and practices of the Catholic faith. We simply accompany him along this pathway.

If you or someone you love needs spiritual assistance, please consult your pastor before beginning any prayers or regimen.

Phase One: Prayer Regimen

The imposition of order is important to getting your life reordered to prayer and the assertion of your will. The purpose of this initial period (minimum of thirty consecutive days) is to establish a baseline of prayer and discipline from which extraordinary diabolical activity becomes much clearer to identify. It also aids in identifying whether the core issue is primarily psychological and/or stemming from character defects/ excesses. These tend to have a greater impact on quality-of-life issues than does extraordinary diabolical activity. The latter responds adversely to ongoing conversion or advancement in the spiritual life. The demonic responds negatively to prayer and discipline as you engage your will and a holy desire for union with God. The operative definition of healing in this process is "reconciliation with God the Father through Jesus Christ and His Church through the sacraments."

The initial prayer prescription is based on your formal, sacramental relationship with God and the Church:

Non-baptized, (the baptism must be in the Trinitarian form):
- Angelus three times per day at 6 a.m., 12 p.m., 6 p.m.

Baptized:
- above Angelus, plus *Auxilium Christianorum* prayers three times daily.[482]

Baptized and first communion:
- above, plus *Confiteor* at noon.

Fully initiated, B+C+C:
- above, plus act of contrition at 6 p.m.

Fully initiated, non-practicing (in habitual mortal sin):
- above, plus pray Psalm 130 three times daily.

---

[482] These prayers can be found at http://auxiliumchristianorum.org/, and Ripperger, *Deliverance Prayers for Use by the Laity*, 89–98.

Other prayers, disciplines, devotions as indicated can be used. In addition:

- Media fast: no social media, internet, games, television, et cetera. Media use is restricted to those activities related to work, vocation, and school.
- Gregorian chant 24/7 at low volume (we recommend the Benedictine monks of Santo Domingo de Silos).
- No reading other than daily Mass readings, that day only, as many times as one wants.
- Pray the Rosary daily.
- Burning of blessed candles to dispel night terrors or evil presence(s), as needed.
- Sacred art and images should replace secular magazines and images.

If you are using this as part of a diagnostic prayer due to suspected diabolic affliction, this regimen should be done under the supervision of your parish priest, confessor, or spiritual director. For those who are doing this as a private devotion, the set prayers/hours should be met, but the other disciplines may be done according to one's prudential judgment.

Appendix B

Suggested Prayers by Lesson

(While some of the prayers here are in public domain, the majority are taken from Father Ripperger's book *Deliverance Prayers for Use by the Laity* and are used here with permission.)

Chapter One: Renunciation of Evil Influences

Lesson One: Identifying Evil Influences

When you identify an evil spirit animating an emotion et cetera, you should rebuke, renounce, and reject it, then sever any ties it may have to you.

Reject, Renounce, Rebuke

In the Name of Jesus Christ, I reject, renounce, and rebuke the spirit of _____ (anger, fear, sorrow, revenge, etc.) and I command it to leave me and to go to the foot of the Cross of Our Lord Jesus Christ to receive His sentence.

If a priest is present, holding a cross, he can sever the spirits with this formula:

In the Name of Jesus Christ, by the Power of the Holy Spirit I come against the spirit of (n.), and I bind it with the Crown of Thorns soaked with the Precious Blood of our Lord Jesus

Christ; I sever with the Sword of the Cross all ties the spirit(s) has with (N.), with Satan and with all satanic assignments; I break all curses and I crush all demonic strongholds with the weight of the Cross; I send the spirit(s), all companion spirits and all remnants quietly, immediately, and permanently to the foot of the Cross of our Lord Jesus Christ for Him to do with as He wills.

Breaking the Spirit of Death

Grave sins such as abortion, sexual abuse, murder, suicide, contraception and sterilization, homosexuality, et cetera can cause a spirit of death to afflict a family or person. In such cases, a prayer such as this can be prayed:

Any spirits of death or anything connected with death, anything associated with abortion, miscarriage, contraceptive use, etc., you and all of your companion spirits, I bind you separately and individually in the Blood of Christ and break all seals, in the Name of the Father, the Son ✠ and the Holy Spirit. I send you directly and immediately to the Immaculate Heart of Mary and the Sacred Heart of Jesus. In the Name of Jesus, begone. (Thrice) I command that you never return. In the name of Jesus never return. (Thrice) In the Name of Jesus, begone. (Thrice) Amen. (Thrice)

Renunciation of Satan and Claiming the Full Victory

I claim the full victory that my Lord Jesus Christ won on the Cross for me. Having disarmed the powers and authorities, He made a public spectacle of them, triumphing over them by the cross. His victory for me is my victory.

In the name of the Lord Jesus Christ, I renounce all the workings of Satan in my life in all its forms, whether brought into my life by my actions or by others. I break all attachments, entry points, curses, spells, and rights Satan may have in my life whether such entry points were gained through my actions or through others. Strengthened by the intercession of the Immaculate Virgin Mary, Mother of God, of Blessed Michael the Archangel, of the Blessed Apostles Peter and Paul, and all the Saints and Angels of Heaven, and powerful in the holy authority of the name of the Lord Jesus Christ, I ask You Lord to command Satan and all his minions, whomever they may be, to get out of my life and stay out. With that authority I now take back the ground in my life gained by Satan through my sins. I reclaim this ground and my life for Christ. I now dedicate myself to the Lord Jesus Christ; I belong to Him alone. Amen.

Severing Ties, Bonds, and Attachments

This is used for severing the ties, bonds, and attachments of deeply rooted spirits in the heart (including traumas, deep hurts, and wounds), mind, or any physical ailment:

With the sword of St. Michael, the sword of Our Lady and the sword of Our Lord's Cross, I sever and break any and all ties, bonds and attachments I have in my heart (mind) or that N. has to me in his (her) heart (mind).

(Making a plunging movement with the cross towards the heart, the top of the head or the general area of the physical ailment, trace a cross in the area of contact, using any or all of these or other suitable words.)

With the sword of St. Michael: Quis ut Deus. (Who is like unto God.) (thrice)

With the sword of our Lady: Ecce ancilla Domini. Fiat mihi secundum verbum tuum. (Behold the Handmaiden of the Lord. Be it done unto me according to thy word.) (thrice)

Magnificat anima mea Dominum. (My soul magnifies the Lord.) (thrice)

Quodcumque dixerit vobis, facite! (Do whatever he tells you!) (thrice)

With the sword of our Lord's Cross: Vade, Satana. (Be gone, Satan.) (thrice)

Exi de homine. (Come out of the man.) (thrice)

Crux sacra sit mihi lux, non draco sit mihi dux. (May the Holy Cross be my light, the dragon will never be my guide.) (thrice)

Lesson Two: Holy and Unholy Alliances

Once you have examined your past and identified unholy alliances, the following prayer can be prayed before the Blessed Sacrament, preferably three times for each unholy soul tie created.

Longer Form of Breaking Soul Ties

Loving Father, I acknowledge that an unhealthy soul tie exists between me and (n.); I repent of this soul tie, and the consequences of the actions that led to this being created. I repent of all my unforgiveness towards this person, and for any unhealthy attachment to that person in thought, word, or deed. Believing that I come before Thee Lord, as forgiven, I now ask Thee, Father, in the name of Thy Son, Jesus Christ, that by the power of Thy Holy Spirit, that Thou sever every unhealthy and unholy soul tie that exists between (n.) and me. I ask Thee to plant the Cross of Jesus Christ, and the shield of His Precious Blood, firmly and completely between (n.) and me so that these unhealthy soul ties can never reconnect. I ask that any relationship between us from this day forward be a relationship filtered through the Precious Blood of Jesus Christ. In the name of Jesus Christ, I bind, chain, and silence any unclean spirit that took root as a result of this relationship, and command them now to leave quietly and without manifestation to the Pit of Hell. Loving Father, please restore the fullness of Thy Fatherly blessing to me and to (n.). Please restore what was lost to us and bless us. Amen.

Lesson Three: The Occult and Generational Sin

Prayer of Renunciation

In the name of Jesus Christ, I reject, renounce, and rebuke the spirit of (n.) that began to afflict me whenever I (n.). I repent of any sins of mine that allowed this spirit to enter into my life. In the name of Jesus Christ, I also reject, renounce, and rebuke the spirit that animated (n.) or anyone associated with this sin. I now take back the authority, power, or permission that I gave to (object or name).

Simple Prayer of Reparation

My loving Jesus, out of the grateful love I bear Thee, and to make reparation for my unfaithfulness to Grace, give Thee my heart, and I consecrate myself wholly to Thee; and with your help I propose to sin no more. Amen.

Prayers for Breaking Curses and the Occult

I ask Jesus to bind in His Most Precious Blood any and all evil curses, pacts, spells, seals, hexes, triggers, trances, vows, demonic blessings, or any other demonic bondages sent against N. or myself, or any of our loved ones or any of our possessions; I ask Him to bind them all and break them. In the name of the Father and of the Son and of the Holy Spirit. (Thrice)

Prayer for Protection Against Curses, Harm, Accidents

Lord Jesus, I ask Thee to protect my family from sickness, from all harm and from accidents. If any of us has been subjected to any curses, hexes, or spells, I beg Thee to declare these curses, hexes or spells null and void. If any evil spirits have been sent against us, I ask Christ to decommission you and I ask that you be sent to the foot of His Cross to deal with as He will. Then, Lord, I ask Thee to send Thy holy Angels to guard and protect all of us.

Prayer Against Every Evil

Almighty God, Father, Son, and Holy Spirit, Most Holy Trinity, Immaculate Virgin Mary, Angels, Archangels, and Saints of heaven, descend upon me. Please purify me, Lord, mold me, fill me with Thyself, and use me. Banish all the forces of evil from me, destroy them, vanquish them, so that I do Thy Holy Will. Banish from me all spells, witchcraft, black magic, malefice, ties, maledictions, and the evil eye; diabolic infestations, oppressions, possessions; all that is evil and sinful; jealousy, perfidy, envy; physical, psychological, moral, spiritual, diabolical ailments. Cast into hell all demons working these evils, that they may never again touch me or any other creature in the entire world. I command and bid all the powers who molest me, by the power of God Almighty, in the Name of Jesus Christ our Savior, through the intercession of the Immaculate Virgin Mary, to leave me forever, and to be consigned into the everlasting hell.

Acts of Rejection

I reject any dedication, consecration, vow, pact, promise, contract or blood contract, covenant or blood covenant to Satan of myself (and insert names of others if you have made generational consecrations or included anyone else when making an offering to Satan), my heart, spirit, soul, body, mind, memory, imagination, intellect, will, dreams, inner thoughts, subliminal thoughts, touch, taste, smell, sight, hearing, stomach, blood, healthy bacteria, immune system, nervous system, and all other internal processes, especially through (insert list at this time) in the Name of the Father and of the Son, ✠ and of the Holy Spirit. Amen. (Thrice) I consecrate myself and my heart, spirit, soul, body, mind, memory, imagination, intellect, will, dreams, inner thoughts, subliminal thoughts, touch, taste, smell, sight, hearing, stomach, blood, healthy bacteria, immune system, nervous system, and all other internal processes, to the Sacred Heart of Jesus and

*the Immaculate Heart of Mary, in the Name of the Father
and of the Son, ✠ and of the Holy Spirit. Amen.*

(After the person has made his rejection, he can then reconsecrate himself to the Trinity and the Blessed Mother.)

Fatima Prayer

(The Fatima prayer is also a prayer of reparation against the offenses against God that occult practice brings.)

My God, I believe, I adore, I hope, and I love Thee! I ask pardon for those who do not believe, do not adore, do not hope, and do not love Thee.

Most Holy Trinity—Father, Son, and Holy Spirit—I adore Thee profoundly. I offer Thee the most precious Body, Blood, Soul, and Divinity of Jesus Christ, present in all the tabernacles of the world, in reparation for the outrages, sacrileges, and indifferences whereby He is offended. And through the infinite merits of His Most Sacred Heart and the Immaculate Heart of Mary, I beg of Thee the conversion of poor sinners.

O my Jesus, I offer this for love of Thee, for the conversion of sinners, and in reparation for the sins committed against the Immaculate Heart of Mary.

O My Jesus, forgive us our sins, save us from the fires of Hell, lead all souls to Heaven, especially those who have most need of Thy mercy.

Act of Reparation to the Sacred Heart of Jesus[483]

O sweet Jesus, whose overflowing charity for men is requited by so much forgetfulness, negligence, and contempt, behold us prostrate before Thee, eager to repair by a special act of homage the cruel indifference and injuries, to which Thy loving Heart is everywhere subject.

---

[483] Ripperger, *Holy Hour of Reparation*, 5–7.

Mindful alas! that we ourselves have had a share in such great indignities, which we now deplore from the depths of our hearts, we humbly ask Thy pardon and declare our readiness to atone by voluntary expiation not only for our own personal offenses, but also for the sins of those, who, straying far from the path of salvation, refuse in their obstinate infidelity to follow Thee, their Shepherd and Leader or, renouncing the promises of their Baptism, have cast off the sweet yoke of Thy Law.

We are now resolved to expiate each and every deplorable outrage committed against Thee; we are now determined to make amends for the manifold offenses against Christian modesty in unbecoming dress and behavior, for all the foul seductions laid to ensnare the feet of the innocent, for the frequent violations of Sundays and holydays, and the shocking blasphemies uttered against Thee and Thy Saints. We wish also to make amends for the insults to which Thy Vicar on earth and Thy priest are subjected, for the profanation, by conscious neglect or terrible acts of sacrilege, of the very Sacrament of Thy Divine Love, and lastly for the public crimes of nations who resist the rights and teaching authority of the Church which Thou hast founded.

Would that we were able to wash away such abominations with our blood. We now offer, in reparation for these violations of Thy divine honor, the satisfaction Thou once made to Thy eternal Father on the Cross and which Thou continuest to renewest daily on our Altars; we offer it in union with the acts of atonement of Thy Virgin Mother and all the Saints and of the pious faithful on earth; and we sincerely promise to make recompense, as far as we can with the help of Thy grace, for all neglect of Thy great love and for the sins we and others have committed in the past. Henceforth we will live a life of unswerving faith, of purity of conduct, of perfect observance of the precepts of the Gospel and especially that of charity. We promise to the best of our power to prevent others from offending Thee and to bring as many as possible to follow Thee.

O loving Jesus, through the intercession of the Blessed Virgin Mother, our model in reparation, deign to receive the voluntary offering we make of this act of expiation; and by the crowning gift of perseverance keep us faithful unto death in our duty and the allegiance we owe to Thee, so that we may all one day come to that happy home where, with the Father and the Holy Spirit, Thou livest and reignest, God, forever and ever. Amen.

Chapter Two: Repentance, Metanoia, and Forgiveness

Lesson Four: The Impediment of Unforgiveness

Prayer to Forgive Others

Heavenly Father, you are holy and righteous. You are perfect in justice. I confess that I have not forgiven as you have commanded me to. Through Jesus Christ, I now forgive these people: _____ (list names and what they did to you). I confess my pride and judgment of those people. Please forgive me Lord and cleanse me from my sin. Please help me to thoroughly entrust these people and the wrongs they caused me into your hands. I pray that your will be done in my life and in their lives. Please help me to no longer think on those wrongs, but instead to focus my thoughts on you. I invite you, Lord, into any painful memories I have concerning what was done. Please heal any wounds I received and help me to have your perspective on what happened. Thank you, Father. In the name of Jesus Christ I pray, Amen.

Lesson Five: Repentance and Metanoia.

Prayer to Reverse Decisions

Lord Jesus Christ, in Thy Name and by the power of Thy Precious Blood, by the intercession of the Blessed Virgin Mary and by the intercession of St. Michael the Archangel, I exercise my authority which was given to me by Thee in giving me freewill over the choices which I have made in the past as presented to me by Satan and his minions. I reject the choices I made N. (here the person names the choices). I reclaim in Thy name and for Thy Glory, those things which I thought I had to abandon in order to preserve the things which I did choose. I beg Thee, in Thy Mercy, to reclaim those which I may have ceded control over to the demons. Protect all of those people and things which I may have relinquished, not knowing that choices laid before me were false. I rededicate myself to Thee by my free choice and by the authority of Thy Name, I bind all demonic influence which is the result of my choices and I command the demons to go to the foot of Thy Cross to receive their sentence. Mary, I ask thee to surround me, my family, my friends, all of those affected people and things affected by my choices with thy mantle of protection and crush Satan's power in our lives. Saint Michael the Archangel, we ask thee and all our Guardian Angels to protect and defend us in battle against Satan and the powers of darkness. Amen. (Thrice, if necessary.)

If a priest is present, he then says:

All you spirits which have sought to gain influence by presenting false choices to N. and all your companion spirits: in the name of Jesus Christ, by His Precious Blood and the authority of my priesthood [with the authority granted to me by Jesus Christ and His Church] I exorcize and bind you separately and individually and break all seals and power gained by you through these choices: I break all influence you have over those people and things as a result of N.'s choices. I bind you from ever seeking to gain power or influence over N., or anyone or anything associated with him (her). You are bound and the seals are broken in the Name of the Father and of the Son ✠ *and of the Holy Spirit.* (Thrice)

Prayer for Healing

(This can be modified and prayed for a loved one)
*Lord Jesus, Thou camest to heal our wounded and troubled
hearts. I beg Thee to heal the torments that cause anxiety
in my heart; I beg Thee, in a particular way, to heal all who
are the cause of sin. I beg Thee to come into my life and heal
me of the psychological harms that struck me in my early
years and from the injuries that they have caused throughout my life. Lord Jesus, Thou knowest my burdens. I lay them
all on Thy Good Shepherd's Heart. I beseech Thee—by the
merits of the great, open wound in Thy Heart—to heal the
small wounds that are in mine. Heal the pain of my memories, so that nothing that has happened to me will cause me
to remain in pain and anguish, filled with anxiety. Heal, O
Lord, all those wounds that have been the cause of all the evil
that is rooted in my life. I want to forgive all those who have
offended me. Look to those inner sores that make me unable
to forgive. Thou who camest to forgive the afflicted of heart,
please, heal my own heart. Heal, my Lord Jesus, those intimate wounds that cause me physical illness. I offer Thee my
heart. Accept it, Lord, purify it and give me the sentiments of
Thy Divine Heart. Help me to be meek and humble. Heal me,
O Lord, from the pain caused by the death of my loved ones,
which is oppressing me. Grant me to regain peace and joy in
the knowledge that Thou art the Resurrection and the Life.
Make me an authentic witness to Thy Resurrection, Thy victory over sin and death, Thy living presence among us. Amen.*

Protection Prayer against Heresy

*All good and holy God; Father, Son, and Holy Spirit to Thee
alone, do we offer right praise and heartfelt worship. Thou
art the author of life, true source of every blessing. Thou
alone are worthy of our adoration.*

*Thou created the world as a gift to humanity that we may
see your goodness and beauty around us and offer praise to*

Thee as the sole creator. By Thine decree, Thou gave us the first commandment that no created thing whether it be the earth itself, any created being or anything formed by the hand of man should be bowed down to as an idol.

Forgive, and be merciful to those who fail to heed this divine law. We implore the maternal protection of the Blessed Virgin Mary, our heavenly mother, Conqueress of all heresy. May she crush the serpent of this age and help us to recognize the dangerous spiritual contagion of our day. Insulate Thy Church from error.

Protect the Pope, all Cardinals, Bishops, and Clergy, and the laity from falling into apostasy, schism, or blasphemy. Amen.

Lesson Six: The Virgin Mary and Spiritual Combat

Sub Tuum Praesidium

This prayer is the oldest known prayer to Mary, from (*circa* AD 250)

We fly to your patronage, O Holy Mother of God,
despise not our petitions in our necessities,
but deliver us from all danger,
O ever glorious and blessed Virgin.

These prayers should be prayed frequently, but especially in times of temptation:

Hail Mary

Hail, Mary, full of grace,
the Lord is with thee.
Blessed art thou amongst women
and blessed is the fruit of thy womb, Jesus.
Holy Mary, Mother of God,
pray for us sinners,
now and at the hour of our death.
Amen.

Hail, Holy Queen

Hail, Holy Queen, Mother of Mercy,
our life, our sweetness and our hope.
To thee do we cry,
poor banished children of Eve.
To thee do we send up our sighs,
mourning and weeping in this valley of tears
Turn then, most gracious advocate,
thine eyes of mercy toward us,
and after this exile
show unto us the blessed fruit of thy womb, Jesus.
O clement, O loving,
O sweet Virgin Mary.
Pray for us, O holy Mother of God,
That we made be made worthy of the promises of Christ.

Consecration of One's Exterior Goods
to the Blessed Virgin Mary

(This prayer is particularly useful for breaking various forms of oppression.)

I, (Name), a faithless sinner, renew and ratify today in thy hands the vows of my Baptism; I renounce forever Satan, his pomps and works; and I give myself entirely to Jesus Christ, the Incarnate Wisdom, to carry my cross after Him all the days of my life, and to be more faithful to Him than I have ever been before. In the presence of all the heavenly court, I choose thee, O Mary, this day for my Mother and Mistress. Knowing that I have received rights over all my exterior goods by the promulgation of the Natural Law by the Divine Author, I deliver and consecrate to thee, as thy slave, all of my exterior goods, past, present and future; I relinquish into thy hands, my Heavenly Mother, all rights over my exterior goods, including my health, finances, relationships, possessions, property, my job and my earthly success (add any exterior good being oppressed) and I retain for myself no right of disposing the goods that come to me but leave to thee the entire and full right of disposing of all that belongs to me, without exception, according to thy good pleasure, for the greater glory of God in time and in eternity. As I now interiorly relinquish what belongs to me exteriorly into thy hands, I entrust to thee the protection of those exterior goods against the evil one, so that, knowing that they now belong to thee, he cannot touch them. Receive, O good and pious Virgin, this little offering of what little is, in honor of, and in union with, that subjection which the Eternal Wisdom deigned to have to thy maternity; in homage to the power which both of you have over this poor sinner, and in thanksgiving for the privileges with which the Holy Trinity has favored thee. Trusting in the providential care of God the Father and thy maternal care, I have full confidence that thou wilst take care of me as to the necessities of this life and will not leave me forsaken. God the Father, increase my trust in Thy Son's Mother. Our Lady of Fair Love, give me perfect confidence in the providence of Thy Son. Amen.

Prayer against Oppression for Those Who Have Consecrated Their Exterior Goods

Most Blessed Trinity, by the authority given to me by the Natural Law and by Thy giving these things and rights to me which I have consecrated to the Blessed Virgin Mary, I claim on her behalf the authority, rights, and power over my N. (income, finances, possessions, etc.) and anything else that pertains to the oppression. By the merits of Thy Sacred Wounds, I renounce any power or authority I conceded to any demon in relation to the oppression and I reclaim on Our Lady's behalf the rights, powers, and authority over anything which I may have lost or conceded, and I ask Thee to remove any demon's ability to influence or affect anything in my life. God the Father humiliate the demons that have sought to steal Thy glory from Thee by oppressing Thy creatures. We beseech Thee to show Thy great glory and power over them and Thy great generosity to me, Thine unworthy creature, by answering all that I have asked of Thee so that I might love Thee perfectly. I bind all demons of oppression, in the name of Jesus, by the power of the Most Precious Blood, the power of the humility with which Christ suffered His wounds, and the intercession of the Blessed Virgin Mary, Virgin Most Powerful, Saint Michael the Archangel, the blessed Apostles, Peter and Paul, and all the saints, and I command you to leave my N. (income, finances, possessions, etc.) alone and go to the foot of the Holy Cross to receive your sentence, in the Name of the Father, and of the Son and of the Holy Spirit. Amen.

Commission of the Care of Soul and Body

(May be prayed at any time, for oneself or one's family, but especially before sleeping.)

Into thy hands, Mary, I commend my body and my soul. I ask thee to provide for them and to protect them. I ask thee to protect them from the evil one. I ask thee to enlighten my mind, strengthen my will, and refrain my appetites by grace. Our Lady and Saint Michael, call down from Heaven the legions of angels under your command to protect me; I ask of thee all the things I ask of my guardian angel. My guardian angel, under thy intellectual and volitional protection I place my body. I ask thee to illumine my mind and refrain my appetites. I ask thee to strengthen my cogitative power, my memory, and my imagination. Help me to remember the things I should and not remember the things I should not. Help me to associate the things I should and not to associate the things I should not. Give me good clear images in my imagination. I ask thee to drive away all the demons that might affect me while I sleep (or throughout the course of the day). (Help me to sleep and, if thou should deem it prudent, direct my dreams. Help me to arise refreshed). Amen.

Chapter Three: Examination of Conscience and Confession

Lesson Seven: *The Development of Virtue*

Prayer to Overcome Evil Passions and to Become a Saint

Dear Jesus, in the Sacrament of the Altar, be forever thanked and praised. Love, worthy of all celestial and terrestrial love! Who, out of infinite love for me, ungrateful sinner, didst assume our human nature, didst shed Thy Most Precious Blood in the cruel scourging, and didst expire on a shameful cross for our eternal welfare! Now, illumined with lively faith, with the outpouring of my whole soul and the fervor of my heart, I humbly beseech Thee, through the infinite merits of Thy painful sufferings, to give me strength and courage to destroy every evil passion which sways my heart, to bless Thee in my greatest afflictions, to glorify Thee by the exact fulfilment of my duties, supremely to hate all sin, and thus to become a saint.

Prayer to Overcome Our Spiritual Enemies

Eternal Wisdom, come down into my soul, that all my enemies may be driven out; all my crimes melted away; all my sins forgiven. Enlighten my understanding with the light of true faith; inflame my will with Thy sweet love; clear up my mind with Thy glad presence; and give virtue and perfection to all my powers. Watch over me especially at my death, that I may come to enjoy Thy beatific vision in eternal bliss. Amen.

Prayer for Help against Spiritual Enemies

Glorious Saint Michael, Prince of the heavenly hosts, who stands always ready to give assistance to the people of God, who fought with the dragon, the old serpent, and cast him out of heaven, and now valiantly defends the Church of God that

*the gates of hell may never prevail against her, I earnestly
entreat you to assist me also in the painful and dangerous
conflict which I sustain against the same formidable foe.*

*Be with me, O mighty Prince, that I may courageously
fight and vanquish that proud spirit, whom you, by the
Divine power, gloriously overthrew, and whom our powerful
King, Jesus Christ, has in our nature, completely overcome,
so having triumphed over the enemy of my salvation. May I
be with you and the holy angels, praise the clemency of God
who has granted repentance and forgiveness to fallen man.
Amen.*

Lesson Eight: The Sacraments and the Flow of Grace

For Breaking the Wall Built up around the Heart

(This prayer can be prayed to help free up the graces of a desire
to return to the sacraments.)

*I bind this wall that is around N.'s heart in the Blood of Jesus
and I break it in the Name of the Father and of the Son ✠ and
of the Holy Spirit.*

At times, severing the demons in connection to the wall will
help to begin the process of the wall coming down on the
side of the person with the wall. This can be prayed for others
according to the instructions in the lines of authority above.

Prayer of Deliverance

(This is a good prayer to use when you identify various spirits, vices, and defects afflicting you or your family. It can be
modified by adding other spirits you are militating against
[rebellion, anger, fear, unforgiveness, generational sins, fear
of suffering, orphan spirit, etc.] with the same response
"We implore Thee, deliver us, O Lord." To modify for the
family, change ". . . my brothers and sisters who are enslaved

by the evil one" to ". . . my family who is being oppressed by the evil one.")

Almighty God and Father, we beg Thee through the interces-
sion and help of the Archangels Sts. Michael, Raphael, and
Gabriel for the deliverance of our brothers and sisters (or,
my family) who are enslaved by the evil one. All Saints of
heaven, come to our aid.

From anxiety, sadness, and obsessions—We implore
Thee, deliver us, O Lord.

From hatred, fornication, and envy—We implore Thee,
deliver us, O Lord.

From thoughts of jealousy, rage, and death—We implore
Thee, deliver us, O Lord.

From every thought of suicide and abortion—We implore
Thee, deliver us, O Lord.

From every form of sinful sexuality—We implore Thee,
deliver us, O Lord.

From every division in our family, and every harmful
friendship—We implore Thee, deliver us, O Lord.

From every sort of spell, malefice, witchcraft, and every
form of the occult—We implore Thee, deliver us, O Lord.

[Here insert other spirits, vices, and defects you are mili-
tating against—We implore Thee, deliver us, O Lord.]

Thou who said, "Peace I leave with you, my peace I give
unto you." That, through the intercession of the Virgin Mary,
we may be liberated from every demonic influence and enjoy
Thy peace always. In the Name of Christ, our Lord. Amen.

Lesson Nine: Making a Good Confession

Pietate Tua[484]

Loosen, O Lord, we pray Thee, in Thy pity, the bonds of our
sins, and by the intercession of the blessed Mary, ever Vir-
gin Mother of God, the blessed Apostles Peter and Paul, and

---

[484] From the *Raccolta*, 49.

all saints, keep us Thy servants and our abodes in all holiness; cleanse us, our relations, kinsfolk, and acquaintance, from our vices; adorn us with all virtues; grant to us peace and health; repel our enemies visible and invisible; curb our carnal desires; vouchsafe us helpful seasons; bestow thy charity upon our friends and our enemies; guard thy holy city; preserve our Sovereign Pontiff (Pope N.), and defend all prelates, priests, and all Christian people from all adversity. Let Thy blessing be ever upon us, and grant to all the faithful departed eternal rest. Through Christ our Lord. Amen.

Prayer to the Precious Blood of Our Lord Jesus Christ

Eternal Father, I offer Thee the Most Precious Blood of Jesus Christ in atonement for my sins, and in supplication for the holy souls in purgatory and for the needs of Holy Church.

Prayer to Be Freed from Evil Habits

Give me, I beseech Thee, O Holy Spirit, Giver of all good gifts, that powerful grace which converts the stony hearts of mortals into burning furnaces of love. By Thy grace, free my captive soul from the thraldom of every evil habit and concupiscence, to restore to it the holy liberty of the children of God. Give me to taste how sweet it is to serve the Lord and crucify the flesh with its vices and concupiscences. Enlarge my heart that I may ever cheerfully run the way of Thy commandments until I reach the goal of my aspirations, the joys and bliss of Thy habitation in heaven. Amen.

Chapter Four: Power and Authority

Lesson Ten: Demonic Compliance and the Rules of Engagement

Prayer against Oppression

(When the demon is harassing the temporal goods, such as your home, vehicle, etc., this prayer can be used to good effect.)

Most Blessed Trinity, by the authority given to me by the Natural Law and by Thy giving these things and rights to me, I exercise authority, rights, and power over my N. (income, finances, possessions, etc.) and anything else that pertains to the oppression. By the merits of Thy Sacred Wounds, I reclaim the rights, powers, and authority over anything which I may have lost or conceded to any demon, and I ask Thee to remove any demon's ability to influence or affect anything in my life. God the Father humiliate the demons that have sought to steal Thy glory from Thee by oppressing Thy creatures. We beseech Thee to show Thy great glory and power over them and Thy great generosity to me, Thine unworthy creature, by answering all that I have asked of Thee. I bind all demons of oppression, in the name of Jesus, by the power of the Most Precious Blood, the power of the humility with which Christ suffered His wounds, and the intercession of the Blessed Virgin Mary, Virgin Most Powerful, Saint Michael the Archangel, the blessed Apostles, Peter and Paul, and all the saints, and I command you to leave and go to the foot of the Holy Cross to receive your sentence, in the Name of the Father, and of the Son and of the Holy Spirit. Amen.

Longer Form of Binding Prayer

I ask Jesus to cover me with His Blood, my hands, feet, arms, legs, head, tongue, mouth, saliva, lips, voice, throat, stomach,

intestines, blood, the immune system, ears, eyes, clothing, in
the name of the Father and of the Son, and of the Holy Spirit.

I bind and render helpless any spirit affecting me: spirits
of never, communication, games, deceit, deception, ministering spirits, dissociation, unforgiving heart, abandonment,
rejection, self-hatred, mocking, controlling, of capital sins,
occult, spirits that cause hiccups, vomiting, fainting, falling,
fear, panic, cowardliness, yelling, rage, explosions, defiance,
amnesia, obscene gestures, tearing of clothing, reading of
hearts, sudden movement, levitation, hot, cold, temperature
fluctuation, upset stomach, bad odors, nausea, abandonment of state in life; of theft, murder, death, lies, brutality,
trauma, resentment, terror, pride, arrogance, bitterness,
confusion, cruelty, hatred, insecurity, adultery, fornication,
masturbation, pornography, prostitution, unnatural sex,
sexual perversions with all their manifestations, contraception, sterilization, revenge, abortion, mutilation, suicide,
blasphemy, sacrilege, heresy, schism, disobedience to authority; contempt for God, for His Name, for the Sabbath rest;
eating disorders, involuntary vices (obsessive compulsive
disorders), envy, jealousy, curiosity, coveting, stubbornness,
perjury, drugs, drunkenness, lewd dancing, molestation,
refusal to speak, false appearance of leaving, distraction,
exaggeration, scrupulosity, presumption, slander, detraction; spirits that attack memory, imagination, mind, spirit,
soul and body, the demons and spirits of freemasonry, the
occult, wicca, covens, hexes, vexes, spells, charms, curses,
snares, traps, obstacles, diversions, divisions, spiritual influences, evil wishes, evil desires, hereditary seals known and
unknown, every dysfunction and disease, negative inherited
DNA, blood sacrifices, generational evil spirits, clinging spirits, and all others known to be present by Saint Michael and
the Holy Angels.

I ask Jesus to sever the transmission of any and all satanic
vows, pacts, spiritual bonds, soul ties, and satanic works.

I ask you Jesus to break and dissolve any and all links,
and effects of links with: astrologers, bohmos, channelers,

*charters, clairvoyance, crystals, crystal healers, fortune tell-
ers, mediums, the New Age movement, occult seers, palm,
tea leaf or tarot card readers, psychics, santeros (Santería),
satanic cults, spirit guides, witches, witch doctors, dungeon
masters, and voodoo.*

*I ask you Jesus to dissolve all effects of participation in
séances, divination, ouija boards, horoscopes, occult games
of all sorts, and any form of worship that does not offer true
honor to Jesus Christ. In the Name of the Father and of the
Son, ✠ and of the Holy Spirit. Amen.*

*If suitable, the person can make the following act of
rejection:*

*I reject all these spirits, vices and wickedness, in the
Name of the Father and of the Son, and of the Holy Spirit.
Amen. (Thrice)*

Chapter Five: Prayer, Weapons, and Tactics

Lesson Eleven: Demonic Tactics

Prayer against Retaliation[485]

*Lord Jesus Christ, in your love and mercy, pour Thy Precious
Blood over me so that no demon or disembodied spirit may
retaliate against me. Mary, surround me with thy mantle,
blocking any retaliating spirits from having any authority
over me. Saint Michael, surround me with thy shield, so that
no evil spirit may take revenge on me. Queen of Heaven and
Saint Michael, send down the legions of angels under your
command to fight off any spirits that would seek to harm me.
All you saints of heaven, impede any retaliating spirit from
influencing me. Lord, Thou art the Just Judge, the avenger
of the wicked, the Advocate of the Just, we beg in Thy mercy,
that all we ask of Mary, the angels and the saints of heaven
be also granted to all our loved ones, those who pray for us*

---

[485] Used with permission.

and their loved ones, that for Thy Glory's sake, we may enjoy Thy perfect protection. Amen.

Prayer of Deliverance

(You can insert the names of loved ones and turn this into an intercessory prayer as well.)

Lord, have Mercy. God, Our Lord, King of Ages, All-powerful and Almighty, Thou Who hast made everything and who hast transformed everything simply by Thy Will. Thou Who in Babylon changed into dew the flames of the "seven-times hotter" furnace and protected and saved the three holy children. Thou are the doctor and the physician of our souls. Thou are the salvation of those who turn to Thee. We beseech Thee to make powerless, banish, and drive out every diabolic power, presence, and machination; every evil influence, malefice, or evil eye and all evil actions aimed against Thy servant . . . where there is envy and malice, give us an abundance of goodness, endurance, victory, and charity. O Lord, Thou who lovest man, we beg Thee to reach out Thy powerful hands and Thy most high and mighty arms and come to our aid. Help us, who are made in your image; send the Angel of Peace over us, to protect us body and soul. May he keep at bay and vanquish every evil power, every poison or malice invoked against us by corrupt and envious people. Then, under the protection of Thy authority may we sing in gratitude, "The Lord is my salvation; whom should I fear? I will not fear evil because Thou art with me, my God, my strength, my powerful Lord, Lord of Peace, Father of all Ages."

Anima Christi

Soul of Jesus Christ, sanctify me.
Heart of Jesus, inflame me with love.
Body of Jesus Christ, save me.
Blood of Jesus Christ, inebriate me.
Water out of the side of Jesus Christ, wash me.

Passion of Christ, strengthen me.
O good Jesus, hear me.
Within Thy wounds hide me.
Let me not to be separated from Thee.
Defend me from the malignant enemy.
At the hour of my death, call me.
And bid me come unto Thee above,
That with the Saints I may praise Thee for all eternity. Amen.

Lesson Twelve: The Weapon of Prayer

Prayer to Saint Michael

Saint Michael the Archangel, defend us in battle; be our defense against the wickedness and snares of the devil. May God rebuke him, we humbly pray. And do thou, O prince of the heavenly host, by the power of God, thrust into hell Satan and all the evil spirits who prowl about the world seeking the ruin of souls. Amen.

Another Form

O glorious Prince of the heavenly host, Saint Michael the Archangel, defend us in the battle and in the fearful warfare that we are waging against the principalities and powers, against the rulers of this world of darkness, against the evil spirits. Come thou to the assistance of men, whom Almighty God created immortal, making them in His own image and likeness and redeeming them at a great price from the tyranny of Satan. Fight this day the battle of the Lord with thy legions of holy Angels, even as of old thou didst fight against Lucifer, the leader of the proud spirits and all his rebel angels, who were powerless to stand against thee, neither was their place found any more in heaven. And that apostate angel, transformed into an angel of darkness who still creeps about the earth to encompass our ruin, was cast headlong into the abyss together with his followers. But behold, that first enemy of mankind, and a murderer from the beginning, has regained his confidence. Changing himself into an angel of light, he goes about with the whole multitude of the wicked spirits to invade the earth and blot out the Name of God and of His Christ, to plunder, to slay and to consign to eternal damnation the souls that have been destined for a crown of everlasting life. This wicked serpent, like an unclean torrent, pours into men of depraved minds and corrupt hearts the poison of his malice, the spirit of lying, impiety and blasphemy, and the deadly breath of impurity and every form of vice and iniquity. These crafty enemies of mankind have filled to overflowing with gall and wormwood the Church, which is the Bride of the Lamb without spot; they have laid profane hands upon her most sacred treasures. Make haste, therefore, O invincible Prince, to help the people of God against the inroads of the lost spirits and grant us the victory. Amen.

Invocation of the Entire Heavenly Court

O Glorious Queen of Heaven and earth, Virgin Most Powerful, thou who hast the power to crush the head of the ancient serpent with thy heel, come and exercise this power flowing from the grace of thine Immaculate Conception. Shield us under the mantle of thy purity and love, draw us into the sweet abode of thy heart and annihilate and render impotent the forces bent on destroying us. Come Most Sovereign Mistress of the Holy Angels and Mistress of the Most Holy Rosary, thou who from the very beginning hast received from God the power and the mission to crush the head of Satan. We humbly beseech thee, send forth thy holy legions, that under thy command and by thy power they may pursue the evil spirits, encounter them on every side, resist their bold attacks and drive them far from us, harming no one on the way, binding them immobile to the foot of the Cross to be judged and sentenced by Jesus Christ Thy Son, to be disposed of by Him as He wills. Saint Joseph, Patron of the Universal Church, come to our aid in this grave battle against the forces of darkness, repel the attacks of the devil and free your son (daughter) N. from the stronghold the enemy has upon his (her) soul. Saint Michael, summon the entire heavenly court to engage their forces in this fierce battle against the powers of hell. Come O Prince of Heaven with thy mighty sword and thrust into hell Satan and all the other evil spirits. O Guardian Angels, guide and protect us. Amen.

Te Deum

(The *Te Deum* is an ancient prayer echoing the praise of the angels and saints before the throne. As such, it reminds the demon of the depth of his fall and the exultation and glory of the angels and saints in heaven.)

O God, we praise Thee, and acknowledge Thee to be the supreme Lord. Everlasting Father, all the earth worships Thee. All the Angels, the heavens, and all angelic powers, All the Cherubim and Seraphim, continuously cry to Thee: Holy, Holy, Holy, Lord God of Hosts! Heaven and earth are full of the Majesty of Thy glory. The glorious choir of the Apostles, the wonderful company of Prophets, the white-robed army of Martyrs, praise Thee. Holy Church throughout the world acknowledges Thee: the Father of infinite Majesty; Thy adorable, true, and only Son; also the Holy Spirit, the Comforter. O Christ, Thou art the King of glory! Thou art the everlasting Son of the Father. When Thou tookest it upon Thyself to deliver man, Thou didst not disdain the Virgin's womb. Having overcome the sting of death, Thou opened the Kingdom of Heaven to all believers. Thou sittest at the right hand of God in the glory of the Father. We believe that Thou wilst come to be our Judge. We, therefore, beg Thee to help Thy servants whom Thou hast redeemed with Thy Precious Blood. Let them be numbered with Thy Saints in everlasting glory.

V. Save Thy people, O Lord, and bless Thy inheritance!

R. Govern them and raise them up forever.

V. Every day we thank Thee.

R. And we praise Thy Name forever, yes, forever and ever.

V. O Lord, deign to keep us from sin this day.

R. Have mercy on us, O Lord, have mercy on us.

V. Let Thy mercy, O Lord, be upon us, for we have hoped in Thee.

R. O Lord, in Thee I have put my trust; let me never be put to shame.

Binding Prayer

(The following prayer may be used in conjunction with the sins, vices, or spirits involved. For a more comprehensive list, see appendix C.)

Spirit of N.,[486] I bind you in the Name of Jesus, by the power of the Holy Cross, by the power of the most Precious Blood of Our Lord Jesus Christ, and by the intercession of the Blessed Virgin Mary, Saint Michael the Archangel, the blessed Apostles, Peter and Paul and all of the saints, and I command you to leave N. (Name of person or object) and go to the foot of the Holy Cross to receive your sentence, in the Name of the Father, the Son and the Holy Spirit. Amen.

Spiritual Warfare Prayer

Heavenly Father, I love Thee, I praise Thee, and I worship Thee. I thank Thee for sending Thy Son Jesus Who won victory over sin and death for my salvation. I thank Thee for

---

[486] A suggested list includes agitation, anger, anxiety, astrology, binding (holding), depression, despair, domination, effeminacy, fear, fornication, fortune telling, incantation, illness, incubus, lust, mental illness, mimicking, necromancy, obsession, Odin, Ouija board, oppression, pacts, pain, palm readings, scratching, sloth, succubus, superstition, and witchcraft.

sending Thy Holy Spirit Who strengthens me, guides me, and leads me into fullness of life. I thank Thee for Mary, my Heavenly Mother, who intercedes with the holy Angels and Saints for me.

Lord Jesus Christ, I place myself at the foot of Thy Cross and ask Thee to cover me with Thy Precious Blood, which pours forth from Thy Most Sacred Heart and Thy Most Holy Wounds. Purify me, O Lord, in the living water that flows from Thy Heart. I ask Thee to surround me, Lord Jesus, with Thy Holy Light.

Heavenly Father, let Thy healing grace flow through the maternal and paternal generations to purify my family line of Satan and sin. I come before Thee, Father, and ask forgiveness for myself, my relatives, and my ancestors, for any calling upon powers that set themselves up in opposition to Thee or that do not offer true honor to Jesus Christ. In the Most Holy Name of Jesus, I now reclaim any territory that was handed over to Satan and place it under the Lordship of Jesus Christ.

By the power of Thy Holy Spirit, reveal to me, Father, any people I need to forgive and any areas of unconfessed sin. Reveal aspects of my life that are not pleasing to Thee, O Father, and ways that have given or could give Satan a foothold in my life. Father, I submit to Thee any unforgiveness; I submit to Thee my sins; and I submit to Thee all of the ways that Satan has a hold on my life. I thank Thee, O Father for this knowledge; I thank Thee, for Thy forgiveness and Thy love. Lord Jesus, in Thy Holy Name, I bind all evil spirits of the air, water, ground, underground, and netherworld. I further bind, in the Name of Jesus, any and all emissaries of the satanic headquarters and I ask Jesus to pour His Precious Blood on the air, atmosphere, water, ground and their fruits around us, the underground and the netherworld.

Heavenly Father, allow Thy Son Jesus to come now with the Holy Spirit, the Blessed Virgin Mary, the Holy Angels and the Saints to protect me from all harm and to keep all evil spirits from taking revenge on me in any way.

Lord Jesus Christ, fill me with charity, compassion, faith, gentleness, hope, humility, joy, kindness, light, love, mercy, modesty, patience, peace, purity, security, serenity, tranquility, trust, truth, understanding and wisdom. Help me to walk in Thy Light and Truth, illuminated by the Holy Spirit so that I may praise, honor, and glorify Our Father in time and in eternity. For Thou, Lord Jesus, are "the Way, the Truth, and the Life," and Thou "have come that we might have life and have it more abundantly."

Appendix C

List of Sins, Vices, or Spirits[487]

The following is one of the lists used by exorcists to determine the sin, vice, or spirit involved. These can also be used as part of a self-examination to see where one may be vulnerable to spiritual attack. These are:

Lying Spirits

Pretension, Unreality, Denial, Delusion/Labyrinth, Convoluted Thinking, Cheating, Neglect of Responsibilities, Irreverence, Circumvention, Folly, Concealment, Blindness of Spirit, Evasiveness, Deceit, Mask, Game Playing, Deception, Illusion, Diversion, Error, Drama, Marionette-Puppet, False, Farce, Hallucination, Smoke and Mirrors, Harlequin Mask, Imitation, Pantomime, Counterfeit, Role Reversal, Fraud, Detraction, Incredulity, Coy, Cunning, Undermining, Aping, Dichotomy, Juggling, Duplicity, Facade, Dual, Showmanship, Theatrics, Show, Acting, Trickery, Magic, Mockery, Appearances, Fantasy, Heresy, Legion, Subversive, Irony, Mimicry, Unclean Spirits, Unclean and Offensive Conditions, Compulsiveness to Clean, Involuntary Vices (Obsessive Compulsive), Compulsion, "I have to," Distortion of Truth, Busybody, Nosey, Curiosity, Violation of Confidentiality, Rumors, Critical

---

[487] This list is taken from Ripperger, *Minor Exorcisms*, 419–28. Used with permission.

Judgment, Perverted Judgment, Perverted Thinking, Scandal, Spirits that Cause Accidents, Theft, Stealing, Greed, Avarice, Materialism, Possessiveness, Hoarding, Covetousness, Collecting, Exclusiveness, Making Excuses for Sin and Infidelities to God, Neglect-Omission, Inability to Pray Because of Worldly Cares, Inability to Give or Share, Stingy, Inability to Give Praise and Thanksgiving to God or to People.

Mental Illness

Dyslexia-Learning Disabilities, ADD, ADHD, Schizophrenia, Multipersonality, Bi-Polar—Manic Depressive, Mania, Insanity, Depression, Borderline, Neurosis, Psychosis, Paralysis, Post-Traumatic-Stress Syndrome, Anxiety Disorder, Panic Disorder, Disconnected Spirit, Disjointed Spirit, Fractured Personality, Split Personality, "Undo," Opposites, Retardation, Tension, Chronic Fatigue, Eating Disorder, Memory Loss, Distorted Thinking, Distorted Hearing, Mental Torments, Confusion, Procrastination, Compromise, Indecision, Doubts, Anorexia, Bulimia, Stuttering, Death-Wish.

Physical Ailments

GI Problems, Diabetes, Heart Disease, Obesity, TMJ—Grinding Teeth, Spoliosis, Night Sweats, Night Tremors, Palsy, Paralysis, Parasites, Crippling Disease, Enuresis, Bleeding, Vomiting, Coccyx Bone Crack, Sinus and Respiratory Problems, Birth Defects, Migraine Headaches, Back Problems, Vision Problems, Hearing Problems, Speech Problems, Metabolic Problems, Gland and Hormone Problems, Tumors, Cancer, Arthritis (Unforgiveness), Smell, Taste, Throat and Vocal Cords, High Blood Pressure, High Cholesterol, Liver, Lungs, Exhaustion, Weakness, Life's Breath, Pneumonia, Tuberculosis, Insomnia, Hay Fever, Deaf and Dumb, Fibromyalgia, Lupus, Allergies, Asthma, Lyme Disease.

False Religions and Philosophies

Jehovah Witness, Christian Cults, Christian Science, Scientology, Eastern Religion, Zen, Buddhism, Ancestor Worship, Taoism, Islam, Karate-Martial Arts, Yoga, Mind Science, Paganism, Pantheism, Druid, Celtic, Bahai, Heathen Worship, Masonic Lodges, Renew 2000, Future Church, Protestantism, Schism, Mormonism, Rainbow Girls, Rosicrucians, Moonies, Unity Churches, Secret Societies, New Age Religions, Social Agencies, Freemasonry, Indian Religions, Socialism/Communism, New Age, Quakers, Shakers, Native American Spirituality, Indian Powwow, Shamanism, Hinduism, Atheism, Agnosticism, Heresy, Anti-Clericalism, Mafia, Nationalism-Nazism.

Abandonment of Religious Practices

Minimalization of Sin, Spiritual Pride, Abandonment of Vows, Abandonment of Vocation, Anti-Christ Spirit, Religious Errors, Apostasy, Doubters of True Faith, Minimalization of Sin, Jansenism/Puritanism, Spiritual Gluttony, Spiritual Wrath Aimed at God, Spiritual Envy of the Gifts of Others.

Those against the Spiritual Life

Spiritual Sloth—Sadness of the Things of God, Sacrilege, Sins against Vows, Scrupulosity, Fear of Vocation, Abandonment of Promises, Feminism, Liberalism, Hatred of the Catholic Church, Fascism, Racism, Marxism, Blasphemy, Apostasy, Contempt for God, Sacrilege of Priestly Sacred Character, Occult.

Superstitious Practices

Satanism, Divination (Methods of Seeking Guidance and Knowledge from the Demonic), Familiar Spirits, Witchcraft-Wizardry, Wicca, New Age Practices, Out of

Body Experiences, Santería, Voodoo, Celtic, Druid, Evil Eye, Bohomo, TM (Transcendental Meditation), Mantras, Crystals, Reiki, Enneagrams, Magic, Evil Levitation, Handwriting Analysis,[488] Seance, Ouija Boards, Yoga, Black Masses, Devil Worship, Palm Reading, Tea-Leaf Reading, Tarot Cards, Horoscopes, ESP, Silva Mind Control, Hypnotism, Centering Prayer, Martial Arts, Any Powers Apart from God, Acupuncture, Homeopathic Remedies with Ritual, Portrons, Channeling, Contacting the Dead or Disembodied Spirits Through: Seances, Dreams, Channeling; Divining with Tree Root, Curses of the Occult Against the Priesthood, Celebration of Halloween—Costumes of the Demonic, Wearing of: Devil's Horn, Rabbit's Foot, Pentagram, Tattoos, Mood Ring; Biofeedback, Dungeons and Dragons, Rock and Roll/Jazz, Bloody Mary, Light as a Feather, Stiff as a Board, Eastern Star, Job's Daughters, Good Luck Charms, Lucky Coins, Magic Eight Ball, Numerology, Spiritism, Astrology, Pyramids, Parental Spirits.

Spirits against Matrimonial Sacramental Unity

Neglect of Responsibilities toward Children Physically, Emotionally, Mentally, Spiritually; Cursing of Children, Child Abuse, Child Molestation, Incest, Betrayal, Abandonment, Inability to Give Love, Detachment and Indifference Due to Self-Absorption, Abandonment of Religious Practice and Teaching the Faith to Children, Lack of Affection, Over Affection, Lack of Tactility, Lack of Affectivity, Lack of Nurturing, Misuse of Authority, Religiosity and Abandoning Children and of Family for Church; Lack of Availability, Competition for Attention with Children for Spouse, Pitting against Spouse with Children-Putting Children in the Middle

---

[488] Here, reference is not made to the science of handwriting analysis to determine similarities and differences in writing but the predicting of the future, the reading of the past of a person's life by the analysis and so forth.

of an Argument, Putting Children above Spouse in the Family Relationships, Living out Your Identity in Your Children, Manipulation, Control, Dominance, Overprotection, Stifling because of Fear, Non-protection-Abandonment, Permissiveness, Allowing: Provocative Clothing, Movies, No Discipline, Over Eating of Junk Food; Swearing, Crude Language, Abusive Language, Unapproachability, Fearful Dominance, Deceiving Children, Over-Doting on and Spoiling Children, Disordered Love and Affection for Children, Preferring One Sibling more than Another, Pitting Siblings against Each Other; Disordered Shame and Guilt about Their Character or Bodies, No Discipline, Disciplining without Explanation or Full Cycle of Love, Teaching Error, Mocking or Belittling of Children; Allowing Cynicism, Sarcasm or Critical Humor, Uncontrolled Use of the Tongue, Preferring Friends to Family, Not Allowing Children to Express Themselves, Fighting with Spouse in Front of Children, Allowing Children to be the Parents to their Parents; Adultery and Its Effects, Any Disorders in Children Produced by any Unnatural Sex in Home; Gossip, Belittling and Allowing Sibling Rivalry; Permissiveness: Teaching Contraception and Giving Contraceptives to your Children, Teaching Immorality to Children, Exposing them to Loose Conduct and Alcoholism, Exclusion in their Rooms; Permissiveness: No Chores around House, No Responsibilities, No Money Management; Occult: Harry Potter, Pokémon. Monster toys, T.V., Books; Non-Protection of Child's Soul or Spiritual Development and Schooling, Non-Protection and Non-Awareness of Relationships within Family Members and Friends, Herding Children with No Personalized Attention (Large Family), Allowing Uncleanness and Chaos in Family; Murder in Womb, Abortion, Contraception, Scheming, Plotting, Deviant Plans; Non-Explaining and Training in Sexual Behavior; Addictions: Alcoholism, Drugs, Smoking, Gambling, Sexual Addiction.

Children

Defiance, Deviant Behavior, Laziness, Unruly and Wild, Out of Control, Temper Tantrums, Hitting Parents; Deceiving-Lying, Curiosity in Sexual Behavior; Procrastination, Rebellion, Stubbornness, Assertiveness and Independence, Leading Parents Around on a Leash; Sibling Rivalry, Fighting, Bickering and Belittling Siblings, Pouting, Daydreaming, Coquettishness, Provocativeness, Mischievous, Impishness, Troubled Behavior, Non-Attentiveness; Coercion of Parents, Manipulation of Parents, Pitting Parents against Each Other; Negative Attention Behavior, Fascination with Occult and Powers, Too Much Time with: Video Games, Sports, TV, Internet; Sexual Perversion, Animal Torture, Stealing and Theft, Anti-Social Behavior, Rebelliousness, Indulgence, Fear, Nightmares, Thumb-Sucking, Bed-Wetting, Nail-Biting; Touchiness and Over-Corrections, Anger and Rage, Fear, Rejection, Sulking and Pouting, Abandonment and Fear of Abandonment In Utero, Fear of Death and Dying, Unwanted Pregnancy, Attempted Abortion, Cord Around Neck, Traumatic Delivery; Following a Miscarriage or Abortion: Suicidal Thoughts, Darkness, Death and Fear of Death, Sadness, Sorrow; Fear of Dark, Nightmares; Emotional Trauma: Panic, Guilt, Shame, Reclusion, Shyness, Ineptness, Low Self Esteem, Bad Self Image, Aggravated Abuse and Jealousy of Others.

Sexual Spirits

Seducing, Perverse, Whoredom, Bondage, Masturbation, Sexual Fantasy, Romanticism, Infatuation, Daydreaming, Pornography, Romance Novels, Lust, Fornication, Promiscuity, Contraception—Condoms, Adultery, Disordered Love Relationships, Bestiality, Necromancy, Unclean Thoughts and Desires, Prostitution, Homosexuality (Baal), Lesbianism (Ishtar), Incubus, Succubus, Pedophilia, Jezebel (Seduction) (N.B. re: Homosexuality, she is called the Pestiferous Queen of the Sodomites), Incest, Voyeurism, Coquettishness, Flirtation, Petting, French Kissing, Fondling, Provocativeness, Internet Porn, Lewd Conduct, Lewd Dancing, Molestation, Oral Sex, Unnatural Intercourse, Lack of Modesty, Nudity, Shame, Guilt, Child Perversity, Sadomasochism, Perverted Acts, Sexual Delusions, Obscenity, Wasting of Seed, Indecency, Pleasure Seeking, Premarital Sex, (Need to Forgive Sex Partners and Remove Hooks and Tentacles), Murder of Spirit, Murder of Purity (Necessary condition to see God), Sexual Gluttony, Sexual Addiction, Ritual Sex, Ritual Sexual Abuse, Insatiable Lusts, Sexual Gratification, Predator, Prey, Orgy (Sexual Carnival), Exhibitionism, Porn Films, Porn Magazines, Dirty Jokes, Squalor (Unclean), Permissiveness, Immorality, Impurity, Sexual Rage (for denying pleasure), Rape, Sodomy, Lack of Custody of the Eyes, Sacrilegious Sexual Abasement (Priests), Gender Mutilation, Ray Knee Kay Fee, Shay Knee Kay Lee.

Fear

Ministering Spirits, Fear, Torment, Violence, Fear of Death, Murder of Spirit, Spirit of Death-Ichabod, Suicide, Impending Death, Tension, Fear of People and their Opinions, Human Respect, Torture, Trouble, Anguish, Darkness, Grief, Night, Black Disordered Grief, Trauma, Weeping, Oppression, Morbidity, Fixation, Helplessness, Hopelessness, Insomnia, Disturbances, Apprehension, Edginess; Phobias: Heights, Crowds, Cars, Planes, Water, Elevators, Hospitals, Claustrophobia, etc.; Inner Conflict, "I am not worthy," Self-Condemnation, Self-Abandonment, Ruminating, Unworthiness, Fear of Disapproval, Fear of Persecution, Fear of Reproof, Fear of Accusation, Fear of Failure, Perfectionism; Crisis, Implosion, Nightmares, Excitement, Turmoil, Horror, Dread, Disgust, Gloom, Doom, Desperation, Disappointment, Anxiety Disorder, Panic Disorder, Fear of Pain, Fear of the Cross, Fear of Being Hurt, Repression,

Suppression of Joy, Suppression, Panic, Anxiety, Worry, Paranoia-Suspicion, Fear of Condemnation, Fear of Judgment, Fear of Rejection, Projected Rejection onto God and Others, Fear of Close Relations, Disordered Fear of God or Hell, Restlessness, Nervousness, Tremors, Tension Headaches, Roaming Around, Nervous Habits, Shackled, Pressured, Viced, Trapped, Barbed Wire, Squeezed, Captive Spirit, Frozen, Isolation, Negativity, Reclusion, Staying Alone, Abandonment-Betrayal, Seclusion, Withdrawal, Indifference, Blockages, Numbness, Closed up, Shut up, Stupor, Locked up, Paralysis, Immobilization, Shut Down, Wall, Coldness, Apathy, Sloth, Escape, Loneliness, Fear of Loneliness, Sluggishness, Listlessness, Sleepiness.

Others

Yawning, Stress, Laziness, Lethargy, Withdrawal from God and People, Stoicism, Discouragement, Foreboding, Darkness, Sadness, Despair, Despondency, Dismay, Distrust, Disheartenment, Powerlessness, Fatality, Melancholy, Joylessness, Fear of Loss, Fear of Failure, Separation Anxiety, Fixation, "Don't touch me," "Leave me alone," Heaviness, Depression, Neglect, Lost, Strangulation, Suffocation, Immobility, Recoil, Defeat, Weakness of Will, Seductibility, Sentimentality, Blues, Bondage, Bound and Gagged, Tied up in Knots, Chained, Caught, Snared, Trapped, Imprisoned, Netting, Webbing, Black Tar—Verbal Barrage in Hearing Faculty, Self-Preservation, Avoidance, Humiliation, Inability to Overcome, Workaholic, Attachment Disorder, Fear of men, Fear of women, Fear of Abduction, Secrecy/secretive, Uselessness, Non-existent, Claiming, Hoarding and Owning Negatives, Holding on to Good Things, Attachments, Bigotry, "I'm not allowed to be here," or "I should be punished."

Womb

Darkness in Mother's Womb, Unwanted Pregnancy, Fear of Pregnancy, Cord around Neck, Undue Sadness from Mother to Child, Birth Trauma, Incubator Abandonment, Adoption, Non-bonding at the Breast, Blood Transfusion, Oxygen Tent or Hospitalization, Previous Abortion, Previous Miscarriage, Premature Pregnancy.

Self

Narcissism, Self-Awareness, Inadequacy, Self-Rejection, Rejection, Self-Pity, No Self-Confidence, Self-Hate/Ugliness, Self-Contempt, Self-Love, Self-Seeking Behavior, Self-Gratification, Self Will, Self-Destruction, Self-Abandonment, Self-Aggrandizement, Ego, Independence, Bad Self-Image, Self-Depreciation, Sensitivity, Inferiority, Self-Absorption, Blockages to God Because of Self-Absorption, Self-Idolatry, Introspection, Insecurity, Timidity, Ineptness, Shyness, Loneliness, Cowardliness, Self-Indulgence, Uselessness, Ideas and Dreams, Agenda, Preconceived Notions, Presumption, Disordered Love, Disordered Responsibility, Disordered Compassion, Self-Assumed Heavy Burdens, Self-Assumed Pious Burdens, Self-Assumed False Burdens, Inability to Receive Love, Inability to Give Love, Faith Crisis, Shame, Guilt, Self-Reliance, Self-Sufficiency, Feeling Accused, Blame, Impulsive, Labor and Toil, Obedient Toil, Drudgery, Aversion, Avoidance, Feeling Unloved, Feeling Unwanted, Pessimism, Indifference, Tepidity, Lukewarmness, Defeat.

Spirits that Say

"I must be punished," "That's not fair," "I am not allowed," "This cannot happen for me," "I am not worthy," "I can do it myself," "I can't," "I won't," "God can't," "God won't," "Oh yes, I can," "You can't make me," "You can't help me," "I can't be healed."

Others, Continued

Mine, Perfectionism, Rigidity, Give Me, Doubt, Incredulity, Unbelief, Paranoia, Suspicion, Irrational, Instability, Unstable, Fickle, Folly, Unmovable, Changeability, Unpredictable, Surprise, Irresoluteness, Weakness of Will, Inconsistency, Sloth, Slovenliness, Non-Forgiving of God, Non-Forgiving of Self, Messiah Complex, Imbalance, Deaf and Dumb Spirit, Distorted Hearing, Perverted Judgment, Perverted Thinking, Indecisive, Scrupulosity, Procrastination, Postponement, Postponing Prayer, Inability to be Influenced by Grace, Trance, Anesthetized, Numbness, Spiritual Blindness, Wall, Dazed, Fog, Indecision, Obstruction, Inability to be Taught, Blockages, Non-Formed Conscience, Analysis Paralysis, Distorted Thinking, Hardness of Heart, Wounded Heart, Disconnectedness of Thoughts and Feelings from Head and Heart, Disjointed Spirit, Fractured Spirit, Split/Severance, Undo/ Breaking, Opposites-Dual, Paralysis, Forgetfulness, Attention Deficit, Memory Lapse, Memory Loss, Obsessive Compulsive, Passivity, Imprudence, Impulsiveness, Compromise, Displaced Feelings, Transferred Feelings, Negativity, Non-Creativity, Grotesque Self Image, Preoccupation with Appearances and Body, Ignorance, Attachment, Concerned with Things Outside One's Own Realm, Passive Aggressive, Finality, Dead End, Stunting, Halting, Interruption, Hesitation, Cutting Off, Dismissal, Defilement, Shock, Entrenchment, Temptation, Passivity, Slave of Constraint, Unfixability, Repudiation and Condemnation, Coveting, Being Served, Not Serving.

Anger

Anger, Rage, Outrage, Blind Rage, Resentment, Unforgiveness, Spite, Animosity, Brooding over Injuries, Vindictiveness, Violence, Temper, Temper Tantrums, Outbursts, Revenge, Lashing Out, Retaliation, Murder, Murder of Spirit, Abortion/Never, Bitterness, Bitterroot, Defiance, Avenging,

Mercilessness, Belittling, Biting, Cruel, Inconsideration of Others' Feelings, Inability to Feel Others' Pain, Wicked Penetration, Agitation, Destruction, Accusation, Disfigurement/Mutilation, Relentless Rage, Pulverizing, Overkill, Compassionlessness, Torture, Predator, Stubbornness, Rebelliousness, Contempt, Vehemence, Contrivance, Strife, Division—Dabbles, Contention, Arguing, Quarreling, Bickering, Fighting, Rejoicing in Evil, Sadism, Masochism, Pouting, Impatience, Marital Discord, Hatred for Parents, Opposition, Disagree, Enmity, Cruelty, Envy, Bludgeoning, Jealousy, Spirit of Wickedness, Spirit of Wicked Penetration, Screaming, Feeling out of Control, Blame, Vulgarity, Foul language, Uncontrolled Use of the Tongue, Name Calling, Cursing, Lying, Discord, Disorder, Dysfunctional Behavior, Havoc, Chaos, Confusion, Calamity, Calumny, Verbal Abuse, Physical Abuse; Addictions: Drugs, Alcoholism, Sex, Smoking, Gambling, Deviant Behavior, Curtness, Gossip, Talkativeness, Spitting, Blasphemy, Sarcasm, Cynicism, Jeering, Wishing Evil, Relishing Evil, Holding Secret Antipathies and Hatred, Coldness, Hatred, Hatred of Men, Hatred of Women, Bigotry, Willfulness, Mockery, Mimicry, Criticism, Yelling, Dirty Jokes, Critical Humor, Cursing of Children by Parents or Grandparents, Tearing of Flesh, Mutilation, Self-Inflicted Pain, Destruction, Spirit of Detraction, Hurtful, Ruinous of Others' Reputation, Destruction of Others' Property and Reputation, Depreciation, Fault Finding, Frenzy, Adversity, Emotional Hostage-Taking, Disunity.

Pride

Boasting, Bragging, Haughtiness, Pride, Arrogance, Detraction, Obstinate Pride, Conceit, Wounded Pride, Aggrandizement of Self, Grandiosity, Judgmental, Spiritual Wrath at God, Pride of Vocation, Nursing Wounds, Insolence, Vanity, Vainglory, Superiority, Indignation, Self-Righteous, Resistance, Non-Submissive, Repelling, Opening Ears to Evil, Cloak and Dagger (political), Reverse Polarization, Repels Self from

God (Magnets), Supremacy, Challenge, Opposition, Spoiled, Will Not Receive Correction, Willfulness, Worldly Success and Achievement, Prowess, Fanaticism, "I will do it," Self-Idolatry, Holding Secret Antipathies, Distortion of Truth, Agitation, Religiosity, False Sense of Confidence, Self-Magnification, Machismo, Egoism, Worldliness, Competition, Exaggeration, Bloated, Control, Manipulation, Dominance, Domineering, Power, Exalted Feelings, Scheming, Plotting, Dishonor, Disprove, Cunning, Conniving, Idolatry, Intellectual Prowess, Intellectualizing, Self-Actualization, Self-Elevation, Judgment Comparison, Acquired Situational Narcissism (Adulation in Early Life, Complicated with Pressure), Buffoonery, Jocularity, Party Foolishness, Uncontrolled Behavior, Intemperance, Drunkenness, Gluttony, Mirth—Gaiety—Foolishness, Debauchery, Minimalization of Sin, Undisciplined, Unruly, Wild, Free Spirit that Obeys and Follows No Law, Lawlessness, Self-Righteous Indignation, Spiritual Superiority, Sacrilegious Communions, Aversion to Others, "Below My Dignity," Unrest, Agitation, Irritation, Spiritual Wrath Directed at God, Because of No Consolation, Emphasizes Letter of the Law and Not Its Spirit, Burning Desire to Justify Self, Burning Desire to Correct Others and Judge Them, Rebelliousness against Leaders and Authority, "I will not serve," "I will not submit," "I will not," Touchiness over Correction, Hypocritical, Self-Righteousness; Judas Spirit: Betrayal, Won't Forgive Self, God Can't Forgive Me; Divided Loyalty, Pharisee, Sanctimoniousness, (Pretending to be of High Morals without Being So), Self-Denial and Discipline for Worldly Gain, Self-Achievement, "I will do it," "Only I can do it," Diabolic Strength—Strength apart from God, Empowerment, Severity, Disciplinarian–Dictator, Workaholic, Stubbornness, Curiosity.

Bibliography

Alacoque, Margaret. *The Autobiography of St. Margaret Mary.* Charlotte, NC: TAN Books, 2012.

Amorth, Gabriele. *An Exorcist Explains the Demonic: The Antics of Satan and His Army of Fallen Angels.* Manchester, NH: Sophia Institute, 2016.

———. *An Exorcist: More Stories.* San Francisco: Ignatius, 2002.

———. *An Exorcist Tells His Story.* San Francisco: Ignatius, 1999.

Anonymous. *Physiologus.* Translated by Michael J. Curley. Chicago: University of Chicago Press, 2009.

Aquinas, Thomas. *Commentary on the Sentences.* Edited by Beth Mortensen. Green Bay, WI: Aquinas Institute, 2017.

———. *Summa Theologica,* 5 vols. Translated by the Fathers of the English Dominican Province. Notre Dame, IN: Christian Classics, 1981.

Assaf, Andrea Kirk. *The Saints' Little Book of Wisdom: Essential Teachings.* Charlottesville, VA: Hampton Roads, 2016.

Aumann, Jordan. *Spiritual Theology.* New York: Continuum, 2006.

Augustine of Hippo. *Expositions on the Psalms.* In Philip Schaff, ed. *Nicene and Post-Nicene Fathers, First Series,* vol 8. Translated by R. G. MacMullen. Buffalo: Christian Literature, 1888.

————. *On the Trinity*. In Marcus Dods, ed. *The Works of Aurelius Augustine, Bishop of Hippo*, vol. 7. Edinburgh: T & T Clark, 1873.

————. *Sermo 169*. In Jacques Paul Migne, ed. *Patrologie cursus completus: series Latina*, vol. 38. Paris: Imprimerie Catholique, 1845-55.

Baltimore Catechism, The New St. Joseph. Official Revised Edition. New Jersey: Catholic Book Publishing, 2011.

Bamonte, Francesco. *Diabolical Possession and the Ministry of Exorcism*. Translated by Cliff Ermatinger. Milan: Paoline, 2014.

————. *The Rebellious Angels: The Mystery of Evil in the Experience of the Exorcist*. Translated by Scott Francis Binet. Milan: Paoline, 2008.

————. *The Virgin Mary and the Devil in Exorcisms*. Translated by Cliff Ermatinger. Milan: Paoline, 2014.

Beal, John P., et al., eds. *The New Commentary on the Code of Canon Law*. New York: Paulist, 2000.

Benedict XVI. *Verbum Domini*. London: Catholic Truth Society, 2010.

Bettenson, Henry. *Documents of the Christian Church*. Oxford: Oxford University Press, 1947.

Boer, Paul A., ed. *The Raccolta: A Collection of Indulgenced Prayers*. Ogden, UT: Veritatis Splendor, 1912.

Bonaventure. *Breviloquium*. Translated by Erwin Nemmers. London: B. Herder, 1947.

Brennan, Robert Edward. *Thomistic Psychology: A Philosophic Analysis of the Nature of Man*. Edited by Cajetan Cuddy. Providence, RI: Cluny Media, 2016.

Carthusian, A. *In Praise of Silence: Poems and Images*. Horsham: St Hugh's, 2009.

Catholic Church. *Liturgy of the Hours According to the Roman Rite, vol. 2*. New York: Catholic Book, 1976.

Catholic News Agency. "Fatima Visionary Predicted 'Final Battle' Would Be Over Marriage, Family" (Oct 13, 2021). https://www.catholicnewsagency.com/news/341 55/fatima-visionary-predicted-final-battle-would -be-over-marriage-family. Accessed 10 June 2022.

Clement XII, Pope. *In Eminenti: Papal Bull Dealing with the Condemnation of Freemasonry* https://www.papalencyc licals.net/clem12/c12inemengl.htm. Accessed 9 June 2022.

Chrysostom, John. *De coemeterio et de cruce, 2*. In J. P. Migne, ed. *Patrologie cursus completus: series graeca*, vol. 49. Paris: Imprimerie Catholique, 1857-66.

———. *On the Priesthood*. In Phillip Schaff, ed. *The Nicene and Post-Nicene Fathers, vol. 9*. New York: Christian Literature, 1889.

Catechism of the Catholic Church. Liguori, MO: Liguori Publications, 1994.

Congregation for the Doctrine of the Faith. *Declaration on Masonic Associations* (November 26, 1983). https://www.vatican.va/roman_curia/congregations/cfaith /documents/rc_con_cfaith_doc_19831126_decla ration-masonic_en.html. Accessed 21 February 2021.

———. *Letter to Ordinaries Regarding Norms on Exorcism*. https://www.vatican.va/roman_curia/congregations /cfaith/documents/rc_con_cfaith_doc_19850924 _exorcism_en.html. Accessed 21 February 2021.

———. *Letter to the Bishops of the Catholic Church on Some Aspects of Christian Meditation* (October 15, 1989). https://www.vatican.va/roman_curia/congregations /cfaith/documents/rc_con_cfaith_doc_19891015 _meditazione-cristiana_en.html. Accessed 4 January 2021.

Cross, Richard. *Duns Scotus*. Oxford: Oxford University Press, 1999.

Damian, Peter. *The Letters of Peter Damian, 1-30*. In *The Fathers of the Church: Mediaeval Continuation*, vol. 1. Translated by Owen J. Blum and Irven M. Resneck. Washington, DC: Catholic University Press, 1989.

Daniélou, Jean. *The Angels and Their Mission According to the Fathers of the Church*. Translated by David Heimann. Allen, TX: Christian Classics, 1957.

De Caussade, Jean-Pierre. *Abandonment to Divine Providence*. Translated by E. J. Strickland. St. Louis: Herder, 1921.

De Chantal, Jane Frances. *Selected Letters of Jane Frances de Chantal*. Translated by the Sisters of the Visitation Harrow. London: Aeterna, 2015.

De Montfort, Louis. *The Secret of the Rosary*. Rockford, IL: TAN Books, 1993.

————. *True Devotion to Mary*. Rockford, IL: TAN Books, 1941.

Department of the Army, *The Official U.S. Army Tactics Field Manual*. Guilford, CT: Lyons, 2020.

Dunnigan, James F. *The Perfect Soldier: Special Operations, Commandos, and the Future of U.S. Warfare*. New York: Citadel, 2004.

Flannery, Austin, ed. *The Documents of Vatican Council II: The Conciliar and Post-Conciliar Documents*. Dublin: Dominican Publications, 1996.

FMSF Amicus Brief—Commonwealth v. Shanley. http://www.fmsfonline.org/links/fmsfamicusshanley.html#note74. Accessed 3 November, 2021.

Francis Mary, ed. *Padre Pio: The Wonder Worker*. New Bedford, MA: Franciscan Friars of the Immaculate, 1999.

General Council of Trent, 1545-63 A.D. Papal Encyclicals, October 12, 2018. https://www.papalencyclicals.net/councils/trent.htm. Accessed January 8, 2023.

Gershon, Livia. "Why Does the Bible Forbid Tattoos?" JSTOR Daily, January 2, 2021. https://daily.jstor.org/why-does-the-bible-forbid-tattoos/. Accessed May 15, 2022.

Gregory of Nyssa. *De Perfecta Christiana Forma*, 46. In J. P. Migne, ed. *Patrologie cur sus completus: series graeca*, 162 volumes, 46, 283-86. Paris: Imprimerie Catholique, 1857-66.

Gregory the Great. *Moralia in Job*. Edited by John Henry Parker, J. G. F. and J. Rivington. Oxford: Oxford University Press, 1844.

Grob, Jeffrey. "A Major Revision of the Discipline on Exorcism: A Comparative Study on the Liturgical Laws in the 1614 and 1998 Rites of Exorcism." PhD diss., St. Paul University, 2013.

Hahn, Scott, ed. *Catholic Bible Dictionary*. New York: Doubleday, 2009.

Hanna, Edward. *"Penance."* In Herbermann, Charles, et al., eds. *The Catholic Encyclopedia: An International Work of Reference on the Constitution, Doctrine, Discipline, and History of the Catholic Church*. New York: Robert Appleton, 1911.

Hardon, John. *Modern Catholic Dictionary*. New York: Doubleday, 1980.

Epistle of Barnabas. In Bart D. Ehrman, ed. and trans., *The Apostolic Fathers, Volume 2: Epistle of Barnabas. Papias and Quadratus. Epistle to Diognetus. The Shepherd of Hermas*. Harvard University Press, 2003.

Hippolytus of Rome. *On David and Goliath*. In G. N. Bonwetsch, ed. *Drei georgisch erhaltene Schriften von Hippolytus*. Göttingen: Vandenhoek & Rupreccht, 2012.

———. *On the Seventy Apostles of Christ*. In Alexander Roberts, James Donaldson, and A. Cleveland Coxe, eds.

Ante-Nicene Fathers: The Writings of the Fathers down to A.D. 325, vol 6. Peabody, MA: Hendrickson, 1995.

Huehnergard, John, and Harold Liebowitz. "Biblical Prohibition Against Tattooing." In *Vetus Testamentum*, 63.1 (2013), 59-77.

Ignatius of Antioch. *Letters of Ignatius*. In Bart D. Ehrman, ed. and trans. *The Apostolic Fathers, Volume 1: I Clement, II Clement, Ignatius, Polycarp, Didache*. Cambridge, Mass.: Harvard University Press, 2003.

John of Dalyatha. In Mary Hansbury, ed. *The Letters of John of Dalyatha*. Piscataway, NJ: Gorgias Press, 2006.

John Paul II. *Crossing the Threshold of Hope*. New York: Alfred A. Knopf, 2005.

———. *On the Mystery and Worship of the Eucharist, Dominicae Cenae: Letter of the Supreme Pontiff Pope John Paul II to All the Bishops of the Church*. Boston, MA: St. Paul Editions, 1980.

———. *Redemptoris Mater*. Vatican City: Libreria Editrice Vaticana, 1987.

———. *Salvifici Doloris: On the Christian Meaning of Human Suffering*. Boston, MA: Pauline, 1984.

———. *The Splendor of Truth (Veritatis Splendor)*. Boston: Pauline, 1999.

Kärkkäinen, P. *Encyclopedia of Medieval Philosophy: Philosophy between 500 and 1500*. Edited by Henrik Lagerlund and Peter Adamson. "Internal Senses." Dordrecht: Springer, 2020.

Kolbe, Maximilian. *The Kolbe Reader: The Writings of the St. Maximilian M. Kolbe, OFM Conv.* Translated by Anselm W. Romb. Libertyville, IL: Marytown, 2007.

Kowalska, Faustina Maria. *Diary of Saint Maria Faustina Kowalska: Divine Mercy in My Soul*. Stockbridge, MA: Marian, 2014.

Laughlin, Corinna and Jennifer Kerr Breedlove. The Almanac for Pastoral Liturgy: Sourcebook for Sundays, Seasons, and Weekdays. Chicago: Liturgy Training, 2008.

Lefebvre, Gaspar. *Saint Andrew Daily Missal with Vespers for Sundays and Feasts.* St. Paul, MN: E.M. Lohmann, 1953.

Leo the Great. *Sermon 95*, 8-9. In J. P. Migne, ed. *Patrologie cursus completus: series Latina,* vol. 54. Paris: Imprimerie Catholique, 1845-55.

Lewis, Charlton T. and Charles Short. *An Elementary Latin Dictionary.* Oxford: Oxford University Press, 1963.

Lewis, Clive Staples, *Abolition of Man.* New York: Harper Collins, 1947.

———. *Mere Christianity.* New York: Harper Collins, 2001.

Liber Christo, "Liberation Conference Manual (2019)." Self-published: Liber Christo, 2019.

———. "Freedom Through Christ Companion Guide: The Catholic Approach to Liberation." Self-published: Liber Christo, 2019.

———. "Four-Phase Protocol Team Training Manual." Self-published: Liber Christo, 2021.

Liguori, Alphonsus Marie. *The Glories of Mary.* Rockford, IL: TAN Books, 1982.

———. *Six Discourses on Natural Calamities, Divine Threats, and the Four Gates of Hell.* London: Aeterna, 2015.

———. *The Sermons of St. Alphonsus Liguori for All the Sundays of the Year.* Charlotte, NC: TAN Books, 2012.

Manly, Carla Maria. "The Pros and Cons of Having a Soul Tie Relationship in Your Life." Genesis Rivas. *Yahoo! News.* Accessed April 24, 2022. https://nz.news.yahoo.com/pros-cons-having-soul-tie-144155513.html. Accessed 10 May 2022. Accessed 4 February 2022.

Marín, Antonio Royo. *The Theology of Christian Perfection.* Translated by Jordan Aumann. Eugene, OR: Wipf and Stock, 2012.

McNally, Richard J. "The Expanding Empire of Post-Traumatic Stress Disorder." In *Medscape General Medicine* 8, 2 (2006): 9–12.

Mills, Mary E. *Human Agents of Cosmic Power in Hellenistic Judaism and the Synoptic Tradition.* London: Bloomsbury, 2015.

Miravalle, Mark. *Mary Coredemptrix, Mediatrix, Advocate: Dedicated to Pope John Paul II and the Bishops of the Universal Church.* Santa Barbara, CA: Queenship, 1993.

Miravalle, Mark, ed. *Mary Coredemptrix, Mediatrix, Advocate, Theological Foundations: Towards a Papal Definition?* Santa Barbara, CA: Queenship, 1995.

Miravalle, Mark and Robert Fastiggi. "Is Mary Co-redemptrix A 'False Exaggeration'?" *Mother of All Peoples.* https://www.motherofallpeoples.com/post/is-mary-co-redemptrix-a-false-exaggeration. Accessed 5 April 2022.

Newman, John Henry. *The Second Eve: From the Writing of John Henry Newman.* Edited by Eileen Breen Mary. Rockford, IL: TAN Books, 1982.

Nevins, Albert J., ed. *The Maryknoll Catholic Dictionary.* New York: Dimension, 1965.

Origen. *Homily* 4,1. In J. P. Migne, ed. *Patrologie cursus completus: series graeca,* vol. 12. Paris: Imprimerie Catholique, 1857-66.

Ott, Ludwig. *Fundamentals of Catholic Dogma.* Rockford, IL: TAN Books, 2009.

Pascal, Blaise. *Pascal's Pensées.* New York: E.P. Dutton, 2016.

Pasquale, Gianluigi and Marsha Daigle-Williamson, trans. *Padre Pio's Spiritual Direction for Every Day.* Cincinnati, OH: Servant, 2011.

Paul VI. *Humanae Vitae: Encyclical Letter of His Holiness Pope Paul VI On the Regulation of Births.* San Francisco: Ignatius, 1998.

Pew Research. "Very Few Americans See Contraception as Morally Wrong." Pew Research Center's Religion and Public Life Project, September 10, 2020. Accessed 25 March 2021. https://www.pewforum.org/2016/09/28/4-very-few-americans-see-contraception-as-morally-wrong/. Accessed 2 October 2021.

Pius X. *Encyclical Letter Ad Diem Illum Laetissimum of the Supreme Pontiff Pius X: On the Jubilee of the Immaculate Conception: February 2, 1904.* Kansas City, MO: Angelus Press, 1999.

Pius XII. *Munificentissimus Deus: The Definition by His Holiness, Pope Pius XII, of the Dogma That Mary, the Virgin Mother of God, Was Assumed Body and Soul into The Glory of Heaven: Issued November 1, 1950.* Boston: St. Paul Books, 1992.

———. *Mystici Corporis.* Colombia: Ediciones Paulinas, 1965.

Ponticus, Evagrius. *The Praktikos and Chapters on Prayer.* Translated by John Eudes Bamberger. Kalamazoo, MI.: Cistercian, 1972.

Pope Leo XIII Institute. "Session IV (November 2015): Resources on Freemasonry." Self-published, 2015.

———. "The Virgin Mary's Role in the Defeat of Satan: 2016 Conference Resources." Self-published, 2016.

Ripperger, Chad. *Deliverance Prayers for Use by the Laity.* Denver, CO: Sensus Traditionis, 2020.

———. *Dominion: The Nature of Diabolic Warfare.* Keensburg, CO: Sensus Traditionis, 2022.

———. *Holy Hour of Reparation to the Sacred Heart of Jesus: For Neglect of and Negligence in Priestly and Religious Vocations.* Denver, CO: Sensus Traditionis, 2004.

———. *Introduction to the Science of Mental Health*. Denton, NE: Sensus Traditionis, 2013.

———. *Minor Exorcisms and Deliverance Prayers: For Use by Priests*. Denton, NE: Sensus Traditionis, 2016.

———. "The Sixth Generation." In *Latin Mass* (Summer 2012), 34-39.

Romero, Mario P. *Unabridged Christianity: Biblical Answers to Common Questions About the Roman Catholic Faith*. Goleta, CA: Queenship Publishing, 1999.

Rumble, L. *Catholics and Freemasonry*. St. Paul, MN: Radio Replies Press, 1964.

Schneider, Daniel. *Eve Was Named an Apostle*. Eugene, OR: Wipf and Stock, 2022.

———. "Weaponry in Biblical Warfare: David's Defeat of Goliath as Prefiguring the Cross in Augustine of Hippo." Paper presentation at the 2022 Midwest Region SBL/AOS/ASOR/RRA ("Warfare in the Biblical World.") February 4-6, 2022.

Schultz, Karl A. *The Art and Vocation of Caring for People in Pain*. New York: Paulist, 1993.

Seigel, Daniel J. *Mindsight: The New Science of Personal Transformation*. New York: Bantam, 2010.

Smit, Johannes. *De Demoniacis in Historia Evangelica*. Roma: Pontificius Institutus Biblicus, 1913.

Snyder, M. M. *Light of an Angel*. Bloomington, IN: Arthur House, 2006.

Sommerfeldt. John R., "Meditation as the Path to Humility in the Thought of Bernard of Clairvaux." In *Mystics Quarterly*, 15: 4 (1989), 177-83.

Spitzer, Robert. *Christ Versus Satan in Our Daily Lives*. San Francisco: Ignatius, 2020.

Strabo and Horace Leonard Jones. *The Geography of Strabo, vol.* 2. Cambridge, Mass: Harvard Univ. Press, 1982.

Tanner, Norman P. "Canons on the Sacraments in General, March 3, 1547," in *Decrees of the Ecumenical Councils: Trent to Vatican II*, vol. 2. London: Sheed & Ward, 1990.

Tanqueray, Adolphe. *The Spiritual Life: A Treatise on Ascetical and Mystical Theology*. Westminster, MD: The Newman Press, 1987.

Tassone, Susan. *Jesus Speaks to Faustina and You*. Manchester, NH: Sophia, 2020.

Telegraph, The. "World's Top Exorcist Saw the Devil in Harry Potter, Yoga, and Thousands of Middle-Aged, Middle-Class Women." National Post, September 22, 2016. https://nationalpost.com/news/world/worlds-top -exorcist-saw-the-devil-in-harry-potter-yoga and thou sands-of-middle-aged-middle-class-women#:~: text=from%20our%20team. ,World's%20top%20exor cist%20saw%20the%20Devil%20in%20Harry%20 Potter%2C%20yoga,Story%2C%20became%20a%20 European%20bestseller. Accessed 16 February 2023.

Teresa of Avila, *The Book of Her Life*. In Kieran Kavanaugh and Otilio Rodriguez, trans. *The Collected Works of St. Teresa of Avila, Volume One*. Washington, DC: ICS, 1976.

———. *The Way of Perfection*. In Kieran Kavanaugh and Otilio Rodriguez, trans. *The Collected Works of St. Teresa of Avila, Volume Two*. Washington, DC: ICS, 1980.

———. *Obras Completas*. Burgos, Spain: Editorial Monte Carmelo, 2002.

Teresa Benedicta of the Cross. *Edith Stein: Essential Writings*. Edited by John Sullivan. Maryknoll, NY: Orbis, 2002.

———. *The Hidden Life.* Edited by L. Gelber and Michael Linssen. Translated by Waltraut Stein. Washington, DC: ICS, 1986.

Thérèse of Lisieux. *Story of a Soul: The Autobiography of Thérèse of Lisieux (the Little Flower).* Washington, DC: ICS, 1996.

Tradition In Action. "A Prayer to Our Lady, Queen of Angels, For Protection." https://www.traditioninaction.org/religious/b006rp.htm. Accessed 14 December 2020.

Unger, Merrill F. and R. K. Harrison, et al., eds. *The New Unger's Bible Dictionary.* Chicago: Moody, 1988.

United States Conference of Catholic Bishops. *The Roman Ritual: Book of Blessings.* New York: Catholic Book, 1989.

———. *Guidelines for Evaluating Reiki as an Alternative Therapy* (25 March 2009). https://www.usccb.org/resources/evaluation-guidelines-finaltext-2009-03_0.pdf. Accessed 21 April 2021.

———. *United States Catholic Catechism for Adults.* Washington, DC: USCCB Publishing, 2006.

Weller. *Roman Ritual, vol 2: Christian Burial, Exorcism, Reserved Blessings, Etc.* Boonville, NY: Preserving Christian, 1952.

Wuellner, Bernard J. *Summary of Scholastic Principles.* Chicago: Loyola University Press, 1956.